Minding the Web

Minding the Web

MAKING THEOLOGICAL CONNECTIONS

Stanley Hauerwas
with **Robert J. Dean**

CASCADE *Books* • Eugene, Oregon

MINDING THE WEB
Making Theological Connections

Copyright © 2018 Stanley Hauerwas. All rights reserved. Except for brief quotations in critical publications or reviews, no part of this book may be reproduced in any manner without prior written permission from the publisher. Write: Permissions, Wipf and Stock Publishers, 199 W. 8th Ave., Suite 3, Eugene, OR 97401.

Cascade Books
An Imprint of Wipf and Stock Publishers
199 W. 8th Ave., Suite 3
Eugene, OR 97401

www.wipfandstock.com

PAPERBACK ISBN: 978-1-5326-5005-5
HARDCOVER ISBN: 978-1-5326-5006-2
EBOOK ISBN: 978-1-5326-5007-9

Cataloguing-in-Publication data:

Names: Hauerwas, Stanley, 1940–, author. | Dean, Robert J., editor and author.

Title: Minding the web : making theological connections / Stanley Hauerwas ; with Robert J. Dean.

Description: Eugene, OR : Cascade Books, 2018 | Includes bibliographical references and index(es).

Identifiers: ISBN 978-1-5326-5005-5 (paperback) | ISBN 978-1-5326-5006-2 (hardcover) | ISBN 978-1-5326-5007-9 (ebook)

Subjects: LCSH: Christian ethics—United States. | Theology, Practical.

Classification: BJ1200 .H38 2018 (print) | BJ1200 .H38 (ebook)

Manufactured in the U.S.A.　　　　　　　　　　NOVEMBER 2, 2018

All Scripture quotations, unless otherwise indicated, are taken from the New Revised Standard Version Bible, copyright © 1989 National Council of the Churches of Christ in the United States of America. Used by permission. All rights reserved worldwide.

To Ephraim Radner and Joe Mangina

Table of Contents

Preface ix
Introduction: Tending the Web – Robert J. Dean 1

PART I: *Matters Theological*

1. Why Language Matters Theologically: On Reading and Writing 21
2. The Past Matters Theologically: Thinking Tradition 32
3. Why Jean Vanier Matters: An Exemplary Exploration 47
4. Why Bonhoeffer Matters: The Challenge for Christian Ministry at the End of Christendom 60

PART II: *University Matters*

5. Kierkegaard and the Academy: A Theological Meditation 77
6. Graduation Address: University of Aberdeen 89

PART III: *Lives Matter*

7. The Good Life 95
8. A Sanctuary Politics: Being the Church in the Time of Trump (with Jonathan Tran) 113
9. Minding the Gaps, Or, Theologians Writing Memoirs 127
10. In Defense of "Our Respectable Culture": Trying to Make Sense of John Howard Yoder 142

PART IV: *The Matter of Preaching*

11. Preaching In the Ruins: Reflections about Words with Sermonic Exhibits 161
12. "Do You Love Me?" 176
13. "Resurrection" 182
14. "The Way, the Truth, and the Life" 187

15. "Wounded" 193
16. "Citizens of Heaven" 198
17. "King Jesus" 204
18. "Repentance: A Lenten Meditation" 210
19. "He Is Our Peace" 215
20. "A Heartfelt People" 219
21. "The Sign That Is Christ" 224
22. "Waiting" 229
23. "The Defeat of Boredom" 234
24. "Do Not Be Afraid" 239
25. "Ambassadors for Christ" 245
26. "Trinity" 251
27. "Celebration" 256
28. "Elected" 260
29. "Sin" 264
30. "Caesar Wants It All" 269
31. "The Politics of Martyrdom" 273
32. "The Never-ending Story" – Robert J. Dean 276
33. "Fake News and Inconvenient Truths" – Robert J. Dean 284

EPILOGUE: A Tale of Two Stanleys, Or, Why We Need More Pointless Sermons from Hauerwas – Robert J. Dean 292

Name Index 311
Subject Index 315

Preface

THE IDEA FOR THIS book was inspired by my colleague and friend Ellen Davis. It is quite handy to have her office across the hall from mine. Ellen thought it time for a collection of her sermons and essays to be published in a single volume. But rather than choosing the sermons and essays herself, she thought it best that someone else select the sermons and essays to make up the book. She asked one of our then graduate students, Austin Dennis, to choose the sermons, as well as organize and create the book. Austin was a wonderful choice, as he is a remarkable preacher, well trained in theology. The result is the terrific book *Preaching the Luminous Word*, for which I had the honor of writing the Foreword.

I understood Ellen's decision to ask the now Dr. Austin Dennis to choose the sermons for the book in order to reflect the connections that others often see, but the author fails to see because they are too close to what they have written. Rob Dean sees connections in the web that are illuminative for me. Austin did the same for Ellen. He did so even though he is a Baptist serving a Baptist church in North Carolina, and Ellen is the exemplification of what it should mean to be an Episcopalian. The resulting book shows clearly that a Baptist/Episcopal merger can turn out to be extremely constructive.

That is how I got the idea of asking Robert Dean to help me put this book together. I have grown tired of trying to justify in Preface after Preface another book by me. I thought, "Why not ask someone who knows me better than I know myself to put a book together in a way that I had not imagined?" Just at the time I was thinking along those lines I read Dean's book, *For the Life of the World: Jesus Christ and the Church in the Theologies of Dietrich Bonhoeffer and Stanley Hauerwas*. Apart from the embarrassment that came from being compared with Bonhoeffer, Dean's book was an account of my work that was extremely illuminating not only for others but for me. In particular, Dean, who had read more of my writing than is good for anyone, focused attention on my early Christological developments. By doing so, he made clear the interconnections in my work that are shaped by those Christological commitments. Moreover, he took seriously Bonhoeffer's claim, as well as my own, about why sermons are such a crucial genre for Christian theology.

So I asked him if he would be interested in performing a role for me in the way Austin had done for Ellen. Rob graciously agreed to do that thankless task, and this book is the result. What a wonderful gift that he was willing to do this without worrying about the cost. Working on this book does not insure that Rob will be credited with any academic contributions. Perhaps even more problematic is that by helping to put this book together, as well as writing the Introduction and Epilogue, he risks being far too closely identified with me. Those reading his book, as well as his contributions in this book, will recognize that Rob is more than capable of developing constructive criticism of my work that shows clearly he has a theological mind of his own. Hopefully the work he has done here will lead some to read not only his book on Bonhoeffer and me, but also his collection of sermons, *Leaps of Faith: Sermons from the Edge*.

Some may wonder, "Why Robert Dean?" We do not know one another. In fact we have never spent time together. I could have asked some of the students I have trained. Yet Rob is just distant enough from me for that distance to be fruitful. At least one of the ways to think of the distance is how young he is and how old I am. Age matters, particularly as it situates one differently in the world. I simply do not know the world that Rob and others his age inhabit. For example, I had never heard of Andy Stanley before I read Rob's extremely insightful comparison of Andy Stanley's understanding of preaching and how I understand what preaching ought to be.

In a similar fashion, I am extremely grateful for how Rob sees the connections between my sermons and the essays. He understands the importance not only of what I say, but how I say it. Perhaps even more importantly, he understands given what I say, why it is what I do not say is equally important. Moreover, Rob seems to enjoy—and that is the right word—what others are often put off by, that is, my use of exaggerated rhetoric. I confess I have never been convinced that what I have said is an exaggeration, but if it is there is a method to the madness Rob helps make not only what I say, but how I say it, understandable.

It seems that I am increasingly better understood by younger scholars like Rob than those in my generation. I am not sure how to account for that, but I am grateful that it seems to be happening. It is not just the difference in age, but it is also the case that I am better understood outside America. That Rob is a Canadian is not, I think, unimportant. It gives us great pleasure, therefore, to dedicate this book to two Americans that have been given a home in Canada—Ephraim Radner and Joe Mangina. Ephraim and Joe are my friends and Rob's teachers and in both capacities they are people who have taught each of us how better to be theologians. So I can only end by thanking Robert Dean for his willingness to help this theologian, who is hopelessly out of fashion but continues to love what it means to be a theologian.

Introduction

Tending the Web

Robert J. Dean

Theological Existence Today

Once, there was no "Stanley Hauerwas." Parroting one of the most renowned opening lines in recent theology, a sentence also previously riffed on by Hauerwas himself, is probably not the most promising way to begin an introduction to a book.[1] That being said, an acknowledgment of the sheer contingency of creaturely existence is never out of place when it comes to discussing Hauerwas's theology.[2] Furthermore, such an acknowledgment may perhaps rightly encourage us to appreciate the gift we've been given through his work. However, the phrase also serves as a reminder for me because in my theological existence there has never been a time when Stanley Hauerwas was not. I'm certainly aware of the pioneering role that Hauerwas played in recovering the importance of

---

1. "Once, there was no 'secular'" is the famous opening sentence of John Milbank's *Theology and Social Theory: Beyond Secular Reason* (Oxford: Blackwell, 1990), 9. Stanley Hauerwas and Samuel Wells begin their essay "Why Christian Ethics Was Invented" with the sentence, "Once, there was no 'Christian ethics.'" See Hauerwas and Wells, "Why Christian Ethics Was Invented," in *The Blackwell Companion to Christian Ethics*, ed. Stanley Hauerwas and Samuel Wells (Malden: Blackwell, 2006), 28.

2. In a recently published collection of interviews with Brian Brock, Hauerwas confirms, "Contingency is the heart of so much that I do." Brian Brock and Stanley Hauerwas, *Beginnings: Interrogating Hauerwas*, ed. Kevin Hargaden (London: Bloomsbury, 2017), 42. The affirmation of contingency is but the flip-side of the Christian doctrine of *creatio ex nihilo*.

character and the virtues, narrative and community for Christian ethics, but by the time I started reading theology these developments were in the past. I began my theological studies in seminary in the same year that Hauerwas was embarking upon his Gifford lectures that would be published as *With the Grain of the Universe*. The first work I read by Hauerwas was *Resident Aliens*, which he co-authored with William Willimon. I read it as a young pastoral major in the context of a worship course where I was wrestling with how to make sense of the apparent success of the seeker-sensitive church movement.[3] Like so many pastors whose attentions were piqued and whose ministries were reinvigorated by the *Christian Century* articles by Hauerwas and Willimon that preceded the book,[4] *Resident Aliens* gave voice to the uneasy sense I had about the state of the Western church at the end of Christendom and helped me to understand why I was right to be concerned.

Since that time I have read more than my fair share of Hauerwas, although I certainly wouldn't claim to have read his oeuvre in its entirety.[5] In spite of my immersion in his writings, as a theologian and pastor working in Canada I remain a less than obvious choice to introduce Hauerwas's work. After all, I have never been a member of the Society of Christian Ethics, nor did I ever study with Hauerwas at Duke Divinity School. However, something about my reading of his work caught Hauerwas's attention.[6] While this may be partly attributable to my decision to

---

3. I am a grateful for the wisdom and patience of my professor Arthur Boers, who allowed me to write a "worship" paper that compared and contrasted *Resident Aliens* with Niebuhr's *Christ and Culture*.

4. Stanley Hauerwas and William H. Willimon, "Embarrassed by God's Presence," *The Christian Century* 102, no. 4 (January 30, 1985): 98–100; Stanley Hauerwas and William H. Willimon, "Embarrassed by the Church: Congregations and the Seminary," *The Christian Century* 103, no. 5 (February 5, 1986): 117–20.

5. In light of his vast literary output and the scattering of his writings across dozens of his own books and, beyond that, throughout a wide-ranging collection of journals encompassing some of the most obscure publications, there is good reason to doubt anyone who claims to have read Hauerwas exhaustively. The rise of the Internet further complicates the task. Future researchers interested in Hauerwas's work will have to decide what to do with the rapidly multiplying number of essays, addresses and interviews, including podcasts and recordings of public lectures, appearing online. In light of Hauerwas's own refusal to draw hard and fast distinctions between academic and popular theology, these rapidly proliferating online sources cannot be ignored by anyone interested in understanding Hauerwas and his work.

6. My most concentrated treatment of Hauerwas's work can be found in Robert J. Dean, *For the Life of the World: Jesus Christ and the Church in the Theologies of Dietrich Bonhoeffer and Stanley Hauerwas* (Eugene, OR: Pickwick, 2016). Also relevant

place Hauerwas alongside of Dietrich Bonhoeffer in a book-length study, I think there is more going on behind Hauerwas's invitation to contribute to this book than his being flattered by my placement of him alongside one of his theological heroes. Interestingly, my own burgeoning interests in matters theological coincided with Hauerwas's self-described theological turn at the beginning of the new millennium.[7] Not only did I come to Hauerwas's work as one animated first and foremost by theological and pastoral concerns, but I read his later, increasingly explicitly theological writings as representative of the theological convictions that were implicitly operative in his earlier work. In other words, I took Hauerwas at his word when he said things like "I understand myself as a theologian and my work as theology proper,"[8] and sought to explore what it might mean to read his work in such a way as to take seriously his assertion that his "primary agenda was and has always been theological."[9]

Taking Stanley Hauerwas seriously as a theologian does not mean expecting that he will conform to the canons of how theology has been done in modernity. He has no time for the perpetual throat-clearing that has characterized modern theology with its preoccupation with prolegomena.[10] Nor does he allow the disciplinary divisions of the modern research university or the modern parcelling up of the theological

---

is Robert Dean, "Unapologetically (A)Political: Stanley Hauerwas and the Practice of Preaching," *Didaskalia*, vol. 25, (Fall 2015): 128–57. Robert John Dean, "For the Life of the World: Jesus Christ and the Church in the Theologies of Dietrich Bonhoeffer and Stanley Hauerwas" (ThD, diss., Wycliffe College - University of Toronto, 2014).

7. Hauerwas comments upon this development in his memoir: "Still, I did begin to notice a difference. I do not know if the difference was enough to say that I was 'changing,' but I noticed I was able to write and speak with less hesitancy about God. I noticed it first when I wrote sermons on the seven last words of Christ for the Good Friday service at Saint Thomas Church Fifth Avenue in New York in 2003." Stanley Hauerwas, *Hannah's Child: A Theologian's Memoir* (Grand Rapids: Eerdmans, 2012), 277.

8. Stanley Hauerwas, *A Community of Character: Toward a Constructive Christian Social Ethic* (Notre Dame: University of Notre Dame Press, 1981), 6.

9. Stanley Hauerwas, *The Hauerwas Reader*, ed. John Berkman and Michael G. Cartwright (Durham: Duke University Press, 2001), 79. This desire to discover a genuinely theological Hauerwas places me "in good company" with the likes of, among others, Samuel Wells, Brian Brock, and Kevin Hargaden. See Samuel Wells, "The Difference Christ Makes," in *The Difference Christ Makes: Celebrating the Life, Work, and Friendship of Stanley Hauerwas*, ed. Charles M. Collier (Eugene, OR: Cascade, 2015), 5–24; Brian Brock and Kevin Hargaden, "Afterword: The End Was There in the Beginning," in Brock and Hauerwas, *Beginnings*, 291–304.

10. Stanley Hauerwas, *A Cross-Shattered Church: Reclaiming the Theological Heart of Preaching* (Grand Rapids: Brazos, 2009), 11.

curriculum to prevent him from rolling up his sleeves and getting down to the work of displaying the truthfulness of Christian convictions that resides in their practical force.[11]

Confronted by the culturally accommodated church of his day and theological faculties that seemed unwilling or unable to address concrete ethical realities, Dietrich Bonhoeffer once exclaimed in exasperation, "Luther was able to write *On the Bondage of the Will* and his piece on usury at the same time. Why can't we do that anymore? *Who will show us Luther!*"[12] Perhaps, somewhat counterintuitively, it may be the self-professed "high-church Mennonite" who, in our time, has shown us Luther.[13] In his transcending of disciplinary divisions, Hauerwas has helped to open the door for the retrieval of a more holistic mode of practicing of theology that previously connected Luther with the Fathers.[14] Furthermore, in his insistence that his own story cannot be properly understood apart from God, Hauerwas has perhaps even provided us, in *Hannah's Child*, with a glimpse of Augustine.[15]

"Watch Out! Here Comes the Spider-Man!"

Hauerwas's commitment to writing a "theological" memoir—a commitment which Hauerwas reflects upon in "Minding the Gaps" in the present volume—is evident from the opening sentence of *Hannah's Child*: "I did not intend to be 'Stanley Hauerwas.'"[16] In light of this opening line, in which Hauerwas attempts to dispel heroic notions concerning himself, it may seem somewhat counterintuitive to compare him to a comic book

---

11. "I have accepted the current academic designation of 'ethics' only because as a theologian I am convinced that the intelligibility and truthfulness of Christian convictions reside in their practical force." Hauerwas, *A Community of Character*, 1.

12. Dietrich Bonhoeffer, *Ecumenical, Academic, and Pastoral Work: 1931–1932*, ed. Victoria Barnett, Mark S. Brocker, and Michael B. Lukens, trans. Anne Schmidt-Lange et al., vol. 11, *Dietrich Bonhoeffer Works* (Minneapolis: Fortress, 2012), 244.

13. Hauerwas has recently stated his admiration for Luther in Brock and Hauerwas, *Beginnings*, 264. Hauerwas introduces his aspiration to be a "high-church Mennonite" in *A Community of Character*, 6.

14. Stanley Hauerwas, *Sanctify Them in the Truth: Holiness Exemplified* (Nashville: Abingdon Press, 1998), 23–29.

15. Hauerwas engages with various reviewers and interlocutors who made connections between his memoir and Augustine's *Confessions* in the afterword to *Hannah's Child*, 295–301.

16. Hauerwas, *Hannah's Child*, ix.

superhero.[17] However, Peter Parker never intended to become the Spider-Man.[18] He simply was in the wrong place at the wrong time (or perhaps it was the right place at the right time) and was bitten by the radioactive spider that forever changed his life. Just as the gangly, angst-ridden teenager was an unlikely candidate to become the defender of New York, it could hardly have been anticipated that the famously foul-mouthed descendant of "white trash" from "hardscrabble land" in Texas would one day be designated "America's best theologian."[19] Yet somewhere along the line Hauerwas was bitten by the theological bug. It may not have resulted in a moment of dramatic transformation, but eventually he came to recognize that his imagination had been seized by the apocalyptic irruption of God's faithfulness to his creation in the person of Jesus Christ.

The apocalyptic thrust of Hauerwas's work is perhaps most clearly displayed in a response Hauerwas once gave to an interviewer who asked him to identify the center of Christianity. Hauerwas replied, "Jesus is Lord and everything else is bullshit."[20] Although this memorable formulation

---

17. That being said, there is something about the larger-than-life public persona of Stanley Hauerwas that could be imagined to emerge from the panels of a comic book. Anyone who has witnessed Hauerwas in action, dressed in an obnoxiously loud tie, riotously laughing at his own jokes, and demonstrating the chutzpah necessary to question long-held and cherished institutional assumptions in public academic and ecclesial settings, knows what I'm talking about.

18. I would simply encourage those who question the appropriateness of such a humorous comparison to read more of Hauerwas's own work. A good place to start would be his recent essay, "How to Be Theologically Funny" in *The Work of Theology* (Grand Rapids: Eerdmans, 2015), 229–249. An excellent exemplification of the use of humor in this vein can be found in William Cavanaugh's entertaining and educative biographical essay, "Stan the Man: A Thoroughly Biased Account of a Completely Unobjective Person" in Hauerwas, *The Hauerwas Reader*, 17–32.

19. For Hauerwas's description of his familial background that employs these terms, see *Hannah's Child*, 22. There is deep irony in the designation "America's Best Theologian" in light of Hauerwas's pronounced and enduring concern that Christians in America have confused being Christian with being American. Furthermore, one wonders what qualifies *TIME* magazine to pronounce upon theology and how one would even go about determining the "best" theologian? For the article that accompanied the designation, see Jean Bethke Elshtain, "Theologian: Christian Contrarian," *Time* (September 17, 2001), 74–75.

20. Justin Brierley, "Stanley Hauerwas Interview: Truthfully Speaking," *Reform*, February 23, 2011, http://oldsite.reform-magazine.co.uk/2011/02/stanley-hauerwas-am-possessed-the-need-know-what-controls-life/. I was alerted to the source of this quotation by Ryan Turnbull in his MA dissertation, "Jesus is Lord: The Particular Imagination in the Work of Stanley Hauerwas," Providence Theological Seminary, Otterburne, MB (2017).

is beloved and frequently invoked by many of Hauerwas's informed—and sometimes not-so-informed—allies, it does not really do justice to the nuance of his thought. As a polemical utterance, the statement is surely intended to contribute to unmasking the idolatrous presumptions that accompany the "and" in grammatical formulations like "God and country."[21] However, the fact that Jesus is Lord does not mean that everything else is bullshit, rather it necessarily entails that everything else matters for "Christ plays in ten thousand places."[22] Douglas Harink astutely observes that "many misunderstandings of Hauerwas's work fail to recognize that he works from a position that can be characterized in the same terms that [J. Louis] Martyn uses of Paul in Galatians: 'Paul's [fundamental issue] is evangelical, cosmic, history-creating christology.'"[23] Although quotations from the Gospel of John do not appear in Hauerwas's corpus with near the regularity as those from the Synoptics, Hauerwas's work could be read as an extended commentary on John's declaration, "the Word became flesh and lived among us" (1:14). The classical Christological dogma of the incarnation is the pivot on which Hauerwas's theology turns.[24] The English essayist Dorothy Sayers waxed in a Hauerwasian key when she addressed the relevance of Christological dogma in a 1940 address entitled, "Creed or Chaos":

> It is not true at all that dogma is 'hopelessly irrelevant' to the life and thought of the average man. What is true is that ministers of

---

21. Hauerwas approvingly quotes Karl Barth, "if you make a start with 'God *and* . . .' you are opening the doors to every demon." Karl Barth, *God in Action* (Eugene, OR: Wipf & Stock, 2005), 138, quoted in Stanley Hauerwas, *Approaching the End: Eschatological Reflections on Church, Politics, and Life* (Grand Rapids: Eerdmans, 2013), 80.

22. The phrase "Christ plays in ten thousand places" is found within a sonnet by Gerard Manley Hopkins. I first became aware of it as result of Eugene Peterson's book *Christ Plays in Ten Thousand Places: A Conversation in Spiritual Theology* (Grand Rapids: Eerdmans, 2005).

23. Douglas Harink, *Paul among the Postliberals: Pauline Theology beyond Christendom and Modernity* (Grand Rapids: Brazos, 2003), 82. Admittedly, Hauerwas and Martyn might inflect the terms "evangelical," "cosmic," and, particularly "history-creating" in slightly different registers. In an essay engaging the work of J. Louis Martyn, Hauerwas suggests that Yoder's apocalyptic account of the Lordship of Christ avoids some of the theological problems associated with Martyn's use of "invasion" terminology and makes obvious the political implications left underdeveloped in Martyn's presentation ("The End of Sacrifice: An Apocalyptic Politics," in *Approaching the End*, 22–36).

24. I have advanced this argument in *For the Life of the World*, 41–71. Wells offers a similar analysis in "The Difference Christ Makes," 5–24.

the Christian religion often assert that it is, present it for consideration as if it were, and, in fact, by their faulty exposition make it so. The central dogma of the Incarnation is that by which relevance stands or falls. If Christ was only a man, then He is entirely irrelevant to any thought about God; if He is only god, then He is entirely irrelevant to any experience of human life. It is, in the strictest sense, *necessary* to the salvation of relevance that a man should believe *rightly* the Incarnation of Our Lord Jesus Christ. Unless he believes rightly, there is not the faintest reason why he should believe at all. And in that case, it is wholly irrelevant to chatter about 'Christian principles'.[25]

Like Sayers, Hauerwas is convinced that the relevance of Christianity is not to be found in its ability to pander to the discriminating tastes and religious preferences of modern men and women, but rather in the condescension of God into the finitude and frailty of human existence in the person of Jesus Christ. The Gospel of Jesus Christ simply *is* relevant because it is the story of "God with us." As a result, the classical Christological doctrine that states that Christ was very God and very man must not be confused with a distillation of the truth of Scripture that can be tweeted in under 140 characters. Rather, it is properly understood as a grammatical cue to aid the church in its reading of Scripture by affixing the church's attention upon the unsubstitutable identity of Jesus Christ as it is narratively displayed in the Gospels.[26]

For Hauerwas, the apocalyptic moment funds what could be construed as catholic sensibilities because the apocalypse has a name: Jesus Christ. Names stand as shorthand for particular stories and the particular name Jesus Christ encompasses not only the story of the first-century

---

25. Dorothy L. Sayers, *Creed or Chaos?: And Other Essays in Popular Theology* (London: Methuen, 1947), 32. The quote from Sayers resonates with John Howard Yoder's reflections upon the ethical significance of the Christological dogma in *The Politics of Jesus: Vicit Agnus Dei*, 2d ed. (Grand Rapids: Eerdmans, 1994), 10.

26. The phrase "unsubstitutable identity" was introduced by Hauerwas's teacher Hans W. Frei in *The Identity of Jesus Christ* (Eugene, OR: Wipf & Stock, 1997). I believe it is difficult to understand what Hauerwas is up to without attending to his two early "Jesus essays" where he unpacks this claim. See "Jesus: The Story of the Kingdom," in *A Community of Character*, 36–52; and "Jesus: The Presence of the Peaceable Kingdom," in *The Peaceable Kingdom: A Primer in Christian Ethics* (Notre Dame: University of Notre Dame Press, 1983), 72–95. See also my discussion in *For the Life of the World*, 45–58. Similar assessments of the importance of these essays are articulated by: Wells "The Difference Christ Makes," 24; Brock and Hargaden, "Afterword: The End Was There in the Beginning," 293; Hauerwas himself in *The Work of Theology* (Grand Rapids: Eerdmans, 2015), 272–73, and in Brock and Hauerwas, *Beginnings*, 269.

Palestinian rabbi from Nazareth who proclaimed the Kingdom of God, healed the sick, drove out demons, ran afoul of the religious and political authorities, was crucified between two thieves, was raised on the third day, and enthroned in power at the right hand of God, but it also enfolds, as the title Messiah indicates, the story of God's chosen people Israel and the new covenant people who bear the Christ's name. Any attempt to tell the story of Jesus apart from the story of Israel and the story of the church is not to tell Jesus's story, but some other story. As Hauerwas starkly frames the matter, "No Israel, no Jesus. No church, no Jesus."[27]

In the recapitulation of the story of Israel and the story of Adam in the apocalyptic advent of Jesus Christ we are given a glimpse of the true humanity that is our destiny and is even now impressing itself upon the present, through the gracious ministrations of the Holy Spirit, drawing a people into the life of Christ.[28] From this apocalyptic perspective it becomes obvious that two of the animating questions that pervade Hauerwas's work—What time is it? and What does it mean to be human?—orbit around a Christological center of gravity. The fact that the apocalyptic irruption of the faithfulness of God to his creation takes the form of a human life reinscribes the timefulness of human existence and gives the world a history. As Hauerwas puts it, "Apocalyptic does not deny the continuation of the history of creation but rather reminds us it is historical exactly because it has an end."[29] The apocalypse of the God of Israel in the life, death, and resurrection of Jesus Christ stories the world through showing us the end, making it possible for us to live patiently as creatures in time.[30]

---

27. Hauerwas, *The Work of Theology*, 39.

28. The apocalyptic character of Hauerwas's work obviously reflects the deep influence of the theology of Karl Barth. However, as the wording of this sentence suggests, there is also a distinctly Irenaen flavor to Hauerwas's apocalyptic theology. See for example his early deployment of the doctrine of recapitulation in "Jesus: The Presence of the Peaceable Kingdom," and a more recent discussion in *Cross-Shattered Christ: Meditations on the Seven Last Words* (Grand Rapids: Brazos, 2004), 86–88. Also noteworthy is the increasing use of the language of "participation" and even "theosis" in his recent writings.

29. Stanley Hauerwas, *Christian Existence Today: Essays on Church, World, and Living in Between* (1988; repr., Grand Rapids: Brazos, 2001), 51.

30. For Hauerwas's explicit discussion of the relation of creation and apocalyptic, see "The End is in the Beginning," in *Approaching the End*, 3–21. For one of Hauerwas's most significant explorations of this eschatological mode of existence, see "Taking Time for Peace: The Ethical Significance of the Trivial," in Hauerwas, *Christian Existence Today*, 253–66.

As a result, themes such as character, virtue, narrative, and community are best understood as tools within Hauerwas's conceptual toolbox that are employed for the sake of accounting for the timefulness of human existence within the apocalyptic time brought into being through the life, death, and resurrection of Jesus.[31] Richard Hays puts it well, when he writes of Hauerwas, "At the end of the day, his work is not defined by the ethics of character, or by pacifism, or by countercultural communitarian ecclesiology. All these elements play important roles in his writings, but they are reflexes or consequences of his more fundamental commitment to think rigorously about the implications of confessing Jesus Christ as Lord."[32] This is not to say that there may not be times when Hauerwas's language "goes on vacation," but only that he is at his best and is most consistent when his conceptual tools are submitted to Christological control.[33]

The mode and method of theologizing must be governed by the reality of the revelation of God in the person of Jesus Christ, if theology is to remain true to its subject matter.[34] As Hauerwas, writing with James Fodor observes, "Its form cannot be separated from its content."[35] According to this apocalyptic logic, theologians betray their calling and subject matter if they seek to establish an epistemological foundation for their work, aspire to carve out a "position" for themselves, or attempt to develop a system of thought. Theologians who attempt to establish an epistemological foundation for their work are implicitly attempting to circumvent the reality of revelation and, in so doing, fail to acknowledge the transcendence of God and the sheer contingency of creation. The apocalypse of the God of Israel in the person of Jesus Christ establishes its own foundation. Reflecting approvingly upon the work of Karl Barth,

---

31. In his skillful interviewing of Hauerwas, Brian Brock has brought to the fore how Hauerwas's somewhat eccentric use of categories like character and virtue are a result of their being qualified by the apocalyptic logic of the Gospel. See Brock and Hauerwas, *Beginnings*, 64, 76, 146–47, 268.

32. Richard B. Hays, foreword to *The Difference Christ Makes*, ix.

33. For example, Hauerwas tells the story of a student who following a public lecture once said to him, "I don't understand where all this virtue talk comes from. We're not called to be virtuous; we're called to be disciples of Christ" (Brock and Hauerwas, *Beginnings*, 243).

34. This, of course, was one of Karl Barth's fundamental insights.

35. Stanley Hauerwas and James Fodor, "Performing Faith: The Peaceable Rhetoric of God's Church," in Stanley Hauerwas, *Performing the Faith: Bonhoeffer and the Practice of Nonviolence* (Grand Rapids: Brazos, 2004), 84.

Hauerwas writes, "Theology rather is the exposition of how God's Word as found in Jesus Christ provides not only its own ground but the ground for all that we know and do."[36] These Barthian convictions lead to Hauerwas's distinctive postfoundational approach to theology, perhaps best encapsulated in his colloquial exclamation, "If you say you need a theory to know if it might be true that God raised Jesus from the dead, worship that *theory*, don't worship the crucified and risen Jesus."[37] This postfoundationalist impulse ties in with Hauerwas's conviction that theologians do not have "positions" because "in a world without foundations all we have is the church."[38] "Theologians do not need to have a position," Hauerwas avers, "because we serve a confessional community that makes our reflections on church practice possible."[39]

Perhaps it could be said that although theologians do not have a position, they do occupy a location. Theologians occupy an office within the church as servants of the Gospel that has called into being a people who through the Spirit participate in the new humanity of the Son unto the glory of God the Father. For this reason, Hauerwas affirms, "The work of theology is a second-order activity that depends on the actual existence of a people who have learned to worship God."[40] This leads into Hauerwas's concerns about construing the work of theology in systematizing terms. Hauerwas worries that "such theology in our time cannot avoid giving the impression that Christianity is a set of ideas that need to be made consistent with one another."[41] However, Christianity is not a set of ideas waiting to be organized by the theologian; it is, rather, a life constituted by a constellation of practices emerging from the story of God's salvation in Christ through which the people of God are inscribed within the network of Trinitarian relations. Theologians, therefore, always begin in the middle, for they find themselves immersed in the

36. Hauerwas, *Sanctify Them in the Truth*, 32–33.

37. Stanley Hauerwas, *Disrupting Time: Sermons, Prayers, and Sundries* (Eugene, OR: Cascade, 2004), 215.

38. Stanley Hauerwas, *In Good Company: The Church as Polis* (Notre Dame: University of Notre Dame Press, 1995), 33. Interestingly, the essay from which the quote is taken, "The Church's One Foundation Is Jesus Christ Her Lord or In a World without Foundations All We Have is the Church" largely consists of a series of sermonic exemplifications through which Hauerwas attempts "to use a practice central to the church's life in which form and matter are one" (34).

39. Hauerwas, *The Work of Theology*, 26.

40. Hauerwas, *The Work of Theology*, 264.

41. Hauerwas, *Sanctify Them in the Truth*, 1–2.

gloriously thick reality of the creating, reconciling, and perfecting work of the Triune God which always precedes them. The attempt to develop a comprehensive theological system would be to deny both the timefulness of our existence as creatures who always find themselves *in media res* as pilgrims and *viators* enroute to the celestial city and to deny that it is, in fact, the God who forever exceeds our intellectual and linguistic grasp that we meet in Christ. Humility, therefore, may be the defining theological virtue for theologians seeking to inhabit the apocalyptic time ushered in by the Spirit in the raising of Christ from the dead, for it turns out the faithful practice of theology requires the recognition that the theologian's work is never done.[42]

These apocalyptically fuelled convictions about theological method are not meant to deny that there is a coherence to the Christian faith. In fact, the various Christian beliefs hang together "like an elegant web that is at once delicate but also strong. Leave out one part and the whole web collapses."[43] Although Hauerwas's brick-laying analogies are perhaps better known, his metaphor of theology as a web, first introduced in *Sanctify Them in the Truth*, has risen to a place of particular prominence in his recent work.[44] It turns out that if we are to understand Hauerwas in his own terms, we must think of him as a kind of Spider-Man. While awestruck readers might be tempted to think of him as effortlessly swinging between skyscrapers bearing the names of Barth, Aquinas, MacIntyre, and Wittgenstein, skimming across the rooftops of countless other more humble structures, it is more in keeping with Hauerwas's own self-understanding to see him scurrying across the surface of the web, diligently working to repair, discover, and make articulate the connections necessary for Christians faithfully to make their way in the world.[45] The web

---

42. For a mere sampling of Hauerwas's comments on the unfinished character of theology, see Hauerwas, *The Work of Theology*, 252, 259, 264; Hauerwas, *Approaching the End*, 20–21; Brock and Hauerwas, *Beginnings*, 44.

43. Stanley Hauerwas and William H. Willimon, *The Holy Spirit* (Nashville: Abingdon Press, 2015), 11.

44. Hauerwas, *Sanctify Them in the Truth*, 2; Hauerwas, *Approaching the End*, 5; Hauerwas, *The Work of Theology*, 257–58, 273; Hauerwas and Willimon, *The Holy Spirit*, 11. Hauerwas cites a line from an essay by Robert Jenson as the originating inspiration for the analogy in "The Church and the Sacraments," in *The Cambridge Companion to Christian Doctrine*, ed. Colin Gunton (Cambridge: Cambridge University Press, 1997), 207.

45. The importance of identifying connections between contingencies in order to properly construe the world is something Hauerwas has learned from Wittgenstein.

is not constructed from ideational building blocks, rather its strands emerge organically from the totality of the reality of the world created and redeemed through the Word enfleshed in Jesus.

This suggests that there is a significant pneumatological dimension to Hauerwas's understanding of the work of theology, as "Jesus can be known only through the connections the Spirit makes possible."[46] To attempt to do theology in such a manner may suggest that theologians find themselves in a rather tenuous position, something akin to a high-wire performer operating without the assurance of a safety net; for if there are no foundations, then theology is "performance all the way down."[47] As Hauerwas and Fodor make clear, "the intelligibility (and hence the persuasiveness) of Christian faith springs not from independently formulated criteria, but from compelling renditions, faithful performances."[48] Therefore, it is crucial for the work of the theologian and for the life of the church to be able to identify the virtuoso performers who have been able to "keep time" with God. This is why Jean Vanier has been such a significant figure in Hauerwas's work.[49] Vanier appears, once again, in this book to play a leading role in "Why Jean Vanier Matters: An Exemplary Exploration." Without faithful performers like Vanier, the church would lack the imaginative resources to know how to go on. However, Hauerwas's emphasis on exemplification arising from his refusal to separate doctrine and ethics, and the "what" from the "how" of belief, presents him and all who have been influenced by his work with an intractable dilemma. Namely, what are we to make of the work of John Howard Yoder now that the horrific magnitude of his sexually abusive behavior toward

---

See, for example, Hauerwas's essay, "Connections Created and Contingent," in *Performing the Faith*, 111–34. The definitive treatment of Wittgenstein's influence on Hauerwas remains Brad Kallenberg, *Ethics as Grammar: Changing the Postmodern Subject* (Notre Dame: University of Notre Dame Press, 2001).

46. Hauerwas, *The Work of Theology*, 39.

47. Hauerwas, *The Work of Theology*, 24.

48. James Fodor and Stanley Hauerwas, "Performing Faith: The Peaceable Rhetoric of God's Church," in *Performing the Faith*, 78. This important essay develops the argument that theology is the faithful performing of a rhetoric.

49. See, for example, Stanley Hauerwas, *Dispatches from the Front: Theological Engagements with the Secular* (Durham: Duke University Press, 1994), 188–89; Hauerwas, *Sanctify Them in the Truth*, 143–56; Hauerwas, *Performing the Faith*, 209–10; Stanley Hauerwas and Romand Coles, *Christianity, Democracy, and the Radical Ordinary: Conversations between a Radical Democrat and a Christian* (Eugene, OR: Cascade, 2008), 103–5, 195–207; Stanley Hauerwas and Jean Vanier, *Living Gently in a Violent World: The Prophetic Witness of Weakness* (Downers Grove: InterVarsity, 2008).

women has come more clearly into focus? While Hauerwas's account is unlikely to satisfy everyone, his unwillingness to shy away from a personally distressing topic that needed to be addressed is to be commended. Furthermore, in taking responsibility for his ignorance of the scope and scale of Yoder's abusive behaviour, Hauerwas has modelled the type of humility that must characterize not only the work of the theologian, but the life of the Christian, if we are to make our lives our own.[50]

There is no doubt that Hauerwas's construal of theology contributes to a rather ambitious intellectual agenda. Put simply, "if the task of theology is to show that the world we experience can only make sense in the light of what has been done through the life, death, and resurrection of Jesus there is no subject foreign to the work of theology."[51] This conviction accounts for the astonishing array of interlocutors represented in Hauerwas's work and contributes to the difficulty of comfortably locating Hauerwas's work amongst any of the disciplinary silos represented within modern theological faculties. While Hauerwas's commitment to understanding theology as an exercise in practical reason often earns him the designation of "ethicist," I believe a case can be made for understanding Hauerwas as, if not a pastoral theologian, then a "pastor's theologian." The concrete realities of everyday life are the fields in which the pastor daily labors. The siloed character of contemporary theological education provides little help to the seminary graduate when they find themselves out in the pastorate, as they soon discover that life is not parceled out in sanitized, stackable Tupperware containers.[52] Furthermore, the attempt to preserve the disciplinary divisions under which they were educated can only result in a disheveled or even schizophrenic pastoral existence, devoid of conviction and power. Hauerwas's work is invaluable for helping pastors to attend to the connections between what they do when they meet with the session around the board table, drink tea with the widow in her living room, give food vouchers to the homeless man who has arrived at the door of their study, and their paradigmatic service of ministering in the presence of the risen Lord in the pulpit and at the Table. Hauerwas's contribution to this end continues in this volume, as he turns

50. See Hauerwas's discussion of repentance in Brock and Hauerwas, *Beginnings*, 151.

51. Hauerwas, *The Work of Theology*, 259.

52. For recent reflections from Hauerwas on the place of theology in ministry, see *The Work of Theology*, 103–21.

once again to the witness of perhaps the most preeminent "pastor's theologian" of the twentieth century and displays "Why Bonhoeffer Matters."

"Your Friendly Neighborhood Spider-Man"

Pastors deal in particulars. Until very recently they almost always ministered in geographically defined parishes. Similarly, the comic book hero Spider-Man made a name for himself thwarting villains in New York City. In light of his convictions surrounding the profoundly contextual, or better occasional, nature of theology, we would be remiss if we did not consider the neighborhood in which Hauerwas, the theological Spider-Man, has made his home.[53] Hauerwas's neighborhood has been dying Western Christendom, particularly as that phenomenon has found expression in the United States. Hauerwas has recently called attention to the following sentence as exemplifying the concerns that have animated his work: "In the shadows of a dying Christendom the challenge is how to recover a strong theological voice without that voice betraying the appropriate fragility of all speech—but particularly speech about God."[54] Recovering a strong theological voice without betraying the appropriate fragility of all Christian speech is a less pressing concern if one does not share the presumption that Christendom is dying. I suspect this is why a significant number of the monograph-length studies of Hauerwas's work have origins outside of the United States.[55] While it may be possible for

---

53. Hauerwas approvingly cites John Webster in expressing his preference for the term "occasional" to "contextual" as a descriptor of the character of the theological task. He fears that proponents of "contextual" theology too often take the context as given and fail to recognize that the context itself must be interpreted theologically. Hauerwas, *Performing the Faith*, 22–23n.19, quoting John Webster, *Word and Church: Essays in Christian Dogmatics* (Edinburgh: T. & T. Clark, 2001), 4–5. In doing so, however, he in no way denies the locally and temporally conditioned nature of theological reflection.

54. Hauerwas, *The Work of Theology*, 113.

55. See, for example, Arne Rasmusson, *The Church as Polis: From Political Theology to Theological Politics as Exemplified by Jurgen Moltmann and Stanley Hauerwas* (Notre Dame: University of Notre Dame Press, 1995); Emmanuel Katongole, *Beyond Universal Reason: The Relation between Religion and Ethics in the Work of Stanley Hauerwas* (Notre Dame: University of Notre Dame Press, 2000); John B. Thomson, *The Ecclesiology of Stanley Hauerwas: A Christian Theology of Liberation* (Aldershot: Ashgate, 2003); Samuel Wells, *Transforming Fate into Destiny the Theological Ethics of Stanley Hauerwas* (Eugene, OR: Cascade, 2004); John B. Thomson, *Living Holiness: Stanley Hauerwas and the Church* (London: Epworth, 2010); Ariaan W. Baan, *The*

Christians in America to convince themselves that the United States still is, or may yet one day be, a great Christian nation, the political situations on the ground in Europe, Australia, and Canada make the demise of Christendom a reality much harder to avoid.

It is Hauerwas's situatedness as a neighborhood theologian that informs his enduring quarrel with liberalism, as the false cosmopolitanism of liberalism represents the denial of place and the historicity of human existence. This is not to deny that liberalism may be socially useful. Hauerwas acknowledges that "liberalism as a practice for organizing cooperative arrangements between moral strangers could be good for Christians."[56] However, he goes on to observe that it is not so clear that liberalism is good for liberals. "Indeed," Hauerwas writes, "I thought my critiques of liberalism were charitable because my criticisms were an attempt to suggest to liberals that there are alternatives to a liberal way of life."[57] The church provides such an alternative to the timelessness and placelessness of liberalism, for it is a people who have been storied by the history of God's covenantal dealings with a people and his dwelling in their midst within Temples built of stones and living stones, and ultimately from the flesh of the Virgin. However, if Christians allow the political presumptions of liberalism to efface the particularity of our story, then the difference Christ makes is lost. Hauerwas continues to develop this argument in the current book through drawing the work of one of his lesser-known teachers, the Yale theologian Robert Calhoun, into conversation with that of George Lindbeck and Alasdair MacIntyre to help us see that "The Past Matters Theologically."

Theologians have a past. They are part of the church's ongoing argument about how to best enact and interpret the Christian story found in the Scripture. Standing within this tradition, they write *coram Deo* for a particular audience in specific contexts at discrete moments in time. (This is quite evident, for example, in the "Aberdeen Graduation Address" included in this volume, where Hauerwas attempts to address a timely word to the graduates that goes beyond the weightlessness and sheer banality that often characterizes speeches delivered on such occasions.) The occasional character of theological work means that there is much the contemporary theologian can learn from the letters found within the

---

Necessity of Witness: Stanley Hauerwas's Contribution to Systematic Theology (Eugene, OR: Pickwick, 2015); Dean, *For the Life of the World*.

56. Hauerwas, *The Work of Theology*, 182.
57. Hauerwas, *The Work of Theology*, 182.

New Testament, elicited as they were by the pressing needs facing the nascent Christian communities. For Hauerwas, theology is inextricably bound to "the necessity to respond to the challenges of trying to discern what being a Christian entails in this place and at this time."[58] One of the foremost challenges that Hauerwas has discerned to be facing the church in his "neighborhood" over the course of his career is the continuing challenge of how to negotiate being a Christian in America. "A Sanctuary Politics," written with Jonathan Tran, takes up the challenge of wrestling what it means for the church to be the church in the time of Trump.

The co-authoring of "A Sanctuary Politics" points to a further clarification that must be made if our whimsical image of Hauerwas as a Spider-Man is to adequately serve our cause. For the comic-book character, the expression "your friendly neighborhood Spider-Man" was a means of combatting the popular notion that he was simply a vigilante or even a nefarious criminal. In our context, to call attention to the "friendliness" of the Spider-Man that is Hauerwas is to suggest that behind what is sometimes perceived to be a gruff and combative public persona there lies a kind and gentle man whose life has been constituted by friendship.[59] Hauerwas must not be mistaken for a black-widow spider jealously guarding her web, even to the point of devouring her mate. Rather, he is more like a member of the *Anelosimus eximius* species of spiders, which work and live together in large colonies, building, maintaining, and cleaning webs that expand to over twenty-five feet in length. Friendship is at the heart of theology, because at its heart theology is about the God who has claimed us as friends. In his patient reading of such a wide breadth of texts, his loyal support and encouragement of his graduate students, and his gracious inclusion of outsiders, like myself, in his ever-expanding circle of friends, Hauerwas has reminded us that friendship must not only find a place in the theologian's body of writing, but must ultimately come to characterize the theologian's body.

---

58. Hauerwas, *The Work of Theology*, 24.

59. *Hannah's Child* could be read as an extended exemplification of the claim that Hauerwas's life has been constituted by friendship. For explorations of the place of friendship in Hauerwas's life and work, see J. Alexander Sider, "Friendship, Alienation, Love: Stanley Hauerwas and J. Howard Yoder," in *Unsettling Arguments: A Festschrift on the Occasion of Stanley Hauerwas's 70th Birthday*, ed. Charles R. Pinches, Kelly S. Johnson, and Charles M. Collier (Eugene, OR: Cascade, 2010), 61–86; Paul J. Wadell, "Friendship," in *Unsettling Arguments*, 265–83; Dean, *For the Life of the World*, 206–14.

"With Great Power Comes Great Responsibility"

Concluding this essay by quoting the famous charge given to Spider-Man by his dying uncle—"with great power comes great responsibility"—may be enough to cause long-time readers of Hauerwas, who up to this point have patiently endured a rather fanciful analogy, to throw up their hands in disbelief. After all, any experienced reader of Hauerwas knows that the category "responsibility" is often nothing more than an empty cipher used by Christian ethicists to rationalize the accommodation of the church to modern liberal democratic social orders.[60] Whether Stan Lee, the creator of Spider-Man, was a Niebuhrian is not my concern. My interest is in the way this saying serves as a commissioning formula that propels Spider-Man on mission. Responsibility can also be understood in a dialogical fashion where it qualifies the human subject who has been addressed by God.[61] This naturally brings us into the realm of vocation.

Stanley Hauerwas is a man on a mission. While his voluminous literary output could perhaps be dismissed by an appeal to some type of pathology, such an explanation does not account for his proclivity for friendship, as discussed a moment ago, or the thousands of miles he has travelled in response to invitations to speak at churches, seminaries, and universities. In his criss-crossing of the continent and circling of the globe, Hauerwas has played a role something akin to that of a travelling evangelist. While he may not be seeking to save the souls of the lost in the manner of the evangelists who led the tent revivals in his hometown of Pleasant Grove, Texas, Hauerwas is very much on an evangelizing mission. I would suggest that this is reflected in the way that preaching has become increasingly important for his work. "Preaching," Hauerwas argues, "is not a matter of apologetics but rather of evangelization. That is, preaching must be understood as part of the whole church's ministry to convert our lives by having them constituted by a narrative that we have not chosen, but which has chosen us."[62] Make no mistake about it,

---

60. See, for example, Stanley Hauerwas, *After Christendom?: How the Church Is to Behave If Freedom, Justice, and a Christian Nation Are Bad Ideas* (Nashville: Abingdon Press, 1999), 31.

61. Dietrich Bonhoeffer is a theologian who understands the concept of responsibility in such a manner. Dietrich Bonhoeffer, *Ethics*, ed. Clifford J. Green, trans. Reinhard Krauss, Charles C. West, and Douglas W. Stott, vol. 6, *Dietrich Bonhoeffer Works* (Minneapolis: Fortress Press, 2005), 254–57.

62. William H. Willimon and Stanley Hauerwas, *Preaching to Strangers: Evangelism in Today's World* (Louisville: Westminster/John Knox, 1992), 10.

Hauerwas is out to convert us all. In this regard, there is a certain Kierkegaardian character to Hauerwas's work. While longtime readers of Hauerwas may recognize the thread of the great Dane's influence running throughout his work, here in the present volume we are finally granted the opportunity to observe a direct engagement between Hauerwas and his Copenhagen-based, fellow theological provocateur in "Kierkegaard and the Academy: A Theological Meditation."

Despite his disavowals of apologetics as an enterprise, Hauerwas often employs a form of *ad hoc* apologetics as part of his evangelizing efforts. These apologetic forays are conducted not on the basis of any systemic correlation, but rather are grounded in the recognition that "Jesus is the shape of natural theology."[63] As a result, we often see Hauerwas allowing, as he does in "The Good Life" in this book, the light of Christ to shine through the cracks of our shattered and sin-riddled existence, in order to awaken our senses to the plenitude of life that awaits us in God. In all of his work, Hauerwas has been diligently laboring to assemble "reminders of the significance of saying Jesus is Lord,"[64] so that Christians, half-Christians, and not-yet-Christians alike, may come to perceive the truth of our existence in the vulnerable beauty of the Crucified One.

Once there was no "Stanley Hauerwas." One day there will be no Stanley Hauerwas, but until then, may the web-slinging continue. If Hauerwas is right, there are always new connections to be discovered, old connections to be recovered and restored, and new friends to be welcomed into the colony. Let us thank God that there is no shortage of good work for Stanley—and for us—to do.

---

63. Wells, "The Difference Christ Makes," 27.
64. Brock and Hauerwas, *Beginnings: Interrogating Hauerwas*, 241.

Part I

MATTERS THEOLOGICAL

1

Why Language Matters Theologically

On Reading and Writing

On Writing

"Call me Ismael." Did Melville begin with that line or find it along the way as he wrote his great novel? I would like to think he found it along the way and that is one of the reasons it is so unforgettable. I would like to believe he found the sentence along the way because such sentences are so important that one suspects they could only be discovered with great difficulty. Sentences like "Call me Ismael" seem so organic, as if they just "happen"; but once they are found, they can never be replaced. Their very existence as a sentence creates a kind of necessity. Once a sentence like "Call me Ismael" exists, we know it cannot not exist.

A first sentence must be written to seduce the reader into reading the next sentence, and the next, and the next, until all the sentences have been read. That is true, for example, of the sentence I have just written. I wonder if the sentences with which I began meant whoever is now reading this could not resist reading this far? I should hope that to be the case, as I hope to seduce any reader of these sentences to read further.

Yet why am I writing about writing when I am trying to convince you to read? The reason that I can only write about reading by writing about writing is, as Verlyn Klinkenborg writes in his marvelous book *Several Short Sentences about Writing*, "You can only become a better writer by becoming a better reader."[1] It may even be true for some that you can only become a better reader by becoming a better writer.

That reading and writing are inseparable crafts is a widely shared presumption by writers and readers. Writers, however, are more likely than readers to argue that you only become a writer by reading what other writers have written. Some writers even report that they learned to write by copying sentence after sentence from another writer's novel or essay. Some readers who have become writers even tell us that in the process of copying one sentence after another sentence before they knew it they had copied a whole novel.

Most readers of this essay, I suspect, are willing to grant that there is an important relation between reading and writing, but they might wonder why reading and writing matter theologically. I want to explore that question by attending to two writers, Rowan Williams and Craig Keen, who have written on the theological significance of writing, or, more accurately, on why language matters theologically. I will also take a side glance at Alasdair MacIntyre's account of language, because MacIntyre develops an illuminating account of language by exploring how other species besides humans may develop innovative modes of communication. MacIntyre helps us see how at once we share many characteristics with other animals, while at the same time making clear the difference language makes. Williams and Keen, however, are crucial for the case I want to make because they are eloquent writers of theology who share in common a sense of how difficult it is to say what we mean. Crucial for both is Williams's contention that "the labor involved in scrutinizing and using language about God with integrity is bound up with the scrutiny of language itself."[2]

I focus on Williams and Keen because they write beautifully about the importance of writing beautifully about God. That is a great achievement because it is generally acknowledged that many theologians do not even write clearly, much less with beauty. The reasons theologians do not write well are no doubt complex, but at least one of the reasons is the relegation of theology to the university with the result that theologians now write mainly for other theologians. That theology has become primarily an academic specialty means theology—like many academic

---

1. Verlyn Klinkenborg, *Several Short Sentences about Writing* (New York: Vintage, 2012), 17.

2. Rowan Williams, *The Edge of Words: God and the Habits of Language* (London: Bloomsbury, 2014), 17.

subjects—has confused incomprehensibility with profundity. Williams and Keen do not make that mistake.

It may be objected that Williams and Keen write primarily not about writing but about language. That is not surprising if you take notice of the fact that without language there would be no writing or reading. There is no correlate between those that write well and reflection on the nature of language itself, yet we should not be surprised that writers cannot resist trying to understand the words they use. Williams and Keen are theologians who not only develop accounts about the theological significance of language, they also write beautifully about why language is so important. I begin with Williams because his account of the incomplete character of language illumines Keen's work.

Rowan Williams on Language

It is not surprising that Rowan Williams chose to concentrate on language in his Gifford Lectures delivered at the University of Edinburgh. It is not surprising because anyone who has followed Williams's work over the years finds familiar themes in the published version of his lectures entitled, *The Edge of Words: God and the Habits of Language*. Deeply influenced by Wittgenstein, at the heart of Williams's theological project has been what Charles Taylor has identified as the constitutive understanding of language. Taylor contrasts the constitutive view of language with what he calls the "enframing" account of communication. The enframing account of language assumes that life, behavior, purpose, and mental functioning can be described without reference to language.[3] In contrast, for the constitutive view of language, a view Taylor attributes to Herder, there is no "outside" of language because any attempt to get at "reality" without language flounders on the reality that "reality" is linguistically constituted.[4]

The constitutive understanding of language, an understanding made possible only by having at our disposal linguistic resources, is the condition of the possibility of our being able to think at all. Yet because we are possessed by language, we are able to have ever changing emotions, goals, and relationships. Language, therefore, by its very nature cannot avoid,

---

3. Charles Taylor, *The Language Animal: The Full Shape of the Human Linguistic Capacity* (Cambridge: Harvard University Press, 2016), 3.

4. Taylor, *The Language Animal*, 4.

nor should language users try to escape, the necessity of new meanings being introduced into the world. Meaning is created because through language new properties—for example, new objects of admiration and/or indignation—are introduced into the world.[5]

I have begun with Taylor's account of language as a way to introduce Williams's very sophisticated account of what it means for us to be language-constituted beings. Though he does not use the term "constitutive," Williams's view of how we become language users is very similar to Taylor's—thus Williams's remark that "the fact of language is a good deal more puzzling than we usually recognize."[6] It is so, even though we normally think our language represents to us and makes present to us the patterns and rhythms of our world. Representation, however, is not a passive process.

Williams challenges the assumption that the primary task of language is to describe the world by distinguishing two ways of thinking about how we speak about our linguistic encounters with the world. Description is the name he gives to our presumption that the task of language is to produce a map that makes possible a structural parallel between what we say and what we perceive. Such a view of language, however, fails to account for what Williams calls the representational work of language that seeks "to embody, translate, make present or reform what is perceived."[7]

Williams's intent in *The Edge of Words* is to illumine the representational process, which he takes to be more significant than our mistaken presumption that description is more basic. The representational character of language presumes, as well as expresses, our ability to be an agent. To be sure, on Williams's reading, we are complex agents, but nonetheless because of speech we are capable of acting in the world. We cannot, however, describe the world any way we want. "We cannot in human discourse simply say what we please."[8] Yet we cannot know the limits of what we can say in principle because we cannot know the full range of possible schemata.[9]

5. Taylor, *The Language Animal*, 47.
6. Williams, *The Edge of Words*, ix.
7. Williams, *The Edge of Words*, 22–23.
8. Williams, *The Edge of Words*, 26.
9. Williams, *The Edge of Words*, 26.

WHY LANGUAGE MATTERS THEOLOGICALLY 25

> This means we cannot place a limit on conceptual possibilities. The diversity of representational possibilities points toward an understanding of our language as fundamentally unfinished. This unfinished character of language establishes us as speakers who must constantly seek to respond to changes in our place in the world. Metaphysically this means that claims to represent our environment presuppose, as Herbert McCabe suggested, that the universe not only looks like, but is a network of communication.[10]

We are at once determined and freed by our ability to speak. The freedom that characterizes language, a freedom that makes it possible to be truthful by what we say, comes through the struggle to say the right words in appropriate contexts. To test our language requires intelligent discernment because our language

> creates a world, and so entails a constant losing and rediscovering of what is encountered. The connectedness of language to what is not language is a shifting pattern of correlation, not an index-like relation of cause and effect. We cannot easily imagine human speaking without the risk of metaphor, without the possibility of error and misprision, without the possibility of fiction, whether simple lying or cooperative fantasy. In other words, the human speaker takes the world as itself a 'project': the environment is there not as a fixed object for describing and managing but as a tantalizing set of invitations, material offered for reworking and enlarging.[11]

This incomplete character of language makes it necessary to reach for the perspective of another. When we speak we are engaged not only with other speakers in our immediate context, but with those represented by time-constituted rituals and fictional narratives. That language is inherently filled with time is an indication of our finitude. Constituted by time, our thoughts and words presuppose as well as indicate the necessity of community for our ability to speak truthfully to one another and to avoid deceiving ourselves.[12]

We are always saying more than we know, but that is simply a reminder that language is, as we are, finite and historical. While language can be used to distort the truth, as well as to lie, the very ability to lie

---

10. Williams, *The Edge of Words*, xi.
11. Williams, *The Edge of Words*, 59–60.
12. Williams, *The Edge of Words*, 86–87.

depends on our ability as language users to use language to represent that which is not itself. In short, without language we would be incapable of being truthful. According to Williams, however, the truth is often to be found in the silences that surround what we say. Silences are testimony to the unfinished character of language manifest by the very fact that we are often aware of what has not been said that needs to be said, even though we are unsure how to say what needs to be said.[13]

The incomplete character of our language is an indication that what Williams describes as "the sacred" is present in our lives. The sacred names the fact that just to the extent that we are able to speak we cannot escape the reality that we are related to something that is other than ourselves. Yet that "something" is closer to us than we are to ourselves because in a certain sense it speaks us. The indeterminate, incomplete, embodied character of our language expressed in metaphor and formal structure is "interwoven with a silence that opens up further possibilities of speech."[14]

"Opening the possibilities of further speech," Williams takes to be a description of how theological language must work. Knowledge of God is not found in the experience of religious ecstasy or when we feel alone in the universe. Rather, to know God is to develop an understanding of how our thinking and feeling become de-centered, if not dispossessed, through the very ability we have to speak. Any claims to represent God are thereby to be tested by whether such a representation entails a dispossession and deepened capacity to be still. Williams sums up his view by quoting Maggie Ross: "Every true sacred sign effaces itself."[15]

Williams disavows any suggestions that his appeal to silence is a way to "prove" the existence of God. Rather, he thinks the complexity of language that he has tried to describe is what we should expect if Christ is, in fact, the Word of God. In short, just as we discover the silence of language through speech, so we discover why Jesus must be known by revelation, that is, we can only know he is the Son of God through his humanity. Christian doctrine, therefore, points to the irony that unconditioned reality communicates itself in the conditioned reality of the death of a Jewish man.[16]

13. Williams, *The Edge of Words*, 167–168.

14. Williams, *The Edge of Words*, 170.

15. Williams, *The Edge of Words*, 175, quoting Maggie Ross, *Writing the Icon of the Heart: In Silence Beholding* (Eugene, OR: Cascade, 2013), 46.

16. Williams, *The Edge of Words*, 180.

Williams concludes his investigation of the character of language by observing that in our day it is worth remembering that it is not simply God's existence that is at issue, but the existence and continuation of what it means to be human. Thus Williams chose to focus on language because our humanity is to be gained through the distinctively human ability to speak. By developing an account of our continuity with as well as difference from animals, Alasdair MacIntyre provides an account of language that I think supplements what we have learned from Williams.

A MacIntyrian Interlude

MacIntyre develops his account of language, an account that reflects his indebtedness to philosophers in the Wittgensteinian tradition, in his book, *Dependent Rational Animals: Why Human Beings Need the Virtues*.[17] I call particular attention to his account in this book because he helps us better understand how communication is possible between animals that do not have a language.

Drawing on studies of dolphins by Louis Herman, MacIntyre observes that no one who has studied dolphins doubts that dolphins have a sophisticated system of communication. They not only communicate to one another, but they also have a remarkable capacity for innovative and creative forms of communication. These include, for example, responses to the challenge of capturing schools of fish for food. MacIntyre argues, therefore, that though animals like dolphins do not have a language, they are best described as prelinguistic because they have the capacity to communicate with us.

MacIntyre directs our attention to the ability of dolphins to communicate to suggest that though we are linguistic animals, like dolphins our linguistic ability draws on prelinguistic capacities. However, as talking animals, in order to speak to each other, we must have at our disposal a stock of expressions with syntactical rules that make possible the matching of names to the bearers of those names. Our sentences must be embedded in forms of social practice—practices often rooted in the body—that make possible our ability to know what kind of speech act has been or is being made—e.g., whether I am asking a question or

---

17. Alasdair MacIntyre, *Dependent Rational Animals: Why Human Beings Need the Virtues* (Chicago: Open Court, 1999), 26–27.

making a request.[18] MacIntyre develops these reflections about language to suggest that adult human behavior and activity develops out of, and in many ways is dependent on, modes of activity that we share with other intelligent animals. Accordingly, the behavior of those species of animals, like dolphins, must be understood as kin to language users such as ourselves. As language users, we rely in large areas of our lives on the kind of recognitions, discriminations, and perceptual attention that shape our linguistic powers.[19]

MacIntyre's suggestion about the life shared by language users at once supports and extends Williams's account of the significance of language. In particular, MacIntyre's emphasis on the dependence of language on a tradition with a stock vocabulary that makes possible innovative interventions is important if we are to understand how Christians talk. In MacIntyre's terms, Christian speech depends on the practices of a people called Christian, but that does not mean the language of the faith is esoteric. It does, however, require innovative interventions because what it means to be Christian is a matter of ongoing discovery.

Another way to put the matter, a way that I have called attention to in earlier work, is that the necessarily innovative character of theology demands we see and make connections.[20] I have long wanted to entitle a book *Connections*, because if I have any talent it is for seeing connections. It is not just seeing connections, for example, between words and sentences, though that is very important, but seeing connections between social and political realities and what and how we say what we say. That is Craig Keen's great gift. He helps us see that our very humanity is at stake in how we speak.

Craig Keen on Writing Theology

In the preface to his book *After Crucifixion: The Promise of Theology*, Keen begins with this surprising sentence: "Not only a writer's pride or

---

18. MacIntyre, *Dependent Rational Animals*, 29–30.

19. MacIntyre, *Dependent Rational Animals*, 40–41.

20. Stanley Hauerwas, *Sanctify Them in the Truth: Holiness Exemplified* (Edinburgh: T. & T. Clark, 2016), 1–3. I begin the preface to *In Good Company: The Church as Polis* (Notre Dame: University of Notre Dame Press, 1995) with the sentence "Christianity is connections" (xiii). At that time I was thinking of connections between people across time and space. Such connections make possible the innovative character of Christian speech.

her humility may lead her to settle on the conviction that the book she has written is extraordinary."[21] That sentence is not in the league of "Call me Ismael," but it does the work Keen meant for it to do. Namely the sentence sets the context for his confession that though he is both proud and humbled he nonetheless believes he has written an important book. He is quick to observe that "an extraordinary book is not necessarily a good book" (x), but it remains clear he is not trying to win the reader's agreement by practicing false humility. He observes that "pride and humility are complicated phenomena that not uncommonly rub off on the work in which they are complicit" (ix)—a beautifully written sentence in which Keen rightly should take pride while being reminded that humility cannot be left behind.

It is not surprising, therefore, that in the sentence that follows his claim to have written an extraordinary book, he reminds us that both pride and humility "come in handy" when we are engaged in prolonged and difficult tasks—like writing books. Keen confesses, and confesses is the right word, that he is sure in the writing of the book he has been both proud and humble, because in the writing of the book he has found himself against himself through comparison with others whose levels of energy are greater than his own. Consequently, as he has written this book he has felt alternatively good and bad about a choice of word, the turn of a phrase, and the way phrases "tumble together" to make paragraphs and sections and chapters and, suddenly, a whole book.

After Crucifixion is a strange book that seems to have tumbled out of Keen's soul. It is a book that defies any easy description about what it is about. It does so because, as Keen acknowledges, he introduces one subject after another with the result that one is not sure how it all fits together. For example, Keen lists the subjects he will treat: "from immigration to education, from the history of metaphysics to the Gospel of Mark, from urban planning to martyrdom, from brain physiology to ecclesiology, from wounded bodies to the forgiveness of sins, from hard work, hard death, from time to resurrection, from theological method to the doctrine of the Trinity" (x)—and much more. Keen is unapologetic about the scattered nature of the book's subjects because he does not understand his book to be a book about anything. It is not a book about anything because, he tells the reader, "what I have written is a prayer, a prayer I have prayed in the writing" (x).

21. Craig Keen, *After Crucifixion: The Promise of Theology* (Eugene, OR: Cascade, 2013), ix. Paginations for Keen's book will appear in the text.

The above paragraphs are meant to call attention to Keen's writing to indicate the art of his sentences that are shaped by what he takes his task to be. After the initial beginnings, he tells us that his book is meant to be an introduction to theology. But he knows it is a *weird* introduction to theology because the "position" taken in the book "will not stay still long enough to stake a claim" (x). Yet he persists in calling the book an introduction because "*After Crucifixion* is an invitation to you, an invitation to dance, to think, to pray, to hear an extraordinary, weird, uncanny beat and move to it—with me" (xi).

Keen's writing has the character of poetry. Indeed, he tells us that he has spent an enormous amount of time agonizing over word choices. He explains such attention to words is required when you are writing, as he is, for so many audiences. He uses puns and etymologies of words to signal the extent to which words often speak with more than one voice. Accordingly, he lets the awkwardness of certain phrases gesture in the direction of "the text's multiple concurrent personalities" (xiii). If you have had any doubt that Keen has a poetic sensibility, "concurrent personalities" should be sufficient to still such worries.

Having directed attention to the care he has used in his choice of words, Keen then makes explicit why he takes this to be so important for theological writing. For Keen, the task of theological writing is "to write words off themselves" (xiii). That words must do such work in and for theology is because words about God are "entangled in an overtly or covertly memorial past and a wonderfully or fearfully anticipated future" (xiii). That our words are so entangled is but the expression of the fact that "to follow Christ is with him perpetually to be emptied" (29).

The way Keen writes as a theologian turns out to be an expression of his theological convictions. As followers of Christ we are led to care for the poor, but such care is a very particular kind of care found in the life, death, and resurrection of that man, the Jewish peasant, Jesus, the Son of God. Keen thus acknowledges that he is to hope and remember the poor with his words. The words must be words disciplined by Jesus who called the poor to be as he was—poor. Keen, therefore, writes in a way to make the words he uses empty themselves in a manner that exemplifies the silence that Williams suggests surrounds all speech, but particularly speech about God.[22]

22. What it means for words to "empty themselves" is echoed in Stephen Mulhall's recent Stanton Lectures, which are now published in his book, *The Great Riddle: Wittgenstein and Nonsense, Theology and Philosophy* (Oxford: Oxford University Press,

Connections

I suggested above that the unfinished character of our language forces us to discover modes of expression that can surprise us. I observed that such discoveries are often made by seeing connections that had not been seen prior to their discovery. Reading Keen is an ongoing training in seeing connections. Connections like his argument that there is an intrinsic relation between ecclesiology and martyrdom, which forces the further question of what it might mean, or perhaps more accurately, what will the church look like when she no longer lives as if she must insure her own existence.

That Keen describes his book as a prayer is the kind of discovery I suspect Williams presumes theology requires if it is to be truthful speech about God. Of course, if theology is prayer that means theology cannot be *about* God, but must be an address *to* God. That I take is Keen's great gift, that is, his studied refusal to write as if theology is but another form of information. As a result, he has written theology in a manner that makes unnecessary any apology. That he has been able to do so is testimony to a soul that has no need to prove itself. We are in his debt.

2015), 57. Mulhall uses the language "kenotic or self-emptying" to describe how words mean. He understands such self-emptying to be a Christological expression.

2

The Past Matters Theologically
Thinking Tradition

The Story That Is Christianity

"Christianity is not one of the great things of history; history is one of the great things of Christianity."[1] Rowan Williams uses this pregnant observation from de Lubac in support of his contention for why Christians must study the past.[2] To "study the past" does not properly suggest the significance of Williams's argument for why the past matters theologically. Christians do not simply study the past, but rather the past continues to be crucial for the present. The past is not "back there" because it is not even the past.

Williams develops de Lubac's claim by suggesting that it is the Bible that makes history necessary. It does so because the people we now call Jews experienced a series of disruptions—e.g., the exodus, the establishment of monarchy, the role of the prophets, the exile—that they could only make sense of by telling a story. Their struggle to tell a coherent story about their history of failures and displacements turns out to be just what makes history what it is, that is, a "set of stories we tell in order to understand better who we are and the world we're now in."[3]

---

1. Henri de Lubac, *Paradoxes of Faith* (San Francisco: Ignatius Press, 1987), 145.
2. Rowan Williams, *Why Study the Past? The Quest for the Historical Church* (Grand Rapids: Eerdmans, 2005), 6.
3. Williams, *Why Study the Past?*, 1.

According to Williams, what is true of the Hebrew Bible is perhaps even more the case in the New Testament. He observes that by the time the first texts of the New Testament were being written Christians were already aware of tensions created by the question of whether they shared the same history with the Jews. Accordingly, the New Testament is not an account of "what really happened," but an attempt to make an intelligible story out of memories of very disruptive events for Jews and Gentiles alike. The New Testament writers had to develop a coherent story that does justice to the novel presumption that in the life, death, and resurrection of Jesus a decisive retelling of God's covenant with the Jews was required.[4]

This process, of course, did not end with the establishment of the New Testament canon. Christians were determined to read and write history in the light of what Michel de Certeau characterized as the revolution begun in Christ. The early Christians associated that revolution with the crucifixion and resurrection of Jesus, which they believed had broken apart the familiar world. As a result, Christians found themselves left with the task of putting the pieces back together in the light of what had happened in Christ. It soon became apparent to Christians that this is an unending process. That is why Christians have had a strong investment in history as a discipline; because, like the Jews, the past is always a problem that must be "talked through, mended and unified, in language. The strange and interruptive has to be made into a unity, has to be made intelligible, yet not reduced and made so smooth that you don't notice there is a problem."[5]

I have begun by calling attention to Williams's understanding of the historical character of Christianity because I think it very important for any consideration of why Christianity is a faith that demands to be articulated through an ongoing tradition. To be sure, some Christians, call them liberal if you like, did and continue to reject some aspects of Christian tradition. This may give the impression that they do not believe tradition to be constitutive of Christianity. Yet, this critical attitude toward tradition cannot help but reject some aspects of the tradition in the name of the tradition. Thus Williams's argument for the acknowledgment that Christians must produce some "history" means there can be

---

4. Williams, *Why Study the Past?*, 6.
5. Williams, *Why Study the Past?*, 9.

no avoiding some account of tradition as constitutive of the task of telling the story of our existence.

Put more polemically, the presumption that one must choose between tradition and what is now identified as liberal theology is a mistake. Liberalism, at least liberalism understood as a stance within Protestant theology, is itself part of the tradition. It is so because liberal theologians could only make a case for why certain aspects of the Christian faith should be left behind or reconfigured in response to developments in modernity by telling a story. No matter how hard Protestant liberal theologians may have tried to distance themselves from past understandings of what was assumed to be forms of orthodox theology they could not help but reproduce the very mode of reasoning they were seeking to escape.

Yet it is certainly true that in recent times a recovery of the significance of tradition has taken place. It is not accidental, moreover, that de Lubac was one of the key figures in what is now identified as the *ressourcement* movement in Catholic theology in the last century. Other figures associated with the attempt to renew Catholic theology by recovering theological alternatives to neo-scholastic theology would include Hans Urs von Balthasar, Marie-Dominique Chenu, Jean Daniélou, and Yves Congar. This significant movement, however, while certainly important for the enrichment of the Catholic theological tradition, was not an attempt, as it was in Protestantism, to recover the role of tradition in order to enrich the theological resources for a theology that was thought to have grown too thin.

Neo-scholastic theologians, like Reginald Garrigou-Lagrange, understood their work to be in a tradition. The *ressourcement* theologians thought, however, that the neo-scholastics' understanding of tradition was too sterile.[6] They sought to enrich the tradition by recovering the theological insights often associated with the Patristic fathers that challenged the neo-scholastic categories. Much of their work found a home in Vatican II.

These developments in Catholic theology are extremely important, but the *ressourcement* movement in Catholicism was a quite different movement than the Protestant recovery of tradition. In this essay, I will attend primarily to developments in Protestantism because there we have

---

6. For an excellent set of essays on the *ressourcement* movement, see Gabriel Flynn and Paul Murray, eds., *Ressourcement: A Movement of Renewal in Twentieth Century Catholic Theology* (Oxford: Oxford University Press, 2014).

a clearer view of the relation of tradition to liberalism. In particular, I will direct attention to developments in Protestant theology associated with the little known, but extremely important theologian Robert L Calhoun, who in the second half of the last century taught at Yale Divinity School. Without Calhoun, the recovery of tradition that has become known, perhaps misleadingly, as the Yale School would not have been possible. Calhoun quite simply created the knowledge of the doctrinal tradition that enabled George Lindbeck and Hans Frei to do their constructive work in theology.

To be sure there are other figures, for example Robert Jenson and Robert Wilken, who are not associated with the "Yale School," but are theologians whose work has shown the significance of the theological tradition for the challenges of the present. By concentrating on developments at Yale, however, I hope to tell an important but little-known story of how a theological perspective was developed that did not entail the rejection of the concerns that had shaped the development of theological liberalism.

The Recovery of Tradition at Yale: The Work of Robert Calhoun

In *After Virtue*, Alasdair MacIntyre characterizes "a living tradition" as "an historically extended socially embodied argument, and an argument precisely in part about the goods which constitute that tradition."[7] His understanding of tradition as argument is very important for the story I want to tell about the recovery of tradition by Robert Calhoun and the subsequent development of what has become known as postliberal theology represented by Hans Frei and George Lindbeck. Lindbeck underscores the importance of Calhoun in a lovely reflection on his own education under Calhoun, observing that "Calhoun called himself a liberal until the time he died, but he was a liberal who actually ended up being more orthodox doctrinally than someone like H. Richard Niebuhr."[8]

---

7. Alasdair MacIntyre, *After Virtue*, 3d ed. (Notre Dame: University of Notre Dame Press, 2007), 222.

8. George Lindbeck, "Israel, Judgment, and the Future of the Church Catholic: A Dialogue among Friends," in *Postliberal Theology and the Church Catholic: Conversations with George Lindbeck, David Burrell, and Stanley Hauerwas*, ed. John Wright (Grand Rapids: Baker, 2012), 125.

I call attention to Lindbeck's judgment about Calhoun because Lindbeck (and Frei) are well known, but Calhoun was not widely known when he taught at Yale (1923–1965), nor is he well known today. Yet Frei and Lindbeck attribute how they learned to approach theology to Calhoun. His courses in the History of Doctrine and the History of Philosophy were renowned among colleagues and students at Yale. Calhoun was an active participant in some of the activities of what was then called the Federal Council of Churches, but that was not sufficient to establish his reputation as a scholar of the Christian theological tradition. For that to have happened would have required him to publish his lectures. He seems to have simply seen no reason to do that. He was quite content to be a teacher. Although he had written his lectures, in the classroom he delivered his lectures without notes. Students frustrated by not having his lectures to read would at various times record and transcribe them. We are in George Lindbeck's debt for finally making Calhoun's lectures on the early development of doctrine available in published form.[9]

Lindbeck's introduction to these lectures is crucial for understanding Calhoun's significance for the developments in theology now associated with Yale. Though "generous orthodoxy" is a description attributed to Frei, it rightly describes what Calhoun represented. Lindbeck remembers him as the greatest lecturer he has ever heard. He lectured in a manner that manifested his extraordinary learning, a learning, I might add, he carried lightly. He lectured, according to Lindbeck, as if he thought through every sentence and paragraph to say what needed to be said about the theologian he was presenting. He was intent to provide as sympathetic account as he could of theologians with whom he might well disagree. In particular, he wanted his students to understand those theologians who would later be called heretics, because without them Christians would not know what they should not say.

Lindbeck draws on one of Calhoun's doctoral students, Virginia Corwin, who describes Calhoun's effect. Corwin says:

> No student who has become a teacher can remember (Calhoun's lectures) without a stab of envy. . . . The thought of someone gone centuries ago—St. Augustine, for example, or Origen— takes shape before the mind, every essential detail in place. . . . the line and structure of the whole dominate, and the part is

---

9. Robert Calhoun, *Scripture, Creed, Theology: Lectures on the History of Christian Doctrine in the First Centuries*, ed. George Lindbeck (Eugene, OR: Cascade Books, 2011).

held in true proportion.... This extraordinary effect of clarity is not achieved by sacrificing a (thinker) or his conception to a scheme of one's own.... Students know that they are watching a master teacher who is also an austerely honest historian, testing the theses of other scholars by reading the sources in their original language, by controlling the less well-known writings and personal letters, and making his independent report. He protests that he knows but little of the domain he traverses, but the listener is not deceived.... The response can only be one of keen pleasure.[10]

As one lucky enough to have taken one of Calhoun's last courses in the history of doctrine, I can testify that Corwin's description is accurate. His commitment to help his students understand the development of Christian theology—developments resulting from controversy and argument—meant, in the words of Robert Cushman, who was to become the Dean of Duke Divinity School, that an appreciation of "pre-modern deposits of philosophical and Christian wisdom" was made possible. This was an achievement because, Cushman observes, it was at a time when theological studies in the mainline denominations and universities were "heavily weighted on the side of sciences of religion and post-Kantian thought."[11]

Cushman, who wrote a dissertation on Plato under Calhoun, judges that no other person did more to open the way "for a sympathetic rediscovery of classical Christian positions both Catholic and Protestant" than Calhoun. Accordingly, Cushman suggests that Calhoun "mightily helped doctrinally illiterate children of liberal American Christianity in the thirties and forties to recover a critical comprehension of the well-nigh unsearchable riches of inherited Christian wisdom." This had an unexpected result, as not only did Calhoun's perspective make possible the reception of "neo-orthodox theology" (i.e., Barth), but it also produced people able to be in conversation in Catholic and Protestant ecumenical movements.[12]

Cushman's judgments are no doubt true, but as Lindbeck noted above, Calhoun always thought of himself as standing in the Protestant liberal tradition. To be sure, he was among those who abandoned in the face of war what was understood to be a far too optimistic account of the

10. Lindbeck, introduction to Calhoun, *Scripture, Creed, Theology*, xi.
11. Lindbeck, introduction to Calhoun, *Scripture, Creed, Theology*, xv.
12. Lindbeck, introduction to Calhoun, *Scripture, Creed, Theology*, xvi.

human condition, but according to Lindbeck that did not mean Calhoun became associated with what was called neo-orthodoxy. Lindbeck suggests, in effect, Calhoun adopted "a view closer to traditional orthodoxy without abandoning his liberal convictions."[13]

"His liberal convictions," however, were primarily his conviction that theology had to be open to challenges of modernity. He was not a "liberal," if liberalism names that form of theology that tries to establish theological inquiry on some basis other than the authority of revelation and reflection on that revelation in the Christian tradition.[14] The very way Calhoun taught doctrine was an argument against the attempt by some forms of liberalism to ground Christian theology in reason qua reason. Calhoun knew the Enlightenment was over, which meant he saw clearly that Kant was not the future for Christian theology.

Calhoun was a "traditionalist," if by that description one means someone who appreciated the mode of argument represented by patristic and medieval theologians. The care with which he explicated all the different sides in the development of the creeds, for example, testified to his conviction that the mode of argument used by the Fathers was appropriate to the subject matter. Hans Frei in an *in memorium* for Calhoun describes the effect Calhoun had on his students this way:

> Calhoun taught us to use the time honored orthodox term "doctrine" once again with ease, and not to be afraid of the word "dogma." In his lectures . . . orthodoxy was a matter of broad consensus within a growing and living tradition with wide and inclusive perimeters. His theological teaching was above all generous, confident that divine grace and human reflection belonged together and that the revelation of God in Christ was no stranger to this world, for the universe was providentially led, and human history was never, even in the instances of the greatest follies, completely devoid of the reflection of the divine light.[15]

Calhoun's commitment to unpacking the arguments in order to understand developments in the tradition meant he was able to combine his liberalism with Christian traditionalism in a manner that did true justice to the integrity of both. For example, Frei observes that Calhoun thought philosophy, and in particular Plato, was essential for the development of

13. Lindbeck, introduction to Calhoun, *Scripture, Creed, Theology*, xxii.
14. Lindbeck, introduction to Calhoun, *Scripture, Creed, Theology*, xxiv.
15. Lindbeck, introduction to Calhoun, *Scripture, Creed, Theology*, xix.

Christian theology. He therefore, according to Frei, agreed with Schleiermacher that, freed of its unwarranted fear of the "secular," Christianity had been from its beginnings a faith that drew on its surrounding culture to be a "language-shaping force." Thus Frei contends that Calhoun "went about the business of showing how the one great, continuing tradition was built with the aid of . . . countless cultural contributions then and now."[16]

It would be a mistake, however, to suggest that Calhoun's theological convictions are or were crucial for how he taught the history of doctrine. Methodologically, he insisted that the historian should be an agnostic. He neither sought nor did he make disciples. Yet he insisted—exactly because the historian has the obligation to represent the character of their subjects—that historians must attend to the religious devotion of the theologian being studied, for it is finally the case that the primary locus of a theologian's work will finally depend on the practices that make the theologian a theologian. Accordingly, Calhoun refused to evaluate the theologians he presented by external standards. Instead, he worked very hard to help students understand why, for example, theological work must be done if Christians are to be articulate about what they believe and why what they believe is necessary if they are to make sense of their lives.

Lindbeck rightly identifies Calhoun as a traditionalist, a category that Calhoun himself did not use, because Calhoun helped us see that the story of the development of doctrine is the condition necessary for any consideration of the validity and/or truth of the Gospel. He, for example, presented the creeds as "crucial for coherent construals of Scripture when it is treated as a unified whole . . . the historic and Trinitarian and Christological formulations, should continue to be regarded as criteriologically though not conceptually normative for mainstream Christianity."[17]

Calhoun helped students understand the inside of the people and movements that made Christianity Christianity. According to Lindbeck, Calhoun worked very hard to provide a sympathetic picture of the theologians he thought crucial for understanding the ongoing exploration of what had happened in Christ. He would explain why Irenaeus thought the way he did, Tertullian the way he did, and Origen the way he did. As a result, when you came to the condemnations of Origen a few hundred

---

16. Lindbeck, introduction to Calhoun, *Scripture, Creed, Theology*, xx.
17. Lindbeck, introduction to Calhoun, *Scripture, Creed, Theology*, lvii.

years later you understood why Origen was so misunderstood and yet you were not out of sympathy with those who had condemned him.[18]

It is not possible to provide a detailed account of the narrative Calhoun developed in his course on the history of doctrine, but I can give a general overview. He began the course with methodological considerations about the relation of revelation and theology. He then dealt with the New Testament and in particular questions surrounding the Jesus of history. He then presented an account of Johannine theology. The latter was important because of how the Johannine books would shape later Christological controversies. The course was designed to climax in the disputes that resulted in the Nicene and Chalcedonian debates surrounding the Trinity and Christology. In order to get there, however, Calhoun dealt with the second-century apologists, heresies, the Apostles' Creed, Irenaeus, Tertullian, Clement, and Origen. The course was designed to help one appreciate that the development of doctrine was the result of the ongoing commitment of Christians to work out the implications of the reality that the God Christians worship is triune.

Lindbeck suggests that Calhoun's approach to doctrine allowed him to be at once a "traditionalist" who continued to understand himself to be in the tradition of liberal Protestant theology. That is particularly true if Schleiermacher is taken to be *the* representative of liberal theology. He treated Schleiermacher as a great theologian in the Reformed tradition who could not be blamed for the use of his theology to support positions that Schleiermacher avoided. Accordingly, we see in Calhoun an account of the development of doctrine that is at once "traditional" and "liberal."

The implications of Calhoun's position are perhaps best seen in Lindbeck's account of doctrine in *The Nature of Doctrine: Religion and Theology in a Postliberal Age*. The early methodological chapters in Lindbeck's book in which he contrasts the experiential-expressive account of theological claims with the cultural-linguistic alternative have tended to dominate discussions of his book in a manner that makes readers miss Lindbeck's primary purpose in writing the book, which was to provide a comparative account of doctrine. Lindbeck's proposal of a "rule-theory" account of doctrine is his attempt to provide a way to understand how doctrines are at once constant, yet subject to change.

The fruitfulness of Lindbeck's rule-theory display of doctrine finds its most illuminating exemplification in his discussion of the development

---

18. Lindbeck, "Israel, Judgment, and the Future of the Church Catholic," 127.

of the Nicene and Chalcedonian creeds. Thus his regulatory principles: (1) there is only one God; (2) the stories of Jesus refer to a genuine human being who lived and died in a specific time and place; and (3) every possible importance is to be ascribed to Jesus that is not inconsistent with the first rule.[19] Lindbeck argues that these principles were clearly at work in the New Testament, which makes intelligible the diverse ways, some better than others, that Jesus was affirmed as God.

The various positions we now call heretical must be part of the story because their mistakes are crucial for helping the church provide an appropriate account of the relation of the three principles. Lindbeck argues that it is probably the case that the "Nicene and Chalcedonian formulas were among the few, and perhaps the only, possible outcomes of the process of adjusting Christian discourse to the world of late classical antiquity in a manner conformable to regulative principles that were already at work in the earliest strata of the tradition."[20] It is hard to avoid the conclusion that Lindbeck's formulation of these Christological principals is the working out of how he learned to think as a student of Calhoun.

It is unclear to me how helpful it has been for the theological developments at Yale after Calhoun to be labeled "postliberal." But that label does at least indicate that, contrary to many critics of the theological developments represented by Lindbeck and Frei, they have not left behind much that has been learned from Protestant liberal theologians.[21] Frei's discussion of Schleiermacher and Barth in *Types of Christian Theology* makes clear that these theologians share much in common.[22] I call attention to Frei and Lindbeck because I think the kind of theology they have exemplified was made possible by the story of the development of doctrine represented by Calhoun.

---

19. George Lindbeck, *The Nature of Doctrine: Religion and Theology in a Postliberal Age*, 25th anniversary ed. (Louisville: Westminster John Knox, 2009), 80.

20. Lindbeck, *The Nature of Doctrine*, 81.

21. John Allen Knight provides a useful and informative account of the liberal/postliberal alternative in his *Liberalism versus Postliberalism: The Great Divide in Twentieth-Century Theology* (Oxford: Oxford University Press, 2013). Knight is a fair reporter of these alternatives, but I think he is quite wrong in his criticisms of Frei, who he criticizes for having no referential account of language. Knight seems not to have learned from Wittgenstein that the realism/idealism alternatives reproduce the modernist presumption that epistemology is everything.

22. Hans Frei, *Types of Christian Theology*, ed. George Hunsinger and William C. Placher (New Haven: Yale University Press, 1992), 34–46.

There is the question, however, whether the politics exist to sustain this theological project. In the last chapter of *The Nature of Doctrine*, Lindbeck observes that the disarray in church and society makes the transmission of the necessary skills to sustain the postliberal way of doing theology increasingly difficult.[23] The skills Lindbeck has in mind are as basic as learning the language of the faith as exemplified in Scripture.

In a foreword to the German edition of *The Nature of Doctrine*—a "Foreword" now happily included in the twenty-fifth anniversary edition of the book—Lindbeck observes that there is much lacking in *The Nature of Doctrine*. In particular, he suggests that "MacIntyre's treatment of what he calls 'traditions of inquiry' would have been helpful in specifying the relations of doctrine, theology, practice and religious communities."[24] I think Lindbeck is right about the importance MacIntyre's work can have for the position represented by Calhoun and, by extension, Lindbeck and Frei.[25] Let me try to explain why I take that to be the case.

MacIntyre on Tradition

MacIntyre is, of course, first and foremost a philosopher, but I believe his work to have profound theological implications. I began the discussion of Calhoun's work with MacIntyre's claim that tradition is an extended socially embodied argument. MacIntyre's emphasis on the importance of a tradition being socially embodied is extremely important because liberalism is not only a philosophical and theological position, but perhaps more importantly liberalism is a determinative social theory and politics. Liberalism so understood means that Calhoun-like positions are necessarily in tension with the politics of modernity.

Of course, liberalism is a hydra-headed beast. There is no strict correlation between the many forms of political liberalism and the equally diverse reality of theological liberalism. There are, moreover, many

---

23. Lindbeck, *The Nature of Doctrine*, 110.
24. Lindbeck, *The Nature of Doctrine*, xxxi.
25. David Trenery has written a terrific book comparing MacIntyre and Lindbeck. What follows owes much to his analysis. See, *Alasdair MacIntyre, George Lindbeck, and the Nature of Tradition* (Eugene, OR: Pickwick Publishers, 2014). For example, Trenery maintains that the text of *The Nature of Doctrine* "is a demonstration of the relevance of MacIntyre's account of tradition to understanding the way in which religions may respond to internal and external challenges to their coherence, and continue to develop their own tradition-constituted forms of rationality" (232).

different kinds of liberal theories that in various ways seek to sustain an understanding of society, politics, and a liberal way of life. However, as I will suggest below, MacIntyre's account of liberalism suggests why the church is a necessary social and political institution if Christian theology is to be properly disciplined by tradition.

MacIntyre develops his understanding of tradition and rationality in contrast to the liberal presumption that an account of rationality is possible that is free of any tradition.[26] The latter he thinks decisively represented by Kant's attempt to give an account of reason free of all contingencies. Kant's ambition was to show that by assuming a universal and impersonal stance it is possible for an agent to reason from the perspective of anyone and thus be free of any particularistic tradition (334). The difficulty with Kant's ambition to construct a morality for individuals free of all traditions—and countless proposals after Kant—was the inability to come to any agreements about what constitutes such universalizability. MacIntyre observes that the book-review section of philosophical journals is the graveyard that marks the failure to sustain the consensus that liberal theory assumes is not only possible but necessary.

Liberalism, MacIntyre argues, is not just a philosophical position, but an ideal many desire to be a social reality. Liberals seek to create social orders in which individuals can emancipate themselves from contingency and the particularity of tradition by each person being "anyone." The work of people such as John Rawls exemplifies MacIntyre's contention that liberalism entails a particular social theory and politics. Liberals sought, as well as continue to seek, to construct a social order on individualistic presumptions in the hope of establishing a tradition-independent mode of political life. The history of that project has exposed that ambition to be an illusion, but that same history has had the ironic result of transforming liberalism "into a tradition whose continuities are partly defined by the interminability of debate about principles" (335).

There is, moreover, a "morality" and corresponding social psychology associated with liberal social orders. Because liberals presume there is no overriding good that can make possible a narrative coherence for our lives, the compartmentalization of our lives cannot be avoided. Each individual is free to live by whatever conception of a good life appeals to them, but they are hounded by the knowledge that their understanding of what constitutes a good life is finally a matter of arbitrary preferences.

26. Alasdair MacIntyre, *Whose Justice? Which Rationality?* (Notre Dame: University of Notre Dame Press, 1988), 326–48. Subsequent paginations in text.

Therefore, the only thing they cannot do is believe that they have the right to impose their conception of the good on anyone else (336–37).

In contrast to the liberal tradition, MacIntyre develops an account of tradition-constitutive forms of rational enquiry. Such enquiry begins in and from some condition of pure historical contingency associated with a particular community. For MacIntyre, the beginnings of a tradition are simply a given, but that does not mean the poetry that constitutes the beginning is arbitrary. To be sure, the authority of a community will be found in certain texts and voices. Such an authority may be obeyed without question for a time. However, if the community is to be capable of maintaining itself across time, a tradition must necessarily develop to account for the changes the community cannot avoid (354). The event that often is decisive for necessitating change that opens up new possibilities in a community's tradition is the encounter with another community with a history that challenges some of the assumed givens of the community (355).

Through such developments, inadequacies in a tradition can be revealed in a manner that results in new formulations designed to remedy the discovered limits. In the process, a tradition will reach a stage in which it is possible to ascribe falsity to earlier judgments and beliefs. MacIntyre suggests that on such a basis a correspondence theory of truth can be established, but such a theory in the early stages of a tradition will more likely take the form of a correspondence theory of falsity. Such a process calls into question Cartesian passive conceptions of the mind in favor of the mind as activity. For MacIntyre, to think is possible because the mind can be adequated "to its objects insofar as the expectations which it frames on the basis of these activities are not liable to disappointment" (356).

Crucial for understanding MacIntyre's account of the rationality of tradition is his understanding of what he calls an "epistemological crisis." According to MacIntyre, traditions are to some degree local. They are shaped by the particularity of language and of the peculiar geography that the language reflects. So a tradition will have its peculiar history and often seem to be independent, if not isolated, from other alternative traditions. That such is the case is why some think MacIntyre has no way of avoiding relativism or perspectivism (361).

MacIntyre's first response to the accusation that he cannot avoid relativism and perspectivism is to observe that those alternatives are based on the assumption that something like rationality as such exists

(352). More significantly, those alternatives fail to take account of the possibility that a tradition can recognize a fundamental challenge to its presumptions and make constructive responses. The latter often requires fundamental changes, but the changes can be located as a working out of the fundamental convictions of that tradition. The solution to a decisive epistemological crisis, such as the reception of Aristotle's work for Christian theology, may well require the discovery or production of new concepts that makes possible the framing of the challenge in a manner that enables those in the tradition to recognize the continuities as well as the discontinuities with the tradition to that point (361–62).

MacIntyre draws on Newman to give examples of successful responses to an epistemological crisis. In particular, MacIntyre thinks Newman's exposition of the crisis in the fourth century over the Trinity is a great achievement. That controversy—a controversy that arose from competing interpretations of scripture—was given a satisfactory resolution by using philosophical and theological concepts that had come from debates rationally unresolved up to the point of Nicaea. Of course, those very philosophical and theological concepts occasioned new challenges that continue to inform thinking around the Trinity. MacIntyre does not regard that as a failure, but rather an accomplishment because a tradition in healthy working order will always be an extended argument (362–63).

MacIntyre also uses examples from science to illumine his account of the significance of epistemological crisis. For example, he calls attention to how late-medieval physics was called into question by Galileo and later by Newton. They identified the phenomena of nature in such a way that a lack of correspondence with what the impetus theory presumed about motion became obvious. What such an example suggests is that an epistemological crisis is not only the result of one alien tradition calling another into question, but an epistemological crisis can also be occasioned by internal tensions within a tradition (365).

MacIntyre acknowledges, however, that a tradition may be in an epistemological crisis for centuries. For some epistemological crises cannot be resolved, which means a tradition may be discredited rationally by appeal to its own standards. What must be denied, however, is that there is some neutral standing ground that can provide the rational resources for an independent inquiry independent of all traditions. To position oneself outside all traditions is to assume a position that not only makes one a stranger to all enquiry but ultimately makes one a stranger to oneself (367).

Such persons, MacIntyre believes, exist. They are post-Enlightenment agents who have responded to the failure of the Enlightenment to provide neutral and impersonal standards by concluding that no set of beliefs proposed for acceptance can be justified. Such persons view the social and political contexts in which they find themselves as falsifying masquerades that hide from us the reality of the nothingness that grips our lives. At best, such people think they are cosmopolitans who are home nowhere other than everywhere.

Ending with a Beginning

I trust that the implications of MacIntyre's work for how theology is understood as a traditioned form of inquiry are obvious. MacIntyre's stress on the importance of a tradition to develop the skills to introduce the young into the tradition is singularly important for Lindbeck's account of doctrine. That is particularly the case given Lindbeck's observation, an observation with which I agree, that Christianity now finds itself in the awkward position of having once been culturally established, but now increasingly disestablished. For Christianity to be so positioned can be seen as an advantage, because to be a Christian now requires a formation that has been missing.

MacIntyre's account, moreover, helps make clear that the arguments Christians continue to have about the Trinity are testimony to the truthfulness of the fundamental Christian convictions. So the tradition of inquiry that is Christianity is integral for any considerations of what it might mean to say what we believe is true. Tradition turns out to be the discovery of the conceptual means to rightly tell the story of Christ and how that story cannot be told without the story of Israel. MacIntyre helps make clear why Williams was right to argue that the past matters for Christians. In holding this conviction, Williams, as we have seen, was preceded by Calhoun, who seems to have sensed that the discovery of history was at once a great benefit for Christian theology and also one of the most powerful threats to Christian presumption. A threat because given the scope of our historical consciousness who could believe that God chose Israel to be his promised people. The only way to respond—a response Mr. Calhoun patiently enacted—was to tell the story, and tell it he did. Lindbeck continued that task—after all, it is never finished.

3

Why Jean Vanier Matters

An Exemplary Exploration

Setting the Stage

Where would Hans Reinders be without Jean Vanier?[1] I ask that question of Hans, but it is a question that is no less important for me. Hans and I need Vanier because we need exemplification of what we try to suggest Christianity ought to look like. For example, when I am asked, "Where is your church?" at least one of my responses is to point to L'Arche. But that use of Vanier is hardly the end of the matter. Vanier is crucial for Reinders and me because we are anti-foundationalists. That claim will need further explanation, but, in brief, to be an anti-foundationalist means there is no place to start other than in the middle, even if you cannot be sure where the middle may be.

The presumption that you can only start in the middle is perhaps better expressed by the contention that moral reflection cannot desire to escape history. Indeed one of the enduring problems of recent ethical theory is the tendency to avoid recognizing the importance of narratives for our understanding of what we do and do not do. What must be acknowledged is that ethical reflection is rooted in a particular politics and the mode of argument will often be in the form of unacknowledged narratives. Narratives are constituted by determinative exemplification. Exemplification is not equivalent to simply providing an example meant

---

1. This essay was originally written as a contribution for a *Festschrift* for the theological ethicist Hans Reinders.

to illustrate a deeper theory. Exemplification is the form of the argument itself.

I want to use this occasion of celebrating the life and work of Hans Reinders to explore this understanding of exemplification and, in particular, how Jean Vanier plays that role in Hans's work. Exemplification makes the positions Reinders develops rationally persuasive. Put in even stronger terms, without Vanier Reinders would lack the ability to think the way he thinks—and so would I. I cannot pretend I know all that is entailed by such a declaration. So at best this essay is an exploration of why Vanier is so important for reflection on the intellectually disabled.

What I am calling exemplification has always been an important aspect of the way I have tried to do ethics. I am, after all, an Aristotelian. According to Aristotle, actions that are just or temperate are the sort that a just or temperate person would do. But one cannot presume that a person is just or temperate simply because they have acted in ways that are thought to be just and temperate. In order to *be* just or temperate they must have done what they have done according to the manner of a just or temperate person.[2] Therefore you only "know" what it means to be just or temperate by the existence of persons who *are* just and temperate. Therefore, for any adequate account of the moral life, at least an account in which the virtues are central, you need examples.

Jeff Stout quite rightly criticized me for claiming that my stress on the significance of exemplification for ethical reflection is an alternative to modern ethical theory that is devoid of examples. In particular, Stout calls attention to John Lyon's book, *Exemplum*, because in that book Lyon had shown the crucial role of examples in Renaissance humanism. Stout goes on to argue that examples continue to play a decisive role not only in modern ethical theory, but in the actual practice of most modern people.[3] David Brooks's recent book, *The Road to Character*, provides strong evidence that Stout is right.[4] I do, however, worry that the phenomenon to which Stout is directing our attention may be closer to what I identified above as examples than to exemplification.

I have no reason, though, to dispute Stout's contention that examples continue to be important for modern ethical theory and practice. As an

---

2. Aristotle, *Nicomachean Ethics*, trans. Terence Irwin (Indianapolis: Hackett, 1999), 1105b6–11.

3. Jeff Stout, *Democracy and Tradition* (Princeton: Princeton University Press, 2004), 168–73.

4. David Brooks, *The Road to Character* (New York: Random House, 2015).

Aristotelian, I would not think otherwise because I believe Aristotle's account of moral formation is a description of how human beings become human beings. I assume, therefore, that Aristotle's account of morality will be illuminating in contexts where he is completely unknown. You do not need to read Aristotle to be an Aristotelian. I do think, however, that particular times and places make it more difficult to become what Aristotle thought we were destined to be.

I believe that may be true of the kind of world in which we currently find ourselves. I am sure that the importance of examples is not absent in modern ethical theory, but to the extent Kant-like accounts of ethics continue to shape our theoretical accounts, examples cannot help but be seen as playing a secondary role. Kant, for some very good reasons, sought to ground morality in a manner that could defeat contingency. Kant did so because he thought that if our moral commitments were contingent on a particular history then they could not avoid being arbitrary. Accordingly, Kant sought to anchor moral judgments in reason qua reason, that is, in an account of rationality that was free of being the expression of a particular history. He did so in the hope that moral reason so construed could help us secure agreements between people without resort to violence. That project relegated examples in liberal political and moral theory to a secondary role.

Of course, not all examples are created equal. Vanier is different, but his difference is exemplary. Yet if I am to say why Vanier's difference matters, I need to say more about practical reason. By drawing on MacIntyre's account of practical reason, I hope to show why I have contended that exemplification is not just an example that illumines a more basic principle, but rather is constitutive of moral reason. MacIntyre's account of practical reason, I will argue, helps clarify why Vanier is so significant for the kind of arguments Reinders makes about disability.

Before exploring MacIntyre's account of practical reason, I need to state one of the issues that many think a problem for the kind of argument I am trying to make. The problem for some is that if practical reason is specific to a particular history there is no way to avoid a kind of irrational choice of one tradition over another. What do you do when two antithetical traditions confront one another? I have tried to explore this issue in what is no doubt a far too indirect manner in an earlier essay entitled "The Non-Violent Terrorist: In Defense of Christian Fanaticism."[5] In that

---

5. Stanley Hauerwas, *Sanctify Them In the Truth: Holiness Exemplified*, 2d ed. (Edinburgh: T. & T. Clark, 2016), 177–191.

essay I used MacIntyre's account of epistemological crisis to argue that argument was possible between antithetical exemplary traditions, but there is no way to guarantee that result in principle. From MacIntyre's perspective, for a tradition to have an epistemological crisis is a great achievement. If a tradition when confronted by another tradition is not put in an epistemological crisis the alternative is war. I mention this set of reflections not only because it suggests that much is at stake, but because I will argue that the role Vanier plays in Reinders's (and my) work is an alternative to war.

Questions about the coherence of Christian belief in God are also entailed in questions surrounding the role of exemplification in practical reason. For example, in "Making Connections: By Way of a Response to Wells, Herdt, and Tran," given at the event celebrating my retirement, I called attention to how I understood my work as an attempt to provide a response to Wisdom's famous paper, simply entitled "Gods."[6] I briefly suggested that my response to Wisdom entailed an attempt to show the difference being Christian makes for how the world is seen. "How the world is seen" is a phrase that can suggest a constructivist epistemology, but I think MacIntyre's account of rationality avoids that alternative because he argues that his position is one that underwrites a realist epistemology. Yet, as I will argue, the way things are cannot be known if we are not knowers of a certain kind. We are part of how the world is what it is and not something else, which means exemplification is necessary if we are to be and see what cannot be other.

MacIntyre on Rationality

Alasdair MacIntyre's account of practical reason is obviously at the heart of the kind of case I am trying to make. Beginning with *A Short History of Ethics*, MacIntyre has written a series of books—*After Virtue* being the most famous—in which he develops the account of practical reason I want to defend. The broad outline of his understanding of rationality is perhaps most fully on display in his book, *Three Rival Versions of Moral Enquiry: Encyclopaedia, Genealogy, and Tradition*.[7] It is so because in this

6. Stanley Hauerwas, "Making Connections: By Way of a Response to Wells, Herdt, and Tran," *The Difference Christ Makes*, ed. Charles M. Collier (Eugene, OR: Cascade, 2015), 77–94.

7. Alasdair MacIntyre, *Three Rival Versions of Moral Enquiry: Encyclopaedia, Genealogy, and Tradition* (Notre Dame: University of Notre Dame, 1990).

book he provides an account of rationality by helpfully giving us a kind of history of alternative accounts of reason. We should not be surprised, given MacIntyre's contention that rationality necessarily takes the form of a narrative, that his account of the alternatives to his understanding of tradition-constituted reason takes the form of a story.

MacIntyre begins his story with the attempt by philosophers in the tradition of the Enlightenment to liberate reason from any historic communities in the hope that reason can be genuinely universal and disinterested. Because such a view of reason found its home in the ninth edition of the *Encyclopaedia Britannica* MacIntyre calls this the Encyclopaedia tradition. Opposed to the Encyclopaedist tradition are the genealogists, that is, Nietzsche and Foucault, who become the great atheists of modernity. They are so because they expose, as well as reject, the universalistic pretentions of the Encyclopaediaist as but a mask to hide the desire for power. In contrast to the Encyclopaedist and genealogist, MacIntyre draws on Augustine and Aquinas to develop an account of rationality in which tradition is constitutive. Such a view of reason assumes that reason reflects membership in a particular moral community with a distinct history. The latter is necessary because, for MacIntyre, rationality is a communal process of judgments that make possible the discovery of goods in common.[8]

MacIntyre makes his account of tradition-constituted reason concrete by providing an extended account of the kind of reasoning characteristic of craft traditions. He does so because he believes the philosophical tradition that Socrates began is best understood as analogous with the development of a craft. One learns to reason philosophically the way one learns to be a potter, that is, by being introduced to a mode of life through which virtues are acquired commensurate with that life. Just as crafts depend on exemplification as intrinsic to their task, so does philosophy.[9]

To learn a craft, including philosophy, one must go through an apprenticeship in order to learn to distinguish what is good to do from what only seems good to do. In order to learn how to make such discriminating

---

8. MacIntyre, *Three Rival Versions of Moral Enquiry*, 59–60.

9. In *Whose Justice? Which Rationality?* (Notre Dame: University of Notre Dame Press, 1988), MacIntyre observes that any account of practical reasoning will entail an account of how examples are to be described, but because how any particular examples are described depends on how the tradition is construed, appeals to examples will not and cannot resolve differences between traditions (321).

judgments, a teacher who has mastered the craft must be present because someone with authority is required so that those entering the craft know who they can look to for guidance. By becoming an apprentice to a master, the beginner can learn how to identify the mistakes they make by applying the standards of the craft manifest in their teacher. In the process, the apprentice learns what is good or best for them to do at their level of training in the craft to that point.[10]

Crucial for the development of the apprentice is the identification of their limitations with respect to the *telos* of the craft. Habits of judgment and evaluations must be learned so that the apprentice develops the self-knowledge necessary to hold themselves accountable for their mistakes as well as for their achievements. These habits are rightly identified with the intellectual and moral virtues necessary for the recognition of the good of the craft. Just as each craft has a history of excellence directed toward the achievement of the good of the craft, so life itself has such a good. The discovery of such a human good also requires a teacher whose authority enables us to develop the moral habits that make possible our ability to be participants in the ongoing enquiry necessary for living well.[11]

MacIntyre makes the extremely important point that the standards of achievement in the craft are justified historically. For those standards are the result of criticisms by predecessors who have remedied past mistakes. Such a strong historicist view of rationality is deeply at odds with the Encyclopaedic alternative just to the extent the Encyclopaedist presumes that to achieve the universal point of view necessary for us to be rational requires us to assume a timeless point of view. The very notion of "timelessness," however, the genealogist scorns as false consciousness.

MacIntyre's emphasis on the historical character of rationality is an alternative to the Encyclopaedic and genealogical positions.[12] That the history of a craft is constitutive of its rationality means that the work of the craft is never complete, as the agents of the craft must remain open to new discoveries and challenges. One of the marks of the authority of the master is that they must know how to go further in order that the craft be extended by recognizing and responding to new challenges. New discoveries can never be ruled out since one of the marks of a good tradition is

---

10. MacIntyre, *Three Rival Versions of Moral Enquiry*, 61–62.
11. MacIntyre, *Three Rival Versions of Moral Enquiry*, 63.
12. MacIntyre, *Three Rival Versions of Moral Enquiry*, 64.

to know how to go further.[13] To "go further" means one must know how to link the past with the future in an ongoing narrative that both cares for the past and anticipates the future. Exemplification is required in this process because it must be seen how the new developments in the craft are in continuity with past developments.

In a "Foreword" to Frederick Will's book, *Pragmatism and Realism*,[14] MacIntyre makes a point crucial for understanding why what I am calling exemplification is necessary given his account of practical reason. In his "Foreword" MacIntyre observes that Will, like most anti-Cartesians, rejects the justification of arguments that arguments are false if they are not grounded in "first cognitions" (x). Will rightly, according to MacIntyre, argues that the justifications of statements as well as inferences drawn from practices will not be discovered beyond or outside the practice itself. Just as innovation in a craft is justified by how that development is seen in continuity with the end of the craft, so what Will calls amplification makes intelligible the innovations associated with that particular mode of enquiry (xi).

Amplification is Will's name for the form of reasoning that is not adequately described as deductive or inductive, but rather is imbedded in practices that make present that which otherwise might be missed. Amplification is the name Will gives to the discovery of a solution to some challenge in a manner that makes possible the correct characterization of the problem to which the amplification was a response. So there is a sense in which amplification, when successful, becomes its own justification, but that does not mean it is "without reason." In fact, MacIntyre praises Will for being committed to a correspondence theory of truth because MacIntyre argues that there must exist between our beliefs and what they are about a goal of inquiry that cannot be discarded if we are to maintain

---

13. MacIntyre, *Three Rival Versions of Moral Enquiry*, 65.

14. Alasdair MacIntyre, "Foreword," to Frederick Will, *Pragmatism and Realism* (New York: Rowman and Littlefield, 1997). Paginations in text. I am indebted to Christophe Rouard for reminding me of the importance of this "Foreword." MacIntyre often makes quite important moves in places that are not destined to have a wide readership. If they are not read, the result is he is not well understood. As someone who has also written many "forewords," I am sympathetic with him because I know I have often made arguments or at least observations in contexts that readers and critics cannot help but ignore. See Rouard's article, "The Thomism of Alasdair MacIntyre: Which Ethics? Which Epistemology," in *American Catholic Philosophical Quarterly*, 88, no. 4 (Fall, 2014), 674–75.

our conviction that there is a congruity between what is sought and what is achieved.

MacIntyre reinforces this last point by observing that Will's position bears some resemblance to a philosopher MacIntyre deeply admires—namely, C. S. Peirce. In a fascinating article, Christophe Rouard calls attention to MacIntyre's reflections on Will's understanding of amplification and, in particular, MacIntyre's suggestion that Will's position is quite similar to Peirce's understanding of what he called abduction, that is, the kind of reasoning that can be found in the sciences whose practice depends on the testing of what we seek by falsification through experimentation.[15] Experimentation is, of course, understood by Peirce as not being limited to the laboratory, but rather is a characteristic that can be applied, for example, to the reading of texts.[16] Like Will, MacIntyre argues that Peirce—who characterized his position as pragmaticism in order to distinguish it from James's pragmatism—is committed to a robust realism.[17] In that respect, the pragmatism Peirce and James championed is often misunderstood. Pragmatism is not a theory that maintains if something works it must be true; rather, pragmatism maintains that the meaning of a concept is determined by its practical effects.

David Trenery, however, does not think MacIntyre's commitment to realism is sufficient to save his account of practical reason from relativism. According to Trenery, MacIntyre's arguments are developed within the Aristotelian tradition, which means the standards and modes of justification are derived from that tradition. As a consequence Trenery argues that MacIntyre has no way of countering the critic who does not share his judgments concerning the cogency of the various arguments. In fact, Trenery suggests that MacIntyre has no way of justifying his rejection of the Enlightenment standards of justification.[18]

---

15. Rouard, "The Thomism of Alasdair MacIntyre," 674. Pierce's name for this mode of reasoning was abduction by which he seems to mean the establishment of a hypothesis that will allow you to carry on.

16. For this account of Peirce, see Jacob Goodson, *Narrative Theology and the Hermenetical Virtues: Humility, Patience, Prudence* (New York: Lexington, 2015), 117.

17. For an account of practical reason that is commensurate with Will's account of amplification, see Eugene Garver, *For the Sake of Argument: Practical Reasoning, Character, and the Ethics of Belief* (Chicago: University of Chicago Press, 2004). Garver's calling attention to what he calls the "ethical surplus" that is discovered through practical reason strikes me as quite suggestive for a way to develop the stress on exemplification.

18. David Trenery, *Alasdair MacIntyre, George Lindbeck, and the Nature of*

Though I remain skeptical that "relativism" can be as clearly identified as Trenery seems to assume, I think there is no question he has named a set of significant problems that I am sure MacIntyre would think are important challenges he must address.[19] In particular, Trenery argues that MacIntyre's rejection of Aristotelian biological teleology in *After Virtue* left MacIntyre without an adequate response to show how one tradition may be superior to another. Within any one tradition there may well be a hierarchy of crafts, but Trenery does not think that sufficient to allow MacIntyre to determine how one tradition is superior to another.

Trenery does think MacIntyre's account of how one tradition may put another tradition into an epistemological crisis suggests that there are ways MacIntyre thinks significant traditions can call another into question. An epistemological crisis occurs when a conceptual scheme through which members of a tradition interpret their world proves to be inadequate to respond to critiques from another tradition. Epistemological crises are, as I suggested above, great achievements, as all too often traditions pass one another as ships in the night.

One way to read MacIntyre, however, is to see his whole project as directed towards putting those identified with the Encyclopaedia tradition, those he calls liberal cosmopolitans, into an epistemological crisis. He wants to convince them that they cannot think for themselves unless they have thought with others. Moreover, they must recognize they have ignored the standard internal to the mind that makes possible their ability to know their deficiencies. For such a person to become part of a tradition that makes their lives intelligible requires something very much like a conversion.[20]

That such a conversion is possible, Trenery suggests, is made intelligible by the development of MacIntyre's position in his late book *Dependent Rational Animals*.[21] In that book MacIntyre acknowledges he was wrong in *After Virtue* to reject a biologically based account of human

Tradition (Eugene, OR: Pickwick, 2014), 87–88.

19. Only at the end of his book does Trenery indicate that MacIntyre is objecting to accounts of relativism correlative of "objectivist" (Trenery's word) epistemologies, but Trenery still seems to assume that relativism is a problem even when it is not a correlative of foundationalist epistemologies (234–38). From my perspective relativism is not the problem. The problem is that we live in a world in which it is often quite difficult to understand someone from another form of life.

20. MacIntyre, *Whose Justice? Which Rationality*, 396.

21. Alasdair MacIntyre, *Dependent Rational Animals* (Chicago: Open Court, 1999).

telos. Accordingly, in *Dependent Rational Animals* MacIntyre develops an account of how our bodily character, which biologically resembles that of many other creatures, means we are by "nature" mutually dependent and vulnerable. It therefore turns out that our dependency on the other is the resource that makes possible the acquisition of the virtues necessary for the good working of our reason.[22]

MacIntyre's underwriting of a *telos* correlative to our bodily nature does not guarantee that radically different traditions of enquiry will see in other traditions recognizable differences and common agreements. It remains the case that our biology must be given form through social and political activities that thereby constitute incompatible alternative traditions. Yet the recognition of our dependence on one another is a resource for the possibility of recognition across traditions. Such recognition will depend on the ability to acknowledge our lack of self-knowledge, which too often is the result of our failure to recognize our dependency on others. It therefore turns out that encounters with the disabled are crucial for the recognition of sources of error in our practical reasoning.[23]

MacIntyre does not refer, as far as I know, to Jean Vanier in any of his work, but I think it is not a stretch to suggest that MacIntyre's suggestion that the disabled are significant for our common ability to reason well is the kind of exemplification that I have tried to suggest is constitutive of practical reason. Indeed, on MacIntyre's grounds Vanier's willingness to have his life shaped by friendship with the disabled makes him a master of practical reason. The conclusion seems obvious: if you want to know how to think, apprentice yourself to Vanier.

What Reinders Understood Because of What He Understands

I want to try to bring all this together by directing attention to an observation Reinders made about one of my essays on Vanier and L'Arche. Reinders edited a book of essays entitled *The Paradox of Disability: Responses to Jean Vanier and L'Arche Communities from Theology and the Sciences*.[24] The book was a collection of essays that were written by

---

22. MacIntyre, *Dependent Rational Animals*, 4–5.
23. MacIntyre, *Dependent Rational Animals*, 137.
24. Hans Reinders, ed., *The Paradox of Disability: Responses to Jean Vanier and L'Arche Communities from Theology and the Sciences* (Grand Rapids: Eerdmans, 2010).

scientists, philosophers, and theologians for a meeting with Vanier at Trosly-Breuil, France. My contribution to the volume was entitled, "Seeing Peace: L'Arche as a Peace Movement."[25] In the "Introduction" to the book Reinders characterizes my essay, quite rightly, as trying to develop the implications of L'Arche for social ethics. In particular, he observes that I call attention to Vanier's claim that sharing his life with the disabled taught him that peace cannot be realized if the gifts of the weak are not recognized. He quotes my observation that "Vanier's great gift, the gift of L'Arche, is to teach us to see pain, to enter into the pain of others, without wanting to destroy those who suffer."[26]

Reinders, however, does not stop with that summary of my essay. Instead, he makes a surprising suggestion. He observes that my essay operates at another level because I want to show how L'Arche embodies a moral epistemology. He explains by observing that in my essay I am trying to show that L'Arche is not just another idea put into practice any more than nonviolence is a moral principle to be politically realized. Rather, he suggests that I am following Wittgenstein's presumption that the order of knowledge works the other way around, that is, "In the beginning was the deed." What I find remarkable is that Reinders rightly recognized that I wrote the essay thinking of Wittgenstein, even though I did not mention Wittgenstein anywhere in the article. Yet Hans spotted what I was trying to do. What I was trying to do, moreover, is exhibit why Vanier is the exemplification of the craft of being with the mentally disabled.

Reinders also gets this just right by observing that Vanier and his friends did not begin by trying to put a politics of inclusion in place, but rather they "tried to live a life inspired by the way of Jesus Christ, whose peace we have received to give to one another. According to Hauerwas, L'Arche is thus more of a sign than a means for a politics of peace."[27] Reinders quite rightly notes that this is not to deny that L'Arche has a politics, but it is of a different order than how politics is understood in advanced societies like ours. It is a politics of time because it takes time to be present to one another when the object is *to be with* rather than *to do something for* one another.[28]

---

25. Stanley Hauerwas, "Seeing Peace: L'Arche as a Peace Movement," in *The Paradox of Disability*, 113–26.

26. Reinders, "Introduction," to *The Paradox of Disability*, 12–13.

27. Reinders, "Introduction," 13.

28. For this sense of "being with" see Samuel Wells, *A Nazareth Manifesto: Being With God* (Oxford: Wiley Blackwell, 2015). Reinders develops this understanding of

In a subsequent essay on Vanier, Reinders explicitly refers to my "Wittgensteinian reading of L'Arche" to explain why Vanier's account of being with people with disabilities could not have been the result of a theory or any preconception of what being with his friends entailed. Vanier, according to Reinders, only gradually learned to understand what it meant to share his life with disabled people. Reinders quotes Vanier's reflection that as he looks back over the formative years of L'Arche he labels that time as one "open to providence and daily life." Vanier, according to Reinders, had a deep awareness that L'Arche was God's project so all he had to do was attend to daily affairs and be on the lookout for where God was leading them.[29]

Reinders develops these "Wittgenstienian" reflections noting that crucial to his reading of Vanier is the significance that the core members in the L'Arche homes are called "teachers." That the core members are called "teachers" makes clear, according to Reinders, that L'Arche is not the result of a preconceived ideal. According to Reinders, the core members are called our teachers because they can open the door to our hearts in a way that is quite distinctive. By their willingness to share their lives with us we discover our deepest fears, not the least being the fear of vulnerability.

So it turns out that Vanier is not the only exemplification of practical reason. The core members of L'Arche are also his and our teachers. They are the exemplification desperately needed for our ability to reason well. As Reinders observes:

> Self-knowledge is essential to what being with persons of intellectual disabilities can teach us, not in the sense of showing us how to become better people, but in the sense of knowing the truth about ourselves without illusions. We will not succeed in being with them—and enjoy life with them, and find time for celebration—unless we learn to face the hidden fears in our own hearts, which will break the bonds of our hypocrisy. The hard lesson for Christians who grow up in a culture that abrogates the reality of the cross to which the Christian faith attests is how to avoid the sentimentalism of being moved by one's own feelings

---

time in his essay entitle, "Watch the Lilies of the Field: Theological Reflections on Profound Disability and Time," in *The Paradox of Disability*, 154–68.

29. Hans Reinders, "Jean Vanier's Theological Realism," in *Disability in the Christian Tradition: A Reader*, ed. Brian Brock and John Swinton (Grand Rapids: Eerdmans, 2012), 470.

for the poor. Vanier's message is as simple as it is confrontational: go and live with them, and you will soon find out whether you are truly a neighbor of the poor.[30]

---

30. Reinders, "Jean Vanier's Theological Realism," 480–481.

4

Why Bonhoeffer Matters

The Challenge for Christian Ministry at the End of Christendom

Bonhoeffer for Pastors

It hardly needs to be said that Bonhoeffer is a theologian that should be studied by those in the ministry. Indeed, I suspect he is one of the few recent theologians who have been read, or at least admired, by those in the ministry. I worry that he may be more admired than read, but I have no way of judging how deeply his theological work has shaped those in the ministry. My worry is not just about whether Bonhoeffer has been read, but the extent to which those in the ministry read anything, much less theology. I do not mean this to be critical because for some time theologians have written primarily for other theologians. They have done so because theologians now think their primary constituency is the university and not the church. As a result, we get the disastrous distinction between theology proper and practical or pastoral theology.

Bonhoeffer was, of course, a university person all the way down. He studied at the University of Berlin and wrote two distinguished dissertations. Yet given the developments in the German universities in response to the rise of the Nazis, Bonhoeffer felt compelled to distance himself from his intellectual home, confessing to a friend, "I no longer believe in the university."[1] However, I think it a mistake—a mistake that

1. Dietrich Bonhoeffer, *London, 1933-1935*, ed. Keith Clements, trans. Isabel Best,

Bonhoeffer's declarations about his work may have encouraged—to think that there is a deep divide between his early university theology and his later more ecclesial theology. This is not the place to argue the matter, but I would contend that there is a deep continuity between his early more academic work and his later theology that was more explicitly written for the church and the ministry. *Life Together* is, of course, the seminal text that embodies Bonhoeffer's commitment to do theology in a manner that recognizes that the challenges facing the church and the world never go away.[2]

Yet I am sure Bonhoeffer would say that it is not him or his theology that should matter for pastors. It is, rather, what he cared about that should matter for those in the ministry. So it is not Bonhoeffer who is important for pastors, but rather it is the Christ who was at the center of Bonhoeffer's theology. I think Bonhoeffer is an important resource for those in the ministry because he did not get in the way of Jesus. As Gerhard Ludwig Müller and Albrecht Schönherr observe in their "Afterword" to the German edition of *Life Together*, Bonhoeffer sought "to show a continuity in the event of revelation, both by grounding the concrete community in the reality and activity of Christ and by seeing it become actual through Christ in the present through Word and Spirit."[3]

Yet one may wonder how Bonhoeffer should be read by those in the ministry in our time. The challenges he faced are so different than the everyday tasks incumbent on those in the ministry in our day. Bonhoeffer confronted the Nazis and Hitler—it's hard to imagine a more dramatic conflict. Dangerous though it may have been, those confronted by the Nazis knew which side they needed to be on. We seldom enjoy such clarity. The result is often a stark divide between activities associated with pastoral care and the social witness of the church.

Those in the ministry today have to negotiate a very different world than the world Bonhoeffer encountered. We are unsure who our enemy is, or if we even have an enemy. We lack the clarity Bonhoeffer enjoyed, which, of course, is not a bad thing. But it leaves us confused about how to discern the primary challenge facing the church in the world in which

---

vol. 13 of *Dietrich Bonhoeffer Works*, ed. Victoria J. Barnett and Barbara Wojhoski (Minneapolis: Fortress Press, 2007), 217.

2. Dietrich Bonhoeffer, *Life Together*, ed. Geffrey B. Kelly, trans. Daniel W. Bloesch and James H. Burtness, in vol. 5 of *Dietrich Bonhoeffer Works*, ed. Wayne Whitson Floyd, Jr. (Minneapolis: Fortress Press, 1996).

3. Gerhard Müller and Albrecht Schönherr, afterword to Bonhoeffer, *Life Together*, 131.

we live. Bonhoeffer saw quite early who the enemy was, though he was surrounded by many who did not see what he saw in the Nazis. Indeed, one of the most significant questions about Bonhoeffer's relevance for pastors in our time involves exploring what enabled him to see the true character of the regime Hitler represented when so many others did not. That he came from the upper classes no doubt played a role, but surely what Müller and Schönherr identify as his "grounding the concrete community in the reality and activity of Christ" is crucial for understanding his early opposition to the Nazis. The question for us is how that "grounding" might help us know better the challenges before us. I suspect it is a mistake—and a quite understandable one—to assume that what you are *against* is sufficient to define your moral identity, rather than what you are *for*.

But to emphasize the "grounding" at the heart of Bonhoeffer's theology may suggest another reason why Bonhoeffer's work is not immediately relevant for the challenges that face those in the ministry today. Bonhoeffer's church, for all of its unfaithfulness, still seemed to be a viable institution. Of course, it was a state-supported church, but at least those in that church's ministry had confidence that the church was just there. Those in the ministry in our time, however, cannot be confident that the churches they serve will survive. At least that seems to be the case for those churches that are identified, an identification that may be misleading, as representing mainstream Protestantism. It simply is not clear if that peculiar form of Christianity is going to survive. Bonhoeffer had a church that was, to be sure, deeply compromised, but the assumption seemed to be that you could assume that church was not going away. That assumption proved to be mistaken, but it was nonetheless operative for Bonhoeffer and those young people he was training for the ministry.

There is, moreover, the problem that Bonhoeffer may represent an alienating example to many looking for resources in the ministry today. He was, after all, a person of immense talent whose talent was enhanced by the class status of his family in Germany. That status insured that he was a person of confidence that seldom had reason to doubt his judgments. That he died a martyr only makes it more difficult for those in the ministry to try to emulate him as a paradigm of faithful service.

It is important to remember, however, that Bonhoeffer was a churchman. That he declared early in his life that he would be a theologian seemed, at least to his family and friends, odd.[4] But even more

---

4. Paul Duane Matheny observes that what compelled Bonhoeffer to make the

curious was his conviction that he should be ordained. To be an academic theologian was an acceptable ambition for someone with the status the Bonhoeffer family represented, but to be ordained was not necessarily part of that package. Yet Bonhoeffer seemed to think, a thought quite intelligible for someone who wrote *Sanctorum Communio*, that he should be ordained. Bonhoeffer had finished writing *Sanctorum Communio* by 1927. The book was published in 1930. He was ordained in 1931.[5]

Sanctorum Communio helps us understand Bonhoeffer's pastoral practice and, in particular, his desire to be ordained, because in that book Bonhoeffer developed his strong argument that the church was "Christ existing as community." Accordingly, the task of theology is a pastoral task because the church and Christ cannot be separated. Bonhoeffer would say, and he knew what he was saying, that the church "is the presence of Christ in the same way that Christ is the presence of God. The New Testament knows a form of revelation, Christ existing as church-community."[6] This is a theme in his theology to which I will return as I suspect his emphasis on the importance of the recovery of the visibility of the church as the expression of Christ is an emphasis that is crucial for sustaining his ministry as well as those currently in the ministry.

Bonhoeffer did not, however, seek ordination to obtain a status. He seems to have sought ordination because he was convinced he was called to the work of the ministry. For example, early on he enthusiastically took on the responsibilities of a pastor, that is, he became of all things a "youth minister." Even more remarkably, he seems to have genuinely cared about

---

decision to be a theologian is unclear. It seems Bonhoeffer never spoke about his decision. Matheny, however, suggests that his reflections on the meaning of death—reflections often contained in his early children's sermons, his essays on Luther, as well as his extended reflections on honor—played a role. Matheny, introduction to *The Young Bonhoeffer, 1918-1927*, ed. Paul Duane Matheny et al., trans. Mary C. Nebelsick with Douglas W. Stott, vol. 9 of *Dietrich Bonhoeffer Works*, ed. Wayne Whitson Floyd, Jr. (Minneapolis: Fortress, 2003), 9.

5. Eberhard Bethge confirms the judgment that Bonhoeffer took very seriously his call to be ordained. Bonhoeffer had to be serious about being ordained because he was given the hard duty of being the chaplain for students at the technical college in Charlottenburg. Bonhoeffer was not a success. Bonhoeffer found them, to use Bethge's word, unresponsive. See Bethge, *Dietrich Bonhoeffer: A Biography*, rev. ed., ed. Victoria J. Barnett (Minneapolis: Fortress, 2000), 221–26.

6. Dietrich Bonhoeffer, *Sanctorum Communio: A Theological Study of the Sociology of the Church*, ed. Clifford J. Green, trans. Reinhard Krauss and Nancy Lukens, vol. 1 of *Dietrich Bonhoeffer Works*, ed. Wayne Whitson Floyd, Jr. (Minneapolis: Fortress, 1998), 140–41.

those who had been placed under his care.[7] As Andrew Root argues in his fine book, *Bonhoeffer as Youth Worker: A Theological Vision for Discipleship and Life Together*, Bonhoeffer's theology was shaped by what he was learning as a pastor charged with the instruction of the young. In particular, Root describes a confirmation class of young boys in Wedding, a section of Berlin, who were so unruly that they were thought responsible for the death of the pastor who prior to Bonhoeffer was trying to have them learn the catechism. This group of young men became known as the confirmation class that killed their teacher. Bonhoeffer was charged with the task of teaching them the catechism.

Root reports that Bonhoeffer won them over by never losing his temper and by always being composed. The latter stance was by no means easy because the young men tried to impose on Bonhoeffer the bedlam that they used to "kill" the last incumbent. Bonhoeffer, however, drew on stories of his own life to create a trust between him and the boys that made it possible for the work of confirmation to take place. Particularly important for Bonhoeffer was his determination to visit the homes of the boys because those visits proved to be an eye-opening experience.

Through such visits he saw the difficult circumstances in which these young men were being raised. Root reports he even wrote to a friend that his theological training was of no help in understanding what he was doing in making such visits. What was missing according to Bonhoeffer was any account of how to do pastoral care at the end of Christendom. In a letter to a friend, Root quotes Bonhoeffer describing his reactions to these home visits:

> *I sometimes or even usually stand there and think I really might as well have studied chemistry.* Sometimes it seemed to me as if pastoral care was where our work broke down. What hours or minutes of torture often pass by when the other person or I try to have a pastoral conversation, and how hesitatingly and drearily it goes on. . . . Some will tell you completely without embarrassment and naively about their very dubious lifestyle, and you have the feeling that if you said anything about it they

---

7. See, for example, the recently discovered correspondence Bonhoeffer had with a young person he had confirmed in England. It seems he understood the importance of staying in touch with those whose lives had touched his life. See Dietrich Bonhoeffer, *Letters to London: Bonhoeffer's Previously Unpublished Correspondence with Ernst Cromwell, 1935–1936*, edited by Stephen Plant and Toni Burrowes-Cromwell (Eugene, OR: Cascade, 2013) for confirmation of his determination to interact with those he had confirmed. Confirmation was extremely important for Bonhoeffer.

would just not understand you. In short, this is a very sad chapter, and I often try to console myself with the fact that I think this whole kind of pastoral care is also something that didn't exist even earlier and is completely unchristian. But maybe it really is the end of our kind of Christianity.[8]

"Maybe it really is the end of our kind of Christianity" is an observation I think extremely important for helping us see why Bonhoeffer is so significant for those in the ministry today. He is so because I suspect that the kind of Christianity Bonhoeffer thought was coming to an end in Germany is not that different from the Christianity that has lived through us. It is a Christianity that has been identified with the ideals of the culture in which it found itself. As a consequence, the Christianity that has shaped us has little defense against Christians believing we are at home in this world.

For example, in August of 1933 in a letter to his Grandmother, Bonhoeffer said it was becoming increasingly clear to him that what they were going to get for "church" is a *völkisch* nationalistic church that in "its essence can no longer be reconciled with Christianity." He then suggested "that we must make up our minds to take entirely new paths and follow where they lead. The issue is really Germanism or Christianity, and the sooner the conflict comes out in the open, the better. The greatest danger of all would be in trying to conceal this."[9]

Bonhoeffer's enduring significance for those in the ministry in our time is on display in his attempt to bring this conflict into the open. For, as he suggests, we may well be coming to the end of a form of Christianity that will demand changes in how the ministry is understood. In particular, it will call for the recovery of the visibility of the church as the necessary condition for bringing into the open the conflict between church and world. One aspect of such a recovery will entail on the part of those in the ministry a confidence in our most basic acts that make us the church of Jesus Christ, that is, the preaching of the word as true and

8. Dietrich Bonhoeffer, *Ecumenical, Academic and Pastoral Work: 1931–1932*, edited by Victoria J. Barnett, Mark S. Brocker, and Michael B. Lukens, trans. Anne Schmidt-Lange et al., vol. 11 of *Dietrich Bonhoeffer Works*, ed. Victoria J. Barnett and Barbara Wojhoski (Minneapolis: Fortress Press, 2012), 98, quoted in Andrew Root, *Bonhoeffer as Youth Worker: A Theological Vision for Discipleship and Life Together* (Grand Rapids: Baker Academic, 2014), 106.

9. Dietrich Bonhoeffer, *Berlin: 1932–1933*, ed. Larry Rasmussen, trans. Isabel Best and David Higgins, vol. 12 of *Dietrich Bonhoeffer Works*, ed. Victoria J. Barnett and Barbara Wojhoski (Minneapolis: Fortress, 2009), 159.

the celebration of the Eucharist. Bonhoeffer rightly reminded us that it is the preaching of Christ and the celebration of his crucifixion and resurrection that makes possible lives that can identify the lies that threaten our lives.

Visibility

In *Performing the Faith: Bonhoeffer and the Practice of Nonviolence*, I suggested that Bonhoeffer's theological politics is best understood as an attempt to recover the visibility of the church. The church in Germany, according to Bonhoeffer, had become "invisible" because Luther—to be sure, in his own peculiar way—had confirmed Constantine's covenant with the church. The result, particularly in Germany, was to institutionalize a minimal ethic for everyone. Such an ethic meant that the existence of the Christian became indistinguishable from the existence of the citizen. Bonhoeffer argued this development had the effect of making the church vanish into an invisible realm.

Bonhoeffer suggested that realm of invisibility had a name. He called it "religion." Religion was assumed to be an unavoidable aspect of the human. Christianity was but one form that religion could take. By calling attention to religion as the concept necessary to make the church invisible, I suspect Bonhoeffer was suggesting how the tradition of Protestant liberalism functioned to make Christianity a legitimation of the high humanism of German life. In that tradition, a generalized anthropology was thought necessary to sustain Christianity as a civilizational faith. Liberal Protestants might emphasize the importance of the church for the formation of individuals, but the fundamental problem remained the same—namely, once Christianity becomes religion it is almost impossible to think of the church, in Bonhoeffer's words, as "Christ existing as church-community."[10]

Bonhoeffer's call in *Letters and Papers from Prison* for a Christianity free of religion was not, as it has often been interpreted, an underwriting of liberal Protestant theology. Rather his call for a Christianity free from religion was an implicit critique of the attempt by Protestant liberal theologians to defend Christianity by identifying what we believe as Christians with the presumed unavoidable religious aspects of the

---

10. Stanley Hauerwas, *Performing the Faith: Bonhoeffer and the Practice of Nonviolence* (Grand Rapids: Brazos, 2004), 41.

human condition.[11] The result from Bonhoeffer's perspective was to legitimate an invisible church by confusing the Gospel with some version of humanism.[12] Bonhoeffer called this apologetic approach to Christianity "methodism" because it attempts to methodically preserve a place for Christianity on the margins of life, but concedes the center.[13]

Bonhoeffer clearly thought the association of Christianity with "inwardness" had prepared the way for the failure of the church to oppose the Nazis. This was made explicit in the Bethel Confession in which these false doctrines were rejected:

> That the church is a religious association formed by gathering together of devout individuals (Enlightenment, pietism, liberalism):
> That the true church is invisible, and that every empirical church is only an imperfect attempt to realize the ideal of the true church (idealism): . . .
> That the church could be the religious organization for a nation, so that it would have to provide the religious foundation for that nation's ethno-national tradition [Volkstum], and that the territorial boundaries of that church should be the same as those of that nation (nationalism).[14]

These were the presumptions Bonhoeffer tried to challenge by the way he trained those studying for the ministry at Finkenwalde. The training he was providing at the seminary, including the way the day was organized, was Bonhoeffer's attempt to train those in the ministry to be people capable of the kind of work necessary to recover the visibility of the church. Geffrey Kelly in his introduction to Bonhoeffer's *Life Together*, quite rightly directs our attention to Bonhoeffer's 1932 lecture, "The Nature of the Church." In that lecture, Bonhoeffer makes explicit the pastoral implications of his earlier work, which is not surprising given the

---

11. See, for example, Dietrich Bonhoeffer, *Letters and Papers from Prison*, ed. John W. deGruchy, trans. Isabel Best et al., vol. 8 of *Dietrich Bonhoeffer Works*, ed. Victoria J. Barnett and Barbara Wojhoski (Minneapolis: Fortress, 2010), 428.

12. For an insightful account of Bonhoeffer's understanding of "religion," see Jeffrey Pugh, *Religionless Christianity: Dietrich Bonhoeffer in Troubled Times* (London: T. & T. Clark, 2008), 69–95. Pugh rightly suggests that Bonhoeffer knew quite well that religion can become the source of answers to questions that perplex us, but Bonhoeffer knew that to be exactly the problem, because religion "too easily becomes captive to abstractions and human needs motivated more by society than God" (88).

13. Bonhoeffer, *Letters and Papers from Prison*, 450.

14. Bonhoeffer, *Berlin: 1932–1933*, 407–9.

task he was taking on, that is, to train young men to serve a church that could resist being invisible.[15]

Bonhoeffer begins his lecture on the church by observing that the visibility of any institution depends on it having a place in the world. But that is exactly what the church lacks because it has tried at once to be everywhere, which results in the church being nowhere. The ambition for the church to be everywhere has, moreover, had the ironic result that the church was turned into the world without the world being transformed by the church. Bonhoeffer, with uncommon insight, suggests that such a worldly church cannot help but try to hide its own unfaithfulness, which results in contempt toward itself and the world. Because a church so constituted has abandoned its place in the world, it is hidden by privilege and exists primarily to meet the needs of the *petit bourgeois*.[16] The God such a church represents is like the church itself: at once everywhere and nowhere having no concrete reality.

According to Bonhoeffer the proper place of the church, the place that makes possible the visibility of the church, "is the place of Christ present in the world. . . . Neither the state church nor some petit bourgeois center, for no human person, but God alone determines this place. The church which is aware of this waits for the word that transforms it into God's place in the world."[17] Bonhoeffer is quick to challenge any suggestion that such a church is an ideal church, but rather the church is a reality in the world being, in fact, "a bit of the world reality."[18] The church is, just as Jesus was, fully human, which means the church must renounce that most deceptive form of invisibility—namely, the attempt to be pure.[19] Thus the church, the visible church, will be "worldly" by renouncing all privileges and property, but never will it renounce Christ's word and the forgiveness of sins. "With Christ and the forgiveness of sins to fall back on, the church is free to give up everything else."[20]

In their afterword to *Life Together*, Gerhard Müller and Albrecht Schönherr quote from a draft of a speech written for pastors in 1942 by

15. Geffrey B. Kelly, introduction to Bonhoeffer, *Life Together*, 10–11.
16. Dietrich Bonhoeffer, "The Nature of the Church," in *A Testament to Freedom: The Essential Writings of Dietrich Bonhoeffer*, rev. ed., ed. Geffrey B. Kelly and F. Burton Nelson (New York: HarperOne, 1995), 84.
17. Bonhoeffer, "The Nature of the Church," 84.
18. Bonhoeffer, "The Nature of the Church," 86.
19. Bonhoeffer, "The Nature of the Church," 87.
20. Bonhoeffer, "The Nature of the Church," 87.

Bonhoeffer. In this fragment, Bonhoeffer addressed what pastors must do in the event of a successful overthrow of the regime. Bonhoeffer called on those to whom he wrote to order their lives anew. He observed they had suffered too long from the desire to go their own way and to separate themselves from their brothers. Such a separation is not in the Spirit of Jesus, but the spirit of individualism, indolence, and defiance. Bonhoeffer makes the surprising suggestion that to be so separated from one another results in the destruction of good preaching. The problem is they sought to perform their duties without faithfully keeping regular times for prayer, contemplation, and study, as well as receiving from one another their personal confession. Accordingly, Bonhoeffer ends by imposing on each of those to whom he writes "the sacred duty to be available to our brother for this ministry. We ask you to come together to pray as you prepare your sermons and to help one another find the proper words."[21]

"To find the proper words" strikes me as the great challenge for the recovery of the church's visibility. Consider, for example, Bonhoeffer's reflections in the *Ethics*—tellingly in the section "Ethics as Formation"— in which he describes how Hitler, the one who tyrannically despises humanity, makes use of the meanness of the human heart by giving it other names. "Anxiety is called responsibility; greed is called industriousness; lack of independence becomes solidarity; brutality becomes masterfulness."[22] The small number of people who oppose and expose such duplicity find that their courage is called revolt, their discipline Pharisaism, their independence arbitrariness, and their masterfulness arrogance. In short this tyrannical despiser of humanity hides his distrust of all humanity behind "the stolen words of true community."[23]

These Orwellian reflections by Bonhoeffer are so interesting because Bonhoeffer connects the church's failure to call into question these "stolen words" to the church's desire to be politically relevant. As a result, Christians have failed to be properly visible. The irony is that the invisibility of the church is a correlative of the church's attempt to be politically relevant—an ambition that tempts the church to use the foreign language—at least foreign for Christians—of what passes for

---

21. Müller and Schönherr, afterword to Bonhoeffer, *Life Together*, 124.

22. Dietrich Bonhoeffer, *Ethics*, ed. Clifford Green, trans. Reinhard Krauss, Charles C. West, and Douglas W. Stott, vol. 6 of *Dietrich Bonhoeffer Works*, ed. Wayne Whitson Floyd, Jr. (Minneapolis: Fortress, 2005), 86.

23. Bonhoeffer, *Ethics*, 86.

political speech. That language, moreover, meant even Christians could be seduced by the Nazis whose cynicism knew no limit.[24]

As I suggested above, we are tempted to think we live in a very different time than Bonhoeffer. We are not threatened by Hitler-like leaders, but the cynicism that produces a Hitler remains alive and well. We do not trust our neighbors, nor do we trust ourselves. Nor do we trust the church. In fact, many in the ministry prefer the church to be invisible. The invisibility of the church means that the primary role for those in the ministry is to be a pleasant person. What seems lacking is anything for those in the ministry to do. But Bonhoeffer gives those in the ministry something to do. Bonhoeffer challenges those in the ministry to imagine how the social significance of the everyday ministerial tasks such as preaching, presiding at the Eucharist, and caring for the dying are practices for the formation of a people who are capable of being a political alternative to the world. Let me elaborate on that claim by directing your attention to the recent work of Jennifer McBride on Bonhoeffer.

In her book, *The Church for the World: A Theology of Public Witness*, Jennifer McBride emphasizes, as I have, the significance of Bonhoeffer's insistence on the importance of the recovery of the visibility of the church.[25] She quite rightly argues that Bonhoeffer's account of the necessity of the church's visibility is an expression of his Christology (57–88). Yet McBride worries that this emphasis on the recovery of the visibility of the church as a correlative of Christ's public witness may fail to do justice to Bonhoeffer's Lutheran understanding of the hiddenness of Christ. For central to Luther's (and Bonhoeffer's) Christology is the reality of the cross, which is a manifestation of God's hiddenness (68). The cross is at once the most visible manifestation of God, but it is a manifestation that is constituted by Christ's humiliation, which means there is a necessary hiddenness at the point God is most determinatively present.

McBride worries that the call for the recovery of the visibility of the church, a recovery she associates with my call for a recovery of the public character of the church, can underwrite a triumphal account of the church's role in the world (23–54). McBride, therefore, suggests that an emphasis on the visibility of the church can give aid and comfort to the religious right, who, she argues, are idolatrous in their support of America.

---

24. Bonhoeffer, *Ethics*, 86.

25. Jennifer McBride, *The Church for the World: A Theology of Public Witness* (Oxford: Oxford University Press, 2012). Paginations for McBride's book will appear in the text.

The result, moreover, turns Christianity into a moralistic faith unable to be a witness commensurate with the hiddenness of the Incarnation.

In order to avoid that result, McBride suggests that the church must embody the humility that the cross demands. Such a witness, she argues, will best be made by the church that is primarily identified by confession and repentance of sin. Such a confession means the church can reflect the humility of the cross in a world dying for an alternative to our prideful self-assurance. McBride argues, therefore, that church and world are not strict alternatives, but rather they overlap in their mutual need to confess and repent of sin. This is the fundamental way the church serves the broader society; that is, "through creative, repentant activity in public life, the church participates in God's healing transformation of the world" (6).

McBride emphasizes the importance of repentance for the church because she thinks a church so formed can better negotiate an increasingly pluralist politics. She worries that the strong distinction between church and world can result in a far too negative view by Christians of the politics in which we find ourselves. Such a view, McBride argues, betrays Bonhoeffer's humanism, encapsulated by Bonhoeffer's insistence that God did not become human that we might be divine, but God became human so that human beings might become more fully human (85). Accordingly, the Pauline admonition that the church is to be "in the world but not of the world" means that the church as a repentant people can never stand in self-righteous arrogance against the world (89).

McBride suggests that this way of understanding Bonhoeffer clarifies his call for Christians to be "worldly." A worldly church remains a church that is an alternative to the world, but not in a world-denying way. For it turns out if the church is a community that has been born of the repentance necessary for making disciples of Christ, the church cannot help but be led into the "messiness and complexity of historical existence, engagement which alone ushers forth concrete redemption" (115). Christian prophetic criticisms of "the world," therefore, are perverse if it is forgotten that the church can only stand as an alternative to the world for the world's sake.

I indicated above that McBride worries that my emphasis on reclaiming the visibility of the church as alternative to the world's violence is too antagonistic. According to McBride, I lack an appreciation for "the Christological fact that the world, like the church, stands under God's judgment and mercy" (221). I fail to account for the fact that the church's primary truthful witness is not to nonviolence, but rather to the church's complicity in sin and violence (221). McBride worries that I cannot imagine that God is also present in those who know not Christ, but live faithful lives of love to the neighbor.

I confess I am not particularly troubled by McBride's criticisms of my account of Bonhoeffer because I do not think her emphasis on confession of sin and repentance as the heart of the witness of the church is antithetical to my understanding of the church as an alternative to the world. Yet I have thought it important to call attention to her account of Bonhoeffer because I think she helps us see why he is so pastorally significant. He is so because, as I suggested above, he helps us see the connections between the everyday practices of the church and the witness of the church for the world.

McBride provides an ethnographic account of the formation of two communities of confession and repentance that show that her and Bonhoeffer's understanding of the church is not some ideal, but can be a concrete reality. For example, she directs our attention to the Eleuthero Community of North Yarmouth, Maine. This is a small community of Christians whose faith takes the form of a stance toward the world of gratitude and repentance. They confess that they live in sharp irony because they participate in a culture that has more power and status than any people who have ever lived, yet it is not clear such a way of life is sustainable. They confess, therefore, that they are a community whose identity and mission grow out of a disposition of confession of sin and repentance. Accordingly, they have taken on as their common effort to found a retreat and study center for the exploration of a Christian spirituality that they know is required to sustain the discipline necessary to practice the care of the earth (153–54).

McBride provides an account of the hard work in community building necessary for sustaining such a community. It is the kind of work I suspect is necessary if we are to be the kind of church that Bonhoeffer points us toward. It is a church that will by necessity raise up those able to make us articulate before the world. I cannot imagine a more significant role for those who find themselves identified as priests or ministers.

The Christ that Is Present

I am acutely aware that you may find the last claim disappointing. You cannot help but feel a sense of "That's it?" Surely you didn't read this far simply to be told that the reason Bonhoeffer remains so important for those in the ministry is his insistence that at the heart of the church and, therefore, at the heart of pastoral ministry, is word and sacrament! Yet what Bonhoeffer helps us see is that the visibility of the church, the ability of Christians to claim place in a placeless world, draws on our confidence that in word and sacrament God is "placed." God is not no-where. God is present in these essential acts that only make sense if Jesus has been raised from the dead.

I should like to think that my emphasis on the church in my work over the years is a theme that is consistent with Bonhoeffer's call for the church to again become visible. I recently discovered a sentence that I should like to think gives expression to what I have been about. It is a sentence, moreover, that I think is not inconsistent with Bonhoeffer's stress on the significance of the recovery of the "proper words" constitutive of our faith. The sentence reads "in the shadows of a dying Christendom the challenge is how to recover a strong theological voice without that voice betraying the appropriate fragility of all speech but particularly speech about God."[26]

Bonhoeffer was a master of the fragility of speech about God. Accordingly we can do no better than to study his work. Through such study we may well learn to use the "proper words" we have been given. For the invisibility that destroys us is the loss of confidence in the words that make us who we are. They are the words that make your preaching and presiding at the altar visible and life-giving. That visibility is crucial for the world, calling into question, as it must, the lies necessary to deny God. I end, therefore, with Bonhoeffer's confident claim in *Discipleship*:

> The church-community has, therefore, a very real impact on the life of the world. *It gains space for Christ.* . . . All who belong to the body of Christ have been freed from and called out of the world. They must become visible to the world not only through the communal bond evident in the church-community's order and worship, but also through the new communal life among brothers and sisters in Christ.[27]

26. Stanley Hauerwas, "Making Connections," in *The Difference Christ Makes*, ed. Charles M. Collier (Eugene, OR: Cascade, 2015), 77.

27. Dietrich Bonhoeffer, *Discipleship*, ed. Geffrey B. Kelly and John D. Godsey, trans. Barbara Green and Richard Krauss, vol. 4 of *Dietrich Bonhoeffer Works*, ed. Wayne Whitson Floyd, Jr. (Minneapolis: Fortress Press, 2001), 236 [italics mine]. For a wonderful account of Bonhoeffer and preaching, see L. Roger Owens, *The Shape of Participation: A Theology of Church Practices* (Eugene, OR: Cascade, 2010).

Or, as I am prone to say, the first task of the church is not to make the world more just. Rather, the first task of the church is to make the world the world. That such a task is given to those in the ministry is surely one of the dramatic commitments that makes the ministry such a demanding and rewarding call.

Part II

UNIVERSITY MATTERS

5

Kierkegaard and the Academy
A Theological Meditation

Getting the Question Right

It is no accident that Christianity developed a scholarly theological tradition that over time found its way into the university. That is to put the matter in a misleading way. It is not that theology found its way into the university, but universities, particularly the universities at Paris and Oxford, were constituted by theologians at work. There were lively debates about what other disciplines might need to be included in the curriculum, but the central role of theology was never questioned.

It is a fascinating question why Christians have needed people who think they have to think about what being Christian means. I think the church needs theologians because she cannot hide from herself that she believes the one that moves the sun and the stars is to be found in the person of a first-century Jew named Jesus. To make such a claim, and even more to make your life turn and depend on it, as we say in the South, requires a good deal of thought. And thought has to take place somewhere. For centuries monasticism was a good home for theology, but then along came the university.

The university, of course, has changed over the years. One of the most important changes was called the Enlightenment. The university gave birth to the Enlightenment and became the primary agent of this movement. That it did so is not surprising given the Enlightenment desire to free humanity from all authority except reason alone. The transformation of the university by advocates of the Enlightenment meant that those who would have theology taught in the university bore the burden of proof. The strategies developed to legitimate theology as a university discipline meant, however, that theology in modernity was no longer an ecclesial discipline. At best theology became but another subject in the curriculum of the modern university.

Theology, so understood, often becomes no more than a report about what Christians at one time believed. This is thought to be a useful task because students who may well be Christians lack a robust knowledge of the Christian tradition. Yet even a report on what Christians at one time believed can be quite controversial if the subject is not taught in a disinterested way. Religious convictions that have cost believers their lives are now presented in a fashion that will let students make up their own minds. So constituted, it is quite difficult for students not to think theology is a matter of "opinion."

Many people who teach theology, or some discipline such as biblical studies, desperately try to avoid any suggestion that they are trying to indoctrinate students. Faculty who now comprise departments of religious studies have strong reasons not to be identified as theologians. Their methods are social scientific or historical because those methods are accepted by the university. Theology on the other hand is assumed not to pass muster. As a result, most students, even students at Christian colleges and universities, have little opportunity to take courses in theology. At least they have little opportunity to take courses in theology that are taught with the presumption that this course can and perhaps should change the life of the student.

It is also the case that there are social and political presumptions that are challenged by courses in theology. Take, for example, the widespread presumption that in religious matters the distinction between the public and the private is a given. That distinction is often assumed to be crucial for sustaining liberal social orders that depend on relegating our strongest convictions to the alleged private realm. That presumption must be challenged if theology is to be taught well. When it is not challenged, the student cannot help but conclude that theological convictions are not subject to questions of truth or falsity, with the added implication that theological claims cannot be subjected to reason.

I suspect Kierkegaard would have found these developments deeply "ironic." He was, of course, a person of extraordinary intelligence, but he seemed to have no desire to be associated with the university. He wrote on his own authority. Moreover, he did not write to be read by other theologians. He wrote to change the world or, at least, the lives of those who read him. That he did so raises the interesting question of whether Kierkegaard could be taught in the current university "objectively" because objectivity would require that the teacher make clear that Kierkegaard is not someone you simply learn "about." When read rightly, the reader experiences an encounter: Kierkegaard wants to change your life.

That Kierkegaard wrote outside of the university does not mean he did not value the university.[1] He not only went to the University of Copenhagen, but he seems to have been an exemplary student. Walter Lowrie observes that in his first years in the university Kierkegaard was extremely diligent, not only because he thought to be so was his duty, but also because "he rejoiced in the opportunity for broader culture which was there offered to him, or which the free life of a university student made possible."[2] Later Kierkegaard would study in Berlin, which at the time represented what most considered the zenith of academic culture. As a result, Kierkegaard was well versed in ancient and contemporary philosophy attending, for example, Schelling's lectures on Hegel.[3] In short, Kierkegaard could not have been the great critic of church and university if he had not received an education that only a university can provide.

These meandering reflections about theology, the university, and Kierkegaard—reflections that would demand acknowledgment that universities come in quite different shapes and sizes—are in the interest of trying to imagine what or how Kierkegaard might help us think about theology and the university. One way to put the matter is to ask if and how Kierkegaard could be taught in most universities. He was unapologetically Christian. He sought to reintroduce Christianity into Christendom. Can his works be taught with the same seriousness with which he did his work? I will return to this question in the conclusion of this paper.

---

1. Paul Holmer observes that Kierkegaard had a high regard for the disciplines of history and the sciences. Moreover, he was extremely well read in philosophy and theology. Though no doubt much of Kierkegaard's intellectual development was the result of his self-education, it is still the case that that education was made possible by the university. See Paul Holmer, *On Kierkegaard and the Truth*, ed. David J. Gouwens and Lee C. Barrett (Eugene, OR: Cascade, 2012), 79–108.

2. Walter Lowrie, *A Short Life of Kierkegaard* (New York: Anchor, 1961), 45.

3. Lowrie, *A Short Life of Kierkegaard*, 119–20.

There is, of course, the question of whether the changed circumstances in which we live mean Kierkegaard's work no longer has the relevance it did in his day. The university in Kierkegaard's time was still a Christendom institution. That is no longer the case. Does that mean we no longer have anything to learn from Kierkegaard's attack on Christendom? I do not think that true, but to say why will require giving attention to Kierkegaard's understanding of Christendom and why he thought such an arrangement made it difficult to be a Christian.

As I have already indicated, most contemporary universities no longer identify with their Christian past. That some still allow theology to be taught can be understood to be a "cultural lag" that may not last much longer. Yet, it is nonetheless the case that even though most contemporary research universities no longer identify with their Christian beginnings, that does not mean they have ceased being agents of—to be sure, a very different—"Christendom." This is particularly the case given John Howard Yoder's account of the mutations Constantinianism has assumed in recent time. For example, Yoder insightfully suggests that Constantinianism can assume a quite secular form just to the extent it is assumed that the movement of history has a singular secular purpose.[4]

These are clearly not theoretical issues for me. I am a declared lover of the university. In *The State of the University: Academic Knowledges and the Knowledge of God*, I was quite critical of universities for being such good servants of the reigning economic and political interests.[5] Yet, in *The State of the University* I offered no account of the university that might be an alternative to the universities we now inhabit. I offered no alternative because I am unsure what such a university would look like. I also worry that a university that paraded its Christianity would find it difficult to maintain a radical perspective. How that might be done—that is, how Christians might reclaim the university as a servant of Christ—I hope to explore by attending to Kierkegaard's attempt to introduce Christianity into Christendom.

That I hope to find resources in Kierkegaard for thinking through how to think theologically about the university, as well as how to do theology, even in the university, may seem quite odd. Kierkegaard could be quite devastating when he satirically depicts professors who write books

---

4. John Howard Yoder, *The Original Revolution: Essays on Christian Pacifism* (Scottdale, PA: Herald, 2003), 143–45.

5. Stanley Hauerwas, *The State of the University: Academic Knowledges and the Knowledge of God* (Oxford: Blackwell, 2007).

about books. He also knew he was destined to be "a" subject of study by professors who would write learned treatises on what he must have really meant by "a leap of faith," or whether he had disavowed "reason," or whether he was a philosopher or theologian.[6] From Kierkegaard's perspective, to try so to "place" him betrays his attempt to help us see that the how of theology is as important as the what.[7]

It is ironic, a category Kierkegaard loved, that Kierkegaard—the one person who had taken his task to be introducing Christianity into Christendom—has become the creature created by professors in the interest of making him just another theologian with a position. By attending to Kierkegaard's attack on Christendom, I hope to recover why his theology should continue to challenge us. Yet, I think the situation in which we find ourselves is quite different than the Christendom Kierkegaard confronted. He wanted to introduce Christianity, which turned out to be Jesus, back into Christendom. We no longer live in a robust Christendom like that of Kierkegaard's Denmark. This may mean we need to rethink what it means to do theology in a manner that defies the attempt to defang what Christians say we believe.

In order to try to get clear on these matters I need to remind us what Kierkegaard thought to be the problem he called "Christendom." His "authorship" was designed to create readers capable of being able to follow Christ in a world in which everyone assumed they were Christians. He wrote to create a "reader." I will try, therefore, to describe his attack on Christendom without that description betraying his desire to make us "individuals."

On Being a Christian in Christendom

Kierkegaard begins *The Point of View for My Work as An Author: A Report to History* by explaining why he has written using different pseudonyms.

---

6. David Burrell gets it right in response to the suggestion that Kierkegaard is an irrationalist because he sought to edify. Burrell observes that Kierkegaard thought one can learn "to speak Christian with impeccable rigor." What those who would make Kierkegaard an irrationalist fail to see, according to Burrell, is that Kierkegaard simply offers a different conception of what proper philosophic inquiry should look like. See David Burrell, *Exercises in Religious Understanding* (Eugene, OR: Wipf and Stock, 2016), 175. Burrell's book was originally published in 1974.

7. For an insightful account of the how of Kierkegaard's "how," see Holmer, *On Kierkegaard and the Truth*, 149–55.

He has done so, he confesses, because "Christendom is a prodigious illusion" that cannot be challenged using direct communication.[8] One cannot challenge an illusion using direct communication because direct communication presupposes the receiver's ability to receive is in good order. But in Christendom the ability to receive has been lost because it is assumed that one is a Christian just as one is a Dane. The problem is deep because the illusion makes it impossible for the one under the illusion to recognize they are under an illusion. That is why one must first use a caustic means, if one is to get a message past the illusion. According to Kierkegaard a caustic powerful enough to challenge the illusion will often take the form of a negative means in which the truth may appear the same as the deception (40).

What is the illusion that forces Kierkegaard to use deceptive strategies in the hopes of creating "an individual?" It is the presumption by the citizens of Denmark that they are Christians because they live in a Christian country. What are we to make, Kierkegaard wonders, of the reality that thousands call themselves Christian yet they live in categories quite foreign to being a Christian? For example, Kierkegaard observes, there are people who never enter a church, people who take oaths in God's name, people upon whom it has never dawned that they might have an obligation before God, nonetheless, they still consider themselves Christians. In a like manner, there are people who are buried as Christians by the church, who are recognized as Christians by the state, who may even call themselves Christians although they may not believe in God's existence. Given the conditions of Christendom, these same people still consider themselves Christians (22–23). This illusion, moreover, is sustained by the assumption that eighteen centuries of Christianity are sufficient to confirm the truth of what Christians believe. Kierkegaard counters that assumption, arguing that those eighteen centuries have contributed not

---

8. Søren Kierkegaard, *The Point of View for My Work as An Author*, trans. Walter Lowrie (New York: Harper Torchbooks, 1962), 22. Paginations will appear in the text. For a defense of *The Point of View of My Work as An Author* as representing Kierkegaard's truthful understanding of his authorship, see Mark Tietjen, *Kierkegaard, Communication, and Virtue: Authorship as Edification* (Bloomington: Indiana University Press, 2013), 61–88. Tietjen's general perspective on Kierkegaard is one with which I am deeply sympathetic. In particular, I think he is right to read Kierkegaard in the tradition of the virtues which puts him much closer to MacIntyre than MacIntyre himself thinks. Tietjen's readings of the pseudonymous literature as works of edification is, I think, also right. These matters have direct implications for the suggestions I will make concerning how Kierkegaard should be taught in the modern university.

an iota of proof for sustaining the truth of Christianity. Indeed the opposite has been the case, as those eighteen centuries have "contributed with steadily increasing power to do away with Christianity."[9]

Kierkegaard does not deny that Christianity has rightly had an effect on the world. Christ's name is proclaimed and believed throughout the world. The doctrines surrounding Christ have changed the face of the world permeating all relationships. Accordingly, many assume that the history of the triumph of Christianity to take over the world is sufficient to establish that Jesus is who he says he was, namely, he was God. Kierkegaard responds to this claim with an emphatic, "No." History has not established who he is because history and the effects of Christianity in history cannot substantiate the claim that Jesus was God. At most appeals to historical effects might show that Jesus was a great or good man. But faith in Jesus as the Son of God is of a different order.[10] Any claim to the contrary is blasphemy.

What must be acknowledged, Kierkegaard argues, is that from any human point of view Christianity is and must be a kind of madness. It is so because only through a consciousness of sin can one come to the one who can save. Accordingly, Christianity must display itself as madness "in order that the qualitative infinite emphasis may fall upon the fact that only consciousness of sin is the way of entrance."[11] Indeed this is the kind of consciousness that is the exact opposite of the kind of awareness that Christendom sponsors, namely, the attitude that expresses admiration

9. Søren Kierkegaard, *Training in Christianity*, trans. Walter Lowrie (Princeton: Princeton University Press, 1941), 143.

10. Kierkegaard, *Training in Christianity*, 28-29. In *Philosophical Fragments* (Princeton: Princeton University Press, 1936), Kierkegaard remarks: "If God does not exist it would of course be impossible to prove it; and if he does exist it would be folly to attempt it" (31). In many ways that sums up the case I was trying to make in my Gifford Lectures, now published as *With the Grain of the Universe: The Church's Witness and Natural Theology* (Grand Rapids: Brazos, 2001).

11. Kierkegaard, *Training in Christianity*, 72. For an incisive account of Kierkegaard's understanding of sin, see Jason Mahn, *Fortunate Fallibility: Kierkegaard and the Power of Sin* (Oxford: Oxford University Press, 2011). Mahn interprets Kierkegaard's understanding of sin as being in the tradition of the "fortunate fall." Mahn's interpretation stems from Kierkegaard's persistent attempt to see grace through the fractures of human fallibility (2). Mahn also makes the extremely important point that when Kierkegaard inscribed his account of sin within his account of human nature he also enfolds that anthropology within his portrayal of Christ's particularity (14). Christendom's resistance to such particularity results in sin being something from which we can assume we have already been saved and therefore no confession or repentance is required.

for Jesus. Such a form of consciousness is a fraud, a self-deceit, but one common to Christendom. It is so because in Christendom Christ is exalted to confirm our self-deceptions; the deepest deception being that we do not have to lose our lives to be a true disciple of Jesus.

What those shaped by Christendom cannot fathom is that there is an intrinsic connection between truth and martyrdom. The crowd is untruth and it was the crowd that crucified Christ. Although Jesus addressed himself to all, he refused to have dealings with the crowd as a crowd. He was not trying to win a popularity contest or be elected messiah. He would be what he is, the Truth, which is the condition necessary to produce that strangest of all characters in Kierkegaard, that is, the individual. That character is to be found among those who recognize that the hard truth, a truth that cannot be acknowledged by the crowd, is that "every-one who truly would serve the truth is *eo ipso*, in one way or another, a martyr" (114).

What Christendom occludes, or even more troubling what Christendom loses, is Jesus. The reason it is so difficult to be a Christian in Christendom is that one cannot help but think being Christian is to identify with the eighteen hundred years of the effects of Christianity rather than with this Jesus who is the Christ. But when Christianity becomes something other than faith in Jesus as the Christ it can no longer claim to be true. For Christ is the truth in a manner that makes clear that the truth cannot be abstracted from any explanation of what the truth is. Thus Kierkegaard's claim that the truth, in the sense that Christ was the truth, is not a collection of sentences, nor a definition of concepts, but rather truth in its essence is the reduplication in us that his life is "the very being of truth, is a *life*, as the truth was in Christ, for He was the truth."[12]

In Christendom, however, Christians assume that knowing about Christ is the equivalent to believing in him, but that cannot be true.[13] It cannot be true because Jesus called those who would follow him to be disciples. To become a disciple is to acquire another self, that is, to become a new creature.[14] A disciple may appear to be a student, but a student may learn without being transformed. In contrast, the disciple undergoes a conversion because the truth that possesses her is one in which the one who is the truth cannot be abstracted from what makes

12. Kierkegaard, *Training in Christianity*, 201.

13. Kierkegaard, *Training in Christianity*, 38.

14. For Kierkegaard's account of what it means to be a disciple, see *Philosophical Fragments*, 13–16.

the truth true. These are complex matters that are often misunderstood because, as Kierkegaard knew, those determined by the habits of Christendom cannot help but find such an account of truth "extreme."

One of the ironies of being a true Christian in Christendom is the necessity to have one's faith hidden. To be a Christian is to have a "hidden inwardness" because if one's Christianity were known some people might wish to honor and celebrate you for being a true Christian. As a result, a true Christian must remain in a hidden inwardness. Kierkegaard observes that there is a great irony that true Christians must remain hidden. In the first centuries of the church, if Christians could be recognized by their enemies they could be put to death. In the "triumphant church," which is the name Kierkegaard gives to the present day Christendom church, the danger is that Christians are not put in danger by being Christian, but rather Christians are rewarded and honored because they are Christians.[15]

In contrast to the triumphant church, the early church was a militant church. The militant church, moreover, alone is the church. The triumphant church, as well as the very concept of Christendom, is but vain conceit. Nowhere is that vanity more apparent than the triumphant church's inability to produce martyrs. The triumphant church has the illusion that she has conquered the world, but in fact the world has conquered her.[16] The triumphant church may make much of the doctrines that allegedly constitute the faith—the triumphant church may celebrate her "orthodoxy"—but she fails to see that Christianity is not doctrine but rather a life named Jesus.

Paul Holmer indicates the connections Kierkegaard is trying to make suggests that at the heart of Kierkegaard's representation of Christian convictions is the "pragmatic significance of the person of Jesus Christ."[17] Holmer observes that Kierkegaard assumed that books can be written about Jesus just as they can be written about Plato. Books can be written to give objective accounts of the teachings of this or that person. An account of the institutions such figures challenged or which institutions supported them can also be described. It is also the case that such studies can try to establish the significance of each man. Yet Kierkegaard's point, according to Holmer, is that historical accounts fail to describe

15. Kierkegaard, *Training in Christianity*, 211–12.

16. Kierkegaard, *Training in Christianity*, 213.

17. Paul Holmer, *Theology and the Scientific Study of Religion* (Minneapolis: Denison, 1961), 203.

Jesus, because he is presented in abstraction from the demands he places on those who would follow him. Jesus can only be known when the interests, the passions, Jesus asks of his followers, the demand that we live by dying, win by losing, receive by giving, are constitutive of what it means to know Jesus.[18]

To do justice to Kierkegaard's understanding of what is required to introduce Christianity into Christendom would require a much fuller account of his work. But hopefully enough has been said to suggest what might follow for the challenges Christians face if we are to serve the university as followers of Christ. The irony of Christendom is central to his work, but this is lost if Jesus's claim on us is not the counterpoint. Kierkegaard undertook the thankless task of trying to help Christians see Jesus in a culture that assumed Jesus could be seen just by looking. We may face a quite different challenge.

Where We May Be Today in Academia

Kierkegaard took his task to be the introduction of Christianity into Christendom. As I suggested above, we may be in a quite different space and time. To be sure we are creatures of a Christendom that is rapidly disappearing. Fragments of its existence still give some the hope that a Christian world can be recovered. Many universities and colleges are institutions that represent some of those fragments, just to the extent they live in the tension between their Christian past and their uncertain future. By "uncertain future" I do not mean whether they will survive—though it appears many will not survive—but rather what kind of self-understanding will be available to avoid becoming "just another university." "Self-understanding" can be but a nice way of saying ideology.

I wish I could pretend to have some suggestion about what a university committed to being of service to the church might look like. I think, however, it is not first a question about the university, but about the church. Do we have a church sufficiently distinctive to produce people with the imaginations to create and sustain knowledge of the world that can be described as Christian? That a college or university is sponsored and supported by Christians is not without use, but the crucial question, as I tried to suggest in *The State of the University*, is whether the

---

18. Holmer, *Theology and the Scientific Study of Religion*, 204.

disciplines that constitute the curriculum of such a university reflect the Christian difference.

That does not mean that every discipline in such a university will be different from its counterpart in a non-Christian university. The assumption, for example, is that many of the sciences will not necessarily have what might be considered Christian content, but there may still be questions surrounding education in the sciences that Christians should care about. For example, I should think that no science in a university supported by Christians should be taught that does not teach the history of that science. Too often, I fear, the teaching of science in the modern university presupposes a reductionist metaphysical materialism that cannot be justified but is never made articulate and, therefore, is mistakenly assumed to be internal to the science itself. That the history of a science must be taught at least offers the opportunity for those in the science to make the fundamental presuppositions of the science open to investigation.

I have called attention to the sciences because they are usually assumed to be the most determinative challenge to the kind of account I am trying to give concerning what a university that calls itself Christian must do. But the "humanities" are no less a challenge. How history, for example, should be understood and taught to reflect how Christians understand their place in the world will be, and cannot help but be, an ongoing debate. Descriptions are everything. For example, why should Christians assume what is called the American revolutionary war was a just war?

One of the other questions that the very existence of such a university would raise is whether the parents of children who have been formed in such a university would be happy with the effects such a university might have on their children. A child educated in such a university will not have been educated to be a success. Students shaped by education in an economics department that took seriously Jesus's strictures against possessions might be ill-prepared to be good players in the market. Would the parents of students formed by a department of economics so conceived want their children back?

What does all this have to do with Kierkegaard? Kierkegaard attacked Christendom. The kind of university I seem to think we need in the light of a dying Christendom may suggest I am trying to reestablish something like Christendom. Sam Wells observed that anytime "Christian" is used as an adjective you have an indication that some kind of

Constantinianism is at work. I think he is right about that. That is why I have not used the description "Christian university," but rather referred to the Christian support of the university. Yet, I cannot deny that no matter how the matter is phrased, the kind of university I want seems to make the church a civilizational reality.

But that *is* what I want—that is, I want Christians to produce a material culture that can find expression through the disciplines represented in a university. If that is Constantinianism, so be it. I find it hard, however, to think such an understanding of the Christian stake in producing something like the university to be Constantinian, if it is remembered that the church that makes such a university possible is one determined by the crucified Christ. A university so conceived, for example, could not organize courses in politics on the presumption that violence must be assumed necessary for the cooperative work necessary for the discovery of goods in common.

Perhaps another way to put the matter is to observe what a loss it would be if Christians lacked a context for the study of Kierkegaard. The challenge, of course, is how to prevent such study from becoming a way to avoid Kierkegaard's challenge to our complacency about how to live as Christians. Kierkegaard can only be taught well just to the extent he is allowed to call into question our very being as Christians. In a like manner, a university determined by Christian practices will by necessity be an institution that desires to change students' lives.

I do not think a university so conceived is antithetical to Kierkegaard's attack on Christendom. We no longer live in Christendom. To be sure, it is not yet clear what status the church will have in the new world aborning, but in the meantime a non-established church can use the shards left from the old dispensation to sustain her life. One of those shards was a strange man called Søren Kierkegaard. How fortunate for us.

6

Graduation Address
University of Aberdeen

June 19, 2017

Pro-Chancellor Torrance, Principal Diamond, Distinguished Guests, Graduates, Ladies and Gentlemen, I am deeply grateful for the honor bestowed on me, as well as being asked to address you. Scotland has been very good to me. I have thought that may be because I am a Texan, which means I have some sense of what it means to come from a country ruled by a foreign power. I do understand, however, that many of you have come to study here from that place. That is an achievement that should not be ignored.

Graduation addresses are in general all alike. The speaker must begin congratulating those graduating for their achievement. Those graduating are then told that the world to which they are being unleashed is in sore need of their talent. The speaker then has the option of describing the world the graduates are to enter as brimming with potential or being a dark and dangerous place. Either way, those graduating are assured that the education they have received has prepared them well for the challenges they will confront. The climax of the speech takes the form of recommendations for how those graduating should negotiate the rest of their lives. These recommendations are commonplace generalizations that are difficult to take seriously because the speaker lacks the authority to say anything that has the ring of truth. As a result, you will discover if asked what the speaker has said you cannot remember anything. I know this because I estimate I have heard over forty-five of these addresses and I cannot remember any.

I begin with this characterization of graduation speeches because, as much as I should like to avoid being boring, I suspect what I have to say may fall within the normal paradigm. I am, however, going to give you some advice I expect you to remember. My advice is designed to give you a life worth living. Such a life is described well in James Rebanks's wonderful book, *The Shepherd's Life*. Toward the end of the memoir, in which Rebanks describes the hard life and work of being a shepherd, he is lying on his back watching the sheep he has let loose in the fells and he thinks, "This is my life. I want no other." An extraordinary claim I suspect few in our social orders can make. So let me give you the advice I think you need if you hope to one day be able to say, "This is my life. I want no other."[1]

Here is my advice: "*Do not lie.*"

You have to be thinking: "Is that it? Is that all he has to say? I have to sit here and listen to someone tell me what I already know?" I am sure you think you do not need me, in my profession as a moralist, or even in the role as a graduation speaker, to tell you never to lie. You may not remember when or where you learned not to lie, but long before this day you knew that though in some circumstances you may have to say what is less than true, in general, lying should be avoided.

Yet, the general agreement that lying should be avoided masks our confusion about what constitutes a lie. Lying may be rightly understood as intentionally saying what we know to be false in order to deceive, but it turns out we often are unsure we know what is true. Thus the Austrian-British philosopher Wittgenstein remarked in *Culture and Value* that "the truth can be spoken only by someone who is already *at home* in it, not by someone who still lives in untruthfulness, and does no more than reach out towards it from within untruthfulness."[2]

What it might mean to be at home in the truth is not immediately evident, but hopefully the training you have received over the time you have spent in this university has given you some sense of what such a home might entail. The university is an institution that is allegedly based on the practice of truth telling. In the sciences, for example, the demand that negative results are as important as positive results is an indication

---

1. James Rebanks, *The Shepherd's Life: Modern Dispatches from an Ancient Landscape* (Oxford: Penguin, 2015), 287.

2. Ludwig Wittgenstein, *Culture and Value*, trans. Peter Winch, ed. G. H. von Wright with Heikki Nyman (Chicago: University of Chicago Press, 1980), 41e.

that truth matters. However, as many scientists can tell you, a research agenda that only produces negative results means funding will not necessarily be as readily forthcoming. The humanities, whatever they are, are committed to saying well what must be said, even though what is said will often challenge our most cherished illusions. To be a citizen of the university means you are committed to accurate, careful, and eloquent speech.

You will need the formation against lying that the university provides, because, as I suspect you have already discovered, not many of us are at home in the truth. We are moderately good people, but because we are only moderately good self-deception is an endemic problem. Genuinely bad people often have less illusion about themselves and the world than those of us who try to be morally pretty good people. We discover, for example, that in our interactions with those with whom we are closest it is quite difficult not to lie. I suspect you will discover, and I suspect many of you have already discovered, that in your most serious relationships, which sometimes will be marriage, you will fear telling the one you love the truth because the truth will threaten the fragile intimacy that originally sustained the relationship. That is why I have never trusted declarations by couples that claim they have always had a happy marriage—that just tells me someone lost early.

Politics, and in particular democratic politics, is perhaps a far too easy exemplification of the lie which masquerades as the semblance of truth. We often criticize politicians for failing to be candid. We condemn them for pandering to their constituency, but we forget that is what they were elected to do. This expectation produces much that is just downright silly in politics, but it is crucial to remember political life is about life and death. Never forget we ask some to kill, as well as to be willing to be killed, in the name of securing our well-being. It is often said that the first casualty of war is the truth, but the truth is that men and women have killed and died for a mistaken set of judgments. If it is true that truth is the first casualty of war, it is important to remember that the lie seems almost impossible to avoid because we do not want anyone to "die in vain."

"Do not lie" turns out, therefore, to be a more complex demand than is usually assumed. That is particularly the case if not lying requires that we be at home in the truth. To be at home in the truth is a demanding business because so often we lie because we are trying to be good. As a result, it is often the case we end up not sure we know what we are talking about when claim we want to be truthful.

The temptation is to think that in order to get a handle on not lying you need a theory of truth, but that is what many think we no longer seem to have. This is not a new problem. I am a representative of a tradition that has at its center the one we believe not only was at home in the truth, but *was* and *is* the truth. When a minor Roman official was told this man was the one who had come into the world to testify to the truth, he asked the skeptic's question, "What is truth?" He received no answer; the ensuing silence indicates that the response to skepticism is not a theory but an exemplary life. Such a life, a life that is at home in the truth, is a life according to Wittgenstein that has undergone the training to keep pride in check.

Universities are institutions charged with the responsibility to train us to speak and write eloquently. To speak and write eloquently, I believe, is a necessary skill if we are to be at home in the truth. The absence of eloquent speech in our societal and political life is an indication that something has desperately gone wrong. Cost benefit analysis is certainly appropriate in certain contexts, but how that language threatens to overwhelm all aspects of our lives is surely an invitation to believe that life is nothing more than having more.

Therefore, if my advice to you is to say what is true, to avoid the lie, I give this advice in the hope you will demand that our life together be forged by the desire to live truthful lives. Lies make our lives ugly, robbing us of our ability even to trust ourselves. As graduates of the University of Aberdeen, you have during you time here been put on the path to being at home in the truth. That is no small thing. Never take it for granted. To live in the truth will give you a life which may be difficult, but one that will make possible your ability to look back and want no other life than you have lived. As my friend, Sam Wells, suggests the only things in our lives that will last are those things that embody the truth. So a well lived life will not be determined by how thick a person's CV may be, but rather those aspects of one's life that abide in the truth.

So again I say to you, "*Do not lie.*"

Part III

LIVES MATTER

7

The Good Life

A Shepherd's Life

In his beautifully written memoir, *The Shepherd's Life: Modern Dispatches from an Ancient Landscape*, James Rebanks helps those like myself who know nothing about sheep to have some sense of what it means to be a shepherd.[1] Rebanks is well prepared to perform this task as he comes from a lineage of shepherds. Rebanks knows sheep and he helps his reader know something of what he knows.

For example, I had no idea there are so many different breeds of sheep. The diversity of breads means, moreover, that the breeding of sheep can be quite specialized. For example there are breeds of sheep that have been and continue to be bred to negotiate different topographies.

Romantic conceptions of what it might mean to be a shepherd cannot survive Rebanks's honest account of the brutality that is often necessary to maintain the flock. The bargaining between shepherds can be a cutthroat business. To maintain the farm, moreover, is sheer hard work and the result is often a barely sustainable living. If you are tempted to become a shepherd you need to remember you will spend a good deal of your life looking into the mouths of sheep because it seems you can tell much about the quality of sheep by looking at their teeth.

Rebanks is a wonderful storyteller and writer. He knows how to write because, as one who hated formal schooling, he improbably ended

---

1. James Rebanks, *The Shepherd's Life: Modern Dispatches from an Ancient Landscape* (Oxford: Penguin, 2015). Paginations in text.

up doing a degree at Oxford. Although he left secondary school as soon as it was permissible, he discovered he loved to read. Every night after a hard day of working on his grandfather's and father's farm he read. While taking a continuing education course, he was discovered and encouraged to take the tests necessary for him to go to a university. He did take the test, and the rest is history.

Having gone to Oxford, he could have pursued a very different form of life other than that of being a shepherd, but he chose to return to the farm. He did so because, as he observes, he had inherited from his grandfather the classic worldview of the peasant. That worldview he identified with the presumption that he was in the line of those people who just always seem to be "there"—a people who though often battered yet endure, and through such endurance come to believe they "owned the earth." Such people, Rebanks observes, are "built out of stories" that are embedded in the everyday necessities of life.

In the last paragraphs of *The Shepherd's Life*, Rebanks, who has now been a shepherd many years, reports on a moment in his busy life. It is in the late spring and he is in the process of returning his flock to the craggy hills. These sheep had been bred to fend for themselves in a rocky terrain. He enjoys watching the sheep find their way in the rough fields because they are evidently happy to be "home." Rebanks imitates his flock's sense that all is as it should be by lying down in the grass to drink sweet and pure water from the nearby stream. He rolls on his back and watches the clouds racing by. His well-trained sheep dogs, Floss and Tan, who had never seen him so relaxed, come and lay next to him. He breathes in the cool mountain air; he listens to the ewes calling to the lambs to follow them through the rocky crags, and he thinks, "This is my life. I want no other" (287).

"This is my life. I want no other" is an extraordinary declaration that one rarely hears today.[2] As odd as it may seem, I want to suggest that the loss of our ability to have such lives, the absence of the conditions

---

2. I am not suggesting that Rebanks's declaration is equivalent to him being morally good, though I think he is a person of rare virtue. Interestingly enough, Alasdair MacIntyre comments in his *Dependent Rational Animals: Why Human Beings Need the Virtues* (Chicago: Open Court, 1999) that "someone can be a good shepherd without being a good human being, but the goods of sheep farming are genuine goods" (65–66). I am sure MacIntyre is right, but I also think the kind of goodness necessary to be a good shepherd puts one on the road to being morally good. I do not think MacIntyre would disagree. It does not follow, however, that the relation between learning to be a good shepherd and a good person holds for every activity in which we are engaged.

that make such a declaration possible in contemporary life, is a clue for understanding our current cultural moment and corresponding politics.[3] Stated differently, that many people feel they are forced to live lives they do not want or understand helps explain the phenomenon called Donald Trump. An extraordinary claim, so let me try to explain.

God knows it is hard to take Donald Trump seriously, but I think it is a mistake to ignore him or, more importantly, to ignore the people that support him. Trump has given voice to an unease that is widespread at this time in our culture. Theories about *who* the people are as well as *why* they support Trump abound. I suspect there is something to most of these theories. I am sure, for example, that racism plays a role for some who support Trump. It is hard to believe we have a person running for the Presidency of the United States promising to be "the law and order President." If you ever wanted an exemplification of the oft-made observation that Americans forget their history, Trump's claim to restore law and order ignores the racist presumption that gave birth to that phrase in the first place.[4] I am also sure that the fear occasioned by September 11 is another factor that attracts some to his pledge to "Make America Great Again."

Yet the racism and fear Trump uses to give the impression that he would be a "strong leader" are, I believe, manifestations of an even deeper pathology—namely, the profound sense of unease that many Americans have about their lives. That unease often takes the form of resentment against elites, but, even more troubling, it funds the prejudice against minority groups as well as immigrants. Resentment is another word for the unease that seems to grip many good, middle-class—mostly white— people.[5] These are people who have worked hard all their lives, yet find

---

3. This essay originated as lecture given at St. Martin's-in-the-Fields in London, England on October 31, 2016, as the Presidential campaign of the United States was drawing to a close.

4. Though the phrase is now associated with the white demand to use the police to put African Americans in their place, that was not the original context that gave birth to the phrase. Paul Ramsey pointed out to me the phrase was first used by African Americans to demand that white police officers make a response to crime in African-American communities. That was, of course, necessary in a segregated society because in the South police forces that were white simply did not apply the law in African-American sections of their towns.

5. One of the questions raised by the Trump phenomenon is what makes the middle class the middle class. There is increasing evidence that the middle class is shrinking.

they are no better off than when they started.[6] They deeply resent what they interpret as the special treatment some receive in an effort to right the wrongs of the past.

The bottom line is many Americans are angry, but they are not sure towards whom that anger is appropriately directed. Their anger needs direction and Trump is more than happy to tell Americans—particularly if they are white—who their enemy is, as well as whom they should hate. There is a therapeutic aspect to Trump's rhetoric because he gives people an enemy that delays any acknowledgment that those with whom they should be angry may be themselves.

All this is happening at the same time that the church, at least the mainstream church in America, is consumed by a culture of consumption. Americans are increasingly discovering they have no good reason for "going to church." The ever-decreasing number of Christians has led some church leaders to think our primary job is to find ways to increase church membership. At a time when Christians need to have confidence we have something to say, in the interest of "church growth" what we have to say is simplistic and superficial. You do not need to come to church to be told you need to be nice to those with less.

Of course, that is not the only way the church has responded to our current political and social challenges. Drawing on the spirit of the civil rights struggle, black and white Christians have again joined with those who seem to represent the progressive forces of history to extend the equality they assume is promised by our democratic convictions. Rightly embarrassed by complicity in past injustices, Christians now try to identify with anyone or group that claims they want to make America a more just society. Accordingly, Christians express their moral commitments by joining with those who think they are having their fundamental rights denied. This is called social ethics. The only problem with this attempt to recover the moral authority of the church is that while it may be a very good thing for Christians to support these attempts to make our social

---

6. It is interesting to ask what it means for people to want to be "better off." Often, when asked, they say they would like for their children to have more opportunities than they have had, but that answer betrays some uncertainty about what that ambition entails. It usually means they would like for their children not to have to work as hard as they have had to work, but it remains unclear what that means in terms of what they would like for their children to get out of life. The oft-made declaration that "I just want them [meaning their children] to be happy," is not very informative or helpful. You seldom hear someone say that they want their child to be a good person. I suspect people do want their children to be good people, but that is seldom made explicit.

order more just it is not theologically clear how the pursuit of justice so understood helps us know how to live. Indeed, I worry that many people now confuse being on the right side of history with having a life worth living.[7]

The church has simply failed to help people live in a manner such that we would want no other life than the life we have lived. Such lives may well be filled with suffering and failures, but suffering and failures are not blocks to having lived a good life. To have lived a good life is to have lived in a manner that we hope we can be remembered by those who have found our lives crucial for making it possible for them to want no other life than the life they have been given. To be happily remembered is to have lived with a modesty that testifies to our dependence on others and makes possible the satisfaction that accompanies doing the right thing without regret or notice.

"This is my life. I want no other" is the expression of what in the past was called "a good life." That language is still used but now it references lives that have not been unduly burdened. To have had a good life now means for many that their second marriage turned out all right, the children did not become addicts, and they had enough savings to retire. That understanding of the good life too often produces people who do not want the life they have lived. They do not want the life they have lived because it is a life without consequence. I suspect the reason so many men want their service in the military mentioned in their obituary is because they believe that service was of consequence.

If any people should know what it means to have a good life, surely Christians ought to have something to say. Yet I do not think Christians have emphasized sufficiently why we think it so important to have a life well lived and, perhaps even more significant, what living well looks like. I am, of course, not suggesting that what it means to live a good life will be the same for everyone. But I do believe to have lived well makes it possible to want no other life than the life you have lived. To want no other life than the life we have lived—a life that often has moments of failures and betrayals—is made possible for Christians because our lives can be

---

7. There are several generations—I am part of "the several"—whose moral identity is dependent on having a cause to support. The first cause was the civil rights struggle, then anti-Vietnam, then support of the women's movement, all of which seems to have climaxed with the protest against prejudice towards gays. Each of these movements was worthy of support, but often the different moral issues that each raise tend to be occluded.

located in a determinative narrative that makes it possible for us to make sense of even those aspects of our life about which we are not sure we can or should make sense.

In his extraordinary book, *After Virtue*, which was first published in 1981, Alasdair MacIntyre observed that the conception of a whole human life is a concept that is no longer generally available in our culture. Such a conception, MacIntyre contends, is necessary to provide the content of non-arbitrary judgments about particular actions or projects that make up our individual lives. The loss of such an understanding of our lives, MacIntyre argues, has gone unnoticed partly because it is not seen as a loss, but as a gain for human freedom. But the result is the loss of the boundaries derived from our social identity and any sense that our lives are ordered to a given end.[8] Why and how this has happened I want to explore by calling attention to John Milbank's and Adrian Pabst's account of our contemporary situation in their book, *The Politics of Virtue: Post-Liberalism and the Human Future*.

The Politics of Virtue

John Milbank has reclaimed the importance of Christian theology for helping us better understand why many no longer think Christian theology can be about truth. He has done that by polemically showing how the very disciplines we use to understand our lives are, in fact, legitimations that make us think that there are no alternatives to the way things are. Accordingly, with his co-author Pabst, he argues in *The Politics of Virtue* that our lives are shaped by narratives that make it next to impossible to be happy with the lives we have lived.[9] Milbank and Pabst argue that people who are citizens of advanced societies like the UK and the US cannot be satisfied with our lives because we no longer have the resources to live honorable lives of virtue. As a result we seem to be living lives that are contradictory or, as I suggested above, lives we do not understand.[10]

---

8. Alasdair MacIntyre, *After Virtue*, 3rd ed. (Notre Dame: University of Notre Dame Press, 2007), 34.

9. John Milbank and Adrian Pabst, *The Politics of Virtue: Post-Liberalism and the Human Future* (London: Rowman and Littlefield, 2016). Paginations in the text.

10. "I am trying to live a life I do not understand" is an observation made by Pretty Shield, a Crow Native American, after the destruction of the Crow way of life. Jonathan Lear provides a haunting account of Plenty Coup, the chief of the Crow, in his *Radical Hope: Ethics in the Face of Cultural Devastation* (Cambridge: Harvard University Press,

According to Milbank and Pabst, we no longer are able to live virtuously because our lives are determined by a hegemonic liberal story. That story comes in two basic forms. There is the liberalism of the cultural left that is primarily understood as the attempt to free people of past forms of oppression. That liberal story is often contrasted with the political and economic liberalism of the right that is primarily focused on economic and political policy within a capitalist framework. Milbank and Pabst argue, however, that these forms of liberalism, though they have quite different understandings of freedom, have increasingly become mutually reinforcing. The left and the right are joined by the common project to increase personal freedoms—even if the result is the atomization of our lives that makes impossible any account of our lives as having a narrative unity. Ironically, societies committed to securing the freedom of the individual end up making that same individual subject to impersonal bureaucratic procedures.[11]

Politically, liberalism increases the concentration of power in the central state, as well as at the same time underwriting the assumption of the inevitability of a globalized market.[12] The latter has the unfortunate effect of destroying a sense of place. In such a social order, the production of wealth increasingly is in the hands of a new, rootless oligarchy "that practices a manipulative populism while holding in contempt the genuine priorities of most people" (1). As good a description of Trump as one could want.

I think it will be helpful in support of Milbank's and Pabst's account of liberalism to call attention to Ron Beiner's understanding of liberalism in his well-regarded book, *What's the Matter with Liberalism*.[13] Beiner,

2006). Lear's account of Pretty Shield is found on page 61.

11. This is one of the determinative themes in Rusty Reno's *Resurrecting the Idea of a Christian Society* (Grand Rapids: Eerdmans, 2016). Reno's book is an ongoing critique of multiculturalism, political correctness, the pro-gay movement, and unisexual developments, but it is to Reno's credit that he sees these liberation projects as being consistent with, as well as the outgrowth of, the American dream of freedom understood as the ability to make ourselves into anything we wish. Such a view of freedom cannot help but end in contradiction because it cannot help but reproduce the coercive power of government to promote freedom for the sake of freedom (25).

12. The best account I know of the implications of a global market for how the nation-state will be understood is Philip Bobbitt's, *The Shield of Achilles: War, Peace, and the Course of History* (New York: Anchor Books, 2003). The great tension Bobbitt sees clearly is how the developing "market state" can maintain the honor ethic of the military.

13. Ron Beiner, *What's the Matter with Liberalism?* (Berkeley: University of

perhaps even more forcefully that Milbank and Pabst, stresses that liberalism is not only a social and political alternative, but more importantly, the recommendation of a distinctive moral way to live. To be sure, Milbank and Pabst know that liberalism is a normative proposal for how best to live, but Beiner helps us see that even if we do not think of ourselves as liberals the liberal story determines our lives. In my language, liberalism is morally the presumption that I am to be held accountable only for what I have done when what I have done is the result of my choice and my choice alone.[14] That is what liberals mean by freedom. As a correlate to this understanding of freedom, equality is understood as the goal of trying to secure for each individual freedom from arbitrary limits.[15]

A liberal way of life, Milbank and Pabst argue, however, is built on contradictory and self-defeating commitments that are only viable because they have been and continue to be parasitic on the heritage inherited from the past and in particular the Roman and Christian traditions. For example, the Christian commitment to the uniqueness of the person conceived and realized through constitutive relations with other persons is lost in the ruthless liberal presumption that our task is to expand our individual domains limited only by contractual agreements made to insure fairness. The result is an inequity that "gives rise to endless discontents" that spill over into atavistic assertions of the absolute identity of race, nation, religion, gender, sexuality, disability and so on (16).

California, 1992), 22–23. For my use of Beiner's account of liberalism, see my *Dispatches from the Front: Theological Engagements with the Secular* (Durham, NC: Duke University Press, 1994), 156–63.

14. My usual way of putting this is to say that modernity is the name for the political and economic ambition to produce people who believe that they should have no story other than the story they chose when they had no story. The only problem with that story is that those whose story it is did not choose that story.

15. Often those who support the ethos of the Enlightenment argue that figures like MacIntyre continue to presume the goals of the Enlightenment, such as the securing of freedom. They fail, however, to comprehend that what MacIntyre means by freedom is quite different than what most Enlightenment thinkers mean by freedom. The latter concentrate primarily on freedom *from*, but MacIntyre is concerned primarily with freedom *for*. The same is true of the importance of equality. For MacIntyre the question is how equality works in some social relationships, but not in others. Accordingly, from MacIntyre's perspective, some account of hierarchy is required. For MacIntyre's reflections on these matters, see his "Where We Were, Where We Are, Where We Need to Be," in *Virtue and Politics: Alasdair MacIntyre's Revolutionary Aristotelianism*, ed. Paul Blackledge and Kelvin Knight (Notre Dame: University of Notre Dame Press, 2011), 326–27.

According to Milbank and Pabst, the contradictory character of liberalism is but an indication that liberalism's most profound mistakes are metaphysical. Liberalism goes against the grain of our humanity and the universe itself because it is based on the presumption that life has no telos other than the arbitrary desires we impose on the world to make us feel at home. From a liberal perspective, all life is finally materially determined. This recognition cannot help but result in a pervasive nihilism. The resulting politics of contractual arrangements, whether it is the politics of Hobbes or Rousseau, tries to ameliorate the violence that is at the heart of attempts to sustain cooperative relations between isolated individuals. Such arrangements cannot help but fail because a genuine politics cannot be sustained without some account of the role of those who represent what it means to live well as people of virtue and honor.

I have no doubt that Milbank's and Pabst's understanding and criticism of liberalism will invite critical responses. Milbank and Pabst will be dismissed for having far too strong a position by liberals who in principle dismiss strong positions yet cannot recognize that they have a strong position. The kind of position Milbank and Pabst represent stands the risk of dying the death of a thousand qualifications, which is the academic equivalent of being nibbled to death by ducks. I have no intention to be part of that flock. That may be because I am in deep sympathy with Milbank's and Pabst's understanding and critique of liberalism, and I have sympathy with some of their proposed alternatives. By exploring my differences with their recommendations, I hope to clarify why I began with a shepherd's story.

Milbank and Pabst call their proposed alternative post-liberalism. Post-liberalism is a blend of two older traditions: "a combination of honourable, virtuous elites with greater popular participation: a greater sense of cultural duty and hierarchy of value and honor, alongside much more real equality and genuine freedom in economic and political realms" (1–2). I am particularly drawn to their understanding of the ethics of virtue that they argue depends on the presumption that our lives have a purpose and meaning that is not just our arbitrary will. When confronted by what may be morally difficult, those whose lives are determined by the virtues do not ask what should be done, but rather ask "what I should consistently be doing *at all*. What sort of shape might my entire life appropriately take? What sort of character do I want to be and how should

I order this desire in an acceptable way to my relationships with others?" (4).

Such questions, and admittedly they observe these are not questions we ask or need to ask on a daily basis, are often asked at crucial transitional points in our lives. I suspect, for example, such a point is when the newly married ask themselves what they have done, or when new parents suddenly have forced on themselves the stark reality that they have brought a new life into the world and they are not sure why. Any answer to these questions, moreover, entails further questions about the kind of society in which we want to live. How does my life fit with the lives of others with whom I must share goods is a question that cannot be avoided, if we would live lives that can be happily narrated. The good news is we cannot have an honorable life without others who also seek to live honorably.[16]

To so live can sound quite burdensome, but Milbank and Pabst do not think that to be the case. To live virtuously does not mean that we must be constantly thinking about what we should do or not do. Rather, Milbank and Pabst observe, most of what we do that is honorable is "an everyday matter of performing your job well, being a good lover, spouse, parent, friend, colleague and citizen, or even enjoying a game or a trip. For if goodness is given in nature and not something we contrive with difficulty from time to time, then simple gratitude is a crucial aspect of virtue" (5).

Milbank and Pabst, who know much of what they are recommending, will be thought by some to be reactionary, for they do not hesitate to take positions that many will think to be outrageous. Their defense of an ethics of honor, for example, will be considered by many as an exercise in nostalgia. Yet they argue, drawing on papal social encyclicals, that a post-liberal ethic is about the everyday process of locating the goods we have in common. Such goods are not, as liberalism would have it, the aggregate of privately owned items, but rather goods that can be shared together such as intimacy, trust, beauty. The goods that should determine how we live are embedded in the practices of honor and reciprocity that

---

16. Milbank and Pabst do not provide an extended account of honor, but I take it they are trying to recommend an understanding of honor that simply has no standing in the modern world. At least that is Alasdair MacIntyre's view. In *After Virtue*, MacIntyre argues that the ancient understanding of honor as the recognition of what is due a person has been lost because any account of our relation to one another as determined by what is due has been abandoned (116).

are developed over time through the habits sustained by a tradition. The formation of such traditions depends on the existence of people of wisdom who can provide the judgments necessary for responding to new challenges while remaining faithful to the past (70).

The substitution of technique for wisdom is one of the main reasons that we have no place for understanding the responsibilities and status of the elderly. In wisdom cultures the elderly are expected to remember the judgments made in the past about matters that can be other. Once a social order no longer depends on memory the old have no responsibility to younger generations. The result, too often, is to make growing old a dreadful development that may increasingly be understood as an illness. To grow old in societies like the United States means your primary responsibility is to get out of the way.

Milbank and Pabst argue we need some account of civic roles in order to have a basis for discerning what resources should belong to those who have specific responsibilities. Such judgments inevitably imply the legitimate place for hierarchies and elites for initiating the young into the tradition of the virtues (74). They think such an ethos and politics is a realistic possibility because increasingly the working class and the middle class share a common commitment to meeting the needs of family and community (76). They argue that a coalition politics so conceived would be an alternative to the liberal commitment to abstract universalism and the corresponding denial of the significance of place.

In support of their views, Milbank and Pabst use George Orwell's socialist vision because Orwell's emphasis on practices of reciprocity, through gift giving and receiving, makes possible the process of mutual recognition. Orwell rightly thought most people pursue association with others because they desire that their contribution to our common life, no matter how small, be recognized. To be so acknowledged is what it means to be honored.

People who so live do not think their first task in life is to become more wealthy or powerful as individuals. Rather wealth is best thought of as what we share in common such as parks or practices to which all have access, such as medicine. In other words the post-liberal strategy is exactly the opposite of the liberal assumption that assumes that social practices of mutual assistance should be eliminated while at the same time encouraging our desires for wealth and prestige. The liberal desire for the well-being of the individual not only ignores the goods built on gift relations but in effect destroys the habits that make such relations possible (79).

To their credit Milbank and Pabst confront straight on what I take to be the most determinative objection to their understanding of postliberalism: the problem of luck. Luck comes in many forms and sizes but the most fundamental manifestation of luck is the brute fact that no one chooses when, where, or to whom they will be born.[17] Yet the family into which we are born determines our future, making us subject to inequalities that are justified in the name of this or that tradition, history, or some other abstraction.

I have always thought the profound moral power of the liberal tradition is to be found in the liberal desire to defeat luck. That is particularly the case when luck may be just another name for fate. The impersonality and abstract universalism characteristic of liberal institutions is an attempt to find a way not to let the accidents of birth determine a person's life.[18] Milbank and Pabst, however, argue that liberalism's ambition to overcome luck results in the destruction of any sense that we have a responsibility to fulfill the duties associated with the ascribed roles we inherit through birth (221).

The importance of luck creates the context for Milbank's and Pabst's defense of hierarchy and the importance of sustaining an aristocracy

---

17. For an extremely important analysis of luck, see Lisa Tessman, *Burdened Virtues: Virtue Ethics for Liberatory Struggles* (Oxford: Oxford University Press, 2005). Tessman develops the notion of moral luck as the presumption that a person of good character has "responsibilities that outrun control." Tessman's nuanced account of moral luck turns on how luck shapes as well as is shaped by our lives. She provides an extremely interesting account of the moral damage that comes from being oppressed or being the oppressor. She quite rightly develops Aristotle's insight that good luck can be bad for us if we fail to have the character necessary to receive such a benefit. These are complex but crucial questions that have not been sufficiently explored in contemporary philosophy or theology. For example, we need to know how to think about the significance of the temperament for our being virtuous. Is temperament luck? Tessman distinguishes between constitutive moral luck and luck we associate with being accidentally "lucky." Temperament seems clearly to be a form of constitutive luck, but that makes it no less significant for our becoming persons of moral character. Tessman suggests that regret is crucial for our ability to make our own what may have happened to us but for which we must take responsibility if we are to have a life worth living.

18. The hegemonic character of liberalism can be made apparent in language we use that is assumed to be descriptions of the way things are. For example, the phrase "accident of birth" is a description shaped by liberal presupposition that there is or should be a non-accidental way to be born.

governed by a monarch. The defense of hierarchy, they argue, is but a correlative of the necessity that there be an established church. If the church is not established, the church threatens to become but another voluntary society rather than a political entity that is the living heart of the nation (230–31). Milbank and Pabst develop a complex theological position—complex is my way to say I am sure I do not "get it"—to argue that the established church also requires that there be a monarch who can receive the sacraments for the whole society.

Milbank and Pabst defend this account of aristocracy by turning the tables on liberalism. They do so by arguing that the liberal respect for persons qua persons can be compatible with the exploitation of the person qua miner, qua father, and so on. As a result of this false idealism, personhood is divorced from vocational role. But Milbank and Pabst argue, if Aristotle is right that the aim of politics is to produce virtuous citizens, and since people develop character through social and economic relations, then these relations cannot be attended to properly if the virtuous formation of people is not the purpose of politics. This will require that each and every person's contribution to common life be valued in a manner that each person can be assured that they can exercise political influence through their workplace and with those they share a common purpose (85–86).

Milbank and Pabst argue that not only is their account of aristocracy consistent with democracy, but that democracy is, in fact, dependent on the existence of elites.[19] Elites are not necessarily incompatible with democracy. What is incompatible with democracy is liberalism exactly because of the liberal presumption that all forms of hierarchy are arbitrary and unjust. The liberal attempt to destroy aristocratic elites can lead to the tyranny of the majority.

Liberalism and democracy are in tension just to the extent that liberalism can result in a populism that is indifferent to matters of truth and goodness. The liberal emphasis on individual preference can result in the spread of a kind of anarchy that "exacerbates the increasing inability of the modern sovereign state to command the loyalty of its citizens"

---

19. It occurs to me that it might well be time to revisit the work of José Ortega y Gasset and, in particular, his understanding of the "masses" in *The Revolt of the Masses* (New York: Norton, 1957).

(186–87). War becomes the necessary means to secure the obedience of people who have been formed to vote their self-interests.[20]

Storied by Christ

The high theory that Milbank and Pabst represent may seem quite foreign to Rebanks's depiction of the life of a shepherd. I suspect Rebanks does not need Milbank and Pabst to understand his life. However, Milbank and Pabst probably do need stories like the one Rebanks tells about his life. They need Rebanks because they need exemplifications of the kind of lives they intimate must exist if their position is to be persuasive. The challenge Milbank and Pabst represent is not that lives such as Rebanks do not exist, but that, under the power of the liberal story, people like Rebanks may lack the resources to rightly tell the story of their life. Even more troubling, people like Rebanks, and people like you and me, may wrongly describe who we have been and who we are yet to be. It is a testimony to his humility and modesty that Rebanks makes neither of those mistakes.

Though I am obviously sympathetic with the general position Milbank and Pabst represent, I think there is something missing in their argument that is not without importance if we are to understand what we need to make our lives our own. What is missing in Milbank and Pabst is a person called Jesus and the people he gathers called the church. Milbank and Pabst are good Christians, and there is no doubt that Christianity plays an important role in their account of an ethic of virtue and honor. But Christianity is not the church. The church is a particular people who have been gathered from the world to worship Jesus. That they do so is the necessary condition for them to have lives that glorify God without their lives being desperate attempts to secure worldly glory.

Milbank and Pabst no doubt assume that such a church exists, but that church seems subordinate to a more determinative reality called England. That they have England gives them the confidence that social, economic, and political practices are possible at a national level to offer an alternative to liberalism. That is why they contemplate alliances

---

20. For an account of the place of war as a moral and liturgical enterprise for Americans, see my *War and the American Difference: Theological Reflections on Violence and National Identity* (Grand Rapids: Baker Academic, 2011).

between the working classes and the middle class. I have trouble keeping blue Labor and red Tories straight.

All of which means I am obviously an American. I do not have an England to think about or with. In truth, I am not sure if Milbank and Pabst have the England they seem to think is somehow lurking in the wings ready to be reborn. I think, moreover, this is not irrelevant for the questions about the politics in which we now seem caught. For unless a people exist who have a narrative more determinative than the story shaped by the politics of the day, I fear we will continue to produce politicians like Donald Trump, people who not only seem to be dangerous but are dangerous. They are, moreover, all the more dangerous because no people seem to exist who are capable of telling them the truth. Of course some quite extraordinary people exist, like the poet and farmer Wendell Berry. But Wendell Berry is not a politics. At least he is not a politics given what most Christians in America assume is "real politics," that is, the politics of elections.[21]

To be a Christian in America is to assume that there is a form of political organization that is not only compatible with our fundamental Christian convictions, but is the expression of those convictions. The name for that political reality is democracy. The discipline I represent, Christian ethics, is a discipline built on the assumption that American democracy is *the* form of Christian politics. Thus Walter Rauschenbusch, the great representative of the social gospel, claimed that Jesus saved God by taking the Father by the hand and by so doing made God the Father a democratic figure. According to Rauschenbusch, Jesus came proclaiming as well as instituting the Kingdom of God to be a movement in history to democratize all our relations with one another. Rauschenbusch could even claim that politics in American had been saved because we were a democracy. The great remaining challenge, Rauschenbusch maintained, was to extend that political transformation to the economic realm.[22]

---

21. I have often compared American national elections to the Roman use of the staged battle to distract the proletariat from noticing who is ruling them. Elections become a form of entertainment that give people the mistaken idea that they are ruling themselves because they get to vote. Donald Trump seems to be a confirmation of this understanding of the electoral process. The association of democracies with elections is a profound but widely held mistake.

22. For an account of Rauschenbusch, see my chapter "Walter Rauschenbusch and the Saving of America" in *A Better Hope: Resources for a Church Confronting Capitalism, Democracy, and Postmodernity* (Grand Rapids: Brazos, 2000), 71–108.

Though Rauschenbusch's naïve underwriting of democracy is often criticized, his fundamental presumption that there is a necessary relation between Christianity and democracy is assumed by subsequent figures identified as theologians and ethicists. Reinhold Niebuhr, one of the sharpest critics of Rauschenbusch, developed a realist justification of democracy that I suspect continues to be assumed by many who seek to express their Christian convictions in a politically significant way.[23] For Niebuhr, democracy was not an ideal, but that is not a problem because there are no ideals. Exactly because there are no ideals is why Christians have a stake in democracy as an expression of the best one can do under the conditions of sin.

What we may now be facing is a challenge to the presumption that democracy is *the* expression of Christian convictions. In 1981 I wrote a chapter in *A Community of Character: Toward a Constructive Christian Social Ethic* entitled "The Church and Liberal Democracy: The Moral Limits of a Secular Polity." In that essay I suggested that the Christian underwriting of democracy as rule by "the people," when the people are understood to be self-interested players in a zero-sum game of power, has resulted in the loss of voice by Christians necessary for the church to be an alternative polity.[24] I continue to think that may be true.

The issues surrounding the relation of Christianity and democracy will not and should not go away. The Trump campaign has raised them with new urgency. In particular Trump has alerted us again to the worry that there is finally no check on the tyranny of the majority in democracy as we know it. Tocqueville's worry that individualism would undermine American democracy is back on the table. Tocqueville saw clearly that democratic citizens pursuing their own interest without regard for the commonwealth would result in the loss of associational forms of life on which democracy depends. Andrew Sullivan, drawing on Plato's critique of democracy, argued in an article in the *New York* magazine that democracy depends on elites to protect democracies from "the will of the

---

23. I have written about Niebuhr's position in a number of essays, but on this matter particularly relevant is my chapter written with Michael Broadway entitled, "The Irony of Reinhold Niebuhr: The Ideological Character of "Christian Realism," in *Wilderness Wanderings: Probing Twentieth-Century Theology and Philosophy* (Boulder, CO: Westview, 1997), 48–61.

24. Stanley Hauerwas, *A Community of Character: Toward a Constructive Christian Ethic* (Notre Dame: University of Notre Dame Press, 1981), 72–88.

people."[25] Sullivan's position has been countered by Jedediah Purdy who argues that it is not majoritarian democracy that is the problem, but the growing economic power of a small group of capitalists who have the power to undermine the kind of rule Trump says he is for.[26]

I have no intention to try to resolve these fundamental questions in democratic theory and practice. I think Milbank and Pabst are right to call attention to the incompatibility of liberalism and some forms of democracy. For example, John Bowlin's understanding of democracy as "resistance to domination through the practices of mutual accountability" is an ideal for which it is well worth trying to imagine the institutional form it might take.[27] I fear we are not even close to having such an imagination in play.

But we do have James Rebanks. I suspect for me to have begun a lecture that was to deal with the challenge of national and global politics by calling attention to Rebanks's account of being a shepherd seemed for many quite odd. It is odd, but also hopeful. I believe as long as we can produce narratives of lives like Rebanks we have a way out of the mess we are in. Alasdair MacIntyre observes that most work is tedious and arduous, but nonetheless fulfilling if the work has a purpose, can be recognized to be our contribution for doing it and doing it well, and that we are rewarded for doing it in a way that enables the realization of goods of family and community.[28] MacIntyre even suggests that such a conception of work is a form of prayer.

Such a view of work is why I think it crucial, no matter what you call the systems in which we now find we exist as Christians, that we discover ways to sustain the truthfulness that is constitutive of learning how to be a good judge of sheep. Such a way of life is only made possible by a people who have good work to do that can only be done if we have the skills to say what is true. Hopefully Christians will be such a people because God

25. Andrew Sullivan, "Democracies End When They Are Too Democratic," *New York*, May 1, 2016, http://nymag.com/daily/intelligencer/2016/04/america-tyranny-donald-trump.html.

26. Jedediah Purdy, "What Trump's Rise Means for Democracy," *Dissent*, May 4, 2016, https://www.dissentmagazine.org/online_articles/andrew-sullivan-trump-concern-trolling-for-democracy.

27. John Bowlin, "Democracy, Tolerance, Aquinas," *Journal of Religious Ethics* 44, no. 2 (May, 2016), 278–99.

28. Alasdair MacIntyre, "Where We Were, Where We Are, Where We Need to Be," 323.

in these times seems to be determined to make us a people who are leaner and meaner. Such a people might know how to tell one another the truth because they no longer have anything to lose. A people who have nothing to lose, moreover, might discover they want no other life than the one we have been given.

8

A Sanctuary Politics

Being the Church in the Time of Trump

with JONATHAN TRAN

The two of us admit that, back when Donald Trump's presidential candidacy was at best a strange curiosity, we entertained its possibility as an adventurous thought experiment: "What would *that* be like?" Now that we live in the world called "Donald J. Trump, 45th President of the United States of America," thought experiments have given way to fear. We, like many Christians, are worried about this administration and wonder how we might be faithful under it. There are no doubt worrisome things about any presidential administration, but this one scares us more.

Christians do not help matters by portraying this current political moment as fundamentally different than prior perilous moments. Still, Christian complicity in bringing about these perils and the recurring opportunity for the church to correct itself and be the church is worth considering if we are to, as the social theorist Naomi Klein puts it, "think our way out of the present."[1] Doing so is not here served by going over all the things that worry us about President Trump. Those worrisome things are these days everywhere and obvious. Some, wanting to diminish such worries, have observed that President Trump is only doing what

---

1. "The Possibility of Hope," directed and produced by Alfonso Cuarón, in the DVD, *Children of Men* (Universal Pictures, 2006).

he promised to do. We think we can sum things up by responding, "That's what makes this so terrifying."

It is unclear what, if anything, can be done about how the 2016 election turned out, but people can prepare themselves for the next four years by understanding how Christian mistakes got us here and how Christians can do better. We begin with the elephant-in-the-room fact that the two of us are often seen as the type of people who have downplayed the importance of politics for the Christian life. For some, this de-emphasis on Christian political participation is what got us in this mess. The result of the 2016 presidential election is, for them, the fault of theologians like us, those whose seeming disregard for good Christian participation in politics created a vacuum for bad Christian participation in politics. We hope to turn that accusation on its head by stepping back and offering a different approach to politics—one that does not destine Christians to wrongheaded political behavior. We believe that doing so in these anxious times offers something of an intervention on how Christianity is practiced and imagined.

The Failure of Political Imagination

Christian participation in politics starts with Christians first appraising the world in which they find themselves. This appraisal involves examining political situations as if God mattered for those situations. This is why for us ethics is a matter of seeing the world in such a way that one can accurately survey one's available options. Those options, moreover, depend on the existence of a people who make options available because of the kind of people they are. In particular, they must be a people who have learned to examine any political situation disciplined by a view of God's activity as described in Scripture and as interpreted by Christian tradition. The failure to attain to such a view, for us, explains what often ensues as a lack of *creativity* in American politics. And it explains much of the Christian vote for Trump, which in many cases followed a form of moral reasoning that portrayed candidate Trump as, for whatever reason, the only viable option. This is astounding, because there were many, many reasons why Christians should have voted otherwise—yet still many voted for Trump. If, as is reported, 81 percent of the white evangelical vote went to Trump, then Christians basically handed Donald Trump the presidency, even though they had every reason not to. (We recognize our argument may be question-begging insofar we have not set about the task of verifying its premise that candidate Trump would not make a good president. We also think President Trump, now two months into his term, has himself done our argument the service of verifying that premise.)

It is simply not true to claim, as some have, that Christians were forced into voting for Donald Trump. Our belief is that believing they *had to* vote for Trump, for whatever reason, followed having already surrendered more basic Christian convictions. One might justify this kind of political behavior (voting for a candidate when there is a preponderance of Christian reasons not to do so) by saying that such measures are necessary in politics; that *that* is what politics is. Christians in America have been thinking this way for so long now in relation to war and state-sponsored violence that perhaps they have grown accustomed to this sort of rationale. Maybe they think that Christian faithfulness just requires political participation and political participation just requires otherwise questionable moral judgments. Maybe they imagine Christian moral commitments as quaint, operating in the larger, meaner world of politics where the subsuming of Christianity is part of the *raison d'être* of political activity. Maybe they think that Christians need to grow up and be realistic (thinking indebted to Reinhold Niebuhr's Christian realism, yet shorn of its most robust elements). The momentum this way of thinking sets into motion will make refusing its terms look like downplaying political participation.

At no point in 2016 were Christians without good options. Christians never needed to feel caught between Trump's obviously problematic candidacy and some imagined worse evil. For instance, Christians were never stuck between Trump and Democratic nominee Hillary Rodham Clinton. If, for whatever reason, they thought Clinton no more suitable than Trump, they still had other options, if only they had the faith to believe they did. For example, conservative Christians could have gotten behind the candidacy of independent Evan McMullin, the impressive decorated veteran who espoused an eminently reasonable conservative agenda. If one interjects, "McMullin could not have won!" we might ask, "How do you know?" There was after all an entire process laid out for how McMullin could garner enough electoral votes to deny majorities to either Trump or Clinton and position the Republican-controlled Congress to elect McMullin. If one could not countenance McMullin, one could have written in another candidate. If one could not find another candidate worth endorsing, one could have, in the strongest spirit of democracy, registered one's protest by actively abstaining. Christians who voted for Trump because they wanted their "vote to count" would have done well to remember that any politics committed to justice will require great patience because unjust systems will make losing quite likely. Christianity and democracy share the view that the possibility of losing is no reason to give up one's commitments.

To us the most troubling thing was not that Christians voted for Trump when they had plenty of reasons and ways not to do so. While regrettable, that mistake follows a more basic one. We are most troubled by the ongoing belief Christians hold that the nation-state, not the church, is the arbiter of Christian political action. This belief obligates Christians to modes of statecraft in order to fulfil their moral commitments. In order to play at statecraft—again, for one's "vote to count"—Christians will have to prioritize those commitments that will survive the state's political processes over those that will not. Christians in America have played this game for so long now and with so many half-baked strategies that they can no longer differentiate between America and God, something Scripture calls *idolatry* (which it seems is actually what President Trump wants of Americans).[2] Once Christians zero in on the state as the locus of political activity, they become blind to those myriad other ways the church might politically act in the broad horizon of democratic possibility.

Take for instance the political issue of abortion, which some Christians cited as their reason for voting for candidate Trump. When Christians think that the struggle against abortion can only be pursued through voting for candidates with certain judicial philosophies, then serving at domestic abuse shelters *or* teaching students at local high schools *or* sharing wealth with expectant but under-resourced families *or* speaking of God's grace in terms of "adoption" *or* politically organizing for improved education *or* rezoning municipalities for childcare *or* creating "Parent's Night Out" programs at local churches *or* mentoring young mothers *or* teaching youth about chastity and dating *or* mobilizing religious pressure on medical service providers *or* apprenticing men into fatherhood *or* thinking of singleness as a vocation *or* feasting on something called "communion" *or* rendering to God what is God's *or* participating with the

---

2. For a substantiation of this claim, see Stanley Hauerwas, "Christians, Don't Be Fooled: Trump Has Deep Religious Convictions," *The Washington Post*, January 27, 2017, https://www.washingtonpost.com/news/acts-of-faith/wp/2017/01/27/christians-dont-be-fooled-trump-has-deep-religious-convictions/?utm_term=.737157c082c3.

saints through Marian icons *or* baptizing new members *or* tithing money, will not count as political.

Looking to the future, it will serve Christians to remember that there are *many* ways to be political. Gathering with others around the given body of Christ—a *polis* through and through—is one such way, and is for Christians the original way. As soon as Christians decide that some issue of importance to them (keeping abortion as our example) can be dealt with only one way (namely, voting in a general election) they are cornered into choosing between limited options (the Republican presidential candidate and the Democratic presidential candidate). When Christians see how that same issue can be served other ways (like praying for empty abortion clinics) or when they find more options (like independent pro-lifer Evan McMullin) everything opens up for them. Though it might be unrealistic, even irresponsible, to commit to a cause that will not pan out, it is no less unrealistic, even irresponsible, to close off options that remain available. Christians compelled by issues of consequence can and should look for every available way and option. Indeed, their faith that God gives God's people ways and options is the reason they participate in politics at all.

One of the most tragic results of Christians having voted for Trump in order strategically to secure his support on the issue of abortion is this: women in America have long worried that Christian pro-life arguments objectify them, reducing them to bodies and glossing over the myriad complexities women face in all facets of contemporary life. After pro-life Christians voted into the White House a person who actually *does* seem to objectify women, their nightmares about Christians appear to have been realized. As people who are anything but happy about abortion, we find it telling that much of the church championed a candidate accused of behavior that cannot but endorse those most culpably associated with abortion—namely, men who refuse to take responsibility for their actions. The 2016 election would see matters play out as Trump supporters demonized Secretary Hillary Rodham Clinton's campaign, making her gender a frontline issue in an ongoing and, we should say, *imagined* culture war. This deeply shameful tactic and the embarrassing spectacle that followed demonstrated how many Christians remain unable to separate their pro-life stance from their misogyny and how willing they are to abdicate Christian witness in order to win a culture war no one else seems to be fighting. All this will prove a deal with the devil for which Christian evangelistic efforts will surely pay.

When Christians can imagine politics in a more imaginative and less circumscribed manner, then the question shifts from *whether* Christians can participate in politics to *how* they can do so. This also resituates the issue of abortion from hinging on whether abortion is legal to whether abortion is imaginable. The former we see as difficult given the cultural legacy of *Roe v. Wade*, and the latter impossible, but for the ministry of the Holy Spirit. That near impossibility requires the church to beseech the Spirit, since any robust Christian challenge to abortion (where "robust" indicates persisting beyond myopic strategies) will require the church to be the church (where the church being the church enables reasons and resources beyond myopic strategies). Faced with that daunting task, the American church has punted to the state and justified itself by proclaiming the state as the only site of Christian faithfulness on the matter of abortion. As a result, clergy ask the state to do what they believe they cannot ask members of their congregations to do. This is an astonishing failure of imagination. And that is what happened with Christians in 2016. In direct opposition to that kind of thinking, we argue that the church offers an account of political life where activities like lobbying against abortion is meaningful inasmuch as it is continuous with many other things that make those activities coherent, an expansive enough picture of politics to make Donald Trump's ascendance less likely in the conflagrations to come.

Populism, Elitism, and Fear

We began by talking about fear and continue here by delineating two kinds of fear operating around Trump's presidency. First is the fear that drove some to vote for candidate Trump even when there were plenty of reasons and ways not to do so. Second is the fear that surfaced in response to his candidacy, a fear that has publicly intensified during, and largely because of, his presidency. At first glance, these two fears appear to represent two very different constituencies, each fearing wildly different things as indicated by the polarizing choice to vote for Trump or not. Some of this true, but it's also the case that these fears and their constituencies share many things in common. For neither constituency was the fear new. For both, the 2016 election did not mean that things were *about* to get bad, since for each things were already bad. For both, things in America have always been bad, and Trump's election confirmed just how bad—for some, so bad they would vote for anyone, including a Donald Trump; for others, so bad only a Donald Trump could make them worse.

When one looks across the expanse of America's disenfranchised—say, those pushed to the underside of the American Dream—one finds ostensibly opposed constituencies suffering surprisingly similar conditions. Comparing disenfranchised whites to the urban poor, who tend to be characteristically not white, one will recognize a common quality of disenfranchisement even if the dynamics of that disenfranchisement radically differ. The differences and, as importantly, the supposed differences, create the sense of a seismic divide. Upon closer examination one comes to see that these constituencies share more in common than they had been led to believe. Poor folks everywhere have been played against each other to the strategic benefit of those who profit off both their disenfranchisement and its perceived oppositions. Similarities in socio-economic class, and the fact that they bear similar consequences, are obscured by exaggerated differences in features like race. This is not to say that things like race do not play hugely important roles (one would do well to recall Stuart Hall's maxim that race "is the modality in which class is 'lived'"[3]) but, conversely, to highlight how identity politics of the kind parroted by Trump misses what roles they indeed do play, and how Trump cunningly and disastrously plays them.

Trump's entry into America's longstanding class war comes in his ability to appropriate a populist agenda and politically manipulate it to elitist ends. Working-class white people interpret the economic disadvantages they experience similarly to how Americans typically view anything—namely, through the lenses of race, gender, nationalism and religion—largely removing class from the conversation. Things, of course, do not always go this way. But they often do. Thence, the scapegoating of non-whites, women, immigrants, and Muslims. Rather than help the white underclass ferret out any associated racism (or whatever) from its economic conditions, Trump fans the racism and exasperates the conditions that in turn exasperates the racism. We can understand the rise in brazen hate crimes across America as enabled by Trump, and the brazenness itself as something he emboldened. The conditions that make for this strain of racism—there are others, including those racisms using disenfranchisement as cover—are the many excesses of capitalism riding roughshod over the local ecologies that poor folks call home.

3. Stuart Hall, "Race, Articulation and Societies Structured in Dominance," in *Sociological Theories: Race and Colonialism* (Paris: UNESCO, 1980), 341.

The nationalism of senior Trump advisor Steve Bannon and the so-called "Alt-Right" presents itself as a compassionate friend to those dispossessed by capitalism, bemoaning the loss of virtue and character and intoning a crisis of Western civilization. But when its antidote to global capitalism turns out to be the establishment of a 1950s version of Judeo-Christian Victorian society, without the recognition of that culture's stewardship of capitalism or America's guiding role in its operations, then its nationalism turns out to be only that, nationalism, and of the most nostalgic kind: to make America white again. The end result will be a nationalist-because-anti-globalist agenda that can achieve little more than a protectionist version of capitalism and a pseudo-intellectual endorsement of white supremacist activity. Not particularly original, but highly dangerous. Combine this with Bannon's apocalyptic "clash of civilizations" Islamophobia and the administration begins eerily to resemble a mirror image of the Islamic State, though without ISIS's pretense of asceticism.

Liberal elites are in no position to challenge Trump on his elitism qua populism since they, like the real estate vision of development driving tycoons like Trump, equate economic growth with historical progress. In the elitist liberal mindset, progress gets conflated with capitalism's advance—to support one is to support the other and to resist one is to resist the other, eventuating in the notion that the material fruits of capitalism are the fruits of historical progress. Though they are too sophisticated to admit it, liberal elites think that history should further the cause of the rich; for them, the rich run the world because they should. They can afford this vision of history because it costs them little to hold it. This is the height of privilege. Washingtonian "swamp" elites like Hillary Clinton cannot compete with Trump's appropriated populism for the simple reason that they, as committed centrists, do not think that the poor vote counts for very much. Clinton was wrong in this assessment. What remains unclear is whether President Trump actually cares about these people or whether he uses their support as fodder for his considerable self-regard. If it is the latter, one can only pray that things might, hope against hope, turn toward the former.

When driven by these kinds of elitist sensibilities, Christians adopt without remainder an expectation that history, even in the face of oppressive cultural conditions, will progress on its own toward justice. Yet without confronting their entrenchment in unjust systems, their classism will impede the justice they seek. The mistake for them, then, can be expecting justice in unjust ways. Christians can compound the mistake by supposing this view to be Christian. It is not. One can understand the confusion given how closely it resembles the Christian claim about God's redemption of history. But saying that history will be redeemed is not the same as saying that history enacts that redemption. The Christian claim about history's redemption is a claim about history's need of redemption, and the invitation for Christians to participate in that redemption by doing the work of justice. Christians believe that history will bear witness to redemption through moments of hope, but they also believe that much in history will remain despairing. What makes Christians *Christian* is their willingness to look for redemption by fighting for justice even if redemption is not evident and even when justice does not readily come. The world cannot survive Christians pussyfooting around those pursuits in expectation that redemption and justice will arrive as a matter of course. Neither can anyone claiming to be Christian.

If Christians can, as they sometimes have, lay claim to history as the theater of political action, they might discover God as the author and perfecter of that action. We believe Christians can in this political moment do so by following the lead of those who, unbeholden to unjust systems, turn their faces to the many who suffer the ravages of those systems. As much as it is a fantasy of elites to believe that suffering is far from them, it rarely is. And this proximity, in the networks all moderns inhabit, might end up being their political salvation. It is in this way that a very different region of politics might lead Christians to Jesus. In turn Christians will find friends they didn't know they had, partners in a vocation they had forgotten. If they do not make this turn, they will continue in a faith emptied of everything but the luxuries of privilege. If they persist with their myths and accommodations, then they will continue self-righteously dumbstruck in the face of eventualities like the election of Donald Trump.

The Church's Sanctuary Politics

Much has been made of President Trump's shaky hold on the truth. When everything disagreeable is "fake news" then reality goes out the window. One approach to this state of affairs is to get the media to pile on as much discrediting evidence as possible with the expectation that Trump will be found to be caught in a lie. While this strategy has worthwhile benefits, we think it also has serious limitations, not least of which is that it positions the media politically in an endless troll/counter-troll game that will over time erode the public trust that is the source of its authority. The strategy also presumes that Trump is capable of lying. The way he presents himself makes us unsure that he is. Lying first requires an ability to distinguish truth from fantasy, an initial capacity to differentiate how things are from how one wants them to be. For anyone who has given himself to self-deception as constantly and continuously as Trump seems to, no amount of evidence will matter. Evidence can prove such and such (that he is lying, that he is helping, that he is harming, that he is a strong president or a weak president) when connected to forms of life that makes that evidence meaningful, truthful of such and such. Within this larger frame, this reality (or what one might just call a politics), the truth of Trump, including the truth of Trump *to* Trump, becomes achievable. We believe the church has not only these political possibilities, but itself is this politics.

In these fear-inducing times, Christians can find sanctuary in the body of Christ as the politics through which God gives God's people everything they need to be faithful. Christians can lean into the church as the impetus for political action, and the church as itself political action, by way of an account of history that inscribes the church as sanctuary for the oppressed wherever and however they are oppressed. One of us has already described in some detail Trump's fortress mentality vision of America, acted upon by executive order in the days following his inauguration.[4] Members of one of our communities recently posted the following statement advocating for church sanctuary movements that would shelter immigrants from those orders: "profession of the Christian faith commits it to the formation of a hospitable, just, and truth-telling community, especially for the sake of its most vulnerable members, in whom Christians discern the face of Christ."[5] We think this statement and others like it speak powerfully to the notion of how the church might be the church in a time of Trump, as literal sanctuaries of grace and truth in the terror of this present moment. The statement displays in bold relief the prophet Isaiah's picture of God: "You have been a refuge for the poor, a

---

4. Jonathan Tran, "Drone Dreaming along the Border: Trump, Immigration, and Rhetorics of Nostalgia," *Christian Ethics Today* 99 (Fall 2015), http://pastarticles.christianethicstoday.com/cetart/index.cfm?fuseaction=Articles.main&ArtID=1559.

5. "Make Baylor University a Sanctuary Campus," 6 February 2017, https://docs.google.com/forms/d/e/1FAIpQLSfkC-kxwl1SZSkMV3Guhd_3qh-ZEY_Q95vvtMyQ-tWjEdC8YQ/viewform?c=0&w=1.

refuge for the needy in their distress, a shelter from the storm and a shade from the heat. For the breath of the ruthless is like a storm driving against a wall and like the heat of the desert" (Isaiah 25:4).

The current work of sanctuary churches, comprised of approximately 800 American churches to date, reprises the church's sanctuary movement of the 1980s, when American congregations sought to shelter refugees fleeing American-engineered civil wars in Central America, a practice of hospitality that pitted, as one immigrant described it, "the law of God" against "the law of man." Acting as the church hospitable, Christians welcome those fleeing poverty, violence, and oppression. As the powers threaten this hospitality because it challenges unjust political orders, the church militant responds with the grace and truth expressed in the sanctuary statement, against the grain of a crucifying world and with the grain of the universe. Upending oppressive arrangements, the church as sanctuary, a true international, attests to the absurdity of borders when millions starve and the thievery of states in a world given as gift. If the Trump administration should follow its brinksmanship logic and begin forcibly to register Muslims, Christians might identify as Muslims—something God in God's extravagance did in identifying with creation for the sake of creation, and something Christians in their closefisted self-regard failed to do with Jews under the Third Reich. A full account of Christian sanctuary will offer a wide enough berth to accommodate the extensive range of contingencies for which the invitation of sanctuary comes as good news. As a place of worship, the church sanctuary receives God, which entails receiving along with God those with whom God in Christ identifies, all migrants in need of sanctuary. Sanctuary as conceptualized through the passage from Isaiah has God's people extending hospitality to anyone poor, distressed, or unsheltered, for any who flee the ruthless, everyone who suffers the desert's heat.

The rationale of sanctuary breaks down ideological categories that pit against each other the urban and rural poor, both of whom bear the ravages of capitalism's reduction of creaturely life to surplus value. After all, Rust Belt whites, Syrian refugees, and Central American immigrants will, if given the chance to find one another, likely discover that they share more in common, including religion in many cases, than they will with Trump or Bannon and other elites who look to appropriate or scapegoat them. The presumption that white elites share common cause with the white underclass just because they are white shows just how unhelpful American identity politics can be, as tortured as the accompanying belief that poor whites and poor ethnic minorities share little in common. Poverty, to be sure, disproportionately affects minorities and women, yet poverty in America is a persistently pervasive enough phenomenon that there remains plenty in which to share. Insofar as it breaks down divisions erected by Trump's parroted identity politics, sanctuary politics avails shared life, including life shared over against the disproportions (what we earlier referenced as the distorting roles given to race, gender and so on) that would otherwise make the gathered enemies of one another. At its inception and in its best moments, the church as Christ's body offered the world communion where there was previously animosity, ploughshares and pruning hooks from swords and spears, the peaceable kingdom come alive. The church not only welcomes the stranger, but *is* the stranger, constituted as she is entirely by migrants, herself a migrant through the world.

America's entrenched political culture has encouraged Christians to short change the promise and demands of Christian discipleship, not to mention a genuinely democratic vision of citizenship, how far hospitality must extend and to whom it can be granted, what justice requires, of what truth tells, and where the face of strangers like Christ turns up. No doubt the idea of sanctuary embedded within our current political climate will look dangerous. In that context, people tend to respond to the idea either by encouraging sanctuary by denying its potential dangers, or by denying sanctuary by stressing its dangers. This zero-sum logic is redeployed again and again in conversations about Trump's various proposed bans, those supporting the bans emphasizing their protections and those challenging them emphasizing their harms. President Trump is responsible for this political culture. And this political culture is responsible for President Trump. Christians, if they are to offer genuine alternatives, cannot in their advocacy for things like sanctuary afford the illusion that sanctuary politics comes without dangers, of all sorts. Denying potential ill effects for the sake of advocacy misconstrues what sanctuary names— a situation where extending hospitality risks something for someone. Just as well, Christians blocking the idea cannot do so by forgetting its real benefits; doing so also misses something about sanctuary—that it is a situation where *not* extending hospitality risks something for someone.

Shockingly there remain to this day Christians who support Trump's anti-migration policies because they believe his policies will "keep us safe." Surely one could not wish for a more misleading understanding of what it means to be Christian. Christians worship at the church of martyrs; they seek fellowship with the crucified Lord. Being a Christian is not about being safe, but about challenging the status quo in ways that cannot help but put you in danger. Thinking it possible to be safe in a world where Christians are sent out like sheep among wolves is about as unfortunate an idea as thinking that war is necessary to secure peace. We can only guess that those Christians who voted for Trump because of his willingness to use questionable tactics to keep them safe have forgotten what it means to be Christian.

A Christian participatory politics requires of Christians an examination of the terms American politics imposes on the church—terms that enfeeble democratic life by narrowing its scope and possibility, use identity politics in a junk populism that further robs the poor, put safety before all other considerations, so on and so forth. Christian politics, therefore, begins with sanctuary, gathering in worship those previously divided by oppressive logics draining American political life. It does so by taking stock of the stakes—or, as we have said, appraising situations as if God matters. The same Spirit that presided over Isaiah was present with Jesus as he read from Isaiah in a sanctuary two millennia ago, inaugurating a ministry of good news to the poor, freedom for prisoners, sight for the blind, setting free the oppressed, and proclaiming the Lord's favor. This same Spirit now presides over sanctuaries across the world, in Christian churches and otherwise as they provide sanctuary to those pursued by every new King Herod. The final inauguration of Christ will be the remaking of the world as God's sanctuary. That animating work of the Spirit begins in Israel and the church.

Through these strategies the church continues its life of worship: gathering, greeting, proclaiming, sending. Worship—which is what makes a sanctuary *a sanctuary*—has the formative effect of firing the imagination in order that Christians see the world and its politics as God's and so possessed of grace and truth. Because Christian political life starts in worship, because actual worship in actual sanctuaries is the first political thing Christians do, they are taught to see the world rightly, which in turn enables them to believe that even though trouble is found in this world, now as much as ever, Jesus has overcome this world. The call to begin in worship does not license doing nothing but enables doing anything, including speaking truth to power, providing sanctuary, and praying for enemies. This is to say that while voting and lobbying and marching and sheltering are all political, more basically political is the gathered body of Christ. We end, then, where we began, with adventurous thought:

Furious Lord,

make us, your lost unfaithful frightened people,
possessed by your Spirit.

Thusly possessed, may we be forced
by the courage so unleashed
to be your imaginative alternative in a world
that seems devoid of alternatives.

Make us a people who trust in your miracles.
May we even pray for the soul of Donald Trump.

May he catch a glimpse of what justice looks like
in a world not ruled by dealmakers.

Above all, save us from the self-righteousness
that comes from our not being part of Trump's people.
Help us remember that many of his people are like us.

In this time, a time out of joint,
give us patience so that we might be
capable of being forgiven
and thus able to forgive such that peace may be a reality.

Amen.

9

Minding the Gaps

Or

Theologians Writing Memoirs

Why Harvey?

Some may find the subject of this article rather odd given the task to celebrate the work and life of Hans Ulrich. But then *Festschrifts* are seldom able to separate the life of the theologian from their work. Therefore, it is perhaps not entirely inappropriate for me to use this occasion to reflect on the relationship between the work of the theologian and the life of the theologian. Often attempts to say what may be the relation between the life of a theologian and their theology is done with no reference to the actual life of the particular theologian. By way of contrast, I am going to write about two theologians: A. E. Harvey and Stanley Hauerwas.

A. E. Harvey and I have both done something quite strange for theologians. We have both written memoirs. By the time I finish the reader may well wonder if theologians should write memoirs, but this, I believe, is beside the point. The fact is we have both written memoirs, and I'm not going to let that fact go to waste. Of course, both theologians and memoirs come in all shapes and sizes, but by attending to the similarities and differences between my memoir and A. E. Harvey's memoir I hope to illumine the relation of the life of a theologian and their theological work. Harvey's memoir makes clear being a theologian may make being a Christian more difficult, while my memoir communicates the surprise that I remain a Christian.

Paul Griffiths has recently argued that you do not need to be a Christian to be a theologian.[1] I take that to be an undeniable empirical observation. However, Griffiths also maintains that given that theology requires the theologian to master the skills of the discourse of theology the theologian may well discover they have a "cognitive intimacy" with the Lord.[2] But theology as a skill of the intellect combined with the tragedies of life can result in the loss of faith, even making the theologian wonder if they are a Christian. As we shall see, Harvey reports with admirable directness on how that has happened to him.

As far as I know, Hans Ulrich has not written a memoir. But I know that his life and his theology are intimately related. You cannot be in the presence of Hans Ulrich for five minutes without having a sense of his humility, his modesty, and his theological integrity. He is a theologian who has gone his own way, refusing to reduce the gospel to what some theologians declare they are ready to believe given the epistemological conceits of modernity. Accordingly, Hans has helped us recover the centrality of the eschatological character of the Gospel. But I have no intention to try to write about Hans Ulrich's life, for no other reason than I know so little about the details. If a person, however, is to be judged by the students they have trained, then Hans Ulrich clearly has lived an exemplary theological life.

The reason I take as my subject what a life in theology might entail, however, is that it is a major theme in A. E. Harvey's *Drawn Three Ways: Memoir of a Ministry, a Profession, and a Marriage*.[3] I cannot resist writing about his extraordinary book and life because, as I will try to show, his life and my life have some similarities I had not anticipated. Moreover, we have both written memoirs and, as I observed above, that is not a normal genre for theologians. Indeed, some may think theologians should not write memoirs because for a theologian to write about their life may suggest that the theologian takes their subjectivity far too seriously. Besides, theologians are not known for having lives interesting enough that others would want to know anything about them. I think,

---

1. Paul Griffiths, *The Practice of Catholic Theology: A Modest Proposal* (Washington DC: The Catholic University of America Press, 2016), 41–42.

2. Griffiths, *The Practice of Catholic Theology*, 24.

3. A. E. Harvey, *Drawn Three Ways: Memoir of a Ministry, a Profession, and a Marriage* (Grand Rapids: Eerdmans, 2016). Paginations will be in the text.

or at least hope, that comparing *Hannah's Child*[4] with *Drawn Three Ways* will prove to be interesting.

The reason that I think it might be interesting to write about A. E. Harvey, however, is not solely because we have both written a memoir. No doubt an exercise in comparing the memoirs would be instructive, and I will do some of that kind of work in this article.[5] However, what makes Harvey's memoir so interesting to me is that we shared a similar fate—we were both married to a spouse that suffered from bipolar illness. Harvey's account of his wife Julian's struggle with her illness is painfully eloquent. I only wish I could have written as beautifully as Harvey about the ravages mental illness can exact on everyone it touches. I could not help but recognize much of my own life in reading Harvey's memoir.

Yet I am not suggesting that Harvey and I have similar lives because of our marriages to deeply wounded spouses. We are clearly very different people with vastly different backgrounds. Harvey is English and I am a Texan. Harvey comes from a class far above my own. I was raised to lay brick. I suspect Harvey had few opportunities in his life to do physical labor. Harvey, moreover, is intellectually brilliant. I get by. We are both theologians, although Harvey is much more the scholar than I can claim to be. I have some sense of how different our circumstances in life have been because I actually met Harvey once.

In 1982, I was teaching in London for the University of Notre Dame. I had read Harvey's book, *Jesus and the Constraints of History*.[6] I thought his "method" in the book suggested a way to read the Gospels that was extremely promising. Harvey had read greats as an undergraduate at Oxford, so he brought to his study of the Bible a historical sensibility that put him at odds with many of the scholars that belonged to the New Testament guild. By focusing on the constraints of history, as he observes in his memoir, he was able to show that it may well be the case that the Jesus of the New Testament is a faithful depiction of the "real" Jesus. Accordingly, Harvey warned against taking the German New Testament

---

4. Stanley Hauerwas, *Hannah's Child: A Theologian's Memoir* (Grand Rapids: Eerdmans, 2012). *Hannah's Child* was first published in 2010. The 2012 edition has a new afterword in which I try to say what I think I was doing when I wrote the memoir. Paginations will be in the text.

5. My friend and colleague, Richard Lischer, is in the process of writing a book on the memoirs of Christians. For a preliminary report on his book, see his "Writing the Christian Life," *Christian Century* 132, no. 18 (September 2, 2015), 22–27.

6. A. E. Harvey, *Jesus and the Constraints of History* (Philadelphia: Westminster Press, 1982).

scholars' presumptions of discontinuity between Jesus and the Jews as a given (88).

It was not just his historical sensibilities that attracted me to his book, I was also fascinated by the theological/philosophical developments in the book. For example, Harvey suggested that Jesus's proclamation of the Kingdom entailed the presumption that all existence can be storied. From such a perspective, Jesus's proclamation of the radical change required to understand him makes sense. Once this is acknowledged, then Jesus's concern for the pattern of human conduct that is dominated by the prospect of imminent and radical change, Harvey suggests, may turn out to be one of the most powerful and enduring elements of his message.[7]

To discover a scholar as accomplished as Harvey making these points about the necessity of narrative was a welcome development given my emphasis on the significance of narrative as the fundamental grammar of the Christian faith. So I began to ask friends in England who Harvey might be. I found it surprising that many had not heard of him, but I discovered he was a canon at Westminster Abbey. I had no idea what it meant for him to be a canon at Westminster, but because we were both in London I assumed I should just call him to see if we could meet. I was no one from nowhere, but he graciously agreed to see me, even inviting me to come to his rooms in the close of Westminster Abbey. I do not remember much about our conversations, other than my sense that I was in water far over my head. He was very gracious, however, and he patiently listened to my ill-formed questions. In retrospect, I suspect he must have found me a bit exotic, but he was gracious and listened to my thoughts about the significance of narrative with patience.

That is the only time I met Harvey. I continued to read his books, but I had no knowledge of his life until I read the memoir. I find it quite surprising that he wrote a book like *Drawn Three Ways* because he seems to have what I can only describe as a reserve characteristic of the English upper classes. But we should be very glad he has given us this book because he is such an honest and insightful author. That said, however, it seems quite an unusual book to me—a remark I will now try to explain.

Harvey's Memoir

Harvey's memoir seems rather conventional until you get to the last chapter. Prior to the last chapter, the memoir is chronologically determined in

---

7. Harvey, *Jesus and the Constraints of History*, 76.

a manner that we learn of his education, his decision to be ordained, to marry, his work, and the birth of his children. It is only when he gets to the last chapter that he unburdens himself by describing the difficulties of his life with Julian, his mentally-ill wife. He begins that chapter by reporting on the strain Julian's illness put on him and their children. She had presented with the symptoms of what was then called manic depression in 1981. At the time, Harvey was the chaplain at The Queen's College, Oxford. He reports that he assumed that the crisis would pass after she was released from the hospital and put on lithium, but that was not to be. It did not take long for him to recognize that her episodes of clinical depression were not going away.

Harvey tells us that though Julian's periods of clinical depression could be quite acute, she did not have, as many bipolar people do, comparable manic phases. Given my own experience with Anne, who did have dramatic manic events, I suspect that Julian often resisted her medication because she missed her highs. Like my former wife, Julian would secretly quit taking her lithium, which usually meant that a psychotic episode was in the offering. Harvey reports that Julian had two or three episodes a year "for the next twenty-five years." For those of us who have had similar experiences, the pathos of "the next twenty-five years" is chilling (146–47).

Harvey reflects on how different our attitudes are toward someone with a serious physical illness in comparison with our reaction to someone who is mentally ill. The former illness evokes deep reserves of empathy and compassion for the sufferer as well as those close to the one who is ill. Harvey observes, however, that the reaction to those that suffer an acute affliction of the mind is different. You keep wanting to say, "You have to get a grip," because the sickness seems like something you ought to be able to will your way out of, but that is exactly what the one possessed by this illness cannot do.

The spectacle of Julian seeming to be someone unknown to those that loved her put Harvey and their children in an ongoing emotional turmoil that made their relations to Julian complex, to say the least. For one of the agonizing aspects of someone so beset is, as Harvey observes, when Julian was well she was incapable of recognizing that anything was wrong with her. Not only did that make it almost impossible to persuade her to take her medication, but the very fact she seemed unaware of the darkness and misery that she and her family were undergoing resulted in an estrangement from those that cared the most for her. Though everyone that loved her made valiant efforts to maintain their affection, loyalty, and love of her and one another, Harvey confesses neither he nor the children could continue in a relaxed and close relationship with Julian (147).

Harvey works very hard in his account of the burden Julian's illness put on him and the children not to place blame on her. She was obviously a talented and accomplished person. Harvey quotes large portions of her writing to exhibit her intelligence and talent. He even suggests that he found it hard to blame her for the denial of her illness because he attributes such a denial to her self-defense, given how the illness led to a horrible lack of self-confidence. If she had remembered her episodes, Harvey worries her memories would have haunted her for the rest of her life. Yet her very inability to recognize her illness only contributed to the tension her illness created in the family.

It is not clear to me why Harvey waited until his last chapter to develop these haunting reflections about Julian's illness and the effects it had on him and the children. He tells us early in the memoir that Julian became sick during and after a trip to Greece, but he provides only minimal accounts of the effects of her illness at that time (94–95). He includes a poem by Julian in an attempt to help us appreciate her talent, as well as to have us sympathize with her, but given the way he tells his story in the early chapters of the memoir he seems to imply that after episodes such as the one in Greece things went back to normal. Yet as he makes clear in the last chapter, when your spouse is possessed by an illness like bipolar affect there will never again be a "normal."

In the preface to *Drawn Three Ways*, Harvey tells us that he was often told that giving an account of his life, particularly an account of the seventeen years he spent as a canon at Westminster Abbey, would be worth recording. He doubted whether the rest of his life was of sufficient interest to record, but as he reflected on the task he found that the phases of his journey—teaching and research in a university, training clergy, and carrying out pastoral duties—were held together by influences that were worth exploring. To write the memoir, moreover, provided him the opportunity to include Julian's writing so that we might appreciate what a remarkable person she was (viii). To display Julian's talents through the memoir is testimony to Harvey's dedication, admiration, and love for Julian. The constancy of his care never wavered even though in the last years of her life she suffered from dementia. Julian died not long after Harvey had retired.

A key word in the above paragraph in which Harvey explains why he wrote the memoir is "record." Prior to the last chapter, the memoir is primarily an account of his various academic and non-academic positions. To be sure his descriptions of the various positions he held, as well as his personal interactions with colleagues, are often insightful and fascinating, but they seldom hint about the struggle he was constantly negotiating as he sought to care for Julian and still fulfill the obligations his work as a priest and academic placed upon him. As someone who has gone through similar situations, I can assure you that it is no easy thing to try to care for someone who believes they are getting secret messages from God about the end of the world at the same time as you are preparing to teach a class on the ethics of Aristotle. Yet we have little sense of how Harvey was struggling to survive until we get to the last chapter.

Harvey begins his memoir describing his time as an undergraduate at Oxford in 1951. He was obviously an extremely intelligent young student who read the greats. He had gone to Eton, where he was not an exceptional student, but there he developed his love of music. However once he got to Oxford he was soon seen as a person of exceptional talent who seemed destined to be a university don. His deep moral sensitivities toward the poor, however, would lead him to take a different route.

He tells us about some of his first encounters with Julian and the development of their relationship. Again, there is a matter-of-fact character to his narrative that betrays his avowal of being deeply in love. Julian and her family resided in Florence where Julian was generally regarded as a bright star in the social scene. She also took the opportunity provided by Florence to become quite a good painter. Harvey was doing post-graduate work in Germany, which made it possible for them to nurture their relationship. Back in England finishing his degree at Cambridge, he reports by the spring of 1957 Julian and he "felt sufficiently sure about ourselves and each other" they were ready to announce their engagement (40). The only difficulty Harvey associates with his wedding was how to negotiate the somewhat strange religious views of Julian's mother (42–43).

Harvey's account of the decision to be married is quite straightforward, but you feel like you would like to know just a bit more about how the decision was made. That is not quite right. You would like to know more about how he would regard their marriage in light of subsequent events. I have the same feeling about his decision to become a priest. Harvey was working for the BBC when he decided to go to a theological college. He tells us that he is unsure when he felt "called" to the priesthood.

He was not particularly pious, although he found going to chapel somehow made him feel at home (36).

In fact, it was not clear to him at the time he decided to be ordained whether he was even a believer. Yet, he tells us that his decision to "go into the church" was not irrational because he continued to read Christian literature and his sense that he somehow belonged in the tradition of the Church of England never disappeared. He believes he was drawn to the priesthood because he desired to do something practical and pastoral while continuing to pursue his academic ambitions. Everyone seems to have regarded him as having a powerful intellect. He read widely in the Church Fathers, as well as in literature associated with ancient Stoicism. Even though he had doubts about his fitness to be a priest, he was ordained in St. Paul's Cathedral in 1958. He served four years as a curate in Chelsea, but as he puts it, "with my academic record, there never seemed to be any question of allowing me to proceed to another post in a parish" (52), which meant in 1962 he was appointed to a newly created research studentship at Christ Church Oxford.

He spent the next seven years at Oxford before becoming the principle of St. Augustine's College at Canterbury. He took up his new assignment in Canterbury with the conviction that theology as an academic discipline should always have a bearing on the Christian life (66). His new position, therefore, brought together what he describes as the two competing motivations within him, that is, the intellectual and the pastoral (73). At Canterbury, moreover, he met some extraordinary Christians. He also became acquainted with and subsequently influenced by the life of the monks at Taizé.

Harvey seems to have been very happy running the college, but for financial reasons it would not last. The college was closed after seven years. The closing meant Harvey needed to apply for a lectureship at Christ Church, which he received. During his second stint at Oxford, he reports that he developed a reputation as a New Testament scholar, though he was not someone who represented the New Testament guild. In particular, he taught his students not to trust over-confident statements about the reconstruction of the New Testament (98).

He represented an alternative way to approach the text because he thought that there is very little we actually know about the history of the ancient Palestinian world that cannot be inferred from the biblical text itself. Harvey made these few certainties that he thought could be derived from the biblical text the subject of his Bampton Lectures in 1982. These lectures "tried to anchor certain moments in the story of Jesus through historical research into the circumstances and culture in which he lived" (98). He understood by doing so his academic work expressed his commitment to show the difference theology should make for daily living.

His second stay at Oxford came to an end when he received a letter from the prime minister inviting him to be the canon theologian at Westminster Abbey. He assumed there was no question that he should accept that invitation because being a canon made it possible for him to be available to Julian when she was having an episode while still fulfilling his duties. Moreover, his role as canon gave him the opportunity to bring his "intellectual understanding of the Christian faith to bear on public issues and pastoral tasks" (99). He was canon at the cathedral for seventeen years (1982–1999), during which he was in charge of the selection of the statues of the martyrs that were to fill the niches above the west entrance to the abbey. He was also the main author of the report by the Archbishop's commission entitled *Faith in the City*. His accounts, as well as his reflections about the politics that went into these tasks, make fascinating reading and testify to his insightful judgment about people.

Through it all, Harvey cared for Julian. He observes that apart from her he might have been considered for more important academic or priestly appointments, but given the priority he gave to her needs, particularly when she was in an episode, such ambitions made no sense. I think there is little doubt, as Harvey says, that throughout their married life, even as Julian toward the end of her life suffered from memory loss, he "remained very much in love with her, and any deliberate failure to give all I could to her and our family would have seemed inconceivable" (167). But his attention to her needs was not without a cost.

In the preface to *Drawn Three Ways*, Harvey tells us one reason for writing the memoir is that others outside his immediate circle might find the account of his evolution from being a stoic Christian to that of a Christian Stoic interesting. To say the least, that turns out to be a massive understatement in light of his confession in the last chapter about his standing as a Christian. In retirement, he not only has the burden of caring for Julian, but also the blow of the death of their daughter Christian. He confesses that the "resources" on which he had drawn to sustain his care of Julian, as well as enduring the death of his daughter, had the eventual effect of eroding his faith (159).

He suggests that people might assume that what sustained him over the years was his Christian faith, but in reality he thinks it was a kind of rigid stoicism that enabled him to keep on keeping on without wavering. As one who had studied, as well as taught, the Stoics, he came to realize that it was not so much their philosophical ideas that identified them, but rather it was their inculcation of a way of life that enabled them to sustain the misfortunes that are unavoidable aspects of being human. He found reading John of the Cross's account of the "dark night of the soul" described his state of mind. But he did not have what was fundamental to the life of John of the Cross, that is, "a continued yearning for the God who seemed so unaccountably absent: I was not 'yearning' for him at all, but simply getting used to doing without him" (152).

Harvey's reliance on his stoic resilience did not, at least at the beginning, lead him to abandon his Christian faith. He had always been subject to doubt, as well as having times of serenity and confidence. Yet he found that the amount of the Christian faith to which he could truly assent continued to diminish. Moreover, he thought any search for some religious experience would be but the satisfaction of a human need, rather than a serious engagement with a God who he rightly suggests is not to be "associated with such moments of psychological reassurance" (161). Though his friends thought he had a remarkable talent for making the Bible come alive, he does not think that due to any commitment to the special character of Scripture. He could just as easily have been commenting on a play by Shakespeare.

That he began to doubt his commitment to the Christian faith made him wonder about whether if even in his earlier life he was ever confident enough in his own faith to pass on to others what it meant to be a Christian. This does not mean that he was not a theologian. He tells us that theology for him is a kind of grammar in which its propositions are logically related to one another. The formula of the Trinity, for example, he thinks to be a great intellectual achievement, but to know the grammar of a language is not to have evidence that the language itself relates to any reality. He worries, therefore, that the more definite, dogmatic, and detailed religious language becomes, the less it could be related to a reality that could be called God (164).

He does not let these doubts stop him from carrying out some of his duties as a priest, but he has the "nagging sensation" that he "was not so much a priest, that is, a genuine interpreter and mediator of the things of God to human beings and of human hopes and needs to God, as a performer" (168). He continues to be told he has a talent for clear exposition both as a preacher and as a writer, but he is haunted by the thought that it is all show sustained by his professionalism that blinds him to the fact he did not have the resources of faith necessary to make his attempts to fulfill his spiritual duties real (169). He concludes his memoir with the poignant declaration that if he dies while still an agnostic—even one that doubts God's existence—he will not be greatly disturbed, because he hopes that in his work as a priest he has done less harm than good (170).

One cannot help but admire, as well as be astonished by, Harvey's honest, candid, and eloquent account of his Christian stoicism. Most readers of his memoir, I suspect, cannot help but feel a deep sympathy with his struggle to say truthfully what his care for Julian has meant and the cost it has had on his life. Twenty-five years is a long time. Few—and I am one of the few—can imagine what it means to have to negotiate someone who seems to be so possessed you no longer know who they are. That I am one of the few, as I acknowledged earlier, is because I too was married to a wife who suffered from bipolar illness. I know what it means to have the one you at one time thought you loved rage against your very existence.

Given Harvey's account, I cannot help but wonder how I have remained a Christian, even though I am a theologian. In order to try to explore that question I will call attention to how my story in *Hannah's Child* is similar to and yet different than Harvey's account of his life. Theologically, Harvey and I seem to share a number of similar judgments, which makes me wonder what has made the difference in how we each understand what it means for each of us to be a Christian.

Hannah's Child

As I indicated above, there are obviously deep differences between my life and Harvey's. We come from radically different places in society. I certainly want to avoid—and I tried very hard in *Hannah's Child* to avoid—the cliché story of poor boy makes good, but that I became a theologian and academic is, in truth, quite surprising. I am smart enough, but I am not as accomplished as Harvey, partly because any place the equivalent to Eton did not exist for me. Yet in some ways that is an advantage, because it means I have never felt part of the world in which I have lived out my life.

That I have always felt like an outsider both as a Christian and an academic may account for the different stances we have toward being a Christian. Given my background, I have never felt confident enough that

I know what Christianity is to be able to reject it. Harvey, in contrast, has always been part of a Christianity that takes for granted a consensus about what Christianity is, as well as what the church was meant to be. I do not want to make more of this difference than is warranted, but I think it has some explanatory power.

During the years I was married to Anne and had to negotiate her illness I did not experience any profound doubts about being a Christian. That does not mean, however, that, like Harvey, my determination to see it through may have been more adequately described as a form of stoicism than whatever it meant for me to be a Christian. I have never thought of myself as much more than half-Christian, and I am never sure which half is that half. I know, however, it is a half that matters.

As I hope is clear in *Hannah's Child*, I was determined that Adam and I would survive Anne's illness. I am not sure I was as dedicated to Anne as Harvey seems to have been committed to Julian, but I did the best I could. I understand well that the attempt to fulfill your responsibilities outside the family while negotiating a wife who is in an episode is not easily done. Keeping all those balls in the air was never easy. Harvey and I were both lucky to have positions that let us order our lives and the use of time in "creative" ways.

Yet, one must be very careful in how one understands the "I" in the above sentence. That "I" existed, but the "I" was constituted by prayers on my, Anne's, and Adam's behalf. Others were praying for us, and I could "feel" that those prayers were making God present. I knew, moreover, I could not make it without those prayers and without that presence. I share Harvey's understanding of theology as a grammar, but I was learning how that grammar was shaped by how it offered what was otherwise an unavailable way of life. In the process, I think I was beginning to have a life that was theologically determined.

I need to be very careful about these observations because they could lead some to draw implications from them I would deeply regret. I am not in any way trying to suggest I somehow got it right and Harvey got it wrong. That I somehow remained faithful to the task of theology and Harvey did not is not a conclusion I would want anyone to draw. In fact, I admire Harvey's honesty about his loss of faith more than I take some comfort that I think I can still call myself a Christian, even after Anne. In fact, I think Harvey cared for Julian longer and with more feeling than I was able to sustain. I tried very hard in *Hannah's Child* not to demonize Anne, but I could not avoid the reality that her illness and her anger wore me out. I did not know if I loved or did not love her because I had no idea who she was. In a sense, then, the anger killed whatever love I may have at one time had for her. I do not sense from Harvey's depiction of Julian that she had the same level of anger that possessed Anne.

Jonathan Tran has written a remarkable essay, "Anne and the Difficult Gift of Stanley Hauerwas's Church," in which he argues that my account of Anne in *Hannah's Child* is a fundamental surd-like story that "holds together the church's entailed hope and the difficulty of its constraints."[8] I can only say that Tran has found a way to say what I should have said in *Hannah's Child*. He has put the matter rightly, calling into question those that would read my emphasis on the centrality of the church as a triumphalist narrative that betrays the reality of an Anne.[9] Tran observes that the story I tell of myself is also the story of the church—and there is no church if Jesus is not the Son of God—because it is the church that has made me Christian. Those stories are intertwined, according to Tran, which means the truthfulness of one bears on the truthfulness of the other.[10]

That Harvey's faith became so grim may have everything to do with his "twenty-five years." His care of Julian is nothing less than inspiring given his descriptions of the cruel effects of her illness on her and the family. I feel sure that I did not let Anne's illness disrupt my life in quite the same way Harvey adjusted his work to care for Julian. Seventeen years as a canon, even a canon at Westminster, is a long time for a person of Harvey's talent. Yet he manifests no bitterness. In fact, his deepest sadness seems to be his worry that Julian's illness prevented others from appreciating *her* talent and cleverness.

What primarily interests me about the difference between Harvey's memoir and *Hannah's Child* is how the latter narrative remains a narrative of hope. That a story could be told is an act of hope. Yet hope can be misguided. A number of years ago a friend's son was diagnosed as a schizophrenic. His father and mother did everything to help him regain his sanity. I told them, however, that their first line of defense was to give up hope, that is, the hope that he would get better. Such hope is a form

---

8. Jonathan Tran, "Anne and the Difficult Gift of Stanley Hauerwas's Church," in *The Difference Christ Makes*, ed. Charles M. Collier (Eugene, OR: Cascade, 2015), 65.

9. Tran, "Anne and the Difficult Gift of Stanley Hauerwas's Church," 68.

10. Tran, "Anne and the Difficult Gift of Stanley Hauerwas's Church," 63. Anyone reading Tran's paper should read Peter Dula's following response, "The Limits of Theology: A Response to Jonathan Tran," 71–76.

of optimism that you cannot help but feel during those periods when the one that is ill seems to be "better." But an optimistic hope will finally not sustain you from one episode to the next.

Yet it is also the case that you cannot survive without hope, though a hope that is grounded in a very different reality than optimism. The kind of hope that sustains you is a hope that makes endurance an ongoing way of life without the refusal to give up destroying you. Such a hope takes the form of prayer, in which God is made present in the lives of those suffering from a debilitating illness, as well as those that care for them. In short, hope is the virtue that sustains us with the conviction that no life is without meaning.[11]

Hope was the virtue that the Stoics could not comprehend. Kavin Rowe has recently written a book, *One True Life: The Stoics and Early Christians as Rival Traditions*, which confirms Harvey's judgment that Stoicism was first and foremost a way of life. According to Rowe, both the Roman Stoics and the early Christians claimed their pattern of life was the truth of all things, but that the truth could be known only if followers took the time to live the tradition that was the truth.[12] Rowe thinks each tradition was internally coherent, though each dealt with aspects of life lacking in the other. In particular, Christians had no word for the world's inscrutable power that results in the helplessness of human beings in the face of such power. Rowe suggests that Stoics did have a word to describe the forces that can make or break human life. That word is "Fortuna."[13]

Harvey does not use "Fortuna" to describe his life, but I think it is a word that shapes Harvey's narrative. It is not the word that shapes the story I tell in *Hannah's Child*. Though I told my friends they must abandon hope that their son would recover from his illness, I did not tell them to give up hope that his life would be comprehended by a meaning yet unseen. I take that as the conviction that is unintelligible if the God we worship as Christians does not exist. It is the habit that hopefully sustains the life of Christian theologians.

In a review of *Hannah's Child*, Mark Clavier suggests that my memoir should be read as a theologian's narrative. If I emerge from *Hannah's*

---

11. For a more extensive account of hope, see Charles Pinches and Stanley Hauerwas, *Christians among the Virtues: Theological Conversations with Ancient and Modern Ethics* (Notre Dame: University of Notre Dame Press, 1997), 113–128.

12. C. Kavin Rowe, *One True Life: The Stoics and Early Christians as Rival Traditions* (New Haven: Yale University Press, 2016), 6.

13. Rowe, *One True Life*, 255.

Child as a construct, than I must, in fact, be a theological construct. That the story I tell is a theological story, Clavier argues, reflects my view that my experiences have not unduly shaped my theology. In fact, Clavier argues it works in the other direction—that is, I interpret my experiences through the filter of theology. According to Clavier, I tell just enough of my life to weave an engaging tale, but I leave much unsaid in the hope that a perceptive reader will see that my real life lies somewhere in the silence. Clavier argues that the real Hauerwas "lurks in the gaps" and this is particularly true for my description of my relationship with Anne—a relationship that was, in Clavier's words, an ocean of pain.[14]

I think there are similar gaps in Harvey's memoir. They are gaps that suggest the God who Harvey so faithfully served over the years is not going to give up on him. As he came to the conclusion of his book in which he treated Stoic and Christian thinkers, Kavin Rowe observed that it is difficult if not impossible to see how either of these traditions could provide an answer to the conflicts in the other. Christians simply had no word for the inscrutable powers that were at the center of Stoic existence. Rowe, therefore, draws the implication that "no matter how many criteria we find for living one way or another, we cannot make them add up to a judgment about a true life before we live it."[15] There is a sadness that suffuses Harvey's narrative, but I nevertheless believe the story he tells is one that could only be told by someone who has lived a life of truth.

---

14. Mark Clavier, "A Reflection on *Hannah's Child*," *Covenant*, March 10, 2015, https://livingchurch.org/covenant/2015/03/10/a-reflection-on-hannahs-child/.

15. Rowe, *One True Life*, 257.

10

In Defense of "Our Respectable Culture"
Trying to Make Sense of John Howard Yoder

On Writing about Yoder

In her sobering and well researched article, "'Defanging the Beast': Mennonite Responses to John Howard Yoder's Sexual Abuse," Rachel Goossen reports on a response Yoder made to Marlin Miller's attempt to convince him his "experimentation" with "non-sexual" touching was wrong. In a memo to Miller, Yoder observed that Miller's arguments "represent simply an appeal to the consensus of our respectable culture. I know what that consensus teaches, for I am its product and its victim. I knew its teachings before I began testing an alternative set of axioms."[1] I call attention to Yoder's use of the phrase, "consensus of our respectable culture," because I will argue that his assumption that such a consensus exists was a profound and deeply costly mistake. Even more surprising, at least surprising to me, I will suggest that there can be some quite positive aspects for Christians in the "consensus of a respectable culture."

Before developing that argument I need to make clear that for me to write about these matters fills me with sadness. I do not want to try to "explain" John's behavior. I find even thinking about that aspect of John's life drains me of energy and depresses me—and I am not a person given

---

1. Rachel Waltner Goossen, "'Defanging the Beast': Mennonite Responses to John Howard Yoder's Sexual Abuse," *Mennonite Quarterly Review*, 89, no. 1 (January 2015), 7–80.

to depression. But Goossen's article stunned me. I had no idea that John's engagement in his "experimentation" was so extensive, both in terms of time and the number of women he seems to have involved. I am not sure, moreover, if I ever recognized how troubling it is that John refused to acknowledge his views about what is possible between brothers and sisters in Christ were simply wrong.[2]

I also hesitate to write about John's behavior because I know John's family and I do not want to add to their pain. John was by all reports a loving father, though one that was often absent. Annie, his wife, is a wonderful person who was a bulwark for John in the last years of his life. I count a number of his children as friends and I know something of the complexity of what it means to be John Yoder's child. The Mennonite world is just that—"a world"—and his children must find their way, as they have, through that world without anything I might say adding to that challenge.

I also find it hard to write because I must respond to those who have wondered about what I think about "all this" because they worry that I have not appreciated the seriousness of what John did. I tried to depict my relationship, my indebtedness, to John in *Hannah's Child*.[3] I also report in *Hannah's Child* what and when I learned of John's behavior, as well as my involvement in the process of John's disciplinary proceedings. I see no reason to repeat what I said there, but what I must do is acknowledge that I did not appropriately acknowledge how destructive John's behavior was for the women involved.

As I noted above, I simply did not understand the extent of activities. I think before I left Notre Dame to come to Duke I had been told by a graduate student that John had some questionable relations with women, but I did not have any idea what that meant. I think the next development was the articles in *The Elkhart Truth*, but I did not read all of them because I did not have access to them in Durham. It was not until 1992 that I learned how catastrophic a situation John's behavior was creating.

---

2. Mark Nation suggests that John's sense of intellectual integrity would not allow him to say he believed what he thought was true was wrong. I am sure Mark is right about that, but that does not mean John was right about what he thought was true. See Nation's and Marva Dawn's essay, "On Contextualizing Two Failures of John Howard Yoder," *Anabaptist Nation*, September 23, 2013, https://emu.edu/now/anabaptist-nation/2013/09/23/on-contextualizing-two-failures-of-john-howard-yoder/.

3. Stanley Hauerwas, *Hannah's Child: A Theologian's Memoir*, 2d ed. (Grand Rapids: Eerdmans, 2012), 146–47, 242–47.

In 1992, Al and Mary Ellen Meyer, his brother-in-law and sister, told me about John's behavior. I was at Bethel College to give a lecture I seem to remember John was to give but he had been disinvited because of his behavior. I realized I was getting the straight story from Al and Mary Ellen, but for some reason I assumed the behavior they were reporting on had ceased and that we were not talking about that many women. I thought maybe three or four women might be involved. Of course, one woman would have been too many, but at the time I could not imagine what now seems to be the large number of women who were caught up in John's destructive behavior. Nor did I appropriately appreciate, at the time, how traumatizing John's actions were for the women involved. For that I can only say I am sorry.

One of the aspects of this whole sad story that saddens me is how I have had to recognize how much energy John put into this aspect of his life. His attempt to maintain these multiple relationships would have exhausted any normal person. But John was not normal intellectually or physically. I am depressed when I think about the time he dedicated to developing justifications for his experimentation. Of course John gave us the great gift of the clarity of his mind, but that same analytic ability betrayed him just to the extent he used it to make unjustified distinctions, such as those about the significance of different ways of touching that could only result in self-deceptive justifications.

In *Hannah's Child* I also gave a far too positive account of the disciplinary process undertaken by the church. It is true that Stassen, McClendon, and I made the phone call to urge John to participate in the process. McClendon was the person that told John no matter how flawed John thought the process might be he should submit. But it is clear from Goossen's account that though he submitted, he was anything but cooperative. The intervention by Jim McClendon, Glen Stassen, and myself in the process was ill-timed and poorly judged.

Another reason I find it difficult to write about these matters is like most of us I do not want to acknowledge my mistakes. But I learned from Yoder that such an acknowledgement is necessary if we are to be people for whom speaking truth matters. I hope in some small way writing this paper may be an example of Matthew 18, because at least one of the reasons I am writing is that I have been told by many that I need to do so.

Yet, I must say in spite of my hesitancy about writing this paper, I am glad I have to write it. The paper gives me the opportunity to confess: I was too anxious to have John resume his place as one of the crucial theologians of our time. I thought I knew what was going on, but in fact I did not have a clue. In my defense, and it is not a very good defense, I think it is true that I simply did not understand what was going on. However, in truth, I probably did not want to know what was going on.

I also find it hard to write this because I do not know what to say. I do not know what to say to "explain" John's behavior. Like anyone grieved by John's behavior, I cannot resist trying to give some account of why John Howard Yoder, of all people, got into such a bizarre pattern of behavior. Of course he had a theory, but this was John Howard Yoder. Surely anyone as smart as Yoder should have known better, but what he did speaks for itself. While it may be true that he had some form of Asperger syndrome, this tells us little. My general assumption that his behavior betrayed a deficit of empathy may be closer to the mark, but I think even if that is true we learn little from such a judgment.

I do not know what to say though I must say something about the relation of a person's moral character and what and how they think. Given my emphasis on the virtues, I obviously cannot deny that there is, or there should be, some relation between who we are and what we say. But that is clearly not a straightforward correlation. I will make some tentative judgments about this question toward the end of this paper. But even if I had the time or space I could not claim to know how to parse this heady matter. Finally, I have to revisit Yoder's life and work because I do not want what he has taught us about how we should and can live as Christians and how we are to think theologically to be lost.

Many of my friends who are former students, students who have written quite insightfully about Yoder, feel that they can no longer have their students read Yoder. They rightly worry that the very shape of Yoder's arguments for nonviolence may also inform his views about sexual behavior between men and women in the church. I think the question about the continued use of Yoder's work for instruction is not quite the same among Mennonites as it is for non-Mennonites, but I have no stake in defending that view. What I do know, however, is that we cannot avoid the question of whether his justification for his sexual behavior is structurally not unlike his defense of Christian nonviolence.

So I do not want to write this paper, but I think I have to write about this part of John's life, because I owe it to him. John Yoder changed my life before I knew it needed changing. I am often credited with making John Howard Yoder better known among those identified as mainstream Protestants. True or not, it is nonetheless the case that I am rightly closely identified with Yoder. That being the case I regard it as a responsibility to try to say why Yoder's behavior was so wrong, yet also why he remains such an important theologian for those like me who are at best about half-Christian. I owe John Yoder the truth about his behavior and why such truth cannot help but implicate him in a way of life from which I am sure that God is now giving him all the time he needs to repent.

What Was Wrong with Yoder's "Experimentation"?

In an insightful article entitled, "Scandalizing John Howard Yoder," the authors argue that Yoder's ongoing experimentation with what he claimed to be nonsexual relations with women was inconsistent with his commitment to nonviolence. They begin their article with a quote from Carolyn Holderread Heggen that describes an encounter with Yoder. Heggen was a new mother. She had received a letter from John inviting her and her infant to meet him at a conference. Heggen recounts that in this letter Yoder:

> went into this bizarre, long, detailed description of what it would be like for him to sit in a chair and watch me sit on his bed, take off my clothes and nurse my baby. He described in vivid detail my breasts and other body parts. When I read the letter, I felt I had been raped. The thought of this dirty old man sitting at his seminary desk fantasizing about my nude body was terrifying to me, and I felt extremely violated and angry. I had never done anything to communicate to him that I was interested in anything but a mentor-protégée relationship.[4]

There only needs to be one such report to establish the violent character of Yoder's behavior. But there is clear evidence that many of the women Yoder invited to participate in his experiment experienced the same reaction that Heggen reports. Of course, Yoder maintained that he never forced any women to participate. That sense of non-coercion appears to have preserved his presumption that what he was about was nonviolent, but it is hard to avoid the assessment that he was repressing the violence inherent in the structure of the event. For God's sake, he surely should have recognized that he was John Howard Yoder, the most

---

4. David Cramer, Jenny Howell, Jonathan Tran, and Paul Martens, "Scandalizing John Howard Yoder," *The Other Journal*, July 7, 2014, http://theotherjournal.com/2014/07/07/scandalizing-john-howard-yoder/.

prominent Mennonite theologian in recent times, and that these women he tried first to seduce intellectually in the hope it would lead further—and I think seduction is the right word—wanted his approval.

The authors accordingly argue that Yoder's understanding of violence as the violation of the dignity or integrity of some being is an appropriate description of Yoder's behavior. They conclude that given Yoder's configuration of Christian discipleship as nonviolence and his identification of the kingdom of God with the church's peaceableness, it is "unclear how he, given his behaviors (even if occasional), could consider himself faithful as a disciple of Christ or as a witness of the church."[5] I find their judgment hard to deny.

If anyone wonders if I ever discussed with John what I had learned from Al and Mary Ellen Meyer, the answer is "yes." I am fairly sure my encounter with John about this matter took place at Notre Dame. I had already moved to Duke, but I had returned to Notre Dame for a conference. I visited John in his office in the basement of the library. As usual, the office was stacked high with paper John collected so that nothing would be wasted. Cleaning off a chair I sat down and told him what I had learned from his sister and her husband.

I had read for many years John's unpublished papers such as "When Is a Marriage Not a Marriage" and "When is Adultery a Marriage." So I had some idea of how he challenged, for example, the presumption that for Christian marriage to be Christian the partners had to be married and prepared to bring children into the world. I did not know about his further justification for his "experiment" with nonsexual forms of touching, but I assumed because he thought Christians were first and foremost called to singleness, he must also think there needed to be ways for men and women to touch one another without those touches implying more than they needed to do. I assumed that is why he only associated marital sexuality with ejaculation. He also had a paper that explored homosexual behavior as no more serious than mutual masturbation. I had no idea at the time he actually had intercourse with some of those he was trying to get to buy into his crazy project.

So I told him what I had learned and I made it clear I was not in the least persuaded by his "arguments." I pointed out that everything depends on how you understand "mutual masturbation," as it can be understood as more intimate than intercourse. I told him, moreover, that

---

5. Cramer, Howell, Tran, and Martens, "Scandalizing John Howard Yoder."

I was extremely doubtful about his assumption that what he was about could be described as nonsexual behavior. But clearly I thought what he was doing could not be right because it could not be shared by the whole community. For it must surely be the case that, whatever it means to be a Mennonite, it must mean that you cannot keep your "experiments" secret. John did not respond other than to express concern about the effects his behavior was having on others.

The authors also observe that John's refusal to cooperate with the accountability processes was inconsistent with his ecclesiology. As Goossen makes clear, he tried to simply out-argue Miller and the others associated with the process in the seminary. His argument that the process was inherently flawed because he was not allowed to confront his accusers was a reading of Matthew 18 that is question-begging, at best. He seems to have positioned himself above the process, which meant he did not respect those he identified as the "Mennonite women's posse."

That Yoder's behavior was inconsistent with his deepest commitments is not the most challenging aspect anyone concerned with his actions needs to consider. The most challenging question is raised by the authors, "What do we do with the places where Yoder's actions were *consistent* with his theology?"[6] In particular, they have in mind Yoder's eschatological convictions that the church is the manifestation of the "original revolution" that entailed the "creation of a distinct community with its own deviant set of values and its coherent way of incarnating them."[7] They observe that this understanding of the new age in which the church lives is the framework that informs Yoder's defense of nonviolence. That does not mean that only Christians can practice nonviolence. Yoder always insisted that what for Christians is a duty is a possibility for anyone. All people, whether they are Christians or not, have the possibility of living nonviolent lives. In a similar fashion, the authors suggest that Yoder understood his exploration of "non-genital affective relationships" to be an expression of the "revolution" inaugurated by the new age. As I suggested above, and the authors make the same point, given Yoder's account of singleness, such touching could be seen as a way the church has found to meet the needs of the "whole person."

I certainly feel the power of the authors' suggestion, but as they also suggest, Yoder's account of "non-genital" affection is bizarre. They rightly

6. Cramer, Howell, Tran and Martens, "Scandalizing John Howard Yoder."
7. Cramer, Howell, Tran, and Martens, "Scandalizing John Howard Yoder."

call Yoder's actions "demonic." This invites a very suggestive account of Yoder's behavior as a manifestation of the power of the powers over our lives. Not only is Yoder's concept bizarre, I also do not think it can in any way be commensurate with his defense of nonviolence. Yoder's suggestion that Jesus's "touching" of women provides precedent for the behavior in which he engaged is clearly not justified by any of the Gospel stories of Jesus's interaction with women. Jesus may have touched some women, but not in the way Yoder was touching women. In marked contrast to nonviolence, there are simply no texts in the New Testament to support Yoder's claims about what is sexually possible between Christians.

Nor is there any precedent in Christian tradition to underwrite Yoder's account of nonsexual touching. This is in marked contrast with nonviolence. Even the presumption that the majority of Christian tradition has entailed justifications for just war has always had nonviolence as its bad consciousness. If Christians did not presume nonviolence, why would they need to provide justification for the use of violence? These are complicated matters, but I do not think Yoder could have written a book like *Christian Attitudes to War, Peace, and Revolution* about his views about non-genital sexual relations between brothers and sisters in Christ. To be sure, New Harmony–type groups can exist for a few years, but they never last.[8]

This brings me to Yoder's claim that Miller's criticism of his behavior and justification of that behavior reproduced the "consensus of our respectable culture." You can almost hear by the use of that phrase Yoder's disdain for what he would identify as middle-class morality. Yet, if that is what he heard or read as the basis of Miller's criticism he was profoundly mistaken. It is as if Yoder had not lived through the sixties. If anything, given the sexual revolution, the "consensus," particularly among the children of the middle class, was closer to Yoder's view than that of Miller. Yoder's experimentation could be seen as but one form of the changing sexual mores and behavior of Americans. From such a perspective his views and behavior were anything but radical. Rather, what he was doing could be understood, just as the "new morality" could be understood, as quite conventional. Given the changing attitudes toward

---

8. New Harmony was the utopian community founded in Indiana in the nineteenth century that had at its head John Humphrey Noyes. He believed in complex marriage that meant you could have sexual relations with other people as long as you did not get personally attached. The community soon went to hell in a handbasket.

sexual expression, it was just another step to conclude that you can do what you want sexually as long as you have the other's consent.

Yoder, of course, argued that he never acted without consent, but he never explored how ambiguous the notion of "consent" is when it involves such power dynamics. How would women know if they had given consent when they were confronted by that "intellectual giant" with the name of John Howard Yoder? It is, moreover, quite possible that a woman may well look back on what happened between Yoder and herself and judge that, though at the time she may seem to have given consent, retrospectively she cannot believe she acted freely.

There is, however, another way to read Yoder's disdain for the "consensus of our respectable culture" which I think is more substantive and important. That "consensus" can be understood as the hard-won wisdom and still-ongoing challenge of maintaining the habits necessary for the sustaining of marriage as the institution of life-long fidelity. To be sure there are perversions associated with those habits and practices, but the discovery of marriage as such a commitment for the sustaining of hospitality for new life is a profound discovery. Such a discovery owes much to Judaism and Christianity, but it is not restricted to those communities. In fact, such an understanding of marriage as the appropriate home for sexual intimacy may be thought to be grounded in natural law. I have no objection to it being so located. But that is a move that Yoder may not have had the resources to develop and, even if they were available, he clearly did not use them.

The point I am trying to make, a point not easily made, may entail a criticism of Yoder's work that I am only beginning to understand. I worry that Yoder may have made too extreme the duality between church and world, particularly when it comes to dealing with our everyday relations with one another. I need to be very careful in making such a criticism because Yoder, contrary to many superficial criticisms of him, never restricted God's redemption to the church. He was always ready to acknowledge that God was doing a new thing among those who were not church. Thus my point above that Yoder always assumed what is a duty for Christians is a possibility for those who are not. The critical question is, however, if his emphasis on the distinctive behavior that is constitutive of what it means to be the church presumes we are capable of being more than we are. The question is whether Yoder failed to understand that, when all is said and done, baptism does not make us angels, rather we remain human beings.

There are methodological issues at the heart of theological ethics entailed in these issues. The question of "the natural," the characterization of "the natural," as well as the status of "the natural" is one way these questions can be addressed. Yoder had little use, or at least he seldom addressed questions, about the status of natural law. He quite rightly worried that appeals to natural law invited modes of moral reflection that were in tension with the Gospel imperatives. But some account of the natural, or I would prefer "creation," is required in order to acknowledge that by the grace of God we exist. That means that nature is the concept that affirms that God has willed that there exist that which is not God.

That reality makes possible reflections of practical reason that offer wisdom to guide our lives. Though I doubt there needs to be a hard and fast distinction between the natural or moral virtues and the theological virtues, it is nonetheless the case that the distinction not only can be made but must be made. This is not the context to develop these issues, but I raise them to suggest that I have long suspected that I hold views about such matters that may put me in some tension with Yoder's general perspective.

The Missing Piece

Let me try to put these issues in a register that is more directly relevant to the challenge of Yoder's behavior; entailed is what I think may be missing in Yoder that led him to engage in such destructive behavior, not only for the women involved, but also for himself. As I noted at the beginning, I am not trying to provide an explanation or a cause for John's experimentation. Rather I am trying to help locate what I think his behavior— and even more his justifications for the behavior—may provide to help us understand some problems with his work. Of course, I write as one deeply shaped and beholden to what John has taught me. But what I think is missing in John's theology is quite simple. What is missing is insight and wisdom about learning to live well as a human being.

The point I am trying to make is, I think, at the heart of Alex Sider's article, "Friendship, Alienation, Love: Stanley Hauerwas and John Howard Yoder."[9] In this article—an article with which I was at first not sure I was in agreement—Sider argues that my account of friendship provides

---

9. Alex Sider, "Friendship, Alienation, Love: Stanley Hauerwas and John Howard Yoder," *Mennonite Quarterly Review*, 84, no. 3 (July, 2010), 417–40.

an opening to psychological insights that are absent in Yoder's work. Sider calls attention to passages in Yoder's work, passages I have celebrated, in which Yoder resists any exploration of what Sider identifies as "the affective registers of desire and delight in others and oneself."[10] Sider suggests Yoder is so intent on the primacy of the social dimension of the Gospel, he ignores the personal and psychological dimensions of practices such as baptism.

Particularly important given the subject of this paper, Sider argues that Yoder should have attended to how guilt after baptism continues to be a shaping psychological force in many lives. A focus on baptism that relativizes guilt, Sider argues, still needs to attend to the guilt that people feel even after they have been inducted into the new humanity. Sider illustrates what he is calling for by focusing attention on Sebastian Moore's reflections on guilt as withdrawal into isolated selfhood. According to Moore, such a withdrawal "may be a sense of robbery, of stealing my private life from the whole in which I am a participant. It may be a sense of the inferiority, the unworthiness, of this privatized life in respect of the life as a whole."[11] Sider suggests that this is the kind of insight about our human condition that is simply missing in Yoder.

Sider summarizes his analysis of Yoder's texts by observing that in each instance at the point where practices, practices as basic as nonviolence, shape the psyche, Yoder turns away from providing a rational psychology in favor of pointing to the task of the community. As a result, Yoder refuses to entertain any notion that Christians have any use for or stake in being happy. Happiness, after all, does not have to be understood in the superficial way that is so characteristic of modern social orders, but rather can be, as Aquinas taught, a way of displaying what it means to be befriended by God.

Sider notes that I have at times identified with Yoder's disavowal of thinking it important that we be happy. Yet he also observes, a suggestion I hope is true, that in the actual practice of friendship I manifest the patience with and sensitivity to the alienation and anguish that bedevils our complex relationships.[12] That said, I think my written work displays some of the same psychology Sider thinks missing in Yoder, insofar as the virtues have been so crucial for me.

10. Sider, "Friendship, Alienation, Love," 434.

11. Sebastian Moore, *The Fire and the Rose Are One* (New York: Seabury, 1980), 66, quoted in Sider, "Friendship, Alienation, Love," 436.

12. Sider, "Friendship, Alienation, Love," 439.

Yoder always thought my emphasis on the importance of the virtues was a distraction. I think the fact that he had little use for the virtues is indicative of what Sider is getting at by suggesting John did not have any stake in our being happy. The virtues reside in wisdom traditions because they require insight about the human condition. Desires and passions must be accounted for because the virtues are the form of the passions. Desire and passion are missing in Yoder's work, but they were clearly present in his behavior.

Moreover the focus on the virtues requires consideration of how the virtues are related and how they are acquired. Those considerations entail judgments derived from traditions of reflection about what makes life worth living. John, however, never saw the need to engage any of those questions. There is, for example, no account of moral formation in Yoder's work. He seemed to see no reason why he needed, to use his terms, to provide an account of how we might become nonviolent. He assumed if you were brought up right, if you were part of a community of nonviolence, you would simply become what it meant to be nonviolent. Yet it is surely the case that nonviolence can become a subtly manipulative form of passive-aggressive behavior. Yoder, of course, was quite well aware that could be the case, but he never explored how questions of formation were necessary if we are to become people of peace. Yoder was so fixated on the social process he seems to have forgotten (or had methodological doubts) that we need to be trained to be Christians.

Another way, a rather tendentious way, to make the point Sider and I are trying to make is to observe that Yoder had no interest in novels. He seldom read novels, nor did he think novels to be morally important. It is not that he did not like to read. But he saw little reason to engage in the kind of literature represented by the novel. Yet the novel is all-important for me exactly because it forces one to imagine other lives. In short, novels are an exercise in the enrichment of the imagination through which we develop empathy that is crucial for the acquisition of the virtues. What one cannot help but wonder is how Yoder failed to appreciate how his advances toward women—like the encounter described by Carolyn Holderread Heggen—could only be received as a form of violence. Something was missing in Yoder, and I think the name for what was missing is called the "moral imagination."

Life and Work

I must finally address the question of the relation between morality and the intellectual life. That question is obviously raised by Yoder's behavior. Does the immorality of a person invalidate what they have had to say? I certainly do not intend at this point, even if I could, to develop a general response to that question. What I can do, however, is at least suggest that if you think that theology is not simply "thought," but rather a form of wisdom, then lives matter. That does not mean that everything a person has had to say must be rejected because they have turned out to be immoral, or even evil. But it does mean how their work is read will require a particular hermeneutic of suspicion.

In the first chapter of his wonderful book, *Edith Stein: A Philosophical Prologue, 1913-1922*, Alasdair MacIntyre argues that the lives of philosophers cannot help but be of philosophical interest. They are so because philosophy is the way "in which a life informed by the activities of philosophical enquiry and guided by its conclusions will be significantly different from the life of someone in other respects like the philosopher, but untouched by philosophy."[13]

MacIntyre observes that this understanding of the relation of a person's life to philosophical inquiry now seems strange because philosophy has become a specialized and professionalized academic discipline that makes possible the assumption that the character of the philosopher's life has no relation to their work as a philosopher. What is now characteristic of a philosophical life is the same kind of status and role-playing games that are characteristic of any professionalized academic discipline. Accordingly, the compartmentalization so characteristic of modern life, the kind of life that found its most perverse form in Eichmann, now determines the lives of philosophers.

MacIntyre argues, however, that even those so engaged in philosophical work often embody a very different conception of the relationship of action to their philosophy. They do so because if philosophy is to be recognizable as philosophy, it must always be recognizable as a continuation of Plato's enterprise. That enterprise MacIntyre identifies as a radical critique of everyday life that will require the philosopher to distinguish themselves from that which they are subjecting to critique.[14]

---

13. Alasdair MacIntyre, *Edith Stein: A Philosophical Prologue, 1913-1922* (New York: Rowman and Littlefield, 2006), 1.

14. MacIntyre, *Edith Stein*, 2-3.

The philosopher cannot help, therefore, becoming different because "the very language that we cannot avoid speaking, our everyday vocabulary and idiom, is itself not philosophically innocent, but to a significant degree inherited from and still informed by past philosophical theories whose presence in our modes of speech, belief, and action is no longer recognized."[15] A philosopher, therefore, cannot avoid the reality that their philosophical work will or should make a difference in how they live.

MacIntyre's way of putting these matters has direct implications for how a theologian's life and work cannot be separated. Plato may be unavoidable for the philosopher, but the theologian must operate with "a language we cannot avoid speaking" that will make or should make a difference in how one's life is lived. That may be true just to the extent that the failure to lead a life commensurate with our language indicates something has gone wrong. That something has gone wrong is a testimony to the necessity that there must exist an interrelation between theology and how the theologian lives.

I have suggested that to read Yoder is not to look for mistakes he has made in what he has said, though such a reading is not without reason. It is, however, a reading that is required of any serious text. What I have tried to suggest, however, is that it is not what Yoder has written that is the problem. The problem rather is what is not there. I am not suggesting that if Yoder had a better understanding of our psychology he would have been less likely to have engaged in his extremely troubling "experimentation." We have no means to know that. Rather I am suggesting that if we are to continue to read and learn from Yoder we must do so by attending to what is not "there."

Where Does This Leave Us? or What Do We Do Now?

I do not have ready answers to either of these questions. Much depends of course on who the "us" or the "we" may be that asks the question. As mentioned previously, I have friends who, in recognition of the offenses committed by Yoder against women, have decided that they will no longer have their students read his work. I respect that decision, but it is not one I can make. I need Yoder's clarity of thought if I am to try to think through what I think I have learned from him.

---

15. MacIntyre, *Edith Stein*, 3.

I think Gerald Schlabach puts the matter well in his reflections on his relation to Yoder in his wonderfully titled essay, "Only Those We Need Can Betray Us." There he observes that "there is simply no way to tell the story of 20th-century historic peace church theology—much less to appropriate it—without drawing on Yoder's thought."[16] Schlabach acknowledges that he can understand why younger Mennonite scholars might be inclined to try to do peace theology without relying on Yoder, but he confesses that "I just don't see how they/we can do without him." Nor do I see how we can do without him.

In particular, I need his readings of Scripture that seem to me ever fresh and powerful. Yet, I cannot deny that this cannot be the decision others can or should make. In particular, I think women would have trouble reading Yoder. But "trouble reading" is not the same thing as "not reading." For it is surely the case that there are aspects of Yoder's work that are of constructive use for the concerns of women.

Karen Guth has suggested, for example, that Yoder might be "redeemed" by attending to his positive commitment to some forms of feminism.[17] Guth obviously thinks my close relationship with Yoder should make me follow her advice to engage feminist theologians. My first response to Guth's proposal was to stiff-arm the suggestion that those Guth identified as "witness theologians" should take "feminist theologians" more seriously. I did so because I objected to what I took to be Guth's presumption that I held a position that was an alternative to a feminist position.

I sent this essay to Professor Guth who wrote an extremely informative response. She observed she used "witness" and "feminist" only as conceptual place holders, not as names for clearly identifiable positions. What she was suggesting, a suggestion with which I wholeheartedly agree, is that the feminist critique of patriarchy and the attending violence or at least coercion associated with the male gaze is an insight that those committed to nonviolence ought to credit.

16. Gerald Schlabach, "Only Those We Need Can Betray Us: My Relationship with John Howard Yoder and His Legacy," Gerald W. Schlabach, July 10, 2014, http://www.geraldschlabach.net/2014/07/10/only-those-we-need-can-betray-us-my-relationship-with-john-howard-yoder-and-his-legacy/.

17. Karen Guth, "Doing Justice to the Complex Legacy of John Howard Yoder: Restorative Justice Resources in Witness and Feminist Ethics," *Journal of the Society of Christian Ethics* 35, no. 2 (Fall/Winter, 2015), 119–40. This article is a further development of the argument Guth began in her book, *Christian Ethics at the Boundary: Feminism and Theologies of Public Life* (Minneapolis: Fortress, 2015).

I have a very ambiguous relation with feminist theology because I often agree with their criticisms of male behavior, but disagree with the basis for those criticisms. That I have not been prepared to discuss feminist theology in principle does not mean, however, that I do not think it unimportant to take account of what women have to say. I should like to think that I have done that, at least to the extent that women like Iris Murdoch, Elizabeth Anscombe, Philippa Foot, Martha Nussbaum, Marie Fortune, Catherine Pickstock, and Ellen Davis have been crucial for how I have tried to think. But I engaged them not because they were women, but because what they were doing was so interesting.

I certainly have deep sympathies with the feminist challenge to paternalism.[18] Even more, I think feminist critiques of masculinity to be extremely insightful. Stan Goff's book, *Borderline: Reflections on War, Sex and the Church*, is a model of how feminist insights can illumine what any Christian should think.[19] The work Goff does in his book makes clear that the feminist challenge to "maleness" is a gift to men.

I also think the feminist challenge to the assumption that marriage is necessary for the fulfillment of women to be right and important. Yoder's account of singleness can be read as a feminist argument. I also think we owe feminists a debt of gratitude for their critique of romantic love. For years in the core course in Christian Ethics I assigned the work of Marie Fortune because I thought her exposure of the violence present in romantic love to be a crucial insight. Fortune was not only important for exposing the violence occluded in romantic ideals of love, but she also helped make clear that nonviolence is not just about war. Yoder would and did think similar thoughts, but he did so because he thought they were commensurate with the Gospel.

Yet the issue remains how to receive Yoder's work without that reception seeming to imply that his behavior does not matter. That surely would be an injustice to the women he harmed. He was the President of the Society of Christian Ethics. Should some notation be put next to his name when past presidents of the society are named? Pete Rose will not get into the Hall of Fame, but Yoder is already there. We cannot act as if he was not the president of the Society. Or what does it mean that Yoder

---

18. In *Christian Ethics at the Boundary*, Guth suggests that Yoder's arguments against Constantinianism are quite similar to feminist critiques of patriarchy (141–142). That seems right, and it is a suggestion that invites more thought.

19. Stan Goff, *Borderline: Reflections on War, Sex, and the Church* (Eugene, OR: Cascade, 2015).

was President of AMBS? I obviously cannot speak as a Mennonite, for which I thank God since I have no idea what to say, but they surely must say something.

Nor do I think it helpful to call attention to the misconduct toward women by Martin Luther King, Karl Barth, or Paul Tillich. Each in their own way seem to have engaged in misconduct toward women or a woman, but I think it does little good to suggest that they help us understand Yoder's behavior. To call attention to these men invites the general claim that when all is said and done "we are all sinners." That is a way to excuse each of us with the result that Yoder is left off the hook. That is clearly a mistake, not only because Yoder should not be left off the hook, but also, just as important, because sin should never be used as an explanation.

That is it. That is all I have to say about this troubling matter. It surely feels like I am ending with a whimper. That is the way it should feel because I have ended with a whimper. I did not want to write this paper, but I have done it. I am not happy that I have done it, but then nothing about this situation is happy.[20]

---

20. For a very critical response to my essay, see Hilary Scarsella, "Not Making Sense: Why Stanley Hauerwas's Response to Yoder's Sexual Abuse Misses the Mark," ABC Religion & Ethics, December 1, 2017, http://www.abc.net.au/religion/articles/2017/11/30/4774014.htm.

Part IV

THE MATTER OF PREACHING

11

Preaching In the Ruins

Reflections about Words with Sermonic Exhibits

1. Words Matter

"In the shadows of a dying Christendom, the challenge is how to recover a strong theological voice without that voice betraying the appropriate fragility of all speech and particularly speech about God." That is the first sentence in my response to the papers about my work by Jennifer Herdt, Jonathan Tran, and Sam Wells at an event in November 2013 to mark my retirement.[1] In truth I did not discover that sentence for that event. The sentence had come to me weeks previously when I was trying to find a language about the language we must use as Christians to speak of God.

In this paper for my longtime friend and colleague, Richard Lischer, the sentence with which I begin is, I think, not irrelevant. Words have always been at the center of his work. That should not be surprising. As he observes in his book, *The End of Words: The Language of Reconciliation in a Culture of Violence*, the stock and trade of a preacher is words.[2] Yet given the horrors of our century he wonders what can be said in the face

---

1. The papers as well as responses by Charlie Pinches and Peter Dula can be found in Charles M. Collier, ed., *The Difference Christ Makes: Celebrating the Life, Work, and Friendship of Stanley Hauerwas* (Eugene, OR: Cascade, 2015).

2. Richard Lischer, *The End of Words: The Language of Reconciliation in a Culture of Violence* (Grand Rapids: Eerdmans, 2005), 6.

of the Holocaust Museum or Dachau. The normative response to such stark realities seems to be silence.

Yet Lischer is a preacher. He has to have something to say, and what he has to say can only be said with words. The preacher's task is "to do nothing less than shape the language of the sermon to a living reality among the people of God—to make it conform to Jesus."[3] Even stronger, Lischer argues that the sermon is Jesus who is trying to speak to his people. This is not a new theme with Lischer, because Christology has always been at the heart of his understanding of preaching.[4]

Lischer draws on Christology to make an essential point about preaching: because Jesus fully assumed our flesh, our fallibility, the power of his word often seems hidden. Lischer suggests this means that just as believers organize their common life around Jesus, so the preacher must model a Christ-like way of speaking. For the sermon to be Christ before a hostile world, the sermon, like Christ himself, must refuse to resort to the coercive strategies of the world to gain a hearing.[5]

To so preach, Lischer acknowledges, is hard. It is hard not merely because we live in a world dominated by cultural and political forces that seem to make the gospel into fantasies that we entertain for our private enjoyment. It is hard, Lischer tells us, because preaching bears "the impossible weight of its own message." Drawing on Bonhoeffer, Lischer explains what he means by suggesting that the God who is the subject of a Christian sermon is the God who was willing to be "pushed out of the world and onto a cross."[6]

Lischer's Christological understanding of the sermon, I think, is not unlike the challenge I tried to articulate with the sentence with which I began. Of course, Lischer is a Lutheran, which means he is identified with a form of Christianity that has had little good to say about those people who worry about how Christendom results in a severely compromised church. Yet I think Lischer's understanding of the social and political implications of "the language of reconciliation in a culture of violence"[7] shares much with figures such as Barth and Bonhoeffer who were intent on challenging the cultural captivity of the church.

3. Lischer, *The End of Words*, 7–8.

4. See his *Speaking of Jesus: Finding the Words for Witness* (Philadelphia: Fortress, 1982).

5. Lischer, *The End of Words*, 8.

6. Lischer, *The End of Words*, 8.

7. The phrase is the subtitle of Lischer's, *The End of Words*.

Christendom was and is a complex and varied phenomenon that in many ways has been a faithful response to the gospel. Yet it is also true, as Lischer puts the matter, that Christendom names the attempt by Christians who, by seizing power, attempt to insure that the crucified Lord could not be pushed out of the world. In Christendom, the cross became a symbol of triumph rather than defeat. The words used in the sermons of Christendom too often confirmed a world in which the worship of a crucified Savior did not call into question the powers of this age.

I take Lischer's criticism of those sermons that "have accommodated their rhetoric to the bloodless cadences of civil discourse" to be a characterization of the sermon in Christendom.[8] Lischer challenges Christendom's presumption that if the preacher wants to communicate, she must try to find some common experience between herself and those to whom she preaches.[9] Accordingly, the sermon too often confirms what is assumed everyone thinks without challenging that very assumption.

In contrast to this view of the task of preaching, Lischer insists that the sermon is first and foremost an ecclesial reality. One might wonder, what else could it be? But Lischer's point is that the church provides the resources that make the words of the sermon work. He is insisting that the sermon is a word from one church to another across time and space made possible by the common use of the Holy Scripture. Accordingly, the common denominator between Christians is not human nature but the church gathered around lectern and pulpit, listening to the word of the Lord.[10]

That is what it means for the sermon not only to be about Jesus, but to be Jesus. Thereby the sermon for those that preach and those that hear participates in the mysterious heart of the universe found in the ministry, death, and resurrection of Christ. The church must preach, because we have the responsibility to communicate "the distinctiveness of the Christian message in a world of counter-messages and conflicting values."[11]

Lischer calls attention to Martin Luther King's rushing to scenes of bombings to hold services of prayer and preaching. King would preach in the still smoldering ruins. Lischer interviewed people who heard those

---

8. Lischer, *The End of Words*, 17.

9. For my more developed critique of this way of understanding the task of preaching, see *Without Apology: Sermons for Christ's Church* (New York: Seabury, 2013), xi–xxxii.

10. Lischer, *The End of Words*, 75.

11. Lischer, *The End of Words*, 133.

sermons to ask them what King had said. They often responded that they could not remember what he had said, but they would never forget where he had said it. Lischer suggests that King understood that preaching in the ruins symbolized the triumph of the word of God over every attempt to destroy it.[12] I take "preaching in the ruins" to be a good description of where Lischer thinks we now find ourselves; namely, we exist in "a sea of words" that results in a debasement of the speech we need if we are to preach truth.[13]

If we are living in the shadow of a dying Christendom, the challenge is how to avoid using words that have grown tired and thus unable to tell us the truth. Lischer's preaching has been a model for how words that have been subjected to sentimental ends can be rescued to do the work they were intended to do by helping us see "reality."[14] I hope I have learned from him how that can be done. Examples are crucial. Accordingly, I offer the following sermons as examples of how I have tried, often without success, to recover in the ruins of Christendom the true end of words.

In the first sermon, I try to recover the significance of "the" in order to emphasize that this was not just any young virgin, but this was Mary. I do so to challenge the sentimental view of Mary that would turn her into an abstraction rather than the first disciple of the new creation who was more than ready to challenge the powerful and rich. The "the" is also a way to emphasize the historical reality that Jesus is not the exemplification of what it means to be, in general, "sacrificial" or to be "a person for other persons." Rather the "the" of Mary is the "the" that denotes that this particular human being, with the name of Jesus, came at a very specific time to a very specific people. Accordingly, I wanted the sermon to challenge the endemic Gnosticism that shapes much of Protestant practice.

The second sermon I have included because it deals with words—and silence. I always write my sermons as a commentary on the texts assigned for the day. In this one, I try to explore the philosophical question of how words are necessary to create a silence. I worry that, in response to the so-called "new atheists," Christians try to say too much. When we say too much, we turn our faith into a mode of explanation that cannot help but give the impression that we know more than we do when we say "God."

12. Lischer, *The End of Words*, 33.
13. Lischer, *The End of Words*, 127.
14. Lischer, *The End of Words*, 126.

2. The Significance of a "the"

"Mary: Mother of God"
Christ Church Cathedral
Nashville, Tennessee
December 22, 2013

Isaiah 7:10–16
Psalm 80:1–7, 17–19
Romans 1:1–7
Matthew 1:18–25

"Do you believe in the virgin birth?" That was *the* question people asked one another when I was a boy growing up in that Southern Baptist–dominated land called Texas. It was *the* question, because how you answered would indicate who you were, what you believed, as well as where you stood in the world. If you expressed any doubts about the birth of Jesus by a virgin, you were identified as one of those liberals that did not believe that the Bible was inspired. That is to put the matter in too general terms. It was not that you failed to believe the Bible was inspired, but you refused to believe that every word of the Bible was inspired.

Refusal to believe in the virgin birth also entailed ethical and political implications. If you did not believe in the virgin birth, you were probably a person of loose morals, which meant you also wanted to destroy everything we hold dear as Americans. In particular, if you did not believe in the virgin birth, it was assumed you did not believe in the sacredness of the family and, if you did not believe in the sacredness of the family, it meant you were an enemy of the democratic way of life. In short, a failure to believe in the virgin birth was a sure indication that you were a person not to be trusted.

One of the anomalies, at least what I take to be an anomaly, of this use of the virgin birth to determine one's standing in the world is that those who used the virgin birth as the test case for moral rectitude often seemed to forget who it was that was the virgin. What was crucial for those who used the virgin birth in the manner I am describing is that *some* woman that was a virgin had given birth. It did not seem to matter if Mary was the one that had been impregnated by the Holy Spirit.

But Isaiah does not say that "a" virgin or young woman will bear a child. Isaiah says "the" young woman will bear a child. "The" is a definite article indicating that not anyone would give birth and still be a virgin, but someone in particular would be a virgin mother. We did not know who the "the" would be until Mary was singled out to be the mother of Jesus, but we knew it would be a "the." Not just any young Jewish girl would do. The one to carry Jesus would be named "Mary."

That "the" made all the difference for how the church fathers read this text. For them, what was significant was that Mary, the mother of Jesus, was the virgin. An indication of how important her singularity was regarded is that at the Council of Ephesus in 431, she was given the name "Mary, the Mother of God." That title means that Mary is not a replaceable instrument in the economy of God's salvation. Rather, she is constitutive of God's very life, making it impossible to say God without also saying Mary.

Such a view of Mary, a view held throughout the Christian tradition, was not how those that used the virgin birth as a test understood matters. They had a high view of virginity but a low view of Mary. They had a low view of Mary because the last thing they wanted was to be identified with the Roman Catholics. Roman Catholics even seemed to think you could pray to Mary. Those whose focus was primarily on the virgin birth assumed that such a prayer bordered on being idolatrous.

Those that used the virgin birth as a test to determine one's character were and continue to be identified as people who are theologically and politically conservative. In general, that assumption is probably true. I think, however, that this way of thinking about Christianity can also be found among those who represent more liberal theological and political positions. Conservatives and liberals alike assume that any account of Christianity that can pass muster in our time will be one in which the Christian faith is understood to be a set of strongly held ideas. Conservatives have the virgin birth and satisfaction theories of the atonement. Liberals have love and justice. Conservatives and liberals both take the Christian faith to be a set of ideas. Understood in this way, Christianity becomes a set of beliefs assessable by anyone upon reflection.

But then there is Mary. She is not just another young Jewish woman. She is the betrothed to Joseph. She has known no man, yet she carries a child, having been impregnated by the Holy Spirit. In the Gospel of Luke, we have her annunciation in which her "let it be" indicates her willingness to be the mother of the Son of God. In Matthew, we have the annunciation to Joseph who is told to take Mary for his wife, and he faithfully does so. Accordingly, Joseph is given the task of naming Mary's baby. He names him Jesus, Emmanuel, because this child is the long-awaited sign that "God is with us." The son of David, the King of Israel, has been conceived and born.

Mary and Joseph are not ideas. They are real people who made decisions upon which our faith depends. Christianity is not a timeless set of ideas. Christianity is not some ideal toward which we ought always to strive even though the ideal is out of reach. Christianity is not a series of slogans that sum up our beliefs. Slogans such as "justification by grace through faith" can be useful if you do not forget it is a slogan. But Christianity cannot be so easily "summed up" even by the best of slogans or ideas. It cannot be summed up, because our faith depends on a young Jewish mother called Mary.

Mary and Joseph are real people who had to make decisions that determined the destiny of the world. Isaiah had foretold that a Mary would come, but we had no idea what Isaiah's prophecy meant until Mary became the Mother of God. This is no myth. These are people caught up in God's care of his people through the faithfulness of the most unlikely people. They are unlikely people with names as common as Mary and Joseph, but because of their faithfulness our salvation now depends on acknowledging those names.

This is the last Sunday of Advent. Advent is a time the church has given us in the hope we can learn to wait. To learn to wait is to learn how to recognize we are creatures of time. Time is a gift and a threat. Time is a gift and a threat because we are bodily creatures. We only come into existence through the bodies of others, but that very body destines us to death. We must be born, and we must die. Birth and death are the brass tacks of life that make possible and necessary the storied character of our lives. It is never a question whether our lives will be storied, but the only question is which stories will determine our living in and through time.

Stories come in all shapes and sizes. Some are quite short, such as the story of a young Texan trying to figure out what it means to believe or not believe in the virgin birth. Other stories are quite long, beginning with "in the beginning." We are storied by many stories, which is an indication that we cannot escape—nor should we want to escape—being captured in and by time.

Jesus, very God, became circumscribed by time. He was conceived by the Holy Spirit and born of a virgin named Mary. Jesus, so born, is very man. He is fully God and fully man, making it possible for us to be fully human. To be fully human means that through his conception and birth, we have become storied by Mary. We are Mary's people.

What could it possibly mean that we are Mary's people? In his monumental book, *A Secular Age*, Charles Taylor characterizes the time that constitutes our time as "empty." By "empty," Taylor means that, as modern people, we think of time as if it were a container that can be filled up by our indifferent likes and dislikes. As a result, our sense of time has a homogeneous character in which all events can be placed in unambiguous relations of simultaneity and succession. Taylor suggests our view of time has a corresponding account of our social world as one constituted by a horizontal space, that is, a space in which each of us has direct access to time without the assistance of a mediator.

If Taylor's characterization of our time as empty is accurate—a characterization I suspect many of us will find forces a self-recognition that we would prefer to avoid—we can better understand why we have trouble knowing how to acknowledge that we are Mary's people. We may be ready to acknowledge that the stories that constitute our lives are ones we may not have chosen, but we nevertheless believe that when all is said and done, we get to make our lives up. But Mary did not choose to be Mary, the one highly favored by God. Rather, she willingly accepted her role in God's salvation by becoming the mother of God—even while asking, "How can this be?"

How extraordinary it is that we know the name of our Lord's mother! The time we live in as Christians is not empty. It is a time constituted by Isaiah's prophecy that a particular young woman will bear a son whose name will be Immanuel. It is a time constituted by a young woman named Mary who was chosen by God to carry and give birth to one fully human and fully God. It is a time that is made possible by Joseph, her husband, who trusted in what he was told by the Holy Spirit. It is *that* time in which we exist. It is a time that gives us time in a world that thinks it has no time to worship a Lord who has Mary as a mother.

"Do you believe in the virgin birth?" was a question generated by a world that had produced people who feared they no longer knew the time they were in. That is, they had no other way to tell time but to think they must force time to conform to their fantasy that they could make time be anything they wanted it to be. "Do you believe in the virgin birth?" was a desperate question asked by a desperate people. It was a question asked by good people lost in a world that they feared threatened all they held dear. Yet it was a question that could only distort the gospel by failing to see that the good news is that Mary is the Mother of God. I fear, however, that question, "Do you believe in the virgin birth?" remains in the hearts of many who count themselves Christians.

If you try to answer that question, I fear you will only distort the gospel. Mary the Mother of God is not an answer to *that* question. Mary, the Mother of God, is not an answer to *a* question. Mary, the Mother of God, is a declarative assertion that makes clear that it was from Mary that Jesus assumed our humanity by becoming a creature of time.

That Mary is the Mother of God means we do not begin with speculative accounts about God's existence or nature. Our God is to be found in Mary's womb. Because our God is to be found in Mary's body, we believe that same God desires to be taken in by us in this miraculous gift of the holy Eucharist, the body and blood of Christ. In partaking of this gift, we are led to ponder, to ask with Mary, "How can this be?" But the gift makes the question possible, because through this gift we become participants in a time that is filled with God's providential care of us. We are Christians. We live in Mary's time.

Such a time is anything but empty. Rather it is a time storied by people whose lives witness to the Lord of time, the Lord who encompasses all life and death. I suggested above that there was a politics often associated with the question: "Do you believe in the virgin birth?" There is also a politics that is entailed by our affirmation that Mary is the Mother of God. The politics of Mary is a politics of joy characteristic of a people who have no reason to be desperate. They have no reason to be desperate because they have faith in the Lord of time.

So on this Sunday, a Sunday when Christmas seems so near, let us remember that because we are Mary's people, we are in no hurry. Let us wait in patience for the Christ-child whose own life depended on the lives of Mary and Joseph. The Word of God was made flesh. He came so that we might experience the fullness of time. Let us wait with Mary and Joseph for the child who will redeem all of time. Let us wait with patience and hope so that the world may discover that time is not empty. Rather, time remains pregnant with God's promise found in Mary, the Mother of God.

3. The Silence of Words

"The Sound of Silence"
Church of the Holy Family
Chapel Hill, North Carolina
June 23, 2013

1 Kings 19:1–15
Psalms 42 and 43
Galatians 3:23–29
Luke 8:26–39

"There is no longer Jew or Greek, there is no longer slave or free, there is no longer male or female: for all of you are one in Christ Jesus. And if you belong to Christ, then you are Abraham's offspring, heirs according to the promise." Finally, like me, you have to be thinking, finally. Finally, we have a Paul that does not embarrass us. We have had to struggle with Paul's seeming indifference to slavery; we have cringed at some of his judgments about the place of women in the church; we have had to put up with his judgmental attitude about sex; but now it seems we have a Paul with whom we share some fundamental convictions.

After all, what could be more precious to us than the democratic commitment to treat all people equally? We want everyone to be treated fairly. We want to be treated fairly. We want to be treated equally not only at work and home but also in the church. The church accordingly should be inclusive, excluding no one. Of course, Christians no longer have a problem about Jews or Greeks, slaves or free, but certainly equality between males and females remains a challenge. In spite of some of Paul's judgments in some of his other letters about what women can and cannot do in the church, in this passage from Galatians, Paul seems to be on the side of equal treatment. He finally got one right.

There is just one problem with our attempt to read Paul as an advocate of democratic egalitarianism. As much as we would like to think that Paul is finally on the right side of history, I am afraid that reading this text as an underwriting of egalitarian practice is not going to work. Paul does not say Jew or Greek, slave or free, male or female are to be treated equally. Rather, he says that all who make up the church in Galatia, and it is the church to which he refers, are one in Christ Jesus. It seems that

Jew and Greek, slave and free, male and female have been given a new identity more fundamental than whether they are a Jew, slave, or free. In so far as they now are in the church, they are all one in Christ.

For Paul, our unity in Christ seems to trump equality. Let me suggest that this is not necessarily bad news for us, because one of the problems with strong egalitarianism is how it can wash out difference. In truth, most of us do not want to be treated like everyone else, because we are not simply anyone. Whatever defeats and victories have constituted our lives, they are our defeats and victories, and they make us who we are. We do not want to be treated equally if that means the history that has made us who we are must be ignored. For example, I think being a Texan is one of the determinative ontological categories of existence. I would never say I just happen to be a Texan, because being a Texan, particularly in North Carolina, is a difference I am not about to give up in the hope of being treated fairly.

But what does it mean to be "one in Christ Jesus"? Some seem to think being one in Christ means Christians must be in agreement about matters that matter. In particular, we must be in agreement about the beliefs that make us Christian. The problem with that understanding of what it means to be one in Christ is there has been no time in the history of the church when Christians have been in agreement about what makes us Christians. To be sure, hard-won consensus has from time to time been achieved, but usually the consensus sets the boundaries for the ongoing arguments we need in order to discern what we do not believe.

That we often find ourselves in disagreement, moreover, is not necessarily the result of some Christians holding mistaken beliefs about the faith. Rather, our differences are often the result of our being a people scattered around the world who discover different ways of being Christian given the challenges of particular contexts and times in which we find ourselves. If we were poor we might, for example, better understand the role of Mary in the piety of many that identify themselves as Roman Catholics.

If unity was a matter of agreement about all matters that matter, it clearly would be a condition that cannot be met. We certainly cannot meet the demand at Holy Family. For example, I happen to know some of you are fans of the New York Yankees. Clearly, we have deep disagreements that will not be easily resolved. So it surely cannot be the case that our unity in Christ Jesus is a unity that depends on our being in agreement about all matters that matter.

There is another way to construe what it might mean to be one in Christ Jesus that I think is as problematic as the idea that our unity should be determined by our being a people who share common judgments about what makes us Christian. Some, for example, seem to think that unity is to be found in our regard for one another. We are united, because we are a people who care about one another. Some even use the language of love to characterize what it means for us to be united in Christ.

The problem with that way of construing our unity is it is plainly false. We do not know one another well enough to know if we like, much less love, one another. Of course, it is true that you do not have to like someone to love them, but I suspect like me you tend to distrust anyone who claims to love you but does not know you. If love, as Iris Murdoch suggests, is the nonviolent apprehension of the other as other, then you cannot love everyone in general. The love that matters is that which does not fear difference. Christians are, of course, obligated to love one another, and such love may certainly have a role to play in our being one in Christ Jesus. But that does not seem to be what Paul means in this letter to the Galatians.

Paul seems to think that what it means for us to be one in Christ Jesus is a more determinative reality than what our personal relations with one another make possible. Indeed, when unity is construed in terms of our ability to put up with one another, the results can be quite oppressive. For the demand that we must like or even love one another can turn out to be a formula for a church in which everyone, quite literally, is alike. A friendly church can be a church that fears difference. As much as we might regret it, I suspect it remains true that those we like, and perhaps even love, are those who are just like us. Whatever it means, therefore, for us to be one in Christ Jesus, it surely cannot mean that we must like one another.

How then are we to understand what it means to be one in Christ Jesus? Paul says that if we belong to Christ, we are Abraham's offspring and heirs according to God's promise that he would make us his people. Once we were no people, but now we are a people who through baptism have been clothed anew by Christ. What it means for us to be one in Christ is to be a people who have been given a new story. We are the children of Abraham, which means the kind of struggle against idolatry Elijah faced is now part of our history. We are one with our Jewish brothers and sisters, because together we face a world that knows not the God who refuses to let Elijah accept defeat.

The very fact that the Old Testament is Christian scripture means the story of Israel's faithfulness, trials, and persecutions must illumine our life as the church of Jesus Christ. For example, I suspect there are few things we do as Christians more important than pray the Psalms. The Psalms give voice to Israel's faith in God even when the enemies of that faith, the Ahabs and Jezebels, seem to have the upper hand. Thus Israel asks,

> Why have you forgotten me?
> And why do I go so heavily while the enemy oppresses me?
>
> While my bones are being broken,
> my enemies mock me to my face;
>
> All day long they mock me
> and say to me, "Where now is your God?" (Psalm 11b–13)

"Where now is your God?" is a question that haunts us. It haunts us not because we do not believe in God, but because we simply don't know how to answer it. We stammer for explanations. We believe God remains present in this world—in our lives. And we want desperately to believe we have been made one with Christ Jesus, but that seems like some ideal that has little bearing on reality. In fact, the evidence seems to testify to God's absence. To read the Psalms is to discover that the current challenges posed by the "new atheists" to the faith are not nearly as significant as those voiced by the Psalmist. Thus Elijah asks God to take his life because, being "no better than his ancestors," he assumes his situation is hopeless. What can it mean for this to be the history that makes us one with Christ?

I think it has everything to do with learning to hear God's silence as Elijah does. Better put: it means that we become for the world God's silence, so that the world may know that the salvation offered by God is not just another failed ideal. Elijah stands on the mountain to be encountered by God. There is a mighty wind, but the Lord is not in the wind. Neither is God in the earthquake, nor to be found in the fire. Rather, God is in what is described as "the sound of sheer silence"—a silence we are told that Elijah heard. We cannot help but wonder how silence can have a sound that can be heard, but then we must remember that this is God who is passing by Elijah.

I suspect if you are like me you would prefer a God who chooses to be in the wind, earthquake, or fire. We want a God who leaves little doubt about what it means to be God. We are not at all sure we want to be a people capable of hearing the "sound of silence." To hear the sound of silence means we face a God we cannot make serve our peculiar purposes. Like Elijah, we must first listen.

In truth, I find listening to be a hard discipline. I am seldom silent. I am, after all, an academic. I am not supposed to be at a loss for words. I am to be the kind of person who always has something to say. To learn first to be silent, to listen, threatens loss of control. My only power is the power of the word. So I try to anticipate what you are going to say, prior to what you say, so I can respond before you have said anything.

I try to play the same game with God. I want God to be loquacious. I want God to be like me. But God is not like me. That God is present in silence suggests that listening to silence is as essential as listening to what God says. This is what Elijah had learned about the God of Israel. And this is what we must learn if we are to hear the word of the Lord today. For the same Word that speaks to us today has spoken through the prophets. And God has not left us without resources for learning to be faced by silence.

What it means for us to be one in Christ, moreover, I think we discover in the silence that engulfs us as we confront the most decisive moment of God's silence, that is, the crucifixion. That is when we learn to listen to the sheer silence of our God. That is the moment we discover we are one in Christ Jesus. During Holy Week, we hear again how our Lord is silent before his accusers. On Maundy Thursday, we kneel in silence as the body and blood of our Savior is carried away, the nave is stripped, and we leave the church. That silence, the stunning silence of the crucifixion, is the silence of our God who refuses to save us by violence. The silence of Jesus is echoed by the silence of those who helplessly stood by with his holy mother to bear witness to his silent submission to the Father's will, for our sake. It is this silence that makes us one with him in a manner more determinative than our agreements or commonalities.

This means that there are times when asked, "Where now is your God?" we best remain silent. Yet it is enough. By learning to be silent, we have learned to be present to one another and the world as witnesses to the God who has made us a people who once were no people. Such a people have no need to pretend we know more about our God than we do. We need not pretend that we do not face the reality of death and how that reality makes us doubt if our lives have purpose. But we believe we have been given every gift needed to remain faithful. Just as Elijah was commanded to eat so that he would have strength for the journey, so we have been given this bread and wine which, through the power of the Holy Spirit, makes us one with and in Christ Jesus.

"There is no longer Jew or Greek, there is no longer slave or free, there is no longer male or female; for all of you are one in Christ Jesus." This is indeed good news, but the new identity we have in Christ is one that cannot be attested to by words. The words we use must be surrounded by the silence of God. To belong to Christ, to belong to one another, means we must, like Christ—and like Elijah before him—trust in the sound of that silence.

4. A Concluding Word

Neither of these sermons makes front and center the agenda of recovering the true "end of words," but I hope they nonetheless suggest how trying to preach after Christendom demands we resist trying to make the sermon "useful." We must try, or at least I tried in these sermons, to refresh our words by calling attention to their scriptural grammar. We must try to help our listeners and readers rediscover how what we have to say about God draws at once on our everyday talk as well as the rediscovery of how odd our everyday talk is. That is not easily done, but we have the advantage of having Richard Lischer's insistence that we must never stop seeking "the true end of words, which is the ultimate purpose of the act of preaching."[15]

---

15. Lischer, *The End of Words*, 132–133.

12

"Do You Love Me?"

Duke Divinity School
Durham, North Carolina
Closing Convocation
April 18, 2013

Acts 9:1–20
Psalm 30
Revelation 5:11–14
John 21:1–19

In this time—a time called modern—a time when those that bear the name Christian always seem to carry the burden of proof—in this time when the church seems consumed by scandal and self-doubt—in this time when those going into the ministry are unsure what that may entail or, indeed, whether they will even have a job after graduating from seminary—in such a time, it is difficult to avoid a defensive posture when asked why we persist in being Christian.

God knows we try. Let us show you, we seem to say to anyone polite enough to listen, why we think believing in God makes all the difference. Let us show you why participating in worship may be refreshment for the soul. Let us show you why the Christian way of life is good for Christian and non-Christian alike. Let us show you how being a Christian can and should put you on the progressive side of history. Let us show you that our faith does justice, making possible a politics otherwise unavailable. I have no doubt we believe such "showings" to be true, but too often such "showings" are desperate attempts to assure ourselves that we know what we are about by calling ourselves Christians.

But then the Lord asks: "Do you love me?" It seems an odd question for Jesus to ask. We can't help but wonder if some redactor got it wrong. Or perhaps some failure in communication may have taken place; someone must have misheard Jesus's conversation with Peter. It was probably the person who counted the fish. We are not even sure we can trust John to have gotten it right. The disciples have been with the resurrected Jesus, but they go on fishing? They go back to the ordinary life they had prior to following Jesus? It seems unimaginable.

Moreover, Jesus is not supposed to ask Peter—or us—to love him. His job is to love *us*. In spite of our failures to be faithful disciples, in spite of our confusions about what it means to be Christian, in spite of our prideful presumption that we are our own creator, in spite of our sins, Jesus is supposed to love us. Is this not the heart of the gospel: "For God so loved the world that he gave his only Son, so that everyone who believes in him may not perish but have eternal life" (John 3:16)? This passage from John seems to have gotten off script; we are to be assured of Jesus's love for us and not the other way around.

God's love of us, moreover, is crucial for what we take to be our fundamental task as Christians, that is, because Jesus first loves us we must and can love one another. Our love for one another is crucial for our "showings" to the world. Thus, the world, the unbelieving world, often gives us credit as Christians, because we at least seem to love and care for one another. Some say: "Look at those Christians. See how they love one another. They may believe some crazy things, but they usually make pretty good neighbors."

It is even the case that because we have been loved by Jesus, the love Christians show in response is not restricted to other Christians. Again, the unbelieving world notes that God's love for us makes possible our love for the world. Those Christians love the outcast, the unlovable, the destitute, those ravaged by illness and pain. They even love their enemies! Such a love is surely only possible because they think they have first been loved by God. That is the way it is supposed to work. God loves us and we love everyone in return.

But in this Gospel passage, Jesus asks: "Do you love me?" Three times he asks Peter if he loves him. Jesus even asks Peter if he loves him more than his other disciples do. We are tempted to think Jesus's question is meant specifically for Peter. Peter and Jesus have had a tangled relationship. Jesus is testing Peter to see if he is a rock on which the church can be built. So there is probably good reason Jesus asks Peter this question three times—one for each time Peter had denied him. Jesus is giving Peter a chance to "take it back," so to speak. But surely he wouldn't ask it of us.

I have no doubt that Peter has a particular role in God's providential care of creation through the church, but I do not think that means we can restrict Jesus's question, "Do you love me?" as one only relevant to Peter. It is surely right that all that Jesus is and does manifests God's love for us, but it is no less true that Jesus asks us, as he asked Peter, "Do you love me?" If you are like me, you would prefer to read the passage as one limited to that particular context in order to excuse yourself from having to answer. How on earth can I answer that question without immediately feeling trite? I suspect I am more ready to believe in Jesus than I am to love him. I am, after all, a theologian.

I fear the education you have received may reproduce a similar effect. Seminaries, at least this seminary, are schools rightly committed to teaching you what the church believes. Those of you who are about to graduate have hopefully been well-formed theologically. You have been prepared to read the Bible as the very word of God. You are prepared to believe in Jesus as God's Messiah. You are prepared to believe that Jesus is God incarnate, very God and very man. You have been prepared to say Father, Son, and Holy Spirit while affirming that God is one. You have been prepared to know that not all liturgical orders are created equally.

By the very fact you have endured your education, your formation for the ministry, you have witnessed your willingness to make sacrifices on behalf of Jesus. Upon graduating, most of you will go into some form of ministry. The ministry is no longer a profession of status. You are willing to sacrifice status. You also are not going to make much money. Moreover, you are going to be subject to the omnivorous desires of people who think you have all the time in the world to meet their needs, because you do not work for a living. In short, you are already—or will soon be—doing everything required by anyone who believes God loves them.

But today Jesus asks, "Do you love me?" I suspect most of us are not prepared to answer that question, because we fear, if we answer honestly, what we may have to say. We are not at all sure we love Jesus. We are not at all sure we even know what such a love entails. What could it possibly mean that Jesus asks us to love him? To ask to be loved suggests a vulnerability that we are not sure Jesus should have. That Jesus might want our love suggests he might even be like us, that is, a human being. We think if Jesus is the manifestation of God's love for us, he must not need our love. What he needs is our belief that he is who he says he is.

"Do you love me?" The question cannot be avoided. The question certainly cannot be avoided by those in the ministry. For, as I think you will discover, the ministry is a playground of manipulative games derived from distrust and envy that too often produce lives of destructive self-hate. If you do not love Jesus, you will find it almost impossible to survive your calling. That God first loved us is true, but that love is designed to make us (and I use this description recognizing its danger) fall in love with Jesus. The Father desires that those whom the Son calls to be his disciples are made to be, through the work of the Holy Spirit, unembarrassed lovers of Jesus.

To fall in love with Jesus is frightening. You have, I suspect, fallen in and out of love a number of times. Falling in love has the frightening effect of losing control of yourself with the result that you end up making one disastrous decision after another. So along the way, we develop self-protective strategies to avoid the costs, if we are again tempted to fall in love. Yet Jesus asks you, Jesus tempts you, Jesus means to seduce you, to fall in love with him—not for his sake, but for your sake and the sake of his sheep. There are interesting resonances between this passage from John's Gospel and the passage from Acts. In both passages, we learn that to love the Lord requires dispossession, losing control.

The Lord asks Peter, "Do you love me?" The Lord asks Paul, "Why do you persecute me?" Both questions have a disorienting effect and both encounters are calls to ministry. What might these passages teach us about the ministry to which we have been called? What does our love look like to the Lord? It is crucial to note Jesus does not ask Peter to tend and feed Peter's sheep. The people Peter is to feed and tend, the people you are to serve, are not yours. They belong to Jesus. This is why the Lord says to Paul, "Why are you persecuting me?" and not "Why are you persecuting them?" His love binds us to him, and our love of him, therefore, binds us to one another. Thus to serve the Lord means to lose oneself—a disorienting, frightening, and even embarrassing prospect. It will mean losing control of our lives—which may sometimes feel like you are losing control of your ministry. And so, from time to time, you will need someone like Ananias, another one of God's servants, to remind you that you are not your own; you are an instrument whom God has chosen to serve and feed his sheep.

But what does such love look like? It will mean finding joy in the work you've been given. Though it is often tiresome, your work is characterized by joy, because we cannot imagine anything better than serving the One we love. For to love Jesus is to be so overwhelmed by his life that we no longer think we must choose between love of ourselves, love of others, and love of God. The beauty of ministry is the holiness that comes from laboring in love. It is hard work to be sure, but it is the work of salvation.

But be careful! Please note I am not recommending that you "try" to love Jesus. "Trying" can be an indication of our continuing attempt to love Jesus on our own terms, and it is often a response to misconceptions about the kinds of feelings we must have if we are "really" in love. Reduced to feeling, love becomes a narcissistic fantasy and ministry becomes tyranny. I began by observing we are often tempted to prove the validity of our faith by showing the world how good and beneficial we are to society. There is no doubt that our Christian witness to the world is important. But when that witness is burdened by "proof" it is no longer a witness to love. The work of love is not about proof; it is about Jesus. The Scripture for today assures us that our work is to love and serve the Lord by serving his sheep. That's it. It is his work, through the Holy Spirit, to draw people unto himself. Like the disciples in the passage from John, our job is to listen and cast our net when and how he instructs. But only the Lord can provide the fish. Like Ananias in the passage from Acts, we must obey despite our fears; for it is the Lord's work to change our hearts, just as he changed the heart of Paul.

So when Jesus asks Peter if he loves him, he is not suggesting that Peter should try harder. Rather his question is meant to help Peter discover the love that has already possessed his life. The Lord knew both Peter and Paul would die martyrs' deaths. He knew their love of him would lead to their dying as he had died, so that he may be glorified. He knew that such a death is only possible when one has been possessed by divine love. And he knew divine love has conquered death.

But what does such love look like for you as you leave this place? Such love is that which will possess you Sunday after Sunday as you lead God's people in adoration of the Lamb who was slaughtered and is therefore the one worthy to "receive power and wealth and wisdom and might and honor and glory and blessing!" To love Jesus means week after week you look forward to engaging the Scripture in preparation to preach God's word for God's people. To love Jesus means people will see, even when you have celebrated the Eucharist a thousand times, that you are overwhelmed by what God is doing through you at the altar. For in this meal, this great meal of love and thanksgiving, we discover what it means to be in love with Jesus.

That is finally what the time you have spent in seminary is about—that is, to help you love Jesus. If we are ardent lovers of Jesus, I think we will find we need no longer take a defensive posture toward the world. The world, distrustful that anyone can be trusted to be loved, is dying to know who might be worthy of its love. "Do you love me?" Hopefully, we can say with Peter, "Lord, you know everything; you know that I love you." With our belts fastened, let us follow him wherever he leads. And may your love of Jesus be manifest in the tending of his sheep.

13

"Resurrection"

St. Thomas's Church, Whitemarsh
Fort Washington, Pennsylvania
April 6, 2014

EZEKIEL 37:1–14
PSALM 130
ROMANS 8:6–11
JOHN 11:1–45

Our texts for today are saturated with death. We should not be surprised. We are, after all, still in Lent. It was not that long ago that we were told that we are dust and to dust we shall return. Emblazoned with ashes on our foreheads, we were reminded that ours is a cruciform faith. I always find it odd that some characterize Christianity as an escapist faith, because we allegedly deny the grim character of life. I cannot imagine a more realistic faith than the Christian faith. At every turn, we are told that we are death-determined creatures and that our lives—our all-too-brief lives—at the very least will be complex, if not difficult.

You may wonder, however, about my claim that our texts for today are about death. I am sure, like me, when you heard Ezekiel 37 you could not resist hearing the familiar refrain, "Dem bones, dem bones, them dry bones, gon' rise again." That song seems to suggest that Ezekiel's vision is not about death, but rather about the overcoming of death through the prophetic word. The bones are reunited by the sinews of the prophetic word. They are given breath by the prophet's calling on the four winds to give life. Surely, this is about life, not death.

Ask yourself, however, what must have happened for such a valley of dry bones to exist? This is a horrible image. A valley filled with skulls and bones so scattered that there is no clear indication of which arm belongs to which body. The valley is no cemetery. The valley is a site of massacre. That is why these bones are described as the bones of the slain. These folk did not die a natural death. They were slaughtered. These are the bones of those who have died a meaningless death in a country that is not their country. These bones may be brought back to life, but death—death in a foreign land—was and will be again their fate.

Yet surely, you may object, the story of the raising of Lazarus is not drenched with death. The very description, "the raising of Lazarus," suggests this is a story about the triumph of life over death. To be sure, Jesus raises Lazarus from the dead, but Lazarus's reprieve will not last long. This is the resuscitation of a corpse, but Lazarus will not be spared death. Lazarus may be one of the most unfortunate human beings to have ever existed. He will have to die twice. What good is that? His second death is still to come, but he must now experience life having already tasted death.

Jesus makes clear in every exchange he has regarding Lazarus's death that this miracle is not about Lazarus; this is about Jesus. If we fail to note that this is primarily about Jesus, we will miss some of the oddities of the text. For example, we are told that Lazarus was someone that Jesus loved. But when Jesus is told that Lazarus was sick, indeed he was so sick he might die, Jesus "stayed two days longer in the place where he was." It seems that Jesus, who says Lazarus's illness is not unto death but rather is for "God's glory, so that the Son of God may be glorified through it," is in no hurry to help Lazarus. He waits two days before moving to Judea where Lazarus lives, because he seems to want to make sure that when he arrives there will be no question that Lazarus is dead.

We dare not miss, moreover, that the trip to Lazarus's home in Judea is a journey fraught with danger and, as it turns out, death. Jesus tells his disciples that it is time to go to Judea, but the disciples suggest to him that this is not a good idea. To go to Judea is to make oneself vulnerable to being arrested and killed by those within Judaism that find him to be a threat. To go to Judea is to enter again the politics of the world—a politics determined by the fear of death. Yet Jesus says he is going to make this journey through death, because Lazarus has "fallen asleep."

The disciples find that to be a hopeful description. If Lazarus has only fallen asleep, then he may recover without the help of Jesus. If Lazarus is only sick, they can stay where they are and not risk the death that awaits them in Jerusalem. And so, Jesus tells them plainly that "Lazarus is dead." He must go to Judea, and the disciples must follow. The disciples are in the process of learning that there is no alternative. They must follow Jesus to Judea—"Let us go, that we may also die with him."

Arriving at Bethany, Jesus is met by Martha. She tells Jesus that if he had been there, Lazarus would not have died. We do not know why Martha thought Jesus could have saved Lazarus. All we need to know is that Martha believes Jesus could have saved Lazarus from dying. Jesus seems to underwrite Martha's understanding of his power, but again a mistake seems to have been made. Martha responds to Jesus's claim that Lazarus will be raised by saying they know that all will rise again on the last day. Jesus, however, is not in the least interested in such speculative accounts of life beyond death. Instead, he tells Martha that "I am the resurrection and the life. Those who believe in me, even though they die, will live, and everyone who lives and believes in me will never die. Do you believe this?"

Martha responds with an enthusiastic avowal that she understands that Jesus is the Messiah, the Son of God, who is coming into the world, but she clearly does not "get it." Mary joins Martha in the exchange with Jesus, but this only results in further speculation about what would have happened to Lazarus if Jesus had been there. Jesus is, as we say in the South, none too pleased by the ongoing discussion about what difference his "being there" might have made. We are told he was "greatly disturbed in spirit and deeply moved" and even shed tears. Whether they were tears of sadness or of frustration, we cannot tell. What we know for sure is that he raised Lazarus, whose body had already been in the tomb for four days, from the grave. He commanded them to unbind the cloth that held him and to "let him go."

Again, we are tempted to see Lazarus being given new life as the climax of this event. But Lazarus, like you and me, still awaits death. The ever-present reality of death—our deaths—is something that we surround with a shroud of silence. Notice, for example, how difficult it is for us to talk candidly with the gravely ill about their approaching death. We say we do not want to rob them of hope, but in fact, we do not want to confront their death. We do not want to acknowledge that they are dying, because we do not know what we should say. Death threatens our speech with futility, because death is not just a biological event. It is a reality that we fear may rob our living of any significance.

Our difficulty with comprehending our death and the death of others has resulted in what Bill May has astutely identified as the pornographic character of death in our culture. The pornography of sex is the depiction of sex abstracted from the human emotions that save sex from reduction to technical gymnastic skills that finally cannot escape being boring. When sex becomes separated from the intimacy that a history of faithfulness has made possible, all that is left is speculative possibilities about what might be done with how many. In a similar fashion, when death is abstracted from human emotion, all that is left are the infinite possibilities of killing as many as possible in ever increasing, imaginative ways. Death, particularly as displayed in movies and video games, reflects our loss of the relation of death and grief.

Consider how death is reported in the news. Those that produce the news seem to know that we have a morbid desire to know how someone died—in an automobile accident—because, as Tolstoy observed, a passion for finding the "cause" of someone else's death can be a way of satisfying ourselves that they died accidentally or fortuitously by virtue of special circumstances affecting the one who died (but not me). It seems that we are at once obsessed by death while striving in every way possible to conceal its power over our lives. Accordingly, we ask those charged to care for us when we are ill to do everything they can to get us out of life alive. This is yet another form of self-protection, as it means we then get to blame health-care providers for any miseries related to keeping us alive at all costs.

Yet the reality of our deaths is hard to repress for a lifetime. I am seventy-three. I am beginning to realize that death is not just a theoretical possibility—even for me. One strategy for dealing with our impending deaths is expressed in Martha's presumption that death can be comprehended by a general theory about life after death. Martha believed that we are all slated to rise at a specific time. Most of us believe that we possess some aspect of eternity that will insure some kind of survival beyond death. The only problem with those strategies is they forget that only God is eternal. We are finite.

Jesus does not say that we are eternal. Rather he says, "I am the resurrection and the life. Those who believe in me, even though they die, will live, and everyone who lives and believes in me will never die." Rather than supplying us with a theory to satisfy our longing for life after death,

Jesus asks us to follow him to Judea where we will face those that would kill us for refusing to live as though death can be fought off through violence. If Christian hope amounts to little more than an expectation that everything is going to be okay in the end, then Christian faith will not be powerful enough to resist the impulse to defend life by enacting violence. Our hope in life beyond death is a hope made possible not by some general sentimental belief in life after death, but by our participation in the life of Christ. This is why life must always be viewed fundamentally as a gift and not a "right" to which we are entitled. We cannot participate in "rights"—we can only exercise them in self-destructive ways.

Such a participation is surely what Paul meant by contrasting our life in the Spirit with that of the flesh. Paul's contrast between the Spirit and the flesh is not a contrast between the ephemeral and the material. Life in the Spirit *is* a fleshly life, if it is the flesh of Christ's body. That flesh, the flesh of Christ's body, is the flesh animated by the Spirit. Paul, therefore, says that to set the mind on the flesh, a flesh that is not Christ's, is death but to set our minds on the Spirit is life and peace. That the Spirit for Paul produces peace is an indication that this miracle is about the formation of a people who Paul believes can make a difference in the world of violence.

The Spirit has a body. We call that body the body of Christ. That same Spirit is the agent that through baptism joins us to Christ's resurrected body, gathering our dry bones and enlivening them unto the one through whom and for whom we are made. This is the life—life with Christ— made possible in the Spirit who ensures that whatever death lies before us, we will not die alone. It is this shared hope that gathers and sends us out courageously to follow Jesus on the way to Jerusalem. As we approach ever closer to Holy Week, let us not forget that it is only by our hope in the one who goes before us that we may look upon his death and participate in his singular victory over our own death. May we no longer cling to the frail theories that offer little hope to a world enslaved to the fear of death. Instead, let us cling, this Lent and always, to the Lord Jesus Christ who by his life, death, and resurrection remains the only hope we have that our bones will be reunited in common worship of the one true God.

14

"The Way, the Truth, and the Life"

Church of the Holy Family
Chapel Hill, North Carolina
May 18, 2014

Acts 7:55–60
Psalm 31:1–5, 15–16
1 Peter 2:2–10
John 14:1–14

We are a people haunted by the murderous character of the past century. We are haunted, because we are at once all too aware of the unbelievable taking of life in the twentieth century, yet we must live as if that reality is not part of our lives. How do you go on when what has happened is so horrific that to acknowledge it seems to call into question the everyday? We may be in denial, but denial seems a preferable strategy to the recognition that the history that inhabits us is so bloody.

We find it hard to acknowledge that the past century was one vast killing field, because we thought it would be a time when all forms of dogmatic fanaticism, which were assumed to be the breeding grounds of violence, would be left behind. We thought the twentieth century would be the time when the human spirit would be unleashed to create a more humane world by being freed from the arbitrary traditions that we thought to be the source of our violence. That world, that more humane world, turned out to be a world of unending war. Indeed, it seems we cannot have a social policy that is not a war. Why, for example, must we have a "war" against drugs or childhood obesity?

Nothing is more indicative of the violent character of the last century than the Holocaust—in Hebrew, the Shoah. In what was believed to be the most advanced civilized country in history, a country characterized by an unmatched intellectual culture, were those more than ready to systematically murder Jews for no other reason than they were Jews. That atrocity, a horror beyond our imagination, is almost impossible for us to comprehend. We know the Jews were subjected to mass murder, but killing on such an enormous scale is so hard to imagine that the Holocaust seems like some fantastic tale more like fiction than what we call history.

We, of course, want to say, "The Germans did it." Yet it makes all the difference who the "we" is who hold the Germans responsible. If the "we" is Christian, we cannot deny that the Christianity that made Germany Germany and Europe Europe was one of the factors that made the destruction of the Jews possible. Centuries of Christian fear and prejudice against the Jews created the background that Hitler knew well how to exploit.

We are not just Christians, however, we are Americans. We become defensive if it is suggested that the story of the violence of the last century, or the Holocaust, is part of our story as Americans. We pride ourselves on being a peace-loving people. We did not will this blood-soaked century or the Holocaust into existence. The extent to which we acknowledge that such a characterization of our century is true becomes the extent to which we feel more trapped—victimized—by such a time than agents and perpetrators of such brutality. We did not kill the Jews. We went to war to end that slaughter. We are innocent.

Yet our Good Friday liturgy included in the "Reproaches" this accusation: "I grafted you into the tree of my chosen people Israel, but you turned on them with persecution and mass murder. I made you joint heirs with them of my covenants, but you made them scapegoats for your own guilt."[1] I think it right and good such a reproach is included in our liturgy, because like it or not, we cannot deny that we are inheritors of a history that makes us a people who should acknowledge we are anything but innocent.

I am not unaware that by beginning with this stark account of the violence that has marked our histories I may be making you uncomfortable.

---

1. *The United Methodist Book of Worship* (Nashville: The United Methodist Publishing House, 1992), 364.

I suspect that may be the case, because I know what I have said makes me uncomfortable. But I have begun in this way to make us just a bit sympathetic with those that killed Stephen. We might not have thrown stones at Stephen, but I suspect we might have, like Saul, been willing to hold the coats of those that did throw the stones. That is particularly the case if we attend to why some thought they should stone Stephen.

Our text for today only reports on the stoning of Stephen, but we need to remember what he had said that so enraged those that killed him. To understand why he was killed, why stoning seemed to be the way he must die, we need to attend to the sermon he gave that motivated those that killed him. After having been arrested on trumped-up charges of blasphemy, supported by the testimony of false witnesses that claimed that Stephen had been proclaiming that Jesus would destroy the temple as well as change the customs that Moses had handed on to Israel, Stephen was given the opportunity to address the Sanhedrin. His sermon was a sweeping overview of the history of Israel that was but a recounting of Israel's sins. From the beginning, the people of Israel were unfaithful. The Patriarchs sold Joseph into Egypt. Enslaved in Egypt, the people of Israel rejected Moses by continually questioning who had made him a ruler and judge of Israel. It was the same people who had made a calf of gold in the hope that they would have a god that would insure their existence through sacrifice. Under Solomon, they had built a house for God, but by doing so they failed to recognize that the Most High does not dwell in a house made with human hands. Stephen concludes this bill of particulars by rhetorically asking, What prophets did their ancestors not persecute? According to Stephen, they are a "stiff-necked people" whose stubbornness has led them to betray God by becoming murderers. There is more than a little irony involved in what happens next, because Stephen's judgment that his people have become murderous is confirmed by their stoning of him, thus making Stephen the first Christian martyr.

What is remarkable about Stephen's sermon recounting Israel's unfaithful history is that it is a history he learned from Israel herself. One of the remarkable aspects of Israel's life is her ability to tell the story of God's care for her in a manner that does not attempt to hide her unfaithful response to God's gifts. That Israel was able to so tell her history, I think, has everything to do with her conviction that her story is first and foremost God's story. That story—that is, the story of God's love of Israel—is the story of God's unrelenting desire that Israel be a light to the nations, so that all people can know that there is an alternative to murderous history.

In an interesting way, this means that on the far side of the twentieth century the roles we might have as Christians and Jews in the light of the martyrdom of Stephen are reversed. The story we must tell as Christians is a story of our unfaithfulness—an unfaithfulness horribly manifest in the Holocaust. As Christians, we cannot avoid—just as Israel could not avoid—telling our history as one shaped by the confession of our sins. For it is only through such a telling that we can avoid the temptation to a self-righteous celebration of our achievements, rather than the glorification of God.

Such a glorification is surely found in Stephen's last words, words from the cross itself, "Lord, do not hold this sin against them." How extraordinary! Stephen does not deny that his murder is a sin, but he asks God not to hold it against his killers. That he had the confidence to ask that his murderers might be forgiven surely has everything to do with his seeing the heavens open, revealing the Son of Man standing at the right hand of God. The one crucified has triumphed, making it possible that our histories, our sin-dominated histories, not determine our futures. That our sins may not be held against us does not mean we do not remember our unfaithfulness, but rather that, by being forgiven, the memory of our unfaithfulness is made possible so that we are given a way to go on. The most destructive effect of sin is how we are tempted to justify what we have done in a manner that ensures that we cannot acknowledge what we, in fact, have done. Without such an acknowledgment, we are condemned to repeat time and time again our unfaithfulness.

Those who killed Stephen used deadly stones, but, as we are told in 1 Peter, we have been redeemed by a living stone. That stone, that living stone, that stone that is Christ, has brought into existence a people who once were no people. That people, like the people of Israel, have a history shaped by forgiveness. Make no mistake about this: our confidence that such a way of life is possible, that a Stephen is possible, entails cosmic convictions. Thus Jesus's declaration to Thomas: "I am the way, and the truth, and the life."

We may be quite ready to acknowledge that Jesus is the way, the truth, and the life, but let us confess we are not at all sure we know what to make of Jesus's subsequent claim that "No one comes to the Father except through me." This claim is unsettling to our modern ears, because we fear such a claim does not comport well with our commitment to being a tolerant people. We believe that our ability to tolerate one another is the best alternative we have to avoid the violence that dominates our history.

We should like to think anyone can reach the Father if she wants to, whether or not Jesus is involved. But such a viewpoint misunderstands the spirit of Jesus's statement. Thomas is fearful that he will not know how to find the Lord once he has gone to the Father. Jesus's words are words of comfort and assurance: Thomas need not worry, because the Father has made himself present in the Son. "If you know me, you will know my Father also. From now on you do know him and have seen him." Those who find Jesus's words intolerant forget that the exclusivity of Christ is not a burden, but a gift to all. The Father has given us the Son so that we might see and know the Father's will. In the passage that follows, Jesus speaks of the giving of the Holy Spirit "whom the world cannot receive because it neither sees him nor knows him" (John 14:17). But those who know and follow Jesus will be led by the Holy Spirit and enabled to keep his commandments, which are from the Father.

What does all of this have to do with martyrdom? Unless Jesus is the only way to the Father, the martyr cannot exist. For the martyr's death is her confession that Jesus is Lord, the Messiah of God. The martyrs are those who have died in a manner that make the cross of Christ unmistakable as God's victory over death. Therefore just as the Father glorifies the Son, the Son glorifies those who suffer for his sake. That is why it is so important that we remember the martyrs, that we remember Stephen. Through such a memory, we know there is an alternative history to the history dominated by violence. The martyrs are killed, but those who kill them cannot determine the meaning of their death. For the meaning of their death can only be determined by the one for whom they have died. The Catholic theologian Johannes Metz, therefore, rightly reminds us that remembering the martyrs is a dangerous act. But it is an act we cannot live without if we, a people who once were no people, are to be an alternative to the violence of history. To remember the martyrs is to throw sand in the gears of the world that thinks war and violence are the engine of history.

To be a martyr is to be a witness to Christ. Accordingly, martyrs remain our most truthful form of persuasion. Theologian David Hart observes, "Christianity can only return to its understanding of peace, its unique style of rhetoric, as the sole source of accord; it must always obey the form of Christ, its persuasion must always assume the shape of the gift he is, it must practice its rhetoric under the only aspect it may wear if it is indeed Christian at all: martyrdom."[2]

2. David Bentley Hart, *The Beauty of the Infinite: The Aesthetics of Christian Truth*

Hart's identification of the martyr with rhetoric may strike you as strange, but such an association rightly reminds us that the grammar of martyrdom ensures that God is not a possession of the church, rather God is the God of all people. The martyr is the gift the Father gives to the enemy, offering the ones who kill an encounter with Christ himself. In the case of Stephen, that encounter comes in the rhetoric of forgiveness as Stephen uses Christ's own words to pardon his murderers. No act of forgiveness so great could occur apart from the power of the Holy Spirit, who makes Christ present both to the martyr and the murderer. Let us not forget that the Great Apostle, while still the great persecutor, bore witness to Stephen's martyrdom and heard his last petition. God alone can make such an encounter possible, subsequently offering a way of life, the creation of a people, who not only offer the hope of a peace the world cannot imagine, but, in fact, are that peace. For finally, the alternative to the violence that surrounds us is the beauty manifest in the perfect love we call Trinity. That love binds us together at this table; it frees us from fantasies of being in control of our own histories. We belong to the Lord and, therefore, we belong to one another—past, present, and future.

We are haunted by our inheritance of a murderous past, but through deaths of martyrs like Stephen we have been given the gift that is necessary not to let those histories continue to determine our lives. In Christ, the economy of violence has been overwhelmed by the sacrifice of the Son, creating a people whose lives shine, because they reflect the glory of a resurrected Lord. In Christ, we have seen the Father who is now made present through the Holy Spirit in the body and blood of Christ. So come to the table to share in this meal of a new age. Come let us celebrate the end of sacrifice, for Christ our Lord has been sacrificed for us. Alleluia!

(Grand Rapids: Eerdmans, 2003), 441.

15

"Wounded"

Abilene Christian University
Abilene, Texas
Summit Conference
September 23, 2014

Genesis 32:3–12, 22–32

We live in a time in which those who identify as Christians walk with a limp. We have been wounded. We have lost the social and political power associated with Christendom. I suspect this may even be true in West Texas. Whether being so wounded is good is a matter of debate. But good or ill, we seem to be walking with a limp.

We should like to think that the wound has been inflicted, as Jacob's was, by God—or at least an agent of God. But we rightly worry that our wound is self-inflicted. We worry that if the wound is self-inflicted, the wound may not make us, as it did for Jacob, identifiable as a people named by God. Jacob's wound, a wound that he received because he refused to lessen his grip on the one with whom he had wrestled throughout the night, was accompanied by his being acknowledged as one who strives with God. Thus, his name is changed. He is to be called Israel. Jacob would be the father of a people.

Unlike Jacob, we are not at all sure our wounding makes us such a people. We are unsure what name we should bear. We fear if we are too strident, we will be accused of that worst of all sins in modernity, that is, we might seem intolerant. We have clung to the false promises and presumptions of egalitarianism and have been appropriately wounded, making us doubt we know what we are about.

Our injuries, however, tempt us to engage in narcissistic fantasies that we can somehow regain what we have lost. Some believe all will be well if we can just get straight on what we believe. Others think if we can just find a more user-friendly way to make worship more entertaining for the "unchurched," we will again fill our churches. The list could be extended, but from my perspective, most of these attempts to heal our limp are enacted by a people who have never struggled with Jacob's God.

There is good reason, therefore, to attend to Jacob. There is good reason to attend to Jacob because Jacob is a reminder that we should hope our wounding is God's doing. What God did with Jacob, a seriously compromised human being, should give people like you and me some hope. For Jacob only survived by the grace of God, and grace may be just another word for God's desire to have us grimly hold on, which means we can yet hope we may be a people named by God. If God can make Jacob one of his servants, then it is not outside the realm of possibility that God can even use us. Let me elaborate on this claim by directing your attention to Jacob.

There is perhaps no more interesting person in Scripture than this Patriarch of Israel. He is a charming and delightful con artist. At least he is charming and delightful as long as you are not the subject of his con. He was adept at his artistry, because he had such a good teacher in his mother, Rebekah. It was Rebekah who had Jacob put on Esau's garments that he might receive the blessing Isaac meant for Esau. It was Rebekah who had Isaac send Jacob to Laban that he might find a wife who was not a Canaanite. Jacob, threatened by Esau, gladly made his way to Laban.

On the way, he had the remarkable experience at Bethel in which he saw a ladder that reached to the heavens on which the angels of God ascended and descended. As he slept, the Lord stood beside him, the God of Abraham and Isaac, who promised Jacob he would be protected no matter where he might be. Awaking, Jacob declared that his dream must mean that this place was a gate to heaven, so he named the place Bethel, marking it with a pillar of stones.

One of the worst sermons I ever heard was on this text. The preacher, desperate to make Jacob a model for our faith, suggested that Jacob had a mystical experience that forever changed his life. He was no longer the crafty Jacob, but he had become a knight of faith. According to this preacher, we know he was changed, because he awoke and made a prayer to God. The only problem was the preacher failed to note that Jacob's vow to be faithful to God was in the form of a bargain in which Jacob expected God to keep him safe and ensure that he would always have sufficient food and clothing. Jacob was not changed in the slightest. He remained the crafty guy more than ready to bargain with God.

The only character in the Bible more slippery than Jacob is Laban. The interaction between Laban and Jacob would make a wonderfully funny novel. That Laban was able to have Jacob work for seven years so that he might marry Rachel only to have Jacob mistakenly marry Leah is a story in itself. Needless to say, we are entertained by Jacob finally getting Rachel as his wife, as well as ultimately getting the best of Laban, by some breeding techniques for sheep we will never understand. What we do understand is Jacob leaves Laban a wealthy man who must now confront his brother, Esau.

Jacob knows he has a problem. Esau, as we say in the South, is none too pleased that Jacob has stolen his birthright. Jacob sends presents in the hope he will temper Esau's wrath. Yet, it is reported to him that Esau is coming with four hundred armed men. Jacob immediately recognizes that this is not a good sign. Jacob being Jacob divides his company into two groups sending one company across the Jordan in the hope that Esau will think killing them is sufficient. He also prays, reminding God that God had promised to do good for him, and Jacob wants God to know he should keep his promises.

This finally brings us to Jacob's famous wrestling match. Jacob is alone. We are simply told that "a man" wrestled with him all night without prevailing. The man struck Jacob on the hip, leaving him with a permanent limp, but Jacob would not let go unless the man blessed him. He got more than he bargained for: Jacob got a new name. Scripture leaves the identity of "the man" ambiguous, and so we must take Jacob's word that it was the Lord who wrestled with him and blessed him with a name and a wound. Receiving Jacob's testimony does not, however, leave the matter open or susceptible to a cynical read by those of us who encounter this story as Christians. It is quite the contrary, for to receive Jacob's testimony is precisely what it means to receive the faith of Abraham, Isaac, and Jacob. And it is this faith—this story—that prepares us for receiving Christ. Perhaps what is most significant about Jacob's claim is that it means he has seen God face to face. However, not only does Jacob see God face to face without dying; he does so without changing. He remains the same old Jacob, that is, the Jacob who survives by "cutting a deal."

What are we to make of Jacob? I suppose some might think the bottom line is God can use scoundrels to achieve his purposes. We might take some comfort from such a conclusion. Christians are usually not as clever as Jacob, but he still gives us hope that God can use even us. I think, however, that trying to find some "message" to take away from Jacob's story is far too moralistic.

I think there is no "message" to take away from this account of Jacob's wrestling match. Rather, I would ask you to consider what constitutes a people who would tell the story of Jacob as a defining story for who they are. Of course, the story of Jacob can be understood as a story told by the underdog that suggests how the weak outsmart the strong. But I do not think that is the primary force of what it means for Jacob to receive the name Israel. Israel can be embarrassingly candid about herself, about the character of her forbearers, because it is God—not Israel—that makes Israel unlike any other people. And this same God who refuses to abandon Israel continues to hold us in his grip.

It is possible for us to know that the God of Israel wrestled with Jacob, because this theophany was a foretaste of the theophany of Christ. We know that, in fact, God did become one of us. Our God is incarnate in the man Jesus. He is very God and very man. By becoming one of us, he has grasped us with a grip so firm that there is no escaping. Jacob had been given a new name indicating that he was the father of a people who would strive with God. We too have been given a new name. We are Christians who have been called out of the world, for the world, that the world might know that God has not abandoned us. We know that to be true, because God has wrestled death for us on the cross, receiving there the wound that heals our wounds.

In his wonderful hymn, "Wrestling Jacob" (1742), Charles Wesley wrote:

> What though my shrinking flesh complain
>   And murmur to contend so long?
> I rise superior to my pain:
>   When I am weak, then I am strong:
> And when my all of strength shall fail
> I shall with the God-man prevail.
>
> I know thee, Saviour, who thou art,
>   Jesus, the feeble sinner's friend;

> Nor wilt thou with the night depart,
>> But stay and love me to the end:
> Thy mercies never shall remove,
> *Thy nature, and thy Name is love.*[1]

We are Christians. We are obviously Christians who have been wounded. But the wound that matters is the wound of love. Our Lord refuses to leave us alone, and having been wounded by his love, we have been given the gift of bearing the name "Christian." Let us, like Israel, make the most of our limp. Let us be a people who, like Israel, are able to confess our sins, because we know the story we have to tell is first and foremost God's story. In the process of such storytelling, we will discover that the wound that makes us limp is the source of the strength we need to be a people who have learned to survive in a world that is intent on eliminating all signs of weakness. May we become cleverer so that like Jacob we can learn to wear our wounds well.

---

1. Stanzas 6 and 11 from "Wrestling Jacob" by Charles Wesley, as they appear in S T Kimbrough, Jr., *Partakers of the Life Divine: Participation in the Divine Nature in the Writings of Charles Wesley*, foreword by Peter Bouteneff (Eugene, OR: Cascade, 2016), 89–90.

16

"Citizens of Heaven"

King's College Chapel
University of Aberdeen
Aberdeen, Scotland
October 22, 2014

Genesis 15:1–12, 17–18
Psalm 27
Philippians 3:17—4:1
Luke 13:31–35

"And he believed the Lord, and the Lord reckoned it to him as righteousness." This sentence, this innocent but all-significant sentence, created the time in which we now live. That time is best characterized as "after the Reformation." Thus Brad Gregory's argument in *The Unintended Reformation: How a Religious Revolution Secularized Society* that the "Western world today is an extraordinarily complex, tangled product of rejections, retentions, and transformations of medieval Western Christianity, in which the Reformation era constitutes the critical watershed."[1]

Our complex and tangled lives are testimony to the significance of how this sentence from Genesis determines how we must now live. In particular, how this sentence was read by Luther has, I believe, made it difficult for us to imagine what it might mean to be Christian in this time when Christendom seems to be waning. More accurately, how Luther's

---

1. Brad S. Gregory, *The Unintended Reformation: How a Religious Revolution Secularized Society* (Cambridge: Belknap Press of Harvard University Press, 2012), 2.

use of this sentence has been employed by many of us has meant we have forgotten that salvation involves making us citizens of a time and space that is in tension with all other forms of citizenship. As a result, we have been robbed of resources we desperately need if we are, as Christians, to know how to live in this time "after the Reformation." These are strong claims that no one sermon—and some of you may doubt this is a sermon—should bear, but let me at least try to suggest why I am taking this tack by first directing your attention to what Luther actually says about Abraham.

With his usual love of exaggeration, a characteristic with which I deeply identify, Luther declared in his *Commentary on Genesis* that the fifteenth chapter of Genesis is one of the most important chapters in the Bible. The fifteenth chapter has such importance, according to Luther, because there we are told that the Lord reckons Abraham as righteous because he believed the Lord. The sentence in which the Lord reckoned Abraham righteous, Luther argued, is one of the most important sentences in the whole Bible. If Luther had been raised in the American South, he would have been even more impressed, because the very fact that the Lord "reckoned" Abraham as righteous clearly indicates that God must have a Southern accent.

Luther supported his claims about the significance of this chapter and sentence by calling attention to Paul's use of the sentence in Romans 4:23 and Galatians 3:6. Luther wrote, "from this passage he constructs the foremost article of our faith—the article that is intolerable to the world and to Satan—namely, that faith alone justifies."[2] Luther continues, explaining that "faith consists in giving assent to the promises of God and concluding that they are true. . . . righteousness is nothing else than believing God when he makes a promise."[3]

Luther argues that faith, the steadfast and unwavering reliance on God's grace in Christ, is what saves—not the works of the Law. After all, Abraham believed before the Law had been given. Luther thundered that "this very believing or this very faith is righteousness or is imputed by God Himself as righteousness and is regarded by Him as such."[4] For this reason, Luther went on to assert that "our doctrine that we are justified

---

2. Martin Luther, *Lectures on Genesis: Chapters 15-20*, trans. George V. Schick, vol. 3, *Luther's Works*, ed. Jaroslav Pelikan (Saint Louis: Concordia Publishing House, 1961), 19.

3. Ibid., 19, 20.

4. Ibid., 21.

before God solely through His accounting mercy has its foundation in this passage."[5] Such a faith justifies, not as our own work, but as the work of God. This understanding of justification by faith through grace is arguably the heart of the Reformation. Just as important, I assume the doctrine of justification remains for Protestants today the heart of our hearts.

What could possibly be wrong, therefore, with Luther's use of this sentence to remind us that our salvation is not our doing, but rather what God has done for us? Surely Luther was right to direct our attention to the centrality of this sentence in the letters of Paul. I have no reason to deny either of these claims. My worry is that the use of this sentence to "sum up" the gospel can tempt those of us who identify ourselves as Christians to forget our salvation comes from the Jews. Moreover, when we lose the Jews, we lose our heavenly Savior, and when we lose our heavenly Savior, we no longer believe that our humiliated bodies will be transformed into the body of his glory, so that we are made citizens of heaven.

You have got to be thinking, "What did he just say?" The connection between God's promise to Abraham, what it means to live lives determined by the cross of Christ, and the glorification of our bodies so that we become citizens of heaven is hardly clear. But let me at least try to make the connections by suggesting that what is at stake is the recognition that our salvation is about the engrafting of our bodies into a politics begun by God's promise to Abraham. The emphasis on justification by faith as the summation of the gospel can tempt us to forget our salvation entails that we are made citizens, a people: that just *is* our salvation.

When I lived among the Lutherans, for example, I discovered that the doctrine of justification by faith alone, a doctrine that should provide a profound sense of joy, often produced a deep anxiety. Lutherans were haunted by the thought they might not be justified by their faith. Accordingly, they worked very hard at believing that they believed they were justified by their belief that they were justified by faith. Faith so understood turned out to be an act of believing that did not require you to actually drag your body to church. Even more ironic, faith understood as trying very hard to believe what was hard to believe is exactly what Luther meant by a work!

There is the other small problem, moreover, that when the emphasis on justification is made the heart of the gospel, it is not clear why Jesus ended up on the cross. If his preaching was to assure those to whom he

---

5. Ibid., 22.

preached that they were saved by faith alone, why was Herod trying to kill him? If the gospel is the proclamation that "You are accepted"—an unfortunately vulgarized but widespread account of justification—it surely seems to be a profound mistake to kill someone like Jesus who allegedly had as his central message that we accept our acceptance.

Nor do I think Luther's reading of God's "reckoning" Abraham righteous to be a problem about the relation of faith and works. Luther had no intention of denying the importance of works. In his *Commentary on Genesis*, he says with no hesitation that "faith brings with it a multitude of the most beautiful virtues and is never alone."[6] The question for Luther was not whether works or the virtues follow upon faith, but rather whether faith justifies sinners prior to our doing good works. Luther, however, forcefully asserted that what must clearly be rejected is the "pernicious doctrine" that faith obtains its value from love.

The problem is not that Luther has no way to account for works, but rather Luther does not attend to the content of Abraham's belief. What Abraham believed is that he would have descendants that would be as numerous as the stars. The LORD reckoned Abraham righteous, because Abraham believed that God would make him the father of a great people. God's declaration that Abraham is righteous—the "it" that was what God "reckoned"—was a declaration about bodies. Abraham, a man past the age of begetting children, believed God would make him the father of a people. The righteousness that God reckoned Abraham to have is Abraham's belief he would be the father of a people who by their very existence are God's glory.

If justification by faith is isolated from Abraham's belief that he would be the father of a people, the results can be, and have been, disastrous. Thus, we see Luther's chilling judgment, articulated near the end of his life, that the Jews are no longer God's people. According to Luther, the Jews have been rejected because of their unbelief. God promised to redeem the Jews at a definite time, but Luther observes that that obviously has not happened. As a result, Luther argues that the Jews cannot explain why for hundreds of years they have had to wander the earth without a home, kingdom, or temple. Luther surmises that "this work of wrath is proof that the Jews are surely rejected by God, are no longer his people, and neither is he any longer their God."[7]

6. Ibid., 25.

7. Martin Luther, "On the Jews and Their Lies," trans. Martin H. Bertram, in *The Christian in Society IV*, ed. Franklin Sherman, vol. 47, *Luther's Works*, ed. Helmut T.

Luther missed the fact that even without a home, God's reckoning of righteousness to Abraham had been fulfilled. From generation to generation, Jews refused to let their homelessness, the persecution they endured often at the hands of Christians, stop them from having children. Abraham looked to the heavens to see what God promised, and his descendants reflected the heavens. God's reckoning of righteousness to Abraham is not some general declaration of acceptance, but rather the fleshy existence of a people who exist so the world might know the God who keeps his promises and refuses to abandon us.

Christians are no less fleshy, but there is a difference. Paul tells the Philippians they are to imitate him by observing those who live according to the example he represents. But Paul is without wife and children. That is, he is without descendants—other than the Philippians and us, and this is a crucial fact. For it turns out that we believe on Paul's authority that those of us who follow Christ are Abraham's heirs. We are, moreover, no less bodily than the Jews. But the bodies we bring to the covenant are bodies determined by baptism through which we are made citizens of heaven.

The Lord told Abraham that his people would be as numerous as the stars of heaven. It is, therefore, no accident that Paul tells the Philippians—and us—that our citizenship is in heaven. Heavenly citizenship does not sound bodily, but at least if we attend to Paul's claim in his letter to the Philippians, it is in heaven that we are given our true bodies. For it is from heaven that we expect the Lord Jesus Christ, whose body will transform our bodies, our humiliated bodies, into the body of his glory.

We wonder what that could possibly mean. In *The Kingdom and the Glory*, the Italian political philosopher, Giorgio Agamben, has suggested that the emphasis on glory by Christians is paradoxical. It is so because glory is the essential property of God's eternity, which means nothing can increase or diminish God's glory. Yet we are told that all creatures are obligated to glorify God. Agamben argues that for God to desire that his creatures glorify him is contradictory, because God's glory means he needs nothing. What Agamben misses, however, is that the glory God would have us reflect is the glorified body of Christ.

That body, the body of Christ, is the body we participate in through this meal we share. It is that body (a body that has learned like Jews to live in diaspora) that God reckons righteous. In this time "after the

---

Lehmann (Philadelphia: Fortress Press, 1971), 139.

Reformation," a time when Christians must learn again how to live in a world we know not, it becomes all the more important that we live as heirs of Abraham. To so live means we will be without security of place other than heaven, but surely that is the grandest security to be had. Even more wonderful, God has given us all we need to go on, that is, he has given us a meal of bread and wine, of the body and blood of Jesus, to sustain us on the journey.

If we are to live faithfully in this time "after the Reformation," let us live as confident and bold bodily creatures who trust, as Abraham trusted, that by so living our bodies might reflect the glory of the one alone capable of making us citizens heaven. At the very least, I should think that might mean that because we have been reckoned righteous through the cross and resurrection of Christ, we manifest an infectious joy, because we have no doubt that the Lord reckoned Abraham—and us—righteous. We are citizens of a heavenly politics that makes it possible for us to be a people who are an alternative to the worldly politics based on the presumption that God has not kept his promise to Abraham. But God did reckon Abraham righteous, and on that our salvation depends.

17

"King Jesus"

Christ Church Cathedral
Nashville, Tennessee
November 23, 2014

Ezekiel 34:11–16, 20–24
Psalm 100
Ephesians 1:15–23
Matthew 25:31–46

I am a person committed to Christian nonviolence. I should like for you to be committed to Christian nonviolence. I should like to use this sermon to convince you that as a Christian, as a follower of Christ, you should be committed to living nonviolently. But this is a tricky business, because unless I am very careful, the sermon can easily become coercive. I can assert, as I just did, that you ought to be committed to nonviolence, but, given the structure of Christian worship, you do not get to say anything in response. As a result, my claim that as a follower of Christ you ought to be nonviolent may make you feel like you have come to church only to be assaulted and roughed-up by a pacifist.

That the sermon can become an instrument of violence is a reminder that nonviolence is not just about war and the disavowal of war. To be committed to nonviolence is to be committed to trying to make everything we do, every relation we have, everything we say, enact a nonviolent way of life. To so live is not easy, because we inherit habits of speech and behavior that are manipulative and coercive—often coercive because they are manipulative—and too often such modes of speech fail to be acknowledged as forms of manipulation. This explains my judgment that Southern civility is passive-aggressive behavior turned into an art form. As a result, Southern civility can be one of the most calculated forms of cruelty ever invented by human kind.

I think I can say I am not a person who has ever been tempted to be civil—even as a Southerner! But in truth I am not a Southerner. I am from Texas. That means I often confuse being blunt with saying what I take to be true. The temptation for me, therefore, is to use the sermon to beat you into submission, because I suspect many of you think nonviolence may be a nice idea, but no one can live it. At the very least, I can try to make you feel guilty for not being nonviolent.

The violent character of a sermon so conceived is compounded by the fact that we do not know each other as well we should to have the kind of exchange I am suggesting we need to have about nonviolence. It is always easier to speak hard truths to those we do not know. As a result, even if the truth is spoken, it may betray itself, because it is not spoken in love. By trying to convince you to agree with me about nonviolence, I might get to style myself as prophetic: "I really let those folk at Christ Church have it." But having paid no price for what I have said, any presumption on my part that I have spoken truthfully would only be an indication of self-deception.

You may well be wondering by this point why I have even begun this sermon with these ruminations about nonviolence. This is the feast of Christ the King. What does Christ the King have to do with questions about nonviolence? Kings, after all, use violence to keep themselves in power. Yet it is still true that, once upon a time, it was thought that kings represented forms of social life that offered relative peace in a violent world. Of course, kings fought against kings, but at least within their realm kings seemed to stand for justice and peace.

That we needed kings to perform that task indicates, even in this day in which we no longer think we are ruled by kings, that we live in a world in which we need forms of authority that can secure a relative peace in a violent world. For example, in our *Articles of Religion*, we are told in article thirty-seven that the power of the civil magistrate extends to all men in all things temporal. Even the clergy must obey civil magistrates in all temporal matters. We are, therefore, admonished to recognize that it is the duty of all who profess the gospel to pay respect to the Civil Authority if that authority is "regularly and legitimately constituted." That article was written at a time in which it was assumed that those in civil authority were monarchs to whom loyalty was owed, because that was the way order was maintained. In short, if you wanted peace, you needed a king or queen.

In Scripture, however, kingship was not always celebrated as a "good thing." From the time of Moses to the judges, Israel had no king. At least, she had no king other than God who, tellingly, was to be called the Lord. Indeed, that God was "the Lord" seems to have been the reason Israel did not have a king. How could Israel have a king if God was her king?

But for Israel not to have a king put her at a distinct disadvantage when she came into conflict with the peoples that surrounded her. Her enemies had kings who commanded standing armies. Israel relied on charismatic leaders called judges who, in response to threats, raised up armies. Such a system put Israel at a distinct disadvantage in the international politics of the Ancient Near East. So the people of Israel told Samuel that they desired to be like other nations and asked him for a king. They did so believing that a king was necessary if they were to be safe (1 Samuel 8:19). The tragic figure of Saul was the result.

David, of course, is often held up as the exemplification of what a good king should be. Thus Ezekiel seems to suggest that a new David will be "set up over them." This new David will, like the judges at the gate, govern justly. But Ezekiel does not envision this new David to be a great warrior king. Ezekiel's David is more the prophet and priest whose task is to be a shepherd to his people. Ezekiel represents the emerging conviction in Israel, a conviction no doubt formed in exile, that to have a king was not a good idea. They had learned, as Psalm 100 suggests, that God is the shepherd, and he alone can make them safe.

That Israel's king will be a shepherd, or, as Isaiah would have it, a suffering servant (Isaiah 42), informs Jesus's acknowledgment in Matthew 20:20–34 that he is the son of David who has come as a servant king. What we learn from Jesus's self-identification as a king is that his kingship is not one of absolute power. That Jesus is king means that our understanding of power is now transformed by what we have learned about Christ. What we have learned about Christ, moreover, is that his rule is enacted when the hungry are fed, the thirsty are given drink, the stranger is welcomed, the naked are clothed, the sick are cared for, and those in prison are not abandoned.

In his letter to the Ephesians, Paul expresses what it means for Jesus to be this kind of king by calling him "Lord Jesus Christ." Jesus has been raised from the dead and seated at the right hand of the Father. Accordingly, he is above all rule and authority. He is above all civil magistrates. All things have been put under his feet, and he has been made head over all things for the church that is his body. Paul spells this out further by proclaiming that through Christ's lordship, the church now manifests God's wisdom to the principalities and powers, which have been subjected to God's eternal purpose in the reign of Christ Jesus our Lord (Ephesians 3).

For Paul, the church is the place where the rule of Christ can be seen. That God has not given up on us is demonstrated in God's calling of the church into existence. Thus, Paul makes the astounding claim that the church determines the way things are by imitating how Christ enacted his lordship. The church is a sign for the world that we are not condemned to live violently. But that means the church must live patiently, for patience is the very form of peace enacted by the Son on the cross.

Patience is not only the form of peace, but patience is the power made present through the works of mercy. Too often I fear Christians say they want justice, but what they want is the power of worldly kings. We do so because we assume it is only by having such power that we are able to do some good or to force some order on a violent world. But what it means for Jesus to be Lord is that we have all the time in the world to rule through caring for the hungry.

A people who have learned to live patiently offer hope to a world that believes there is no alternative to violence. All this is expressed in our collect for this morning: "Almighty and everlasting God, whose will it is to restore all things in your well beloved Son, the King of kings and Lord of lords: Mercifully grant that the peoples of the earth, divided and enslaved by sin, may be freed and brought together under his most gracious rule; who lives and reigns with you and the Holy Spirit, one God, now and forever."[1]

Our prayer that the peoples of the earth be freed from sin so that they can be brought together might be considered by many to be a bad idea. As a species when we confront one another, we are just as likely to dislike, fear, and kill one another as we are to live at peace. But that is why it is so important that we are brought together under the kingship of Christ. King Jesus has given us something to do. We are to feed and care for one another. We are able to live in peace with one another, because he

---

1. *The Book of Common Prayer* (New York: Seabury, 1979), 185.

has given us good work to do. It is through having good work to do that we are freed from our fear of one another, which is the breeding ground of our violence.

Just in case you are still not sure what the relation between peace and the declaration of the kingship of Christ may be, let me invoke an authoritative source. In 1925, Pius XI established the Feast of Christ the King with the encyclical *Quas Primas*. He did so because he, like so many, had been stunned by the waste of life in World War One. He observed in his encyclical that the affirmation of Christ as king, particularly in a time when we no longer have kings, is often interpreted as Christ having a metaphorical reign over our hearts and minds. But Pius observed if we ponder the matter more deeply we cannot help but see that the title and power of kingship belong to Christ in the proper and strict sense. In the face of political developments that we now call Fascism, Pius in startling language asserted that peace among nations could only be established through "the restoration of the Empire of Our Lord."[2]

"The restoration of the Empire of Our Lord" seems to suggest that Pius XI wanted to have Christendom restored, which meant that the Catholic church would be given legal standing not had by Protestant churches. He may, in fact, have wanted that, but he thought such recognition must begin with something as simple as the establishment of a feast day such as Christ the King. He did so because he observed that we are bodily people. Accordingly, we need festivals so that "the sacred rites, in all their beauty and variety, may stimulate us to drink more deeply of the fountain of God's teaching, that we make it part of ourselves."[3] Thus, in our closing prayer we give thanks to the God who has "graciously accepted us as living members of your Son our Savior Jesus Christ."[4]

I certainly think and hope Pious XI was right to think peace might be more likely if we had a celebration in the church year of the Feast of Christ the King. I have no idea how the inauguration of the Feast of Christ the King made its way into Episcopal life, but I am glad that at this moment we are celebrating that Christ is king. So I do not need to try to use this sermon to convince you to be nonviolent. I do not need to do so because, if what Pius says is true, we are already discovering what

---

2. Pius XI, *Quas Primas: Encyclical of Pope Pius XI on the Feast of Christ the King* (Vatican City: Libreria Editrice Vaticana, 1925), par. 1, https://w2.vatican.va/content/pius-xi/en/encyclicals/documents/hf_p-xi_enc_11121925_quas-primas.html.

3. Ibid., par. 21.

4. *Book of Common Prayer*, 365.

it means to fall in love with the God of peace whose Son is rightly called King Jesus. That king has made peace possible, because that king refused to use violence to free us from violence. Welcome to this meal of peace in which we become for the world God's peace.

18

"Repentance: A Lenten Meditation"
Church of the Holy Family
Chapel Hill, North Carolina
February 22, 2015

GENESIS 9:8–17
PSALM 25:1–10
1 PETER 3:18–22
MARK 1:9–15

Theologians often make doubtful Christians. I do not mean they make other Christians doubt whether they are or want to be Christian. That may happen, but that is not what I mean by describing theologians as "doubtful Christians." The doubt that I think often characterizes the lives of theologians is that theologians are often unsure if they are Christians. This may be partly attributable to being exposed to intellectual developments that seem to make many Christian convictions problematic. But the problem is deeper than such challenges to the faith. The problem is quite simple—theologians get paid to believe in God.

I have made a good living by being a theologian. If I had ever quit believing, at least if I were a person of integrity, I would have had to find another job. But the very fact I have been paid for being a theologian cannot help but create in me questions about my identity as a Christian. The matter is complicated by the fact that most people identified as theologians in our day are more likely to be servants of the university than the church. Theologians cannot help but wonder if we are Christians not only because we assume an objectivity characteristic of the university that demands a distance from what we assume is our subject, but for the further fact that we get paid by universities to be, or at least to pretend to be, Christians. As a result, we cannot help but entertain the thought that we are more likely to be playing at being a Christian than actually being one.

Why am I imposing on you these pathetic anxieties from the world of theology? I do so because I suspect in some ways the kind of worry that may bedevil the theologian pervades many lives beyond that of the theologian. I think this is particularly true at a time like this—namely, Lent. Lent is a time when we are to examine our lives in the hope that, through such an examination, we will discover and repent of those sins, those impediments, that stand in the way of our being disciples of a crucified Savior.

We are able to undertake such an examination because, as we are told in 1 Peter, "Christ suffered for sins once and for all in order to bring us to God." Yet, it is hard to avoid the sense that we are playing at being sinful. We cannot help but think this is some kind of game. It is almost as if God wants us to be sinful, because God is, or at least we are told that God is, a God of forgiveness. So in order to help God be a forgiving God, we have to play at being sinners—at least during Lent.

For example, think about our Gospel for today. After John was arrested, Jesus came to Galilee proclaiming the good news of God. He said "the time is fulfilled, and the kingdom of God has come near, repent, and believe in the good news." We, of course, are quite glad that the kingdom has drawn near, but it is by no means clear why the kingdom drawing near means we need to repent. Nor do we know what we have done or not done for which we should repent. We are not even sure we know what it means to repent.

But this is Lent, so we are willing to try to come up with something. After all, we often have some sense that we have done something we now regret, so we know we are not perfect. For example, I realize that I should not have been as candid with Mrs. Smith as I was, but there's no denying that she can really get on my nerves. Or, I know I am a bit selfish, but when everything comes out in the wash, I do my bit for others. Or maybe I know I should not lie, but if I had told the truth to X or Y they would have been hurt. You can add to this unending list of our petty failings. After all, we confess we have sinned not only by what we have done, but by what we have left undone. What we have left undone cannot help but cover a range of behaviors that are sufficient to make us sinners.

That said, however, it remains the case that though we know we may be sinners, we have trouble taking that self-description all that seriously. We know we are not perfect, but most of us think we are good enough. The truth is most of us are conventional people who lead good conventional lives. It is not at all clear to us that we are all that sinful, but as I suggested, we are willing to try to play at being a sinner for God's sake—at least during Lent.

That we may have the haunting thought we are only playing at being a sinner, I suspect, involves the more general worry that, in the world in which we now find ourselves, we are not at all sure if we know what it means to be a Christian. I suspect we are not even sure we know what being a Christian looks like. Surely, to be a Christian means more than being a nice person that believes stuff about God. There is, after all, the Sermon on the Mount. But then that is one of the problems: we cannot imagine living out the demands of the Sermon. But because we cannot imagine living the type of lives the Sermon seems to envisage, we cannot help but fear that we are only playing at being Christian.

Something seems to have gone decisively wrong with our attempt to be a repentant people. I think the problem is quite simple. The reason we find it hard to avoid a sense that we are playing at being sinful during Lent is itself a manifestation of our sinfulness. No sin is more basic than the presumption, a presumption schooled by our pride, that we can know on our own what it means to say that we are sinners. Too often, I fear, our attempt to examine ourselves to discover our sins turns out to be an invitation to narcissism.

We do not come to Jesus because our sins need to be forgiven. Rather, we know we need to be forgiven, because Jesus has come to us as the one alone capable of revealing who we are without that knowledge destroying us. Never forget that every Palm Sunday we shout, "Crucify him! Crucify him!"

Sin is not a generalized category to designate that we have done something for which we are later sorry. Sin is an offense against God who, as our Psalm indicates, is a Lord of compassion and love, and it is exactly because God is so that we have revolted. We only know we are sinners, because we are first loved by God. To confess that we are sinners turns out to be a theological achievement, because sin is not a general description that anyone can understand whether they are a Christian or not. In short, sin is not a naturally given category. That non-Christians use sin to describe some failing in their life is a left-over from a past age when Christian speech was assumed as a "given," but that time is quickly disappearing.

As Christians, we believe that we must be taught to be a sinner. That training comes by being confronted by the Son of God who, as Karl Barth has put it, "has accused us by turning and taking to Himself the accusation which is laid properly against us, against all men, against every man. He pronounced sentence on us by taking our place, by unreservedly allowing that God is in the right against Himself—Himself the bearer of our guilt.... This is the humility of the act of God which has taken place for us in Jesus Christ."[1]

The good news is we do not get to be our own judge. We do not get to determine what our sins may be. The devil, the great tempter, would have us believe that we should want to be like that false god, who we assume to be self-sufficient, self-affirming, self-desiring, the supreme being, self-centered and rotating about himself. The problem, of course, is that he is not the God who has come to us in Jesus Christ. That God—the God that has come to us in Christ—is sufficient to Himself, but that sufficiency is the love that has constituted the life of the Trinity from all eternity. Our sin, quite simply, is our refusal to be loved by such a God.

What could possibly account for such a refusal? In a lovely book of prose poems entitled, *Tears of Silence*, Jean Vanier writes:

> I fear
> the mysterious power of compassion
> compassion requires that I have found myself
> and no longer
> play the game
> of putting on a mask, a personage
> pretending to be
> appearing.
>
> Compassion requires
> that I become myself
> accepting my poverty
> letting the Spirit breathe
> move
> live

---

1. Karl Barth, *Church Dogmatics*, vol. IV.1, *The Doctrine of Reconciliation*, trans. G. W. Bromiley, ed. G. W. Bromiley and T. F. Torrance (London: T. & T. Clark, 2004), 445.

love
in me
opening my being
without fear
to the delicate touch
of God's hand
accepting that I am loved
as I am
with my fears and frailties
with my intelligence and competencies
with my heart and with my hopes
free to be myself.[2]

What a startling thought by Vanier. Could he possibly be right that we fear the mystery of compassion? I suspect he is right that we fear compassion, because God is compassion "all the way down." Accordingly, we fear God because we fear knowing who we are. But God has overwhelmed our fear by compassion itself. The name of that compassion is Jesus. We have been made part of that compassion, the compassion that is Jesus, through the sharing of his body and blood. Accordingly, we have little use for our doubts about whether we are really Christians. So do not worry that you worry about whether you are really a Christian. You may think you are only pretending to be a Christian, but by God's grace, God makes us into what we pretend.

This is Lent. Repent! Recognize that those self-centered worries about whether you are really a Christian do neither you nor God any good. Rather, use this time—this sacred time—to prepare to meet the Christ, who for our sake "suffered for sins once and for all in order to bring you (and me) to God."

---

2. Jean Vanier, *Tears of Silence: A Meditation* (Toronto: Anansi, 2014), 58.

19

"He Is Our Peace"

St. Mary's on-the-Highlands Episcopal Church
Birmingham, Alabama
July 19, 2015

Jeremiah 23:1–6
Psalm 23
Ephesians 2:11–22
Mark 6:30–34, 53–56

What we believe as Christians—or better—what Paul says in this passage from Ephesians about what God has done to make us a new people, should stun us. That we exist is almost beyond belief. In fact, it is beyond belief, because we do not have to believe in what we can see. Of course, there is the interesting question of whether we can see the Spirit at work, because most of what we see is our unfaithful response to what God has called us to be. But for all our unfaithfulness, for all our warts, for all of our worries about what it means to be Christians, it matters that we exist. Let me try to elaborate on that observation by directing your attention to our passage from Paul's letter to the Ephesians.

Paul begins by telling the Ephesians that once they were no people, but now through the work of the Spirit they have been made participants in a new humanity. According to Paul, before the Ephesians became followers of Christ, they were people without a shepherd, which means they had no way to know where they were or who they were. They were quite literally lost in the world. The people of Israel were often unfaithful, but

Israel was not lost, because God had storied her, that is, given her a locus, through the covenant. Gentiles were not included in that covenant.

Because Gentiles were a people who were no people, they were without hope, making them strangers to themselves and one another. Yet Paul claims, through the flesh and blood of Christ, God broke through the walls of hostility between Jew and Gentile, making those who once were far off, who were without Christ, citizens in the household of God. That is what is called, using the language of the current academy, a grand narrative.

It is a story, however, that we are not sure "fits" over our lives. The division of the world into Jew and Gentile is not the way we normally think the world can be divided. We know we are not Jews, but we seldom think of ourselves as Gentiles. Nor are we sure we know what it might mean for us to be aliens from the commonwealth of Israel. Will Willimon and I wrote a book entitled *Resident Aliens*, but the aliens most people assumed we were suggesting Christians might be compared with were from Latin America.

Of course, we think we are Christians, but we are not quite sure what to make of Paul's extraordinary claim that by being Christian, we have been made citizens of a new commonwealth. Even more startling, he suggests we have been made citizens of a new commonwealth that is constituted by a new humanity. We just thought being Christian meant we came to church on Sunday. Paul's claims about our status seem exaggerated. After all, we are first and foremost good democratic citizens. That means we are very careful not to offend the egalitarian and tolerant presumptions of the democratic order in which we live by claiming to be a people with a special status.

Accordingly, we are not at all sure how this famous passage from Paul's letter to the Ephesians applies to us. Paul's extraordinary claims about what Christ has done to reconcile Jew and Gentile simply does not seem to map on to our current understanding of what it means to be a human being, nor does such an understanding of ourselves reflect our ecclesial practices. We may have been made one people, but given the character of the current church, such a claim seems to be just that, namely, an arrogant claim that makes us more than we are. Moreover, how claims of Christian distinctiveness have resulted in persecution of Jews by Christians is something we rightly want to avoid.

At the heart of our worries about Paul's extraordinary claim about who we are is his remark—a remark that he seems to throw out as a side comment—that Jesus is our peace. What could Paul possibly mean by suggesting that Jesus is our peace? How can peace be a person? We tend to think of peace as an ideal for which we ought to strive, but seldom achieve. Yet Paul suggests that through the cross, Jesus inaugurated and enacted a new creation and by doing so constituted a new humanity that just *is* peace. According to Paul, Jesus thus became peace for those who were far off as well as for those who were near. Indeed, it seems that such a peace is but a way to say that through Him we have been drawn into the very life of the Trinity by the Spirit who, with the Son, makes the Father known.

What an extraordinary set of claims. Claims that I hope make clear why I began by observing what a stunning text we have before us. These sentences from Paul are stunning because they force us to recognize that to be a Christian means we are made citizens of a people who believe all reality was transformed by an obscure Jew who died over two thousand years ago. We believe that God has made us, his church, the exemplification of the new humanity through word and sacrament. Just as "he is our peace" so we, his church, are a people of the new age making possible a peace otherwise unknown.

I became aware of the extraordinary character of Paul's claim that "Jesus is our peace" in, of all places, Japan. I had been asked to preach by my host in Japan. I was honored to be asked and accepted without much thought. The text for the day was this passage from Ephesians. It occurred to me to ask the Japanese if they had ever met a Jew or if they had any idea what it meant to be a Jew. No one in the congregation had ever met a Jew, nor did they have any idea what it meant to be a Jew. Yet they were being told that they have been made one with the people of Israel through the blood of Christ. What could it possibly mean for Japanese Christians to understand that they have been grafted into the people of Israel and thus become for the world God's peace? Israel's story of God's faithfulness to her is now the story that makes Japanese Christians, and American Christians, Christian.

I call attention to my experience of reflecting on this passage in a Japanese context in order to suggest to you that Paul's claim should strike American Christians as being just as strange and radical as it is to Japanese Christians. We should never take for granted Paul's radical suggestion that the hostility between those who were near and those who were far off has been overwhelmed, put to death, through the cross of Christ. We have been made through Christ a people of peace. This means that we cannot help but be a missionary people scattered throughout the world, so that the peoples of the world might come to know whose they are and no longer be lost.

At Babel, God confused the language of the earth and scattered the peoples (Genesis 11:1–9). What God meant as a gift to counter the prideful attempt to be God was transformed into a violent alternative in which some tried to secure their survival, going so far as to sacrifice the lives of others for the sake of that security. Unable to understand one another, they lived and continue to live in fear of one another. War was the inevitable result of Babel, for in such a world there seems no alternative to kill or be killed.

God, however, had a response to our violence. He called Abraham out of his country to be the father of a people who had to learn to exist by trusting in the one alone who can be trusted (Genesis 12:1–3). We, that is, his church, now stand in that project. We do so because, as Paul says, in Christ we have been made one with God, Israel, and with ourselves and our neighbor. Thus, the extraordinary claim that we, that is those that have been called into God's church, are the alternative to violence. Accordingly, we Christians are not called to live nonviolently because we believe nonviolence is a strategy to rid the world of war. Rather, we are called to live nonviolently in a world of war because as faithful followers of the one who is our peace we cannot imagine living in any other way.

In *Becoming the Gospel: Paul, Participation, and Mission*, Michael Gorman argues that Paul's understanding of this gift of peace enacted in Christ is not an addendum to salvation. It is salvation. It is, therefore, not an idle gesture when Paul writes to his various churches, greeting them in the name of Christ and wishing them to live in peace. He does so because the peace that is Christ is cosmic, making possible a way to live that was once unimaginable. To confess that Jesus is our peace means we, his church, are God's peace for the world. What an extraordinary story. You might almost think it more fantasy than reality, but it is real because Christ was crucified and resurrected with the result that we, his church, exist. "He is our peace," and because he is our peace we are that peace for the world.

20

"A Heartfelt People"

St. Mary's on-the-Highlands Episcopal Church
Birmingham, Alabama
August 30, 2015

Deuteronomy 4:1–2, 6–9
Psalm 15
James 1:17–27
Mark 7:1–8, 14–15, 21–23

We love this exchange between Jesus and the Pharisees. We love it because it is clear who the bad guys are. The Pharisees are the bad guys, because they are clearly self-righteous hypocrites. Jesus's defense of his disciples seems just right to us. We simply do not think the keeping of the law is what makes us good or bad. What matters is who we really are. So we think Jesus is right to commend the inner person, that is, the heart. If our hearts are not right, it makes no difference what we do or do not do, because what we do or do not do must be done with a true heart, if what we do is to be genuinely good.

We also think Jesus is right to defend the disciples because we do not think much is at stake in preserving traditions, particularly if those traditions are associated with purity. That the Pharisees think it important to have their hands washed before eating is the kind of legalism we associate with people we do not want to be around. We generally think we should not sweat the small stuff. What really matters is how we treat one another. Whether we are just or kind is what matters, not whether we obey societal conventions.

We need to be careful, however, before we decide we are on Jesus's side against the Pharisees. Upon further reflection, the contrast between the "inner" and the "outer" may be more complex than it first appears. For example, the contrast between the "inner" and the "outer" may be particularly dangerous for people like us, that is, Protestants. We have inherited from the Reformation the contrast between Law and Gospel. We associate the Law with external behaviors that cannot justify. We are Gospel people, who think that what justifies is what we believe and how we feel about what we believe.

This contrast between the inner and outer, between Law and Gospel, has been reinforced by certain stereotypes that possess our imaginations no matter how much we may claim they have no hold on us. For example, Jews are identified as a people determined by the Law. That characterization we assume is justified by a certain reading of Paul that was the result of the polemical situation of the Reformation. Of course, it was not the Jews that Protestant Christians cared about. It was the Catholics whom the Protestants thought to be the Pharisees of Christianity. Thus, the presumption that Catholics do not care what kind of person you are. They only care that you obey the law. Even worse, Catholics think if they break the law, all they have to do is confess, be forgiven, and get on with their life.

The problem with these stereotypes is they make it difficult to make sense of our text from Deuteronomy and our Psalm for today. In Deuteronomy, we are told that if Israel diligently obeys the Law, she will be a people of wisdom and discernment. After all, that is what Law demands. Wisdom and discernment sound like the kind of virtues we associate with the "inner." But for Israel, the giving of the Law was a gift, a grace, making possible a way of life that would evidence the glory of Israel's God. To obey the law meant freedom to enjoy the gift of holiness which comes from sharing a life with God unimpeded by sin. It is this intimacy with God, maintained through obedience to the Law, which leads to wisdom and discernment. That the Pharisees seemed to lack wisdom is but a testimony to the fact that there is no good gift that we humans cannot pervert.

From this perspective, the sharp contrast between the inner and outer, the Law and the Gospel, clearly represents a false dichotomy. Nowhere is Israel's understanding of the importance of the Law for forming the kind of people God has called out and set apart more apparent than in Psalm 15. Those who would walk blamelessly, who would do what is right, and who would speak the truth from their heart are people who stand by their word. These are the very characteristics that form the basis for Jesus's condemnation of the Pharisees. By contrast, drawing on the prophet Isaiah, Jesus characterizes the Pharisees as those who would honor God with their lips, while their hearts are far from God. The problem is not the Law, which enables our becoming blameless, truthful, and trustworthy. The problem is the Pharisees' hypocrisy.

But let us not forget that the Pharisees' "legalism" was a strategy to stay true to God's covenant with Israel while under Roman occupation. The Pharisees were attempting to remain holy even when the Romans made that very difficult. It's a worthy intention. But even the best of intentions can lead us astray. Jesus was not rebuking them for appealing to the Law. His rebuke centered on their forgetfulness of why the Law was given in the first place.

I began by suggesting we enjoy the presumption that in this exchange between Jesus and the Pharisees we are clearly on Jesus's side. But I think we need to worry a bit about that presumption, particularly in our day. I think our problem is not whether we risk being hypocritical by legalistic observance of the "Law," but rather our problem is we do not think we are law-determined people, when, in fact, we are.

We do not think we live in a time when moral conventions (which is just another word for the Law) determine our lives, but we do. We may not quite be in a Jane Austen world, but we are close. Jane Austen lived in a world of clear social conventions in which everyone knew what was the right thing to do or say, particularly when you were at dinner. Her novels are relentless investigations of whether people who always seem to do the right thing, in fact, have a true heart. If you live in conformity to what everyone assumes is the good, how do you know if you are who you think you are? How do you know your heart is true? We do not think we live at a time when there is agreement about such conventions, but, in reality, we are creatures of such conventions.

For example, there is no convention, no law, more significant than the law that the only law we live by is the law we have chosen for ourselves. The presumption that what really matters is not whether we keep or do not keep the law, but what kind of person we are turns out to be a law. Moreover, this law is an invitation for self-deception, precisely because we do not think it to be a law. We may think we are people whose hearts are true, because we are what we want to be, but, in fact, most of us go through life with little reflection about the person we are becoming.

The Pharisees thought you needed to wash before eating. We think you need to think for yourself. There are few more conventional law-like assumptions than the presumption that when all is said and done, we each need to make up our own minds. We associate this law with being a person who is true to herself. But the notion of being true to oneself undermines the very notion of truth. How could I possibly know to what I am being true when I am a creature who is utterly contingent? It's like aiming at an ever-moving target. The modern convention of being unconventional results in a profound insecurity about what it might mean to have a heart that is true.

One way to test this is to ask yourself if you really want to know who you are or why you may have done this or that. Queen Elizabeth I is said to have remarked that she had no desire to "make windows into men's souls." By that I assume she meant she did not care why subjects obeyed her, but they had better obey. She did not need to know why they subjected themselves to her. She just needed to know that they did subject themselves to her. We are, of course, not Queen Elizabeth, but the question remains whether we would want to see into the windows of our souls.

In the book of James, we are told that many have become hearers of the word rather than doers of the word. They are like those who look at themselves in a mirror, but as soon as they go away they forget what they looked like. However, there is a mirror—a law—that makes possible our knowledge of the self that makes what we do and do not do reflect the truth. That mirror has a name. His name is Jesus. According to James, he is the implanted Word that has the power to make us more than we could ever imagine. That Jesus fulfills the Law rather than abolishing it means that he has become for us the law of life. This is the good news of the gospel. By being conformed to him, we too find the grace of holiness and communion with God. Through that Word, the Word that is a perfect law—James calls it "the law of liberty" (2:12)—we are enabled to persevere in a world that is under occupation by the Romans.

Let us reflect on that mirror: the one who helps us remember who we are as St. Mary's on-the-Highlands. For it is here that we receive the baptism of the Holy Spirit that liberates us from the conventions of the world and sets us free for a life of joyful obedience to the Word. And it is here that the Word teaches us that few things are more important than to care for the widows and orphans. Through such obedience, we will discover the freedom opposed to the oppression of being our own measure of truth. That is surely what the world has been longing for. That is surely what you have been longing for. If that is not true, how else can you explain why you are here?

The disciples were hungry and ate without washing their hands. Yet the hands of the celebrant will be washed before handling these sacred elements. And we too will come to this table as those washed in the waters of our baptism. Let us receive our Lord in these holy gifts so that we may be for one another and the world mirrors of truth. For this, we have been freed.

21

"The Sign That Is Christ"
St. John's Scottish Episcopal Church
Aberdeen, Scotland
October 11, 2015

Joel 2:21–27
Philippians 4:4–9
John 6:25–35

The South—that strange geographic designation for that part of the United States identified by people who talk like me and who pride themselves on being straightforward and uncompromising in their interactions with others—is a place constituted by stories. One story that is particularly relevant for how our texts for this morning might be read is about a farmer who sold a mule to a neighboring farmer. This transaction took place before there were tractors. Mules were invaluable for plowing the fields in preparation for endless cotton crops. The farmer who bought the mule was assured that the mule he was buying was a superior plowing mule.

However, after hitching the mule to the plow, the farmer discovered that he could not get the mule to move, much less plow. In Joel, the soil and the animals are addressed on the assumption that they could respond to the prophet, but as far as this farmer was concerned, his mule would not have responded to God himself. The farmer used every verbal command he knew, which included some language not to be used in polite company. He used his whip on the mule's rear, but with no result. He stood in front of the mule and pulled on the mule's halter, but the mule refused to budge. Finally, he went to the neighbor who had sold him the mule to ask for his money back. He observed that the animal was clearly an inferior plow mule, as he could not even get the mule to move.

The farmer who had sold him the mule did not say anything, but took his neighbor by the arm and led him back to the field where the mule was standing. On the way, the farmer who had sold the mule went by his barn and picked up a two-by-four. Two-by-fours are substantial pieces of lumber often used to frame the walls of buildings. The farmer who had sold the mule walked in front of the mule, raised the piece of lumber as high as he could, and hit the mule as hard as he could right between his eyes. He then said "git" and the mule begin to plow.

The new owner of the mule was impressed, confessing that he had used every trick he knew to get the mule going, but nothing worked. He asked the farmer who had sold him the mule how he knew what to do. The farmer responded that the mule was more than happy to follow commands, but first you had to get his attention. A two-by-four between the eyes was an attention-getter.

The crowd that has followed Jesus, a crowd that appears to consist of many who had just seen Jesus feed five thousand with five loaves and two fish, asked Jesus for a sign. "What sign are you going to give us so that we may see it and believe you? What work are you performing?" They seemed to want Jesus to use a two-by-four to show what he is about. They did so explaining they needed a sign that, as they put it, would enable them to perform the works of God.

They assumed the request for a sign was legitimate. After all, Moses had provided a sign by giving the people food in the wilderness. What was Jesus going to give them? In response, Jesus tells them that he will give them the true bread from heaven that comes, just as it did for Moses, from the one in whom they are to believe. That is the one that Jesus is making known. That is the one, Jesus tells them, who alone has the power to give them bread from heaven. That is the one who has given Jesus work to do, because the work he does is to testify to the one who has sent him. Accordingly, the bread that Jesus now gives them is of a completely different order than the bread that was given in the wilderness, because the bread Jesus provides gives life to the world. His bread is life itself, because it ensures that those who believe in him will never go hungry or thirsty.

What the crowd fails to understand, a characteristic common to their being a crowd, is the inseparability of the works of God and the one who is the work of the Father. That is why the feeding of the five thousand is not a club to the head that compels belief. We may want Jesus to be God's two-by-four, but it turns out that Jesus is the sign that captures our attention precisely because he is not a club. He is instead God's Messiah.

There is an essential relation between the signs Jesus performs and his very being. The Gospel of John is organized around a series of signs meant to help us understand the sign that is Christ. Yet it seems none of the signs compel belief. At the wedding feast in Cana, Jesus turns water into wine. He not only turns water into wine, but the wine he supplies is better than what had been previously served. It is not clear if the quality of the wine is the reason that the disciples began to believe in him. The miracle at Cana seems to have gotten their attention, but we know that their belief in him did not stand the test of time. The sign was not sufficient to sustain the disciples' ability to stay the course.

The performing of signs remained a vital part of Jesus's ministry. Traveling throughout Israel, Jesus performs signs everywhere he goes. Again in Cana, he heals an official's son (John 4:46–54). He then goes to Jerusalem where he encounters the invalid who had long waited to be helped so that he could be washed in the pool of Bethesda (John 5:1–14). Jesus heals the man, but he does so on the Sabbath, incurring the wrath of the Pharisees. He continues to perform signs that attract large crowds.

But as I have suggested, crowds are just as likely to get it wrong as to get it right. The feeding of the five thousand is a clear example of the ambiguous character of the signs. Jesus feeds the five thousand with the five loaves and two fish, which leads some to make false inferences. They become theologians, which leads some to speculate that Jesus must be a prophet, while still others think he should be made a king.

That such conclusions could be drawn makes it clear that John understood that the signs Jesus performed, not the least being the resurrection itself, were not sufficient to turn those in the crowd into disciples of Jesus. Therefore, we should not be surprised that after Jesus raises Lazarus, some believed but others went to inform the Jewish authorities (John 11:46). Even more startling, we are told that after the discovery of the empty tomb, some disciples "returned to their homes" (John 20:10).

The ambiguous nature of the signs is clearly indicated toward the end of the Gospel of John. There we are told that Jesus did many other signs in the presence of his disciples that are not written in this book. Those that do appear in the Gospel, we are told, are meant to aid us in coming to believe that Jesus is the Messiah, the Son of God, "and that through believing you may have life in his name" (John 20:31).

What are we to make of all this business about the signs? Our inclination is to want the signs to be conclusive evidence that Jesus is who he says he is. In particular, in this time when we find ourselves as Christians not sure we believe what we say we believe, we would like the signs to confirm our commitment to the gospel and to confound those who think what we believe to be incoherent nonsense. Why can't they see that the resurrection is meant to make us believe? Our desire to turn the signs into two-by-fours reflects our profound insecurity.

The reason the signs Jesus performs are not meant to be a blow between the eyes is because their character reflects the character of the one who performs the signs. In other words, the signs partake in the mystery of the incarnation. There is an essential relationship between the signs and the humanity of Jesus. For our sake, as we are told in the prologue to this Gospel, God has taken on our flesh so that we might see that this is not a God who would force us to believe in him. Jesus is the visible presence of the Father. In him, we see the Father's glory, but it is a glory that is just as likely to create doubt as faith. For what we find hard to believe is that God is fully present in this man Jesus without ceasing to be God.

The humanity of Jesus means, in the words of Karl Barth, that God's deity is no prison. That God has become a man is the essential sign that God refuses to abandon us. To look on Christ, therefore, is to recognize that God's deity does not exclude but includes his humanity. That humanity cannot compel belief, but rather invites us to recognize that God refuses to coerce us to love him. God became one of us so that we might live as his people.

That is why the signs are so often associated with the "I am" declarations of Jesus. "I am the bread of life. Whoever comes to me will never hunger, and whoever believes in me will never be thirsty." He is the manna that comes from the Father, because he and the Father are one. The very character of the signs Jesus enacts characterizes this bread and wine that will become for us the body and blood of Christ.

So come and receive this gift. It is a sign we desperately need. It is a sign that the world desperately needs. For it is a sign that partakes in the very character of the one who loves us so completely he refuses to force us to love him in return. That the signs Jesus performs do not compel belief is the sign that they are of God. They do not coerce us, rather they caress us, just as Jesus's humanity pulls us into the life, the love, of God.

But that is not the most surprising thing about these mysteries. Rather, the miracle is that by learning to love this God, we discover we have been made a sign of God's love for the world. Such a people have no desire to be or to use a two-by-four. Instead, we have this meal in which we are transformed to be for the world God's sign that a people of peace have been loved into being. Here God has gotten our complete attention.

22

"Waiting"

The Cathedral Church of St. James
Toronto, Ontario
November 30, 2015

Jeremiah 33:14–16
Psalm 25:1–10
1 Thessalonians 3:9–13
Luke 21:25–36

I fear we Christians are not good at waiting. We are more likely to play at waiting than to be people who actually know what it means to wait. Those who have really learned to wait usually have been taught how to do so by necessity. Israel learned to wait by God's gift of the Law that made her a people who had to learn to live out of control. To be sure, she was often less than faithful to what her Lord had given her, but through the ups and downs of her history, she learned what it means to wait on the Lord. God's chosen people, the people of Israel, were often forced to learn to wait, but what came as a necessity was transformed into faithfulness.

We should not be surprised, therefore, that our psalmist asks God to "make me to know your ways, O Lord." "Make" is strong language, but it reflects the recognition that the people of Israel often were unwilling to be "led in truth." "Make" reflects Israel's hard-won wisdom that she seldom willed herself to be obedient, but rather she discovered how to wait faithfully on the Lord. One name for learning to wait is exile.

Christians are a people who seldom use a word like "make." In particular, we are not a people who would pray to be made to wait for anything. To our ears, "make" sounds far too coercive, perhaps even violent. At most, we believe that God, because God is a God of love, should entice us to be a people who have learned to wait. Yet when understood in this manner, waiting seems more like some form of delayed gratification than having to wait indefinitely without a clear sense of when or whether the wait will end.

But this is Advent. Advent is a time, and time is at the heart of what it means for us to be a people who have learned to wait. Therefore at Advent, we think it important to at least act as if we are waiting. I suspect that is what we in fact do—we act, or better, pretend to be a people who know how to wait. So during Advent, we play at being Jews for a few weeks, but we do so as if we are in a drama with designated roles for us to play. However, once the play is over, we have no reason to play the roles associated with waiting.

You may well think that my use of the word "pretend" to characterize our attempt to mimic Israel during Advent is far too strong a description of what we do at this time. I think, however, Advent is a word that rightly describes a stance many of us cannot avoid at this time in the church year. Pretense seems built into our very lives, because we are, after all, a Christmas people. We have been habituated, that is, our bodies and our expectations have been shaped by the rituals associated with the giving and receiving of gifts at Christmas. Those Christmas rituals, moreover, make it quite difficult for many of us not to feel that our waiting is something less than authentic. The problem, moreover, seems intrinsic to the very grammar of the Christian faith.

Let me try to explain what I mean by the suggestion that Christmas makes it very hard for us to think that we know how to wait as Christians. I suspect our problem with waiting has to do with how we were formed by the celebration of Christmas when we were children. Children are often encouraged to ask Santa for a special present for Christmas. Usually children, at least children of a certain class, know that they are going to receive the gift for which they've asked. Yet they keep themselves in doubt by pretending to be unsure if, in fact, they will get what seems so important to them at the time. Accordingly, their wait before Christmas is filled with anxiety, because they fear they may not get what they want. The anxiety that comes with the waiting is intrinsic to the game-like character of receiving the gift. By pretending to wait, the pleasure children receive when they get what they wanted is enhanced.

You may think this account of waiting may be true for when we were children, but we have grown up. Yet habits formed in childhood are hard to break. As adult Christians, we believe we have gotten what we wanted, but during Advent, we have to act as if we are still waiting. But we cannot hide from ourselves the fact that we have gotten that for which we pretend we are waiting.

Consider, for example, how we hear today's reading from Jeremiah. We believe we have been given, as Jeremiah predicted, the "righteous Branch to spring up from David." Though we may say we are a Jeremiah-like people who must wait to be liberated, we believe, as we celebrated last Sunday, that our liberating king has come. We have gotten what we want. So Advent, a time of waiting, finally seems less than real, because we believe our wait is over. We believe the promise "made to the house of Israel and the house of Judah" has been fulfilled.

The truth of the matter, however, is we are not quite sure if what we have wanted is what we got. What, for example, are we to make of apocalyptic pronouncements of Jesus like the one from the Gospel of Luke? We may be ready to welcome a baby in a manger, but we are not at all sure we want a Son of Man who will come with power and great glory. Jesus even seems to suggest, moreover, that dramatic coming will occur before "this generation will pass away." What does it mean for us to learn to wait in the light of this kind of apocalyptic event in which the very powers of heaven are shaken?

I think that what Jesus says would be accomplished before the passing of "this generation" did, in fact, take place. What was accomplished is called the crucifixion. When Jesus was crucified, the light of the sun failed, and the curtain of the temple was torn in two. In agony, Jesus cried, "Father, into your hands I commend my spirit" (Luke 23:46). Jesus's death was an apocalyptic and cosmic event.

Jesus's crucifixion, moreover, rattled the very constitution of the universe, because death could not hold him. Three days later, he is raised. He walks with two former followers on the road to Emmaus, teaching them how to read Scripture. Such instruction was required, because they found it difficult to understand how the one to liberate Israel could end up on a cross. In a similar manner, he instructs the disciples to read the scripture so that they would understand that the Messiah that was to come had to suffer only to be raised from the dead on the third day. A new age and time has been inaugurated.

Jesus's death, resurrection, and ascension are dramatic events. But this drama, I believe, is crucial for helping us understand the kind of waiting that is at the heart of the gospel. The crucifixion of Jesus, the crucifixion of the second person of the Trinity, the death of the One who has come in power and glory, makes clear that our God refuses to save us by coercing us to be what we were created to be. The crucifixion is the manifestation of God's patience. The crucifixion is the demonstration of God's willingness to wait on us to respond to the love that moves the sun and the stars.

The crucifixion does not force us to be a disciple of the one crucified. Rather, we discover that we can finally rest—wait—in the light of this man's crucifixion, because death has been defeated. Accordingly, we can be for the world a people of time that do not fear the end of time, because through the crucifixion and resurrection of Jesus, we have been given all the time in the world to live patiently. Entering into the season of Advent is all about participating in this waiting.

Advent is a time that rightly begins the church year. But as Christians we wait not only at Advent. Rather, waiting is a time that is constitutive of every time of the church year. We are called to wait, because we serve a God who transformed time by being patient—even willing to die that we might live. Waiting is the fundamental stance of God's nonviolent love that would give us the time in a hurried world to be a people who have learned to wait.

But what does it mean to say we are able to wait, because we believe as Christians that Christ inaugurated a new time? We may say we are a people of the new age, but the old age seems all too present. Yet the new age is the age of God's time made manifest by what we do here when we eat and drink with our Lord. This is the feast of the new age: an age made possible by God's patience. Accordingly, we have all the time in the world to be a people of time. We do not need to be in a hurry, because God has given us all the time we need to perpetrate on the world small acts of kindness through which the world is saved.

So our waiting at Advent is not a pretense. We are a people who have learned to wait, because we worship the God of patience. To be sure, that makes us often appear to be slow, but we refuse the temptation to use means that result in the destruction of others in the name of a good cause. In the process, we become for the world a manifestation of God's time, so the world may know that the desperate attempt to defeat death by speed can only result in terror.

Let me try to make this as concrete as I can. I am a person committed to Christian nonviolence. I try to make that commitment public, because I hope by doing so I will create expectations in others that will make me live in a manner I know to be true. I do this because I have no confidence I can live nonviolently without the help of others. To be committed to nonviolence takes out massive metaphysical drafts on time, because often there seems to be no alternative to violence. But it turns out that we, God's church, simply are the alternative to violence.

I began by observing that Christians are not particularly good at waiting. I continue to think that true, but the good news is that God has given us all we need to wait for the one who has made it possible for us to be a people who have learned to wait. Namely, the Father has given the Son that we might be empowered by the Holy Spirit to live lives of patient waiting. Let us light the Advent candles, but let us not forget that the waiting that is Advent is a waiting that shapes what we now do, that is, to have the time to eat and drink with the Lord of time.

23

"The Defeat of Boredom"

Trinity-by-the-Cove Episcopal Church
Naples, Florida
December 6, 2015
A Sermon for the Ordination of Daniel Moore

Isaiah 6:1–8
Psalm 132:8–19
1 Peter 5:1–4
John 10:11–18

"Mine is a parish like all the rest. They're all alike. Those of to-day I mean. . . . that good and evil are probably evenly distributed, but on such a low plain, very low indeed!"[1] So begins Georges Bernanos's sad, yet hopeful, 1936 novel *The Diary of a Country Priest*. The title well describes the book, which is a journal written by a young and nameless priest. Neither he nor the village he serves is attractive or in any way exceptional. As one might expect, the young priest begins with high hopes for the work he has been given, but he soon encounters his parishioners who treat him unkindly, gossip about him, and even cheat him. The village grocer offers to send him three bottles of wine and then charges the priest, who can just barely get by on his meager stipend, for what he had presumed to be a gift.

---

1. Georges Bernanos, *The Diary of a Country Priest*, trans. Pamela Morris (Cambridge, MA: Da Capo, 2002), 1.

Very little happens in the novel. There are conflicts, but they are not between good and evil, rather the conflicts are between boredom and faith. Indeed, in the first pages of his journal, the priest reflects on his parish as one "eaten up by boredom." He observes that boredom is like dust that you never notice, but you breathe it in. These reflections lead him to wonder if humankind has ever before experienced this contagion, this leprosy of boredom, which he describes as "an aborted despair, a shameful form of despair in some way like the fermentation of a Christianity in decay."[2]

The fermentation of a Christianity in decay is a good description of the Christianity that characterized pre-Second World War France, which served as the setting of this particular priest's parish. It was a Christianity that is like the mud that the priest must walk through as he negotiates the roads of the village. Just as the mud makes it difficult to walk through the village, so the village sucks the energy out of all the attempts the priest makes to be a shepherd to his flock. Moreover, he is aware that he is guileless and lacks both eloquence and "management expertise," and he knows his people know his limits. While he has some pastoral moments of grace, most of his people neither need him nor want him around.

His journal is a relentless analysis of his faults, such as his tendency to be overly sentimental, and his social ineptitude, which is the result of his being from the lower classes. He is a timid person, terrified by the "dark night of the soul," who worries about his inability to pray and his ineffective care of the people under his charge. Though a person with no knowledge or love of sport, he plans a sport club for the young men of the parish that turns out to be a spectacular failure.

His one comfort is his being befriended by the Curé de Torcy, a priest in a nearby village, who guides him through his difficulties and failures. From Torcy, he learns that service to God is often experienced as mundane and unfulfilling, but that is where God is to be found. For example, Torcy tells him "Nothing could be more idiotic than an impulsive priest always letting himself go, for no reason—just a pose. Yet all the same our way is not the way of the world. You can't go offering the truth to human beings as though it were a sort of insurance policy, or a dose of salts. It's the Way and the Life. God's truth is the Life. We only look as though we were bringing it to mankind; really it brings us, my lad."[3]

---

2. Ibid., 3.
3. Ibid., 90.

From the beginning, the priest suffers from stomach problems that turn out to be cancer. He travels to Lille to see a competent doctor from whom he learns he will soon die. Taken aback by the news that he has incurable cancer, he does not immediately return to his parish, but instead visits an old friend from seminary. After catching up with one another, our nameless priest, who is not feeling well, accepts an offer to stay with his friend for the evening. That night he dies. A priest could not be found in time to give him last rites. As a result his dying words were, "*Does it matter? Grace is everywhere. . . .*"[4]

The Diary of a Country Priest may be a great novel, but it is an odd one to call attention to on this day when Dan is to be ordained a priest. Bernanos was a member of a Catholic intellectual movement that challenged the positivism of French intellectual life. He was committed to the renewal of the moribund character of French Catholicism. He was, moreover, an ardent anti-fascist, which means for the church and for the world, he was a person looking for something more. That is all quite admirable, but it seems quite a long way from Naples, Florida, and Trinity-by-the-Cove Episcopal Church. Our texts for today, moreover, seem to suggest a very different understanding of what it might mean to be a priest than the nameless priest in Bernanos's novel. This classic text of Isaiah's call cannot help but seize our imaginations. Perhaps a priest can be a prophet. Cleansed by a live coal, Isaiah, in response to the Lord's question of who should be sent, declares, "Here am I; send me!" This is a tempting narrative for one who is to be ordained—until we remember that the prophet is told to make dull the minds of those to whom he is sent!

Peter's advice for elders not to "lord it over" those under their charge seems like good advice for anyone who is or will be a priest. We tend to interpret Peter's admonition for elders to be examples for those they serve as good advice for anyone in a position of authority. Basically, we assume such advice means priests should be "good guys." In other words, they should try very hard to be just like us. After all, most priests discover that to the extent they have any authority at all in the churches they serve, their authority depends on their being a good and likable person with an attractive personality.

Though most of us do not like to think of ourselves as sheep, it is hard to resist the presumption that a priest should be a good shepherd, not a hired hand. A hired hand only cares for the sheep, because they

---

4. Ibid., 298.

have been hired to do so. The priesthood is not a job. To be a priest is to be the kind of person that cares for her people in a way that may require sacrifices she had not anticipated. This is why many in ministerial offices, after some years, feel like they have been nibbled to death by ducks. They have had no defense from their congregants who assume that because priests do not work for a living, they can be asked to do anything.

These readings of our texts, tendentious but common and persuasive readings, miss the heart of *The Diary of a Country Priest*. For the heart of Bernanos's novel is that all that our nameless priest does or does not do—his doubts as well as his faith, his successes as well as his failures—depend on God being in everything he does. To be sure, most of the good that this country priest did remained hidden even to the priest himself. But then that is exactly Bernanos's point, namely, that most of God's work goes unseen. The life of Bernanos's priest turns out to be one lived in imitation of the God we find in Jesus Christ. In Jesus, God's presence is hidden by the very fact that he assumed of our flesh. That is why the man Jesus can only be recognized as Lord when seen with the eyes of faith. He is always either just a good man or he is Lord. It's faith that makes the difference for how he is seen.

It is the same faith in Jesus's lordship that defeats the boredom that gripped the village the priest served, as well as the boredom that threatens us today. The "leprosy of boredom" cannot help but be the condition of those who have learned to live lives that seem to make sense even if God does not exist. For if God, a God hidden in the everyday, is simply not "there," then what is life but to eat, drink, have sex, and die? Such lives are ruled by a ceaseless desire for distraction in the hope that even our failures may serve to hide from us the desperation fueled by the fear that, when all is said and done, our lives—little more than sound and fury—flicker, signifying nothing. Thus, Pope Francis's recent observation that: "The culture of prosperity deadens us, we are thrilled if the market offers us something new to purchase. In the meantime, all those lives stunted for lack of opportunity seem a mere spectacle; they fail to move us."[5]

That is why it is so important that what will soon be done to Dan is not but another distraction. It is rather an essential act that is a crucial weapon against boredom. It is so because today God will make him priest. Hopefully his work as a priest will be more satisfying than that of

---

5. Pope Francis, "Evangelii Gaudium," Vatican Website, November 24, 2013, sec. 54, https://w2.vatican.va/content/francesco/en/apost_exhortations/documents/papa-francesco_esortazione-ap_20131124_evangelii-gaudium.html.

Bernanos's country parson. Whether it is or is not does not matter as long as he remembers that all he does and does not do is to help us see God in the mundane.

We will want him present in our most vulnerable moments. He will know us as we lose our jobs, as our marriages fail, as our children betray us, as we suffer illness and move to death. We will want him to be with us in those times when we are unsure God is present. But God is present in those times, because Dan is not called to be a prophet, nor a leader, nor a shepherd. He is called and will be made a priest to help us discern that God is present in the silences of everyday.

I fear we may be living in a time in which our faith in Christ has been captured by the leprosy of boredom. It may be a time in which we can smell the fermentation of a Christianity in decay. In such a time, that God would call people like Dan into the priesthood is a sign of hope. It is the defeat of boredom, because what could be more dramatic than the power bestowed on Dan to let God loose in the world through word and sacrament? Dan has learned that as a witness to God's presence, a presence that often seems like an absence, he has been called to always be there. For he must help us learn to say, even if we die without last rites, "Does it matter? Grace is everywhere . . ."

24

"Do Not Be Afraid"

Christ Church Cathedral
Nashville, Tennessee
February 21, 2016

Genesis 15:1–12, 17–18
Psalm 27
Philippians 3:17—4:1
Luke 13:31–35

"Do not be afraid," the Lord tells Abram. Abram should not be afraid because the Lord promises to be his shield, in addition to promising to give Abram a very great reward. Yet it is not clear that God needed to tell Abram not to be afraid. Abram shows no sign of being afraid. You might think he should be afraid having left his home in Ur of the Chaldeans in response to God's command, but Abram shows no sign that he is afraid of being made homeless.

Abram does not even seem afraid of God. Abram does not hesitate, therefore, to put God to the test. He wants to know what God is going to give him. In particular, he asks how God is going to deliver on his promise to make him the father of a great nation. Abram points out to the Lord that the promise to make him the father of many people seems quite empty given the fact he has no children of his own. The Lord responds by directing his attention to the heavens, promising that Abram's descendants will be as numerous as the uncountable stars. We are told Abram believed the Lord and was thereby "reckoned righteous."

The Lord, who is only identified as the God who brought Abram out of Ur of the Chaldeans, rather ambiguously promises to give Abram "this land" to possess. Abram again proves he is not in the least cowed by God. He wants to know how he will possess the land of Canaan. God assures him he will possess the land by telling Abram to bring him a three year old heifer, a goat, and a ram, as well as a turtledove and young pigeon. Abram is told to cut the heifer, the goat, and the ram in two and lay each half over the other. The birds are to be laid on this gruesome sacrifice. Abram was left to drive away birds of prey that were attracted to the carcasses.

I do not have any idea what Abram's strange behavior in the sacrifice of these animals has to do with giving him confidence that he will possess the land. Indeed, it is fascinating that we are not told whether Abram believed the Lord. Rather, all we know is that he fell into a sleep in which we are told "a deep and terrifying darkness descended upon him." "Terrifying" suggests that he is not free of fear, but we remain unsure what he fears. It does not seem he needs to fear that he will not be given the land from the Nile to the Euphrates, because the Lord makes a covenant with him insuring that his descendants will inherit the land.

I have rehearsed this exchange between the Lord and Abram, because it is not clear why God tells Abram not to be afraid. What does Abram fear? As I have suggested, he does not seem to fear God. He may be afraid that God's promises will not be fulfilled, but God reassures him that he will become the father of a great nation, and they will occupy the land of Canaan. Abram seems to trust God to fulfill his promises. Yet it is unclear how Abram's trust in God to fulfill his promises has any implications for his fears, because it is not clear that Abram is possessed by fear.

The ambiguity surrounding God's "do not be afraid" is not peculiar to God's exchange with Abram. Fear is a complex passion. There are, for example, what might be called the more philosophical questions surrounding the emotion of fear that make us wonder why God thought he needed to tell Abram not to be afraid. After all, fear is not a matter of the head—fear is a matter of the gut. That is why it usually is of no use to tell anyone (including ourselves) not to be afraid. To try to will one's way to be free of fear is about as unrealistic as trying to will not to love someone with whom you have fallen desperately in love. This seems particularly true of certain kinds of fears, such as a fear of elevators or of terrorists. It does little good to tell a person possessed by what is often identified as "irrational fears" to just "get a grip."

There are, moreover, theological questions about fear. The Lord may tell Abram not to be afraid, but that does not mean that there is not an appropriate fear of God. Isaiah was appropriately afraid when he was confronted by God's glory, because he was a man of unclean lips (Isaiah 6:5). The disciples that accompanied Jesus at his transfiguration were overcome by fear. Jesus touched them and said, "Get up and do not be afraid" (Matthew 17:7). There seem to be times, as well as situations, in which we are appropriately filled with fear and times when we are not.

Who you are, moreover, makes all the difference. The courageous know fears the coward can never know. Of course, cowards may be overwhelmed with fear, but they do not know the fears of the courageous, because the fears of the courageous are fears honed by being courageous. The courageous, because they are courageous, make the world more dangerous for themselves and others exactly because they force a confrontation with dangers cowards may not even know exist. In short, the world of the courageous and the world of the coward are different worlds.

Our Psalm for today is a fascinating exploration of the relation between our trust in the Lord and the fears that threaten to take over our lives. Psalm 27 begins with this stunning declaration:

> The Lord is my light and my salvation;
> > Whom then shall I fear?
> > The LORD is the strength of my life;
> > Of whom then shall I be afraid?
> When evildoers came upon me to eat up my flesh,
> > it was they, my foes and adversaries, who
> > stumbled and fell.
> Though an army should rise up against me,
> > Yet will I put my trust in him.
> One thing have I asked of the Lord;
> > One thing I seek;
> > that I may dwell in the house of the Lord all the days of my life;
> to behold the fair beauty of the Lord
> > and to seek him in his temple.
> For in the day of trouble he shall keep me safe
> > In his shelter;
> > he shall hide me in the secrecy of his dwelling
> > and set me high upon a rock.

What is particularly interesting is the psalmist presumes that those who would behold the "fair beauty of the Lord" will not be free—just as Abram was not free—of dangers and betrayals. The psalmist suggests, for example, that those who have sought the Lord, who have beheld his beauty, may even be forsaken by their father and mother. To be so abandoned surely is one of the things we fear most, because few betrayals are more challenging than to be betrayed by those we believe should love us. The psalmist continues detailing an extraordinary list of what can go wrong for those that trust the Lord.

This Psalm can be read as a commentary on the Lord's command to Abram not to be afraid. If the Lord is our "light and salvation," what do we have to fear? The Lord's command for Abram not to be afraid presumes Abram can trust God to keep his promises. Against all the odds, Sarai and Abram will have a child. From that one child, a mighty people will come. How the promise is fulfilled, to be sure, is somewhat surprising, but the fact that Isaac is born when Abram and Sarai are old makes clear that it is God's doing.

To fear God rightly, therefore, requires that we trust God. To learn to trust God sounds like something we should want to do, but in actuality, it is no easy task. For just as Abram's trust in God resulted in his facing dangers that he otherwise might have avoided, so, as the Psalms make clear, learning to trust God often brings us face to face with the dangers we rightly fear. Yet the good news is that we can trust God to be God.

I do not want to be misunderstood, so I need to make clear what I am not saying. I am not saying that if we trust God then we can "damn the torpedoes," because we think we can take risks that under normal circumstances we would rightly fear and try to avoid. Thus, the presumption by some that if you trust God everything will turn out all right. To trust God surely will make a difference for the risks we take. After all, our everyday lives are filled with dangers—some we rightly want to avoid and others we cannot or should not want to avoid if we trust God. To trust God is not an invitation to engage life filled with false courage, but to trust that God does make possible a way to live that is otherwise unavailable.

In his book, *Be Not Afraid: Facing Fear With Faith*, Sam Wells observes that "in some ways" Christians should think that fear is a good thing. It is so because, as Wells argues, what we fear is an indication of what we love. The good news is that our God has refused to abandon us, making it possible for us to live lives determined by our loves and not by our misplaced fears. I fear too often that our fears are perverse, because we love the wrong thing.

I think this has deep implications for how we currently live as Americans. It has become commonplace after September 11, 2001, to describe America as a nation that runs on fear. That description indicates that the fear that possesses us is a fear that goes well beyond the challenges of the everyday. We can even give that fear a name—Donald Trump. I make this observation primarily to be funny, though some of you may not be laughing. Trump may not be all that frightening, but what he represents certainly is quite fearful. For Mr. Trump and many that support him manifest a fear that has the American people in a death grip. The irony seems lost on many of them that their efforts to remain the strongest country in the world is fueled by a seemingly pathological fear—especially a fear of the other. That kind of fear cannot be sustained if the commandment to love our neighbor is taken seriously.

As Americans, we seem determined to carve out a safe haven for ourselves in the very midst of a world consumed by chaos. Our attempts to be safe in a dangerous world require that others must live in a world made more dangerous by our determination to give ourselves the illusion that we are or can be safe. Put starkly, we simply do not know how to live as people destined to die. We thus entertain the illusion that when all is said and done, if we just get good enough at medical interventions or bolstering our nation's defense, we may be able to get out of life alive.

After September 11, we have increasingly let our fears determine our living by trying to be in control. This is a project doomed to fail. We are no more in control of our lives than Abram was in control of his life. Our lives are overwhelmed by uncertainties. For example, we fear the loss of the love of those we have come to love. Fearful of such loss, we end up not being able to love anyone or anything. Or, we fear being sick, not only because we know we may not get well, but because we fear the vulnerability that comes with illness. We hate the prospect that we may become dependent on those who care for us. We fear the loss of friends as well as the opinions that others may have of us. We fear having to acknowledge who we are because we prefer to think we are who we pretend to be. Unsure of who we are, we fear having to recognize that we may lack the courage for self-knowledge.

The good news, however, is the Lord did fulfill the promises he made to Abram. We are the result of the fulfillment of that promise, because we are Abram's children. That we are to be counted among those peoples that are Abram's progeny is God's surprise. The name of the one who made that surprise possible is Jesus, the Son of God who trusted the will of his Father even to the point of dying on a cross. He refused to let his life be determined by fear. For example, in Jesus's confrontation with the Pharisees, it was assumed that he would try to escape when told that Herod meant to kill him. Yet Jesus refuses to let the Pharisees' presumption that he would fear Herod deter him from his mission.

Jesus does not fear Herod, but the "Herods" of this world fear Jesus. They fear Jesus, because Jesus challenges the presumption that tyrants like Herod are necessary to make us safe. They promise us protection by threatening anyone they think may tell us the truth. For the truth is that we live in a dangerous world in which reliance on those who promise safety only makes the world more dangerous. It turns out, therefore, that the people who are the offspring of Abram are a political alternative to the politics of fear.

In a metaphor loved by Luther, Jesus tells us that he is our brood hen. He has gathered us under his wings. To be so gathered does not mean that we will be free of dangers. We do live in a dangerous world. But we can trust God to keep his promises. That God has kept his promises makes it possible for us, his people, to face down the fears that would make us less than we have been made in Christ. So "do not be afraid." We have been made citizens of heaven. Trust the God of Abram who may ask us to travel to distant places, or who may ask us to receive the stranger who has traveled that same distance, protected only by God's promise. The name of that promise is Jesus. May we prepare our hearts and minds for receiving the one whose love transforms our fears to hope and emboldens us to trust in the will of his Father.

25

"Ambassadors for Christ"

Church of the Holy Family
Chapel Hill, North Carolina
March 6, 2016

Joshua 5:9–12
Psalm 32
2 Corinthians 5:16–21
Luke 15:1–3, 11b–32

I grew up in a society ruled by Southern Baptists. First Baptist Church of Pleasant Grove, Texas, was in the center of town directly across the street from Pleasant Grove High School. What it meant for the Southern Baptists to rule was clear—the Baptists did not think you should dance, which meant only the Methodists, and I was a Methodist, went to the senior prom. The Baptist youth group, who bore the name, "Royal Ambassadors," could think of themselves as Christians because they did not even come to the prom, but instead held an alternative event.

The irony about this state of affairs in Pleasant Grove, as well as in the South in general, is that Baptists are allegedly committed to maintaining the freedom of the church by refusing to coerce others through the offices of the state to conform to their way of life. Thus my observation that the Southern Baptist people are the first form of the free-church tradition that created their own civilization. It is called "the South." I suspect some of you from small-town North Carolina have had experiences not unlike mine in Pleasant Grove.

Why do I begin with this piece of trivia from my past? I do so because I hope it may help us locate where we may now be as Christians. Not that long ago, in places like Pleasant Grove, some Christians thought they knew how to identify the difference it made to be a Christian. The fact that the difference was marked by the prohibition of dancing is an indication that what it meant to be a Christian in Pleasant Grove was not distinguishable from what it meant to be a good American. The prohibition on dancing was a desperate attempt to find a difference.

The Baptists, like most Christians in America, assumed that there was little difference between the American "we" and the Christian "we." There are no doubt many reasons that the First Baptist Church of Pleasant Grove is now closed, but surely its identification as the bastion of American life had something to do with the fact the church is now boarded up. Why do you need the church if you have the Republican Party? In some ways it is quite sad that the end of Christendom for the Baptists turned out to be more of a whimper than a bang.

What does it mean to suggest that Christendom has come to an end? I think it means that we are beginning to rediscover how unusual it is for us—Episcopalians of all people—to be the church of Jesus Christ. Christendom had taught us to think that we Christians were not all that different from those who are not Christians. At least, we were not all that different unless some marker such as not dancing could be located. Could it be, however, that God is giving us the time in this moment to rediscover what it might mean, as Paul suggests to the Christians in Corinth, that we are a new creation, ambassadors for Christ? The church, and we are the church, is God's embassy amid the nations so that all people might see what God's new creation looks like.

We are not quite sure what to make of the dramatic claim that we are a new creation when we seem so ordinary. But if we are living in a time when we rediscover how strange it is that we are Christians, such claims may not be all that odd. That the world seems determined to make us acknowledge what an odd thing this thing called Christianity is, is a gift from God. It is almost as if we are being forced to acknowledge that the difference that makes us Christians is Jesus. We worship a God who became one of us. We follow a Lord who was fully human, who was a first century Jew named Jesus, but who is also the one alone capable of reconciling us through cross and resurrection.

The discovery of the oddness of being a Christian may also offer the opportunity to recover the significance of the strange things we do at the

Church of the Holy Family. Think about the joy that seizes us when we witness the immersion of infants in baptism. A stranger who happens to wander in when we are in the process of baptism might well ask: "Are you people crazy? Are you trying to drown that child?" And, of course, we have to say: "Yes, that is exactly what we are trying to do. We are drowning this child in the Holy Spirit so that this child, in the language of Paul, becomes the gospel." At the very least this means the church is not another friendly group of people who get together because we like one another. We are in Christ a new creation.

One of the effects of this transformation is that it calls into question the familiar. In his letter to the Corinthians, Paul suggests that we no longer know Christ from a worldly point of view, but as the resurrected one who reigns at the right hand of the Father. This means the familiar not only can but must become quite strange. Let me try to develop that thought by calling attention to what I suspect is the best loved parable in the Gospels—the parable of the prodigal son.

I suspect, like me, you assume that you know what the upshot of the parable should be. The take away is that the lost son is rightly received back by his father even though by his own admission he has "sinned against heaven and before you." He tells his father he is no longer worthy to even be considered to be his son. He asks to be treated as one of his father's hired hands because that way he at least will not go hungry. But the father refuses his request ordering that he be given the best robe, a ring, and sandals. The father then commands that a festive celebration take place to welcome this son who was dead, but has now returned to life.

All this is familiar. We know we are to celebrate this forgiving father. We assume, moreover, that the father is really meant to be God the Father who welcomes us, his prodigal children, back into the family. This is a God always ready to forgive. We may even come to understand that the description of the parable as the parable of the prodigal son is misleading. It should have been called the parable of the forgiving father. In truth, most of us are not sure we have done anything as destructive as the prodigal, but in order for God to be a forgiving father we are willing to play the part.

But then we need to remember that there is the older brother. He turns out to be the real prodigal. He is the self-righteous prig who, unlike his father, is unable to welcome back his brother. He is the kind of person we love to hate. He has always done what his father commanded him to do, but the father has never even given him a young goat that he might celebrate with his friends. He is, therefore, not at all happy about the celebration to welcome back his brother.

Let me suggest, if you are like me, you are a little embarrassed by this focus on the older brother as the prodigal son. We are embarrassed because we cannot help but identify with him. We are Episcopalians—we have always gotten to work on time, we have always respected those in authority, we have always done what we have been asked to do, we have even done the jobs no one else would touch, so like the older brother we are not all that happy to get the short end of the stick. But this extraordinary father, just as he had gone to meet the son that was lost, came out to the older brother to plead that he join the celebration. The father points out that the older brother is still in line to inherit everything, so there is no reason he should not join the party.

I assume that the reading of the parable I have just provided is a familiar one. It is a reading, moreover, that we cannot help but find comforting. We may fear we are more like the older son, but we assume the father remains no less forgiving toward the elder son as he was toward the younger son who had squandered his inheritance. So we get a God who is always ready to forgive. But a God who forgives sinners without giving them something to do turns out to be a God of sentimentality. A people who worship such a God turn out to be incapable of challenging the lies that sustain the status quo.

That the parable is usually read to confirm our presumption that God is the Father that is always ready to forgive is not surprising given our state as Christians, who, like the Southern Baptists, have no idea how to challenge the status quo. But if I am right, that is a status quo not long for this world. The problem with the familiar reading of the parable as a parable of the father's willingness to always forgive is that such a reading is abstracted from the life of the one who alone has the power to forgive our sins. In short, we fail to read the parable through the eyes of Paul—that is, we overlook the reality that the father invites both sons to enjoy a restored relationship.

Prior to Jesus's telling of the parable we are told that the tax collectors and sinners came close to listen to Jesus. Jesus did not send them away. This elicited from the Pharisees and the scribes the judgment against Jesus that he not only welcomes sinners, but eats with them and invites them to the table. Jesus tells the parable in response to this grumbling by the Pharisees and scribes about the kind of people with whom Jesus is breaking bread. His response indicates that Jesus welcomes people like you and me—sinners—and he feeds us, making possible for us to feed one another.

What I think we may miss when we make the centerpiece of this parable the forgiveness offered by the father is that the parable says nothing about the father forgiving either son. To be sure, the parable may be about forgiveness by implication. The younger son does not return to the father because he wants the father to forgive him. He returns because he is desperate and he wants to survive. The father does not say to the younger son that he is forgiven, but rather "Thank God you have come home! I thought you were dead. I am going to throw a party!"

In like manner, the father responds to the elder brother, who construes his father's generosity as favoritism. The father, after listening to his complaints, does not chastise the older son, but invites him to join the celebration. Rather than being about forgiveness, the parable shows us that what constitutes a family, what maintains a communion, is not a love that is earned, but a love that is received and given freely—although not without a cost. That cost is crucifixion.

The younger son returns to his father because he is at the end of his rope and wants a good meal. That is not a bad place for any of us to begin. Christians tried to make a home in the world in a manner such that we became unintelligible to ourselves. We ceased being ambassadors for Christ and instead took on forms of life that seemed to make sense even if God had not shown up in Jesus Christ. Now we're wondering if we'll survive, or whether like Pleasant Grove Baptist Church, we'll end up boarded up and empty. Do we have anything to offer a world that has it all?

What we have to offer, what God offers the world through us, is a celebration. It is a celebration of the life and death of Jesus Christ. We each come to the table. Like the younger son, some of us are simply hungry. Others of us are simply here out of duty or faithfulness. Regardless of the motivation, the miraculous occurs. The Lord welcomes us and offers himself as a sacrifice in the bread and the wine so that we might be joined in celebrating Christ's victory over death. We are invited to a feast in which we participate as children whose joy upon being received by the Father, through the Son, and in the Holy Spirit, is so profound that it sounds, smells, tastes, and feels like a new creation, because that is exactly what it is.

The difference we enact each Sunday through participation in the liturgy is determinative for the difference we have become by being made ambassadors of Christ. Interestingly enough, that difference often does involve dancing. Possessed by the joy of being reconciled to God, we cannot help but be a people who move to the rhythm of the music of redemption. What a wonderful time to be a Christian! No longer in control of the world we once thought was "ours," we have been given the grace to discover our true family—it is called the Church of the Holy Family—God's outpost in a world of fear and despair.

26

"Trinity"

St. Paul's Christian Church
Raleigh, North Carolina
May 22, 2016

Proverbs 8:1–4, 22–31
Psalm 8
Romans 5:1–5
John 16:12–15

This is Trinity Sunday. Across Christendom preachers are trying to explain "Trinity" to their congregations. God is one, but God is three. How can one be three we ask? Attempts to explain the Trinity I fear often result not only in dull sermons but, even worse, heresy. Even more debilitating is the reality that the heresy evoked by such attempts is not recognized as heresy. It is not even clear if the person that represents the heresy thinks being a heretic is a "bad thing."

We live in a time when many Christians think what we think as Christians is our "own damn business." Thus the presumption that what matters is not whether you believe that God's primary name is Father, Son, and Holy Spirit, but whether you are a good person. I do not want to sell short that being a good person is important, but I do want to suggest that for Christians what it means for us to "be good" is inseparable from our worship of God as the Father, Son, and Holy Spirit.

One of the worst sermons I ever heard was on Trinity Sunday. At an Episcopal church in Northport, Minnesota, the priest began by declaring that, of course, the Trinity is an absurd doctrine. We know this, he said, because Bishops Pike and Spong, good liberal theologians, have declared that the Trinity is one of those relics of the past that makes no sense. But because we have inherited the language of the Trinity from the past and it is all over the Book of Common Prayer, the priest said we have to try to make some sense of it. So he set out to give an explanation of the Trinity that he hoped his listeners might find reasonable.

He observed he is one person, but he is loved by his wife, his son, and his dog. Each of those loves has him as the subject, but each love is different, which makes him different. That means that metaphysically God is subject to change. We know this because Hartshorne and the process metaphysicians have shown us that just as we are subject to change so is God. So God is part of the metaphysical furniture of the universe.

He tried to spell out the implications of this way of understanding God by describing the difference the love of his wife, his son, and his dog have made for making him who he is. How the different loves work should help us understand the Trinity just to the extent that the love of his wife, his son, and his dog are distinctive, yet he remains the subject of each love. He knows this to be true, because in some mysterious way, he is able to recognize himself as subject to the three loves. He then suggested that is the way we ought to think about the Trinity; namely, each of the members of the Trinity love God in a distinctive manner.

This account of the Trinity is not only embarrassingly self-centered, but the priest managed to represent the heresy of modalism without any recognition he had done so. Like most heresies, modalism was a gift to the church, because we seldom know what we believe until someone gets it wrong. Advocates of modalism maintained that each person of the Trinity is but a different mode of God's being rather than a distinct person. Accordingly, Christians who were and are modalist maintain that the distinction between the Father, Son, and Holy Spirit are but successive roles God plays by creating, redeeming, and sanctifying. The suggestion that the language of Father, Son, and Holy Spirit be replaced by creator, redeemer, and sustainer reproduces modalism.

An alternative attempt to safeguard the unity of God is found in the heresy known as subordinationism. Subordinationists are primarily concerned to protect God's oneness by making the Father the primary God, which reduces the Son and Spirit to some intermediary beings between the Father and creation. Like most heresies, subordinationism represents a valid theological concern, namely the desire to affirm that there is only one God. However, the theological moves made by subordinationists end up making our worship of Jesus a form of idolatry. In theology, balance is everything.

By now you have to be thinking, "We did not come to church to get a lecture by an academic theologian! This guy has to be kidding. He has been appointed to preach. This may be Trinity Sunday, but we are here to worship God, not to get a lesson about how we should think about God. Getting straight on the Trinity does not seem all that important to the task of worship." The account I have just given of the Trinity may even alienate some of you from the Church. After all, for anyone who is trying to make up their minds about this "Christian thing," the language of the Trinity does not seem all that relevant for negotiating how to live.

But I must tell you, if God is not the three-in-one, then our salvation is in doubt. It is not any God that saves us, but the God that saves us is the Father, Son, and Holy Spirit. In his letter to the Romans, Paul makes clear that it is through Christ that we are justified by faith. It is in Christ that we share in the glory of God. Accordingly, Christ is not playing at being God. He is fully God and fully human. He was before there was a beginning, and yet he is also a first-century Jew called Jesus. He is fully God and fully human. He is, therefore, as we say in the Nicene Creed, of one being with the Father.

Yet Christians could not make sense of the God we worship if we only confessed that Jesus is the Son. As our Gospel for today makes clear, Jesus has sent the Spirit of truth who will guide followers of Christ into all truth. The one Jesus sends, moreover, does not speak on their own, but Jesus tells us they will declare what is to come. We, therefore, are taught to say that "we believe in the Holy Spirit, the Lord, the giver of life, who proceeds from the Father (and the Son). With the Father and the Son he is worshiped and glorified. He has spoken through the Prophets." God is Trinity, three-in-one and one-in-three.

It took Christians four centuries to discipline our speech so that we might say what we say in the Nicene Creed. At the heart of that task was the Christian refusal to leave behind God's promise to Israel to be God's chosen people. Christians did not forget that Israel had prayed and continued to pray the Shema: "Hear, O Israel: The Lord our God, the Lord is one" (Deuteronomy 6:4). With that prayer, Christians learned from Jews that the God of Israel is known by the calling of Israel into the world, so that the world might know the righteousness of the One who alone is worthy of worship.

For Israel, however, the claim that the "Lord is one" is not a numerical claim. Rather, her conviction that the Lord is one is an affirmation that it is the same Lord who called her out of Egypt, who was with her in Exile, and who sustained her by the gift of the Law. In other words, Israel's confession that the "Lord is one" is the expression of Israel's faith that what makes her Israel is God's promise never to abandon her.

Robert Jenson, for example, rightly rejects the idea that Judaism or Christianity are monotheistic religions. He calls attention to Michael Wyschogrod and Peter Ochs, prominent Jewish theologians, who refuse the notion that God is one and that is all that can be said about God. Rather Jenson, as well as Wyschogrod and Ochs, maintains that the oneness of God is the oneness of the story Israel tells about God's calling and care of the people of Israel.

Trinity is, therefore, the outworking of the miracle that has made us, the Gentiles, joined to God's promise to love the people of Israel. Accordingly, Trinity makes no sense if we Christians are not as peculiar a people as the Jews. Trinity is the grammar that the church discovered was necessary if we are to tell the story of our being called into existence by Jesus. Trinity is the necessary affirmation that the love that constitutes the relation between the Father, the Son, and the Holy Spirit, the same love that moves the sun and the stars, has called us, people of diverse cultures and histories, to be one people through the work of the Holy Spirit.

We are the church of the Trinity. What one person of the Trinity does is done by the other two. The Son does nothing that is not the Father's will. Nor does the Father do anything by Himself that the Son does not conjointly enact. The Son, moreover, has no special work that is not also the work of the Holy Spirit. In the language of Gregory of Nyssa, "every operation which extends from God to Creation, and is named according to our variable conceptions of it, has its origin from the Father, and proceeds through the Son, and is perfected in the Holy Spirit."[1]

The relation between the persons of the Trinity, therefore, is what it means to say God is love. There is no competition between the Father, Son, and Holy Spirit. There is no competition, because each person of the Trinity delights in the work of the other persons of the Trinity. The Father sends the Son, the Son reveals the Father, the Holy Spirit incorporates us, making us participants in the love of the Father for the Son.

---

1. Gregory of Nyssa, "On 'Not Three Gods': To Ablabius," in *Nicene and Post-Nicene Fathers*, ed. Philip Schaff and Henry Wace, vol. 5, *Gregory of Nyssa: Dogmatic Treatises, etc.* (New York: Christian Literature Company, 1893), 334.

Some may worry that this emphasis on the Trinity may seem to make even more difficult the Christian negotiation of the world in which we now find ourselves. Given our increasing recognition that we live in a world of difference, should we not be emphasizing what we might have in common? Trinity seems to suggest that Christians have an understanding of God that is peculiar to our being a people set apart. Would we not be better off being identified as a people who are quite content to say we believe in god *qua* god? To be sure, such a god dwells in the land of vagueness, but better a vague god than one as concrete as the Father, Son, and Holy Spirit. But when our god becomes the "vague ultimate," we lose the story that makes us who we are.

That is why it is so important that we learn from our mothers and fathers in the faith how to read passages such as the one from Proverbs we read this morning. Our forefathers and mothers identified the wisdom that created all that is as the animating life of the Trinity. God did not become Trinity with the conception of Jesus; God has always been triune. We should not be surprised, therefore, as missionaries often discover, that those to whom they have gone to make Jesus known often seem already to know the Lord.

Because God is Trinity, Christians have no fear of the truth no matter where it may be found. Jesus tells his disciples that the Spirit of truth will guide them into all truth. All that is has been created by the Holy Spirit, so that all truth testifies to the one who makes the Father known. Christians, therefore, have a stake in the wisdom found through the contemplative wonder inspired by the glory of God's creation. All truth, if it is truth, will finally testify to the Trinity. Such testimony may take many years to be recognized, but we need not be in a hurry because, as Paul tells us in Romans, the Holy Spirit has been given to us that our suffering might produce endurance, endurance produce character, and character hope, and hope will not disappoint, because by hope, we are made participants in God's very life. Endurance is but another name for learning to live as creatures who have all the time in the world to be God's good people.

This is Trinity Sunday, but every Sunday is the time made possible because our Lord is triune. So may we rejoice in the glory of the Trinity, which has made us God's people that the world may know and see the goodness of the Father, the Son, and the Holy Spirit.

27

"Celebration"

Aldersgate United Methodist Church
Alexandria, Virginia
October 23, 2016
60th Anniversary Service

Jeremiah 14:7–10, 19–22
Psalm 84:1–7
2 Timothy 4:6–8, 16–18
Luke 18:9–14

You suddenly wake up one day and think, "How did this happen? I am sixty years old! That must mean I am growing old, but I am not sure what that means." For most of us, however, to have lived to be sixty seems like a long time. So we think it a considerable achievement for Aldersgate to celebrate its sixtieth anniversary. But Aldersgate stands in the Christian tradition that has been two thousand years in the making. Sixty years in a 2000-year-old tradition does not seem all that impressive. However, for a church to have survived and even flourished for sixty years in a time like this is rightly to be celebrated. The crucial phrase in the last sentence is "in a time like this." By calling attention to that remark, I mean to reference the fact that we live in a time marked by a decline of what is known as the mainstream Protestant church. We have been shrinking for some time, churches have been closed or sold, and before long, many seminaries will soon be closing their doors. But you are celebrating your sixtieth anniversary for which we can only thank God.

Aldersgate United Methodist Church was founded in that strange, but seemingly normal, time we call "the fifties." The fifties were a time when everything seemed all right, if not better than all right. Dwight Eisenhower was president. He quite cleverly seemed to be doing nothing, when, in fact, he was doing a great deal. Our enemy was identified as communism, which was incarnated in the Soviet Union. Elvis commanded the world of music and, despite some parental worries, rock and roll became everyone's music. The Montgomery bus boycott was underway, and churches were bombed. The civil rights struggle had begun, but that long-delayed work of justice seemed to suggest that America was a nation with a sense of what is right and good.

But then something happened. It is not clear what happened, but whatever happened means sixty years later we live in a very different world than the world of 1956. Everyone seemed to assume in that world that you would grow up, get married, have two children, pay your taxes, and go to church. It is not news to you that world no longer exists. Now there are a variety of lifestyle choices, and it is not clear that one is better than another. What is clear is you are not to be judgmental about the lifestyle of someone else.

Whatever happened, moreover, had dramatic consequences for the church. No longer is it assumed that one ought to go to church. Going to church became and remains another lifestyle choice that is neither good nor bad. That is not quite true, as many non-church people often justified their objection to Christianity by suggesting that the church is filled with self-righteous people who do not understand that they should not be judgmental. Those that make such an accusation seldom acknowledge that they are being quite judgmental about those they regard as judgmental. Drawing attention to that contradiction, however, rarely gets people to church.

It is important not to romanticize the past, but at one time people went to church because they thought they had a duty to worship God. That is obviously no longer the case. The language of duty is not used about anything, much less about going to church to worship God. The church now exists in a buyer's market. Even more troubling is that the consumer now gets to determine the product. The continued loss of membership in the mainstream churches of America—the churches of the 50s—no doubt has many causes, but surely one of the reasons for our decline is it is no longer clear what makes the church the church.

It is a great and good thing that you have been here sixty years. The good news is you have had a good sixty years, but it is not clear the next sixty years will be as fruitful. I pray that you will be here for the next sixty years, but if you are to be here for another sixty years, you will need to be quite clear about the difference being Christian makes.

Our texts for today I find at once sobering and challenging for helping us to know how to celebrate the sixty-year anniversary of the birth of Aldersgate, as well as for how to sustain hope in the face of questions about how the church is to survive for the next sixty years. To celebrate having made it sixty years may put us in the position of the Pharisee, who we know is the bad guy in this parable. Yet he is quite confident that he is doing everything right. He has not only refrained from those forms of evil behavior such as stealing and adultery that are generally thought to be wrong, but he also seems to be genuinely pious. That he fasts and tithes is an indication that he is serious about righteousness.

The Pharisee seems to be a good person whom we might well want to copy. To be sure, he appears to be a bit self-righteous, thanking God he is not like the tax collector. He is, after all, a Pharisee. He is about the difficult task of keeping the Law in a world dominated by Gentiles. Of all the various groups in Israel during Jesus's life, it was the Pharisees with whom he held the most in common.

In contrast to the Pharisee, we have the tax collector. Tax collectors came in different shapes and sizes in ancient Israel, and all of them were bad. In particular, Jewish tax collectors often did the dirty work of collecting taxes for Rome. They were also often associated with manipulating those from whom they took money by raking money off the top for themselves in a way that amounted to theft. So it is no surprise that the tax collector in our parable is profoundly sorrowful about his life. All he has to offer God is his sin. Accordingly, he prays for God to be merciful.

Yet Jesus commends the tax collector. In fact, he declares the tax collector to be justified, rather than the Pharisee. What Jesus seems to mean by declaring the tax collector justified is that the tax collector's confession and acknowledgment of his sin puts him on the road to holiness. For it turns out that holiness is to be found in lives that acknowledge their sinful pride. Such an acknowledgment makes the humility possible that is an essential characteristic of being part of God's good kingdom.

Keeping the Law, as the Pharisee has done, is not a bad thing. But keeping the Law can result, as it seems to have done for this Pharisee, in a prideful stance that robs one of the self-knowledge necessary to keep the Law. Keeping the Law and worship are intimately related just to the extent that by having our hearts set on God we discover the humility necessary to acknowledge who we are. That is, we are a people who would be no people if we did not have this Savior to guide us.

Humility, of course, is a tricky virtue. Have you ever known of anyone who successfully tried to be humble? Humility is usually something that happens to us, rather than something we do. I was once having a conversation with a friend in Ireland about sexual misconduct by priests. I asked him if the acknowledgment of this crime as sin might teach the church humility. He thought for a short time and then said, "Possibly, because there is no humility without humiliation." The tax collector was humiliated, which made him an appropriate witness to the one alone worthy of worship.

But if we put ourselves in the place of the tax collector, do we end up making the Pharisee's mistake of thanking God for not making us like other people? Is celebrating sixty years in existence an attempt to make ourselves not like other people? Truth be told, Christians, in recent times, have generally tried to avoid being identified as different from other people of good will. We have done so out of the fear of being identified with fundamentalist or moralistic Christians. But because we have not wanted to appear different, it has been unclear why anyone would want to be like us, much less become a member of the church.

I have not forgotten this is a sermon to celebrate the anniversary of your sixty years in existence. Such a celebration does not sound like humiliation. Yet the celebration that makes us who we are is called Eucharist. In that celebration, we are made one with the one whose humiliation on the cross turned out to be a victory that defeated sin and death. That is the celebration that unleashes Paul's declaration that he has fought the good fight, having been given by Christ the strength to witness to the Christ who now reigns in glory.

I know not what the future holds for Aldersgate United Methodist Church, but I know we will have a future if we, like the tax collector, ask God for the mercy that is the humbled Christ. The world is hungry to know the truth that is that Christ. So let us thank God for not making us like other people. We are Christians; we are followers of Christ. We once were no people but now through word and sacrament, we are God's people. Our great privilege is to be that truth for the world. It matters little whether in the future we are many or few. What matters is that we are "Jesus people" who know what a delightful duty it is to worship a merciful God.

28

"Elected"

Duke Divinity School
Durham, North Carolina
November 8, 2016

Isaiah 65:17–25
Psalm 98
2 Thessalonians 3:6–13
Luke 21:5–19

Jesus just does not seem to "get it." We should not be surprised, as he often did not seem to understand what should or should not be said if he wanted to have followers. He just did not get how there are better and worse ways to say certain things that need to be said—things that should be said carefully. As we have been reminded of late, "words matter." Jesus should have tried to find a less direct way to say what he feared might happen to the Temple.

Speaking directly, however, seems to have been a habit Jesus could not break. For example, Jesus surely overstated his case when he suggested that we must hate father and mother, wife and children if we are to follow him. Hating brothers and sisters is closer to the mark (Luke 14:26), but even that seems an exaggeration. But the real howler is his claim that the temple will end in ruins. You just do not make those kinds of claims if you want to be elected Messiah. At least, you do not make those kinds of claims about the Temple around the people of Israel. He surely must have known how to say what needed to be said so what is said could be heard.

That Jesus spoke so directly is an indication that he was not trying to create a democratic coalition. He held the ancient offices of Israel. He was prophet, priest, and king. Those positions were not bestowed on him by an election. Moreover, how his life reconfigured each of those offices is a story in itself.

Even as he taught as one with authority, he did not act as if his authority depended on a majority vote. Rather his authority seemed to come directly from who he was—that is, he was the Messiah who is truth itself and thus the one who speaks the truth. The truth is the Temple will be destroyed, and Jesus can speak that truth because he speaks of his own destruction. Jesus is the priest who is at once the altar and the sacrifice. In troubling his listeners, Jesus doesn't attempt to persuade, but rather trusts that the Spirit will reveal, without ambiguity, to those who have ears to hear that he is the Messiah, the one who will be raised again in glory.

In our epistle reading for the day, we come across yet another striking example of someone who lacked political savvy. Saul was knocked off his horse in an encounter with the risen Christ. As a result, Saul becomes Paul and assumes the title "apostle." As far as we know, Paul was not elected by anyone other than God to be an apostle to the Gentiles. Yet he assumes he has authority to tell the Thessalonians what to do. So he issues a command. To be sure, it is a command "in the name of our Lord Jesus Christ," but it is still a command made by Paul. Paul does not lead by suggesting, "I think you would find this a good idea." He says: I command you to stay away from those who live in idleness. Those living in idleness may assume that there is no need to work because they think they heard me say that all things are coming to an end, but they are mistaken about what I am about and they thereby should be avoided. Paul even has the audacity to say, "Imitate me."

Accordingly, Paul does not think that he must say what the Thessalonians want to hear. Majority vote will not determine what the church should or will be. Nor will a poll be taken to determine what the general will might be. Paul has no use for those who will not work. Idleness is surely the breeding ground of the lie, and the lie makes violence inevitable. The lie leads to violence because people who have nothing better to do than to do nothing turn out to be a people who spend their lives making other people miserable because by doing so they at least avoid boredom. Thus, Paul exercises his authority, but his authority is the authority of an apostle.

I have called attention to the kind of authority Jesus and Paul enact as a way to suggest that there may be some tension between the political order that is the church and that form of social and political organization called democracy. I need not tell you this is the day Americans elect their president and a host of other offices. We will be told this is the day the people rule. That sounds like a good idea, but you need to remember that there was a democratic moment in the Gospels, and the people asked for Barabbas.

Voting is often said to be the institution that makes democracies democratic. I think, however, that is a deep mistake. It is often overlooked, but there is a coercive aspect to all elections. After an election, 50.1% get to tell 49.9% what to do. I do not mean to underestimate the work elections may do to make our lives less subject to violence, but elections are not ends in themselves. In classical democratic theory, elections are only the means to make a people have the kind of exchanges necessary for the articulation of the goods we have in common. I think I can honestly report that the campaign climaxing in election today does not seem to fit that description.

It is tempting to blame Donald Trump for that result, but I think the problem goes deeper than Trump. The problem, quite simply, is *us*. A sobering thought, but I fear a true one. We get the people we deserve running for office. What made Trump stand out is he seemed to speak something other than bureaucratic speech. But you know you are in trouble when the kind of speech that is the speech of television sitcoms is identified as plain speech.

We did not elect Jesus to be President. We did not elect Jesus to be the second person of the Trinity. We did not elect him Messiah or Savior. We did not vote on whether there should or should not be a people gathered to worship Jesus. We thought our leadership could even be determined by lot. We did not vote to legitimate what we now call "the Bible." There were times Christians took votes and there will continue to be times Christians take votes, but often it takes centuries for what was determined by a vote to be received by the whole church. Elections are no substitute for argument. Thus, the observation made often by non-Christians that Christians must surely love one another, because how else could we explain their willingness to engage one another in argument?

Truth matters. We are to be people of truth. The truth that makes us Christians means we are a people who are not destined to be celebrated in any social order, whether it calls itself democratic or not. Do not misunderstand! I am not suggesting that there are not better and worse forms of social and political organization. We do not live in a night when all cows are grey. But it is also the case that Christians are a people that believe what we believe is true. Such a people cannot help from time to time coming into conflict with those regimes organized on the assumption that there is no truth other than what "the people" say is the truth.

Jesus tells his followers that we will be arrested and persecuted because of his name. This should be received as good news because Jesus tells us we will therefore have the opportunity to testify. To testify is to tell the truth before a world that often does not believe it possible to say what is true. Jesus assures us that we will be given the words and the wisdom to say at the appropriate time what is true. And this, thank God, is the truth: *Jesus is Lord.*

Lord is not a democratic title; it is a truthful designation for the one we worship. We have the authority to testify to the truth that is Jesus because that Jesus is Lord is not some general truth that can be known without witnesses. That what is true is known by witnesses to Jesus cannot help but be a deep and profound challenge to the *status quo*. It is a challenge because the *status quo* is based on the assumption that whatever is true must be available to anyone. Christians are not anyone. We are Jesus people who Jesus says will be hated and some of us will even be put to death. But if Jesus is who he says he is, what choice do we have? After all we did not elect Jesus. He elected us.

29

"Sin"

Saint Mark's Church
Philadelphia, Pennsylvania
March 5, 2017

Genesis 2:15–17; 3:1–7
Psalm 32
Romans 5:12–19
Matthew 4:1–11

Harold Pinter's 1963 movie, *The Servant*, is seared in my memory. Dirk Bogarde, the great English actor, plays the servant, a gentleman's gentleman, who brings to ruin a wealthy young English nobleman named Tony. Being from the English upper classes, Tony does not have a clue about how one can and should negotiate the everyday. Accordingly, as the English upper classes were wont to do, Tony hires a servant to offer him advice on a variety of issues, including: how to decorate his rooms, what sort of friends to have, what club to join, how to put on a party, what views he should have as a representative of the higher class, and how to treat women, in particular, his girlfriend, Susan.

At first all seems to go well, but Bogarde slowly introduces Tony to the underside of life—gambling, drugs, perverted sex—which ultimately results in Tony's destruction. The movie ends with Tony facing financial, social, and moral ruin. We, the viewers, are left waiting for Bogarde to step in and save him. Instead, Bogarde turns his back on his former master and in an unmistakably deliberate manner walks away with a self-satisfied demeanor.

Leaving the theater after having seen *The Servant*, you can sense there is an uneasiness within all who have seen the movie. That uneasiness, I think, is due to Pinter's refusal to explain why the servant so successfully destroyed his master. You hear your fellow moviegoers speculate about why the servant seems to have set out in such a calculated way to turn Tony into a pathetic human being. Repressed homosexual desire, class revenge, proletariat anger are all mentioned as possibilities by those leaving the movie. While there is obviously something rational about such explanations, the movie itself gives no indication that any singular account is sufficient. Rather, the movie simply depicts Bogarde's calculated destruction of Tony.

I call attention to *The Servant* because I think our text for today about our first parents' disobedience is similar to the film's refusal to explain why Bogarde set out to ruin his master. Eve had all that she could desire. But she could not resist trying to be more than human. In response to the serpent's misshapen question about from which trees she and her partner might eat, Eve could not resist trying to be more than she was created to be. Accordingly, in response to the serpent's question she adds to God's command, telling the serpent that they should not eat the fruit of the tree of knowledge of good and evil. But Eve doesn't stop there, she goes on to add that not only should they not eat the fruit of the tree of knowledge of good and evil, they should not even touch it.

God had said nothing about not touching the fruit of the tree. Eve's attempt to make God's command more strenuous than it actually was helps us see that it was a moral legalist who commits the first sin. It seems Eve is in the business of minding God's business. This observation led Augustine to conclude that Eve's sin was not her decision to eat the fruit; the eating of the fruit was merely an outward sign that a more fundamental turning against God had already taken place.

We are offered no explanation for why Eve felt it necessary to try to be more godly than God. Rather, like the movie, *The Servant*, all we get is the story. That is not accidental. A narrative is necessary if we are to comprehend a singular reality that would otherwise defy comprehension. Sin should not exist, but it does. Accordingly, sin cannot be explained, nor is sin an explanation. Sin is, in Karl Barth's terms, an "ontological impossibility." We may think the story of what we Christians call "the Fall" exists because these were ancient people who had no other way to think about such matters than to tell a story. But, in fact, there is no better way to comprehend the character of sin than through such a story. For it turns out, moreover, that that story of our first parents' sin was not finished until Christ, the new Adam, defeated the power that sin has over our lives.

For that is what sin is—a power. We tend to think sin is something we do, but that is to make sin far too easy to identify. To think of sin as "bad things we do or have done" reduces sin to a matter of morality and fails to understand the full extent of our predicament. Sin is not so much something we do. Rather, sin is a power that can take many different forms, but each form draws on the one power that we know is our destiny, that is, the power of death. Paul suggests in our passage from his letter to the Romans that death is a dominion, a kingdom, that sin has created. But that dominion has now been made subject to another dominion we know as the Lordship of Christ.

This is the beginning of Lent. Lent is a time for the examination of our lives in the hope we can discover what stands in the way of God's love being the loadstar that gives shape to our lives. Sin, therefore, should come into focus for us during Lent. Yet, I suspect, just to the extent we try to explain our sins we become all the more tangled in those modes of life we rightly call sin. We are tempted to think we must will our way out of the death-determined dominions, but when we do so we only make ourselves even more subject to the dominion of the kingdom of death.

Consider how each of the temptations the devil offers Jesus involve powers we think necessary to accomplish some good to keep death at bay. Turning stones to bread would feed the poor, to be the center of religious devotion would heal the divisions between religions, to be Lord of all the kingdoms of the world would make peace possible. Jesus, unlike Eve, counters these temptations by knowing scripture better than the devil. But note: it is not a small thing that the devil knows scripture.

That we are taught to confess our sin, particularly during Lent, is not something to which we look forward. We are not at all sure an emphasis on sin is a good idea. We are in a time of a dramatic loss in membership in mainline Protestantism. We need to attract new people. Telling people they are possessed by sin does not sound like a good church-growth strategy. People come to church because they want to be loved, not to be told that their lives are determined by destructive forces. The best it seems we can do is to say things like "when everything is said and done we are all sinners"—a generalization and platitude that is as meaningless as it is destructive. Destructive because the presumption that when all is said and done we are all sinners in effect works as an excuse in waiting, making possible for us to do what we know will alienate us from the love of God.

I suspect if you are like me and you try to remember a sermon on sin you will have difficulty doing so. We are after all Episcopalians. There are just some things better left in the closet. During Lent we know we are to try to think of some aspect of our lives that we associate with being less than Christian, but if we are honest with ourselves it is almost as if we are trying to play a game called "I am a sinner." We play the game of trying to imagine what it might mean to be a sinner, but we are not at all sure our lives are impressive enough to be called sinful. After all we are decent enough people who may not be all that morally impressive, but then neither do we think we are people of great immorality. We live lives of modest respectability, which means to claim that we are "sinful" can appear like we are putting on airs.

Sin, however, is not a general description of something we have done that we wish later we had not done. No, sin is to be possessed by presumptions of righteousness that assure us our lives make sense, even if the Lord that is Jesus Christ was not raised from the dead. Accordingly, sin often is not what we have done, but what we have *not* done or been. That is why "sins of omission" are so hard to discover. I suspect that like me, you often blanch at the phrase in the confessional prayer in which we ask forgiveness for what we have left undone.

One of the great advantages of being a Christian is that we are in a lifetime project to discover how to confess our sins. To be able to confess our sins is a theological achievement that our baptisms have made possible. For sin, as Karl Barth maintained, is only known in the light of Christ. Thus from Barth's perspective, our fundamental sin consists in the presumption that we can know our sin without having become a disciple of Christ. In short, to be a Christian means we must be trained to be a sinner. Christ has not only freed us from the power of sin, but through Christ we are offered more than we could imagine. The salvation wrought in the cross heals our brokenness by giving us wonderful and compelling work to do that breaks the back of the self-fascination our sin invites.

I fear the American revival tradition, the tradition of the tents, has distorted our understanding of sin. That tradition assumed that you must be convinced that you are first and foremost a sinner before you could be forgiven for what you have done. In some contexts, this could lead to quite entertaining lists and descriptions of sins that had been committed.

That made it possible for those tents to become football stadiums and more recently enormous church buildings that seem to have been inspired by warehouse architects. Though such accounts of sin could be quite entertaining—particularly when sin became primarily thought of as "sins"—sin so conceived is fundamentally mistaken. It is mistaken because it lets sin determine the work of Christ, rather than recognizing that the work of Christ determines our sin. You only know your sin on your way out of it. In short, God refuses our rejection by giving us the very life of his Son who has come that we might have the abundant life called love.

We have been given a tree that stands in continuity with the tree of the knowledge of good and evil in the garden. The name of that tree is Jesus Christ. We are invited not only to touch and eat of that tree, but to cling to that tree with everything we have. In the process, we are consumed by what we consume at the meal that is to come. So consumed, we are freed from the fascination with our sins. We discover that sin no longer has dominion over us and—miracle of miracles—we not only have an alternative to the world, but we have become God's alternative, lively people in a death-determined world. What good news!

30

"Caesar Wants It All"

St. Michael's Episcopal Church
Raleigh, North Carolina
October 22, 2017

Isaiah 45:1–7
Psalm 96:1–9
1 Thessalonians 1:1–10
Matthew 22:15–22

My general impression is that most Christians in the world in which we find ourselves are not quite sure if we, in fact, are what we say we are—that is, Christians. We want to be Christians, but some of the traditional moral commitments associated with Christianity just do not seem workable for us. Take no thought for the morrow does not seem like a good policy for retirement planning, investment strategies, or even life insurance. Do not resist evildoers, turn the other cheek, seems just a bit "idealistic." Turing the other cheek will usually mean that both cheeks end up being, at best, bruised and, at worst, broken.

So we cannot help but rejoice that Jesus's exchange with the Pharisees and Herodians in our Gospel reading seems finally to result in a recommendation we can keep. By "we" I mean we Americans. America is the name of that people who believe that through the instrument of the law we have found a way to be loyal to God and state. We are able to do so because we are a democracy—no emperors need to apply. We call the arrangement that makes possible loyalty to state and God the separation of church and state. To be sure, it took some centuries to get this right, but thanks to the Protestant Reformation, we believe we got what Jesus wanted when he said we were to give to the emperor what is his and to God what is God's. The result is a limited state in which we are free to believe whatever we want without fear of the state meddling with our beliefs.

The institutionalization of Jesus's recommendation to give to Caesar the things that are Caesar's and to God the things that are God's in our society depends on the further distinction between what is appropriately public and what is appropriately private. In general, we think the state has jurisdiction over matters that are public, which is often associated with the body. Few matters, moreover, are more bodily than money. But we believe we are free to think and be whatever we want to be. We are free to be whatever we want to be because what we want to be is our private business.

It turns out, moreover, that one of the main aspects of that which is private is what we think of as religious faith. The state we believe must respect our private convictions, particularly those that have to do with God. We can, therefore, entertain what we want to believe or disbelieve, as long as we play by the rules in the public arena. The only problem is that the relegation of faith to the realm of the private makes it very hard to maintain any discipline in the church itself, because even members of the church believe that no one, not even their priest or bishop, can tell them what they are to believe. Every Christian gets to make up their mind about what it means to be a Christian. It turns out there is an emperor—the emperor is us!

This last remark may suggest that to read this exchange between Jesus, the Pharisees, and the Herodians through the eyes of the church/state divide can result in giving Caesar more power than is good for Caesar. "Give to the emperor the things that are the emperor's and to God the things that are God's" is not a formula for instituting peace between church and state. God and emperors just do not get along. They do not get along because they both want it all. Caesar may appear from time to time to only want some parts of our lives, but when push comes to shove, which is but another way to say in times of "war," we know Caesar will demand everything.

The Pharisees were a movement in Judaism who very probably were the group most like Jesus in Roman-occupied Palestine. They tried very hard to keep the law in a world governed by pagans. They had to obey the law in a manner that did not invite the suspicion of the Romans. They were trying to resist in their own way without Rome catching on. In contrast, the Herodians were collaborationists who thought the only route to survival was doing what Rome wanted. The two groups shared enough in common, however, to make them enemies of Jesus. Jesus, after all, had a much more severe position when it came to Rome. Never forget he died on a Roman cross.

The Pharisees and Herodians begin their interaction with Jesus with flattery, "Teacher," a term of respect, "we know that you are sincere, and teach the way of God in accordance with truth, and show deference to no one"—a true description that makes clear that liars can speak the truth. The question they ask, however, is designed to put Jesus in an impossible position. If Jesus says pay the tax, it will make him appear to be on the side of the Herodians who have sold out to Rome. If Jesus says not to pay the tax, he will become a rebel against Rome.

Jesus does not respond to the question, but instead asks for the kind of coin required to pay the tax. For Rome not only required the tax, but expected the tax to be paid in Roman coinage. It is particularly important that Jesus did not have the coin at hand. For the coin bore the image of Caesar. To carry such a coin was thought by many Jews to commit the sin of idolatry. In Exodus 20:4–5, the second commandment of the Decalogue, Israel was commanded not to "make for yourself an idol, whether in the form of anything that is in heaven above, or that is on the earth beneath, or that is in the water under the earth. You shall not bow down to them or worship them." A coin with Caesar's image on it clearly counted as an idol. That someone that was testing Jesus was carrying the coin meant they bore the burden of truth, not Jesus.

Jesus's claim, therefore, to give to God the things that are God's turns out to be the kind of command that turns the world upside down. In his response to the Pharisees and Herodians, Jesus is not suggesting that we learn to live in the tension between church and state or that his followers should get used to living with divided loyalties. Rather, he is saying that coins with the image of the emperor should be sent back to the emperor.

That Jesus would have the coins sent back to the emperor indicates that Jesus knows of no distinction between religion and politics. Render to Caesar what is Caesar's will turn out to be a challenge to all politics that do not know God. Those who have asked him whether they should pay taxes to Caesar are revealed to be faithful servants of the emperor by the money they possess. After all, Jesus had earlier made clear "No one can serve two masters; for a slave will either hate the one and love the other, or be devoted to the one and despise the other. You cannot serve God and wealth" (Matt 6:24). Wealth just turns out to be another word for emperor.

That God and the emperor cannot both be served is not solved when the emperor is identified with "the people." The people often turn out to be more omnivorous in their desire for loyalty than emperors. Nor is that problem solved by the separation of church and state—a phrase that is to be found in a letter by Thomas Jefferson and not in the constitution. Too often, I fear, the use of that phrase results in legitimating the state to do what it wants while sequestering the church into the mythical realm of the private. Christian accommodation that results from playing the game called "Caesar's coin" insures that the separation of church and state will make Christians faithful servants of states that allegedly give the church freedom.

In an observation about American Protestantism, Bonhoeffer put the matter this way: "Freedom as an institutional possession is not an essential mark of the church. It can be a gracious gift given to the church by the providence of God; but it can also be the great temptation to which the church succumbs in sacrificing its essential freedom to institutional freedom. Whether the churches of God are really free can only be decided by the actual preaching of the Word of God."[1] As Luther was wont to say, "Let that be written in gold."

The church will never be free, nor will the church keep Caesars limited, if there is not in existence a people who have learned to say "no." Such a people will not come from nowhere. Rather they will come from the formation they have received by worshiping rightly the only one that is rightly worshiped. So as you come to eat this body and drink this blood, praise God that by doing so God is making us a people who will always have a problem with Caesars. That problem—that is, how to negotiate the state that fears a free church—will always be an insoluble problem, but that should not be a problem for us. For we know we have a problem, at least if we are disciples of Jesus, when we do not have a problem.

---

1. Dietrich Bonhoeffer, "Protestantism without Reformation," in *Dietrich Bonhoeffer: Witness to Jesus Christ*, ed. John W. de Gruchy (Minneapolis: Fortress Press, 1991), 206.

31

"The Politics of Martyrdom"

Duke Divinity School
Durham, North Carolina
November 1, 2017

REVELATION 7:9–17
PSALM 34:1–10, 22
1 JOHN 3:1–3
MATTHEW 5:1–12

The image of the saints robed in white, surrounding the throne of the Lamb in the book of Revelation, is a powerful depiction of the significant place of the martyred saints in the Christian faith. Put as simply as I can, I think it true that if there were no martyrs there would be no Christianity. That the doors of many churches are painted red is to remind us that we are only able to be Christians by the sacrifice of the martyrs.

That the martyrs play such an important role in our faith is a reminder that to be a Christian is to enter a way of life that trains us in how to die. It is not an empty gesture that in the baptismal liturgy we say "We thank you, Father, for the water of Baptism. In it we are buried with Christ in his death."[1] For the Christian, death is always a possibility given the presumption that as Christians we would die before we betrayed the one who has given us life. Thus Herbert McCabe's observation that for

---

1. The Episcopal Church, *The Book of Common Prayer and Administration of the Sacraments and Other Rites and Ceremonies of the Church: Together with the Psalter or Psalms of David* (New York: Seabury, 1979), 306.

Christians, "there is no casual death, there is only a choice between martyrdom and betrayal."[2]

Martyrdom, so understood, is a reminder that the willingness of Christians through the centuries to be killed because of who they worshiped represents an intense form of the politics of Jesus. That politics—the politics of Jesus—means we never as Christians live in a time or place where martyrdom is not a continuing possibility. Training in how we should die is the heart of every politics, just to the extent politics is always about that for which it is worth dying. That for which it is worth dying means some draw the conclusion that you must also be willing to kill to sustain that which is so valuable.

We, that is we Americans, are quite good at hiding the significance of death for our politics. We tell ourselves that politics is fundamentally about the satisfaction of interests, but it nonetheless remains the case that politics even in liberal societies is but another name for the distribution of risks that are intrinsic to an economy of death.

The political character of martyrdom was strikingly evident in the struggle between Christians and Rome. It took some time for the Romans to even notice that a small band of people called Christians existed. From a Roman perspective the Christians did not seem to be a threat so there was little reason to kill them. Pliny thought they were but another burial society. He was not wrong about that, but he did not have a clue about the significance of how the way Christians died raised questions about the pride that was at the heart of the project called Rome.

The Romans were not completely without insight about these matters. It did not take them long to understand that the Christians were anything but just another religious association. The Christians worshiped Jesus. They thought it was only in that name that you could live a life that you might lose early. Accordingly, Christians called into question the Roman worship of the gods that legitimated the decisions Rome made about who should be killed and who should be tolerated. The Christians, therefore, had a story about the way things are that was fundamentally at odds with the stories on which Rome depended. As a result, Christians refused to be tolerant because they were anything but ambivalent about who had made their lives free.

Confronted by such a people there is only one thing you can do if you are Rome. You must kill them and in the process show that their

---

2. Herbert McCabe, *The New Creation* (New York: Sheed and Ward, 1965; reprint, London: Continuum, 2010), 127.

willingness to die makes clear that the narrative that shapes their deaths cannot be true. Yet there was an unpleasant discovery that awaited Rome. Rome discovered that they could kill the Christians, but they could not determine the meaning of their death.

Rome would even put those who were to die through degrading forms of torture in the hope of making their deaths meaningless. But the Christian refusal to let Rome determine the meaning of the death of martyrs made clear that the church was an alternative politics to the violent politics of glory that made Rome Rome. The citizens of Rome desperately fought to insure Rome was eternal, so no memory would be lost. If Rome fell, who would remember them? Christians had a quite different polity because they knew God would remember.

The white-robed army that surrounds the throne makes the church here and now actual. They have been identified as those who have been made who they are by the blood of the Lamb. They have been told by God who they are. They are not "heroes" or "heroines." They are martyrs. They are witnesses to the inauguration of a new time by a man named Jesus. He has defeated the violence of a politics that tries to sustain itself by killing those who threaten the presumption that it is eternal.

These reflections on martyrdom as a politics may seem quite foreign for American Christians. We do not think of ourselves as living in a country in which our lives as Christians are threatened because we are Christians. So we do not think of ourselves as a church of the martyrs. Yet we do have this prayer in *The Book of Common Prayer*: "Almighty God, who gave to your servant *N.* a boldness to confess the Name of our Savior Jesus Christ before the rulers of this world, and courage to die for the faith: Grant that we may always be ready to give a reason for the hope that is in us, and to suffer gladly for the sake of our Lord Jesus Christ; who lives and reigns with you and the Holy Spirit, one God, for ever and ever. *Amen.*"[3]

We are a people who celebrate and thus remember the martyrs. Let us not forget that this is dangerous business, but let us not fail to remember that those who have triumphed—that is, those called martyrs—have made us members in a fellowship inaugurated by Jesus, so that the world may know a people exist who are willing to die, yet who refuse to kill. To be part of such a people is what it means to be saved.

---

3. *Book of Common Prayer*, 246–47.

32

"The Never-ending Story"
Burns Presbyterian Church
Ashburn, Ontario
November 12, 2017

Robert J. Dean

Isaiah 52:7–10
Romans 1:1–7
Luke 4:14–21

Letter writing has become something of a lost art in our day. I guess it really shouldn't surprise us. After all, with the rise of technology that allows us to communicate instantaneously across vast geographical distances, why would anyone bother to sit down with a sheet of paper before them, pen in hand? It seems rather old-fashioned, not to mention terribly inefficient. While I am not at all contemplating getting rid of my smartphone, I do wonder what we might be losing in this cultural shift. For example, a significant part of the New Testament consists of letters. I wonder what would happen if our passage this morning from Paul's letter to the Romans were replaced with a series of emojis? Although, I can't even begin to imagine which emojis one would choose to represent these pregnant opening verses of the letter! I mean it's all right there, the whole gospel, in this tightly formulated introduction to Paul's letter.[1] Any attempt to

---

1. I was first alerted to the apostolic density of this passage some years ago by David Yeago's discussion of these verses in his yet-to-be published manuscript, "The Apostolic Faith: A Catholic and Evangelical Introduction to Christian Theology," Vol.

portray these verses as a collection of funny symbols would be trite and trivial. It seems like we cannot get by without the words if we want to come to grips with this thing called the gospel.

At the very beginning of the passage, Paul introduces himself. Only it seems that he cannot introduce himself without also speaking of the gospel. Paul seems to be telling his readers that it is impossible to understand who he is apart from understanding how he had been singularly seized by the risen Lord on the road to Damascus. Here in the opening verse of Romans, Paul identifies his master—Christ Jesus; his office—an apostle; and his purpose—sent out to preach the good news or gospel.[2] Paul is a man under authority—he is a servant of Jesus Christ. He is neither a volunteer nor a religious entrepreneur; rather he has been called or chosen to be an apostle—God's messenger to the Gentiles.

The next four verses consist of a series of subordinate clauses in which Paul explains just what he means when he speaks of "the gospel" or "the good news." He begins in the second verse by describing the gospel as that which God had "promised beforehand through his prophets in the holy scriptures." Throughout his letters Paul is at pains to demonstrate that the gospel is in accordance with the Scriptures. Remember, in Paul's day, the New Testament writings had not yet been collected, so when Paul speaks of the Scriptures he is primarily referring to the writings of the Old Testament. Paul understands that the gospel is not the nullification or cancellation of the promises God made to Israel, but is, in fact, their very fulfillment. The gospel does not emerge from a vacuum. Rather, the gospel is rooted in the soil of the long history of God's dealings with his people Israel. Outside of this context the execution of a 33-year old man and his reported resurrection is merely puzzling—an Unsolved Mystery or some type of X-file—but it is certainly not good news. Isolated events or situations make little sense apart from some larger context in which to understand them.

Several years ago when my dad purchased his first digital camera, he got into the habit of regularly sending me e-mails that included digital photographs documenting his weekly exploits. On one occasion, when I opened his e-mail I somehow missed his written message and was left trying to make sense of the pictures he had sent. As I scrolled through them I was baffled. There were a few pictures of some type of river or waterway.

1, "The Gift of the Life of the Triune God in Jesus Christ" (Spring 2005), 52–54.

2. Douglas J. Moo, *The Epistle to the Romans*, New International Commentary of the New Testament (Grand Rapids: Eerdmans, 1996), 40.

There was another of my mom standing with some friends in a boat with a life jacket on. Then there was one of people I didn't know dressed up in Victorian-age costumes. As I scrolled down, I came to a picture of a small bedroom with antique-looking furniture that appeared could have been taken in a museum or maybe some type of bed and breakfast. I was at a loss. Had my parents gone on some type of trip? Where were these pictures taken? Why had my dad sent them to me? What did they mean? As I continued scrolling down, the last two pictures I came to featured large vultures perched high in a tree. These pictures I could make sense of, however, because I was familiar with the story that went along with them. I had previously heard the news of how a venue of vultures had taken up residence in the trees in my grandmother's backyard. I had even seen them myself when I had visited my grandmother's house, but the other pictures remained a complete mystery. It wasn't until later in the day that I discovered my dad had indeed included a brief message explaining that he and my mom had visited various historic sites around Southwestern Ontario as part of the province of Ontario's Open Doors program. It was only in the context of the whole story that I was able to make sense of the discrete scenes depicted in the photos.

So it is with the gospel. The Old Testament provides the necessary context for properly understanding the gospel or good news of Jesus Christ. In fact, the word gospel itself comes from the second half of the book of Isaiah. In our reading from Isaiah, we heard the prophet declare: "How beautiful upon the mountains are the feet of the messenger who announces peace, who brings good news, who announces salvation, who says to Zion, 'Your God reigns.'" From Isaiah we learn that the gospel or good news is associated with the announcement that God's reign is coming because God himself is coming. He will, at last, redeem his people from slavery and shepherd them, and all the ends of the earth will see his salvation. It is, therefore, highly significant that when it came time for Jesus to preach his first sermon, the Gospel of Luke tells us he chose a text from the book of Isaiah. As Jesus stepped into the pulpit in his hometown of Nazareth he read these words from the prophet, "The Spirit of the Lord is upon me, because he has anointed me to bring good news to the poor. He has sent me to proclaim release to the captives and recovery of sight to the blind, to let the oppressed go free, to proclaim the year of the Lord's favor." Apart from the law and the prophets of Israel, it is impossible to truly understand this message called the gospel. That is why, with all due respect to the Gideons, the Old and New Testaments should never be separated. Apart from the Old Testament, we will inevitably end up promulgating news that sounds good to our ears, but which inevitably leaves us enslaved to the spirit of the age and hence is not really good news at all.

When I was a doctoral student at Wycliffe College, I spent a lot of time commuting to and from campus on the subway. On one occasion, I was seated by one of the doors reading a fairly dense theological book entitled *The Identity of Jesus Christ*.[3] As the train slowed down approaching Bloor station, a young man on his way to the door stopped in front of me and said, "I noticed the title of the book you're reading. Do you really want to know the identity of Jesus Christ? The identity of Jesus Christ is recognizing your limitations and overcoming them."[4] And with that, he was out the door and on his way to wherever he was going. Interestingly enough, the exhortation of this subway theologian was actually the exact opposite of what the apostle Paul is saying in our passage this morning, and also, ironically, of the book I was reading. The gospel is not an idea, like recognizing your limitations and overcoming them. Nor is it a principle, like "Everyone is Included." Nor is it a theory, not even one that attempts to present a series of steps for how sinners are made right with God. These may or may not be implications or benefits of the gospel, but they are not the gospel itself. While the Old Testament was the context of the gospel Paul was proclaiming, Paul tells us in verse three that the content of the gospel is a person—the person of God's Son Jesus Christ. Because the content of the gospel is a person and persons are known by their unique life-stories, the gospel takes the form of a story. For this reason, the great Protestant Reformer Martin Luther could assert that, "The gospel is a story about Christ, God's and David's Son, who died and was raised and is established as Lord. This is the gospel in a nutshell."[5]

At this point, Luther is doing nothing more than riffing on the apostle Paul, who presents the CliffsNotes version of the story of God's Son over the course of our passage this morning. In verse three, Paul tells us that Jesus was "descended from David according to the flesh." In

3. Hans W. Frei, *The Identity of Jesus Christ: The Hermeneutical Basis of Dogmatic Theology* (Eugene, OR: Wipf & Stock, 1997).

4. My subway friend's "identity" statement was accompanied by specific gestures, which I incorporated into the sermon when it was preached. Upon saying "recognizing your limitations" he fully extended his arms in the form of a cross. He then proceeded to point upwards with both arms when he said, "overcoming them."

5. Martin Luther, "A Brief Instruction on What to Look for and Expect in the Gospels," trans. William A. Lambert, in *Word and Sacrament I*, ed. E. Theodore Bachmann, vol. 35 of *Luther's Works*, ed. Helmut T. Lehmann (Philadelphia: Fortress, 1960), 118.

other words, Paul is saying that Jesus is the fulfillment of Israel's Messianic hopes. He is the righteous branch from the root of David anticipated by the prophets and the long-awaited good shepherd sent to tend and nurture the flock of God. Paul is telling us that Jesus is the true king of Israel. However, a crucified king is a very strange thing indeed. Yet this is already anticipated in verse three by the phrase "according to the flesh." This short, little phrase stresses Jesus's complete participation in the frailty and finitude of our sin-riddled existence.[6] The entirety of Jesus's distinctive human life, including its ignominious end on a cruel Roman cross is encompassed by the phrase "according to the flesh."

However, the story of Jesus cannot be fully comprehended from solely a human or fleshly point of view. If it could, then the story of Jesus would simply be another human tragedy ending as every other purely human story does in the silence of the tomb. But the story of Jesus does not end engulfed in the darkness of death, rather, Paul tells us that Jesus "was declared to be Son of God with power according to the spirit of holiness by resurrection from the dead." This whole verse reflects Paul's conviction that God has done a new thing! Through the exercise of the Spirit's power in raising Jesus from the dead, the Messianic age has dawned and the end of the ages has come. Right in the very midst of continuing history, God has raised up this Jesus as the first fruits of the general resurrection of the dead. This is why one of the earliest and most succinct summations of the gospel took the form of the simple proclamation, "He is risen!"

Of course, who the "he" is makes all the difference in the world. It would not be good news to say that Hitler or Bin Laden is risen. However, to say that Jesus is risen is to say that God has raised up the one who made the lame to walk and the blind to see. It is to say that God has vindicated the one who fed the multitudes and broke bread with the least, the last and the lost. It is to affirm that God has pronounced his "Yes!" over the one who forgave sins and proclaimed the year of the Lord's favor. The resurrection is the divine verdict pronounced upon the life of Jesus that makes plain to all that Jesus is who he says he is—God's Son.

Paul concludes verse four by telling us that the one who in his earthly life was born into King David's family line and the one who was shown to be the Son of God when he was raised from the dead by the power of the Holy Spirit is one and the same person, "Jesus Christ our Lord." The crucified Jesus of Nazareth is the Lord who now sits in power at the right

---

6. Moo, *Romans*, 47.

hand of God. It was this confession of Jesus Christ as Lord that set the early church on a collision course with Rome, for it was a rather audacious thing for the recipients of Paul's letter in Rome to affirm that Jesus, and not Caesar, was Lord! The Roman imperial propaganda frequently spoke of the "good news" or "gospel" of the birth and military triumphs of the Caesar and how through these military conquests the Emperor had brought "peace" to the world.[7] Yet, here was Paul sending a letter to Christians living in the very shadow of Caesar's throne, audaciously proclaiming the gospel of a different king who reigns not by the sword, but from the cross. Such opposition to God's anointed king was nothing new. Since the beginning of time, fallen human beings have been rebelling against God's rightful rule and it continues right up to this very day. In the midst of a world groaning for redemption, the gospel inevitably sets God's people at odds with the ruling powers and reigning cultural paradigms of the day. The great British Baptist preacher Charles Spurgeon compared Christians with fish that always swim upstream against the current. "If the fish comes down the stream," Spurgeon tells us, "and you see it floating with its white belly on the top of the water, you know that it is dead."[8]

Over the course of his ministry, Paul had been given a front-row seat to observe how the announcement of the gospel set people free to swim against the stream. From a biblical perspective, the fundamental problem with the Gentiles is that they were enslaved to idolatry. The gospel is the power of God that sets people free from the grip of that which by nature are not gods and transfers them into the kingdom of light, life and love. The gospel is a royal summons directed towards all the world, "Come and live under the reign of God! Come and live the life for which you were created." This is why Paul, in verse five, can describe himself as having received from Jesus "grace and apostleship to bring about the obedience of faith among all the Gentiles for the sake of his name." There is a close connection between faith and obedience that runs right through Romans and is even re-stated in the concluding sentence of the letter, where Paul emphasizes that the good news of Jesus Christ has been made known to

---

7. K. Schenck, "Gospel: Good News," in *Dictionary of Jesus and the Gospels*, 2d ed., ed. Joel B. Green, Jeannine K. Brown, and Nicholas Perrin (Downers Grove: InterVarsity, 2013), 342–43.

8. Charles Haddon Spurgeon, "The Beloved Pastor's Plea for Unity," in *Spurgeon's Sermons*, vol. 39 (1893; reprint, Grand Rapids: Christian Classics Ethereal Library), 398. Adobe PDF ebook.

all the nations in order "to bring about the obedience of faith" (16:26). For Paul there is absolutely no disconnect between faith and obedience. Today we tend to confuse faith with mere belief, but for Paul, faith is the presence of the new creation. While the descendants of the Protestant Reformation might be confused about faith, Martin Luther himself was quite clear. Luther wrote, "Faith is a work of God in us, which changes us and brings us to birth anew from God. It kills the old Adam, makes us completely different people in heart, mind, senses, and all our powers, and brings the Holy Spirit with it. What a living, creative, active powerful thing is faith! It is impossible that faith ever stop doing good. Faith doesn't ask whether good works are to be done, but, before it is asked, it has done them. It is always active."[9] Through the proclamation of the gospel, the Holy Spirit sets men and women free to love the Lord their God with all their heart, soul, mind and strength and to love their neighbors as themselves. Faith and obedience go hand in hand, for the gospel is God's means of restoring righteousness upon the face of the earth. Faith and obedience are inseparable, because the good news of the gospel is about the one who is both the Savior of all people and the Lord of all nations.

It might be helpful at this point to stop and assess where we're at in our quest to come to grips with this news Paul calls "the gospel." Drawing upon what Paul has said in first five verses of Romans we could venture to say the gospel is the story of King Jesus. Yet this doesn't quite get us all the way there. A slight detour may help us to get where we need to go. When I was in elementary school, I remember being transfixed by a movie called *The NeverEnding Story*. The movie is about a bookish, socially awkward boy by the name of Bastian who came across a mysterious book entitled *The Neverending Story*. The book introduced Bastian to the young hero Atreyu's quest to save his home world of Fantasia from its impending destruction at the hands of "The Nothing." While the special effects of the film don't quite measure up to today's standards, at the time there was something compelling about the fantastical cast of characters. However, the truly staggering moment in the movie occurred when the boy who was reading the book was directly addressed by the characters in the story. All of a sudden, Bastian came to realize that he was not simply

---

9. Martin Luther, *Preface to the Letter of St. Paul to the Romans* (reprint, Grand Rapids: Christian Classics Ethereal Library), 6. Adobe PDF ebook. This translation lends itself more readily to preaching than the translation found in vol. 35 of *Luther's Works*.

an interested observer, but that he himself was implicated in the plot of *The NeverEnding Story*.

Something similar occurs in verse six of the opening chapter of Romans. Leading up to this verse, Paul has retold the story of the Messiah Jesus in swift and bold brushstrokes, but now he calls upon the Christians in Rome to recognize that they are not simply bystanders, but characters in the story. Paul tells the Christians in Rome that they are included among the Gentiles "who are called to belong to Jesus Christ." The story of Jesus is their story. Jesus is risen and on the loose. His story continues in the life of his people. Jesus is the key that unlocks the whole mystery of creation, and we are all invited to see our stories taken up in his story. In him we have been blessed with a priceless privilege and granted a clear sense of purpose. As Paul puts it, "To all God's beloved in Rome, who are called to be saints." We are all included in this "all." The gospel is good news not only because it is a wonderful and compelling story, but because through it we have found ourselves swept up in the tsunami of God's love, as we are written by the Spirit into the continuing story of Jesus Christ.

The gospel, as the apostle Paul likes to say, is the power of God for salvation. The gospel is the power of God for salvation because the gospel is the Never-ending Story of King Jesus. Because the gospel is the Never-ending Story of King Jesus, it also means that the sermon doesn't end when I sit down. Rather, it continues as we go out into the world in the power of the risen Lord to be his witnesses in our homes and schools and places of work. His story continues in and through you and me as the Holy Spirit cultivates within us faith, hope, and love. We are gospel people, inscribed into the Never-ending Story of King Jesus, which means there really is no way for me to conclude this sermon other than to say, "To be continued . . ."

33

"Fake News and Inconvenient Truths"
Sunday, October 2, 2016

Robert J. Dean

Exodus 20:16
1 Timothy 6:11–16
John 8:12–32

What does it mean to tell the truth? The events of this past week have certainly brought this question to the fore. It is difficult to deny that there is something particularly provocative about the juxtaposition of our biblical texts with their emphasis on telling the truth and the unfolding United States Presidential campaign.[1] Both candidates appear to have what we could diplomatically call unique perspectives on what it means to tell the truth. This was evident in the first presidential debate that took place this past Monday, although, technically speaking, it is difficult to classify what went down as a debate. The *Collins English Dictionary* defines a debate as "a formal discussion . . . in which opposing arguments are put forward."[2] Now, Monday's spectacle was a "formal discussion" in the sense that the date was set in advance and the participants stood behind

---

1. This sermon was preached in Canada. Many Canadians watched the American Presidential campaign with alternating senses of bemusement, consternation, and deep concern. In light of how this sermon features in the argument of the following essay, I have opted to withhold the location of its preaching to protect the innocent.

2. *Collins English Dictionary*, sv. "debate," https://www.collinsdictionary.com/dictionary/english/debate.

lecterns, but anyone who tuned in to see the two candidates constantly interrupt and speak over each another, as well as the moderator, would be hard-pressed to maintain that there was much formality to the discussion or, for that matter, that there was even a discussion occurring. The dictionary definition goes on to specify that a debate is "a formal discussion . . . in which opposing arguments are put forward." While what transpired was certainly argumentative, there were relatively few arguments put forward. Arguments require reasoning on the basis of generally agreed upon truthful premises, but what we got in the debate was each candidate putting forward their own so-called "facts" with the intention of scoring points against their opponents and creating the most memorable soundbite or quote to be tweeted. Genuine arguments require a concern for truth, but with respect to the contemporary political scene—not only in the United States, but often also here in Canada—it appears to be often nothing but spin.

When politics is reduced to cultivating carefully manicured public images, it should not surprise us that the veracity of our politicians would come into question. However, I'm reluctant to jump to the conclusion that they are all liars. It seems to me more likely that since they are constantly engaged in spinning the facts, over time they simply come to believe their own publicity. This is what generally happens to human beings like ourselves. When the truth is disregarded or abandoned, it is only a matter of time before we are captured by the lie. There is a story from the Middle Ages of a village sentry who was a bit of a practical joker. On one occasion he decided to give the townspeople a bit of a scare by sounding the alarm. As a result, he was the last one to join the rush to the city walls.[3] But make no mistake about it, rush to the wall, he did. There comes a point when it is no longer we who speak lies, but it is the lie that come to speaks us.

The Protestant Reformer Martin Luther famously remarked, "This much is certain: anyone who knows the Ten Commandments perfectly knows the entire Scriptures."[4] If we wanted to be particularly audacious, we could go one step further and say that whoever knows the commandment we are considering this morning knows the entirety of Scripture.

---

3. Hannah Arendt, *The Portable Hannah Arendt*, ed. Peter Baehr (New York: Penguin, 2000), 566, cited in Stanley Hauerwas, *Performing the Faith: Bonhoeffer and the Practice of Nonviolence* (Grand Rapids: Brazos, 2004), 69n43.

4. Martin Luther, *Small Catechism*, quoted in Carl E. Braaten, "Sins of the Tongue," in *I Am the Lord Your God: Christian Reflections on the Ten Commandments*, ed. Carl E. Braaten and Christopher R. Seitz (Grand Rapids: Eerdmans, 2005), 217.

This is an overstatement for sure, but it is not without warrant. For in the Scriptures we are encountered by the story of the true God who speaking truly calls creation into being. However, God's good creation is marred through humanity's descent into falsehood, and the Scriptures depict the disastrous consequences of humanity's exchange of the truth for a lie. However, the story doesn't end there. The Scriptures also depict the ultimate triumph of truth over falsehood through the reconciling work of Christ on the cross and the perfecting work of the Spirit in drawing all of creation into the truth that is Jesus.

The ninth commandment directs us toward truthfulness in our dealings with one another. The verse reads, "You shall not bear false witness against your neighbor." The original context for the verse appears to have been the law courts and the presentation of legal testimony. It is somewhat fitting then that this commandment would follow commandments prohibiting murder, adultery, and theft, as conviction for any of these offenses would require a careful trial and honest testimony. While the original context for the commandment appears to have been the law courts, later biblical authors and interpreters rightly recognized that the prohibition speaks against all forms of lying. Lying is a plague upon God's people. The Jewish collection of rabbinical writings known as the Talmud asserts that the lying tongue is responsible for three deaths. It murders the listener, it murders the speaker, and it murders the subject matter.[5] The lie is a slap in the face to the God who, in the fullness of truth, spoke creation into being. For this reason, Solomon in the book of Proverbs can categorically state, "There are six things that the Lord hates, seven that are an abomination to him: haughty eyes, a lying tongue, and hands that shed innocent blood, a heart that devises wicked plans, feet that hurry to run to evil, a lying witness who testifies falsely, and one who sows discord in a family" (6:16–19).

God's people are to be children of the truth, but what it means to tell the truth is not always obvious or immediately apparent. The German pastor, theologian, and martyr Dietrich Bonhoeffer wrestled with the question, "What does it mean to tell the truth?" during the first few months of his imprisonment following his arrest by the Nazis in the spring of 1943.[6]

---

5. *Arakhin* 15b, cited in David Patterson, "Response" in *The Ten Commandments for Jews, Christians, and Others*, ed. Roger E. Van Harn (Grand Rapids: Eerdmans, 2007), 196.

6. Dietrich Bonhoeffer, "What Does It Mean to Tell the Truth?" in *Conspiracy and Imprisonment: 1940–1954*, ed. Mark S. Brocker, trans. Lisa E. Dahill, vol. 16 of *Dietrich Bonhoeffer Works*, ed. Eberhard Bethge et al. (Minneapolis: Fortress, 2006), 601–8.

The question was not merely an academic matter for Bonhoeffer; prior to his arrest he had been involved in a conspiracy to topple Hitler's government and he had helped to smuggle a dozen Jews out of Germany. Now he found himself facing stern interrogation and even torture at the hands of the Gestapo. The German philosophical tradition he had inherited did not seem to provide much help. The eighteenth-century German philosopher Immanuel Kant had maintained that if a murderer came to your door asking for the whereabouts of a friend you were hiding, truthfulness required that you reveal your friend's location to the murderer. Bonhoeffer recognized this as absurdity and was not prepared to hand his friends and co-conspirators over to the Nazi gallows out of some perverse, self-righteous notion of what it means to tell the truth. Bonhoeffer recognized that the truth that everyone must ultimately contend with is the crucified and risen Christ. He is the supreme truth-teller, who is himself the way, the truth, and the life. Recognizing this reality, Bonhoeffer observed that one may only see things clearly and hence speak truthfully, to the extent that one sees the world in the light of Christ. To speak or to act truthfully is to speak or act in accordance with Christ, the God who became human. Bonhoeffer observed that where a factually true utterance is detached from life and abstracted from the context of one's personal relationship to another, the statement "has only the appearance of truth but not its essence."[7] Statements that betray our obligation to love our neighbor, are also a betrayal of the truth. Statements, however factually correct they may be, that are intended to tear down and destroy fall short of the bar of truth. Truth cannot be brandished as a weapon or made to serve personal advantage, for truth is measured by its conformity to the Son of Man who did not come "to be served but to serve, and to give his life a ransom for many" (Mark 10:45). This is why the apostle Paul can instruct the church of Ephesus by saying, "But speaking the truth in love, we must grow up in every way into him who is the head, into Christ" (4:15). The truth can only be spoken in love, because the one who is the truth is the incarnation of the God who is love. However, speaking the truth in love is no easy enterprise; it requires great discernment. As a result, Bonhoeffer insists that "telling the truth must therefore be learned."[8]

This comes to the fore in the Gospel of John where Jesus remarks, "I am the light of the world. Whoever follows me will never walk in darkness but will have the light of life." And again, "If you continue in my

---

7. Bonhoeffer, "What Does It Mean to Tell the Truth?" 604.
8. Bonhoeffer, "What Does It Mean to Tell the Truth?" 603.

word, you are truly my disciples; and you will know the truth, and the truth will make you free." It is in walking in the light of Jesus that one is enabled to see the world clearly. It is in obeying his commandments and holding to his teaching that disciples come to know the truth. We must learn to be truth-tellers and this learning occurs as the Spirit of truth directs us in the way of Jesus. It is the Spirit of the Living God who is at work within the life of the people on the road with Jesus to form them in the image of the one who, as Paul told Timothy in our reading from the Epistles this morning, "in his testimony before Pontius Pilate made the good confession." The Spirit fashions a people who are free to testify to the truth in word and deed before the various tribunals of popular opinion and public sentiment in the world. The Spirit of the risen Lord empowers us to utter and embody a variety of inconvenient truths. Inconvenient truths like:

> We are not going to get out of this life alive.
> Our true identity is not found in our race, our class, our job, our gender, or our sexuality, but rather in our being claimed as the beloved children of God.
> He who dies with the most toys does not win, but may in fact be the most pitied of all.
> A planet of finite resources cannot sustain an economy based upon infinitely increasing production and ever-expanding desire.
> Sincerity is well and good as far as it goes, but one can be sincerely wrong.
> The Free Hand of the Market cannot save us, but neither can Big Government.
> Security cannot be found at the point of a gun.
> "A community of peace can exist only when it does not rest on *a lie* or on *injustice*."[9]
> One cannot serve God and Mammon.
> We *are* our brother's keeper.
> Or to sum them all up, "Jesus Christ is Lord!"

Such inconvenient truths do not sit well with the world. Although the truth of Jesus is the world's salvation, these are not truths that the world wants to hear. But this is nothing new. The world has always resisted

---

9. Dietrich Bonhoeffer, *Ecumenical, Academic, and Pastoral Work: 1931–1932*, ed. Victoria J. Barnett, Mark S. Brocker, and Michael B. Lukens, trans. Anne Schmidt-Lange et al., vol. 11 of *Dietrich Bonhoeffer Works* (Minneapolis: Fortress, 2012), 365.

the truth that is Jesus and it is for this reason that it is from the Greek word for witness or testimony that we get our English word "martyr." A martyr is one who testifies to the truth at the cost of their life. Although they are burned, and drowned, and cut down by the sword, the testimony of the martyrs cannot be silenced, for their blood is mingled with the blood of the Lamb. In one of his visions, John of Patmos heard a loud voice in heaven say, "Now have come the salvation and the power and the kingdom of our God and the authority of his Messiah, for the accuser of our comrades has been thrown down, who accuses them day and night before our God. But they have conquered him by the blood of the Lamb and by the word of their testimony, for they did not cling to life even in the face of death" (Rev 12:10–11).

Pope John Paul II famously described the twentieth century as a "new age of martyrs," as it has been estimated that half of all Christian martyrs from the entire history of the church were killed during the past century. Maximilian Kolbe was one of these many martyrs of the twentieth century who did not cling to life even in the face of death.[10] When he was a child living in his native Poland, Kolbe had a vision in which the Virgin Mary came to him holding two crowns: one white, the other red. The white crown represented a life lived in purity, the red represented the crown of martyrdom. When asked whether he was willing to accept either of these crowns, Kolbe replied that he would receive them both. Kolbe became a Franciscan friar and completed doctorates in philosophy and theology. He was ordained a priest and undertook a series of missions to Asia—founding monasteries in Japan and India. Poor health forced him to return to Poland in 1936. Following the Nazi invasion of Poland, Kolbe organized a temporary hospital at his monastery, which also served as a publishing house for a number of anti-Nazi publications. On one occasion, Kolbe published the following comments in his newspaper:

> No one in the world can change Truth. What we can do and should do is to seek truth and to serve it when we have found it. The real conflict is the inner conflict. Beyond armies of occupation and the catacombs of concentration camps, there are two irreconcilable enemies in the depth of every soul: good and evil,

---

10. For brief introductions to the life of Maximilian Kolbe, see Regis J. Armstrong and Ingrid J. Peterson, *The Franciscan Tradition*, Spirituality in History Series, ed. Phyllis Zagano (Collegeville, MN: Liturgical, 2010), 50–56; and "St. Maximilian Kolbe: The Saint and Martyr of the Immaculate," Franciscans of the Immaculate, https://saintmaximiliankolbe.com/biography/.

sin and love. And what use are the victories on the battlefield if we ourselves are defeated in our innermost personal selves?[11]

From the outbreak of the war until his arrest on February 17, 1941, Kolbe and his fellow monks sheltered over one thousand Jews in their monastery. After his arrest, Kolbe continued to serve as a priest ministering to his fellow inmates, hearing confession, and leading worship, even though he was frequently harassed and beaten by the guards for doing so. Kolbe eventually ended up at Auschwitz where he was branded with the number 16670. In July of 1941, a prisoner escaped from the concentration camp at Auschwitz. In an act of reprisal and to deter further escape attempts, the commanding officer assembled the prisoners and announced that ten men would be chosen to go down to the underground bunker where they would be starved to death. Upon hearing his name called out, one of the prisoners who was a non-commissioned soldier, cried out, "Oh my poor wife, my poor children. I shall never see them again." Before the man could be led away, Kolbe calmly stepped forward and took his place. Over the next number of days, Kolbe led the ten men condemned to die in prayer and song. After three weeks, Kolbe was the only remaining survivor in the bunker. He was given an injection of carbolic acid and was sent to receive the crown that had been prepared for him. In his act of self-sacrificial love, Kolbe had borne true witness toward his neighbor. One of the survivors of Auschwitz described Kolbe's death as "a shock filled with hope, bringing new life and strength.... It was like a powerful shaft of light in the darkness of the camp."[12]

A statue of Maximilian Kolbe now appears above the west entrance of Westminster Abbey. The statue stands alongside statues of Dietrich Bonhoeffer and eight other martyrs from the twentieth century. Through their testimony, we are encountered by the truth of Christ. In the light of their faces, we are given a glimpse of the light of Christ. However, this reality is not reserved for those enshrined above the doors of Westminster Abbey. The commandments are ultimately a description of the Kingdom of God. They contain the promise of the day when God's intentions will be done. Our commandment this morning assures us that a day is coming when we will be so possessed by the truth that not even

---

11. Diana Dewar, *The Saint of Auschwitz* (San Francisco: Harper & Row, 1982), 94, quoted in Armstrong and Peterson, *The Franciscan Tradition*, 52.

12. Patricia Treece, *A Man for Others* (San Francisco: Harper & Row, 1982), 1, quoted in Armstrong and Peterson, *The Franciscan Tradition*, 54.

fleeting shadows of falsehood will remain in, with, or around us. We will be truthful to one another. In a few moments we will tangibly receive the sign of that promise as we come forward to receive the communion elements. The bread and cup that are placed in our hands reassure us that as a result of Christ's death and resurrection, we will be found worthy to sit at the banqueting table of our Lord at the great marriage supper of the Lamb. Hear the good news of the Gospel, "See what love the Father has given us, that we should be called children of God; and that is what we are. The reason the world does not know us is that it did not know him. Beloved, we are God's children now; what we will be has not yet been revealed. What we do know is this: when he is revealed, we will be like him, for we will see him as he is" (1 John 3:1–2).

EPILOGUE

A Tale of Two Stanleys

Or

Why We Need More Pointless Sermons from Hauerwas

Robert J. Dean

Getting to the Point of Preaching

With the publication of the present volume, there are now over one hundred of Stanley Hauerwas's sermons appearing in print. In terms of published sermonic output, this surely makes him one of the most prodigious theologians—if not published preachers—of the past one hundred years. Undoubtedly, some may wonder whether we really need more sermons from Hauerwas. The burden of this epilogue will be to show that while Hauerwas's sermons are, in fact, "pointless," the church, particularly in its North American instantiation, cannot do without them.

  A friend who started out in ministry in the late 1980s once succinctly described to me the challenge he faced in the early years of his ministry as being a choice between Bill Hybels and Eugene Peterson. On the one hand, there was the path of the nascent seeker-driven megachurches encapsulated in the figure of Willow Creek's founding pastor Hybels. On the other hand, there was the "long obedience in the same direction" represented by Peterson's contemplative spirituality firmly rooted in the soil of Scripture.[1] It seems that preachers today may be faced with a similar set of alternatives that takes the form of a choice between two Stanleys. This became apparent to me after I preached the sermon included in this book entitled "Fake News and Inconvenient Truths."

While the sermon has been well-received in written form, on the day of its actual preaching it was far from a rousing sermonic success. The congregation seemed overwhelmed by the sheer profligacy of the biblical references, the introduction of unfamiliar saints, and the traipsing through Western intellectual history. Afterwards, one congregant pulled me aside and said, "If I'm hearing you correctly, you're saying that Jesus is not like our contemporary politicians." While I don't want to minimize the significance of this recognition, I would like to think that the sermon had a little more than that to offer. It is quite possible that the sermon moved too quickly and some of the tightly scripted moves needed more space to breathe. However, I suspect the root issue was that the congregation was simply not used to hearing such preaching.

The pastor, perhaps out of concern that I had not communicated as effectively as I might have, approached me afterwards and pressed me to articulate the one point that I wanted the congregation to remember and take home with them. If I had been quicker on my feet, I might have responded, "I don't have a point I want them to take home, I want them to go home with Jesus." Instead, I was flummoxed, unsure how to even begin to answer the question. The temptation would have been to say that the point of the message was "Jesus is the truth," but to say so would have betrayed the grammar of the very message I had just preached. For Jesus is not the kind of truth that can be reduced to a programmatic statement or proposition available for affirmation. "The truth of God," Mark McIntosh rightly observes, "is not some *thing* we can 'find out' about God, it is simply the concrete form that our encounter with God begins to take in our lives, in works of love and words of faith, in ways of life and habits of thought."[2] In other words, the truth that is Jesus can only be known as one's life is drawn into conformity to Christ through discipleship. In the face of my inability to succinctly summarize "the point" of my sermon, the pastor prescribed the book *Communicating for a Change* by Andy

---

1. *A Long Obedience in the Same Direction: Discipleship in an Instant Society* is the title of one of Peterson's early, influential books (Downers Grove: InterVarsity, 1980).

2. Mark McIntosh, *Mysteries of Faith*, vol. 8 of *The New Church's Teaching Series* (Lanham, MD: Cowley, 2000), 22.

Stanley and Lane Jones in the attempt to cure me of my pointless preaching and restore me to health as a communicator.

Andy Stanley and the Point of a Sermon

Andy Stanley is the founding pastor of North Point Ministries, Inc., an organization devoted to "creating churches that unchurched people like to attend."[3] With six different campuses and over 30,000 people attending weekly services, North Point may be the largest evangelical megachurch in the United States. The son of the prominent Southern Baptist preacher Charles Stanley, Andy Stanley is often considered to be one of the most influential preachers in America.[4] Co-authored with Lane Jones, a director of one of North Point's campuses, *Communicating for a Change* sets forth Stanley's homiletical strategy.

The first half of the book takes the form of an imaginative narrative that depicts the cross-country journey shared by a struggling pastor and a truck driver, the latter of whom is also an experienced evangelist. The fictional account is winsome and engaging and serves in some ways as a metaphor for the journey that each sermon must take. Every sermon, the wise truck driver insists, can be thought of as journey: "You start somewhere, you go somewhere, and ultimately you end up somewhere."[5] The goal of this communication journey is nothing less than life transformation. However, in order to accomplish the goal of life change, preachers must abandon some of their cherished approaches to preaching that have been far too intellectually driven.[6] Stanley writes, "Preaching for life change requires far less information and more application. Less explanation and more inspiration. Less first century and more twenty-

---

3. North Point Ministries, http://northpointministries.org/.

4. See, for example, Michael Duduit, "The 25 Most Influential Pastors of the Past 25 Years," Preaching, https://www.preaching.com/articles/the-25-most-influential-pastors-of-the-past-25-years/.

5. Andy Stanley and Lane Jones, *Communicating for a Change* (New York: Multnomah, 2006), 38. Hereafter, page references will appear in the text. In the introduction to the book, Stanley claims that it his approach to communication that informs the book and that Jones has contributed the parable in the first half based upon this approach. In light of these comments, for the sake of convenience I will refer to Stanley as the author of the book.

6. The assumption that information-driven models of preaching, or "teaching," must be refuted, could perhaps be read as Stanley's reaction against his own formation in a rationalistic strand of evangelicalism.

first century" (96). Preaching for life change boils down to taking one simple truth and lodging it in the heart of the listener (12). Every sermon therefore should have a single point, that is, "every message should have one central idea, application, insight, or principle that serves as the glue to hold the other parts together" (103). The preacher should be able to summarize such a one point message with a short, simple statement (39).

Once the preacher has picked their point, they must determine the best route that enables their hearers to arrive at the intended destination. It is at this point that Stanley puts forward the idea of a relational outline as a way to map the message (46). Stanley sums up his outline with a five word formula: "ME, WE, GOD, YOU, WE" (120). In the "ME" section of the sermon, the preacher begins by talking about themselves as a way of establishing relational capital with their audience. The "WE" section of the sermon is about establishing "emotional common ground" with one's hearers "around the topic or idea of the message" (47). The preacher attempts to accomplish this task by evoking a felt need among as many different groups in the audience as possible. Once the interest level has been sufficiently piqued, the preacher may then pivot to Scripture in the "GOD" section of the sermon to demonstrate how Scripture provides the solution to the question raised by the previously established felt need. The principle that is unearthed in Scripture is then applied in the "YOU" section of the sermon. This section of the sermon is driven by the questions "So what?" and "Now what?" and, for Stanley, often involves challenging people to commit to some type of practice for a certain length of time (127). The final "WE" section of the sermon is used to inspire the hearers by casting a vision of what life would be like if Christians everywhere embraced the point of the sermon.

There is much wise and eminently practical advice in *Communicating for a Change* that would profit any public speaker. Stanley's emphasis on having a clear sense where the sermonic journey is going, his stress upon the importance of transitions (66), and discovering your own voice (72), as well as his discussion of the necessity for every preacher to have a "burden" for the message they have been called to proclaim (113–14) will be edifying for most preachers. However, there is a theological lacuna standing at the heart of what is perhaps Stanley's most important homiletical insight: "*our approach to communicating should be shaped by our goal in communicating*" (93). The "communication" language that Stanley employs in this sentence and throughout the book and his eschewing of the terms "preaching" and "preacher"—going so far as to refer to North

Point ministry personnel as "communicators"—gestures towards the underlying theological malaise. It comes further into focus when Stanley asserts, "*Presentation trumps information when it comes to engaging the audience*" (146). The central verb employed in the previous sentence is fascinating, if not prophetic, in light of current political realities in the United States. When presentation *trumps* information, preaching—and all other forms of communication for that matter—devolves into nothing other than pure propaganda. While Stanley's impulse to push back against the information-driven, rationalistic sermons of his evangelical Baptist tradition by emphasizing the inseparability of the "how" and "what" of preaching is warranted, he ironically ends up re-inscribing the binary and placing the emphasis on the opposite pole. The didactic sermons of his forbearers is replaced by a pragmatic, Pelagian moralism, which is the result of his emphasis on presentation combined with the underlying hermeneutic of his "relational outline," which appears to be nothing other than the cold leftovers of theological liberalism's correlational method heated up for two minutes in the microwave.[7] By starting with the preacher and the felt-needs of the congregation before turning to Scripture, Stanley's hermeneutical method risks domesticating the testimony of Scripture by forcing it to conform to the questions and expectations of modern men and women. When this hermeneutic is combined with Stanley's homiletical insistence that every sermon must have a single point, preachers are left to dispense nothing more than moralistic bromides that allow their culturally captive congregants to somehow cope with their immersion in Western consumeristic society. This becomes apparent when one peruses the list of "sticky statements"—memorable articulations of the single point of the sermon—Stanley provides as examples. The "sticky statements" range from common-sense maxims, such as "Your friends determine the direction and quality of your life," to vaguely theological platitudes, like "Good people don't go to heaven, forgiven people do" (111).

While Stanley does not make explicit his theology of preaching, there are occasional hints that his anthropologically-driven homiletical method is accompanied by a theology of preaching that has distinctive Pelagian overtones and is centered on the communication techniques

---

7. Stanley Hauerwas's recent comment comes to mind: "You get, in evangelicals, in their preaching, Protestant liberalism on a stick and they don't even notice it" (Brian Brock and Stanley Hauerwas, *Beginnings: Interrogating Hauerwas*, ed. Kevin. Hargaden [London: Bloomsbury, 2017], 254).

employed by the preacher. For example, Stanley writes, "God went to great lengths to make Himself known to this world. Seems to me we should be willing to do the same thing. Jesus was the living Word. Shouldn't we do all we can to make the written Word come alive for our audience?" (149). If Jesus is no longer the living Word, no amount of animated gesticulating on Mount Carmel is going to revive the silent God from his slumber. Perhaps I am unfairly highlighting a moment of theological carelessness on Stanley's part, however if what he has said here is true, preachers would be better served not by acquiring a new method of communication, but by an exit strategy that gets them out of the pulpit entirely.

While I suspect that Stanley's own sermons may transcend some of the shortcomings of his homiletical method and theology of preaching, my concern is not with *his preaching*, but for the many preachers struggling to come to terms with what it means to preach in the confusing times in which we find ourselves. The success of his multi-campus ministry may suggest to some preachers that Stanley has found the communicator's silver bullet that is able to slay the beast of encroaching secularism and make in-roads into the hearts and minds of previously uninterested men and women. My fear is that such an approach to preaching will only further exacerbate the culturally-accommodated character of the church and result in congregants who are indistinguishable from their neighbours and lead lives that are utterly uninteresting to people of other- or no-faith.

Stanley Hauerwas's Pointless Preaching

In the sermons of Stanley Hauerwas we see an alternative to Andy Stanley's culturally-accommodated approach to preaching for life transformation. It cannot be denied that Hauerwas, as one of the leading theological ethicists of his generation, is also concerned with life transformation. (Although I suspect he would wish to replace the rather nebulous language of "life transformation" with a thicker theological description, such as "the sanctification of the Christian community," or perhaps even, "theosis.") However, a fundamentally different set of theological convictions animates Hauerwas's sermons.[8] As a way of surfacing these convictions,

8. I have previously attempted to elucidate the underlying theological politics of Hauerwas's understanding of preaching in Robert Dean, "Unapologetically (A) Political: Stanley Hauerwas and the Practice of Preaching," *Didaskalia* 25 (Fall 2015): 131–60.

I would like to draw attention to a sermon in the present volume that I believe is representative in many ways of Hauerwas's preaching.

Hauerwas begins his sermon "The Way, the Truth, and the Life," with the terse, yet evocative, observation, "We are a people haunted by the murderous character of the past century." As he does at the beginning of many of his sermons, Hauerwas exposes the social-material conditions of our current existence that stand in the way of our receiving the testimony of Scripture as good news. There is certainly a type of apologetics on display in the opening paragraphs of the sermon that, like Andy Stanley's methodology, aspires to connect with the contemporary "WE." However, unlike Stanley's approach, this is a form of *ad hoc* apologetics that emerges as the realities of our daily life are laid bare before the "strange new world of the Bible" encountered in the lectionary readings for the day. This becomes evident if one traces the way the "we" functions in the opening paragraphs of the sermon. *We* are a people in denial of our bloody history. *We* are enlightened Western individuals who thought our tolerance would put an end to violence. *We* are not Nazis responsible for the murder of the Jews. *We* are Americans, drawn into battles not of our choosing, who fight reluctantly out of our desire to put an end to war. Ultimately, through the employment of a figural reading of Scripture, Hauerwas suggests *we* are Saul—if not throwing stones than at least holding the coats of the people that did. Hauerwas acknowledges that such a reading of the violence that has marked our histories is enough to make us uncomfortable. It would seem that such uncomfortable sermon openings are the result of Hauerwas's conviction that sermons are intended to be exercises in truth-telling, and as such they cannot help but expose the conflicting loyalties of modern Western Christians like ourselves who are often no more than half-Christian at best.

While Andy Stanley's homiletical method has the preacher turning to Scripture to answer the questions of modern American men and women, Hauerwas shows us that in the church's engagement with Scripture, it is we who find ourselves questioned. Joseph Mangina clearly elucidates the profound difference in heremeneutical posture between these two approaches to Scripture in the service of preaching when he writes "to ask the question of the Bible's 'relevance' is to commit a terrific category error, since the Bible does not want to be relevant to our concerns, but to make *us* relevant to *its* concerns."[9] Andy Stanley presumes that our fundamen-

---

9. Joseph Mangina, "Getting People into the Story: On Not Getting Anything out of Sermons," *The Living Church*, January 1, 2012, 13.

tal problem is that we are lacking in some way and need a principle or tip to provide us with the necessary know-how; Stanley Hauerwas knows that *we* are the problem. We are alienated from the source and goal of our lives in the living God. As a result, we have fallen captive to the original lie of the serpent and the derivative myths and falsehoods of our own making. The assimilative capacities of the fallen human ego imprisoned within the self-incurvature of sin must not be underestimated. Even the words of Scripture can be domesticated and made to serve the illusions of our pious sentimentalities. For this reason, Hauerwas understands one of his tasks in the pulpit is "to find ways to defamiliarize the text."[10] In the sermon under consideration, Hauerwas does this by challenging us to reconsider Stephen's sermon before the Sanhedrin. Upon closer inspection, we see that Stephen's speech is nothing more than a lengthy litany of Israel's sins. Stephen has clearly not read *How to Win Friends and Influence People*! After such an oratorical performance, we should perhaps not be surprised that Stephen would end up being stoned by his audience. But then Hauerwas draws our attention to the most peculiar aspect of Stephen's speech, namely, that he was doing nothing more than retelling the story of Israel that had been preserved by Israel herself. Hauerwas observes, "One of the remarkable aspects of Israel's life is her ability to tell the story of God's care for her in a manner that does not attempt to hide her unfaithful response to God's gifts. That Israel was able to so tell her history, I think, has everything to do with her conviction that her story is first and foremost God's story."

If we are to receive the Gospel as good news, we must be "repositioned" with respect to the biblical text by being re-placed into right relation with the one who is the Truth to which Scripture bears witness.[11] Because the Truth with which we must ultimately reckon is a Person, to be placed into right relation with that Truth is to find oneself engrafted into the ongoing history of God's relationship with his people. Point-driven sermons, therefore, run aground on the rocky shore of God's people Israel. The continuing story of God's way with his people resists premature closure and the fleshly bodies of the sons and daughters of Israel resist facile summation. In fact, the complexity of that story and irreducibility of the body politic of God's people requires the continual

10. Brock and Hauerwas, *Beginnings*, 263.

11. "Repositioning the congregation in relation to the text" is a phrase introduced by Brian Brock in his attempt to describe the type of figural reading Hauerwas employs in his sermons. Brock and Hauerwas, *Beginnings*, 251.

retelling of the story.[12] Therefore, sermons may not have a point, but they do have a purpose. The purpose of the sermon is not to provide people with helpful tips or advice that enables us to cope with the way things are. Rather, "preaching is the gift God has given the church so that our lives can be located within God's life by having our existence storied by the Gospel."[13] At the heart of the Gospel stands the figure of the crucified Messiah of Israel, who, Hauerwas states in his sermon, "has triumphed, making it possible that our histories, our sin-dominated histories, not determine our futures."

In the paragraph that immediately follows, Hauerwas pivots from the "deadly stones" used to kill Stephen to the "living stone" spoken of by Peter in the lectionary reading from the epistles. Whereas many homiletical textbooks presume that preachers will focus their attention on a single text,[14] Hauerwas's sermons regularly engage with the full slate of readings for the day. It is Hauerwas's Christologically-formed imagination that allows him to move seamlessly between the assigned texts for a given Sunday. Following Jesus's own homiletical method on the Road to Emmaus (Luke 24:13–35), Hauerwas understands the person of Christ to be the interpretive key to Scripture.[15] Jesus is the nexus in which the various weekly lections cohere. Ephraim Radner in his erudite study of the theological interpretation of Scripture, has observed that "a key parameter for figural reading" is that "it is essentially Christological."[16] Hauerwas's homiletical practice, therefore, may be understood as his attempt to read Scripture *as Scripture* through recovering the ancient art of figural

---

12. Stanley Hauerwas, foreword to Ellen F. Davis with Austin McIver Dennis, *Preaching the Luminous Word: Biblical Sermons and Homiletical Essays* (Grand Rapids: Eerdmans, 2016), xi.

13. Stanley Hauerwas, *Without Apology: Sermons for Christ's Church* (New York: Seabury, 2013), xvii.

14. See, for example, Thomas G. Long, *The Witness of Preaching*, 3rd ed. (Louisville: Westminster John Knox, 2016), 80–82; Haddon W. Robinson, *Biblical Preaching: The Development and Delivery of Expository Messages*, 2nd ed. (Grand Rapids: Baker Academic, 2001), 54; John Stott, *Between Two Worlds: The Challenge of Preaching Today* (Grand Rapids: Eerdmans, 1982), 213–20; Paul Scott Wilson, *The Four Pages of the Sermon: A Guide to Biblical Preaching* (Nashville: Abingdon, 1999), 36–37.

15. For one of Hauerwas's early "sermonic exhibits" that exemplifies this claim, see "The Insufficiency of Scripture: Why Discipleship Is Required," in *Unleashing the Scripture: Freeing the Bible from Captivity to America* (Nashville: Abingdon, 1993), 47–62.

16. Ephraim Radner, *Time and the Word: Figural Reading of the Christian Scriptures* (Grand Rapids: Eerdmans, 2016), 280.

interpretation.[17] While I dare not presume to know how Radner would assess the fruit of Hauerwas's homiletical efforts, there does seem to be some resonance between Hauerwas's sermons and Radner's description of preaching fueled by figural reading. Radner maintains that:

> a sermon based on figural reading will necessarily move beyond a single text and, in a way that is suitable both to comprehension and formation, engage some aspect of the network of scriptural forms whose constellation marks the work of God that is his truth. Such a sermon will find some appropriate way by which the biblical texts, in some manner of fertile replication, lead the listener to this resting place of expanded vision.[18]

The path to "this resting place of expanded vision" runs through wilderness. When the preacher enters the pulpit on a Sunday morning they enter into close combat with all of the false narratives and lies which have sought to hold sway over the hearts and minds of the members of their congregation over the past week, armed only with "the sword of the Spirit which is the word of God" (Eph 6:17). It is for this reason that Hauerwas can speak of sermons as being arguments.[19] However, they are arguments from faith for faith, based upon the premise, "Jesus Christ is Lord!" Any attempt to subject this premise to validation at the hands of a different rationality is to betray the grammar of the profession itself. In "The Way, the Truth, and the Life," Hauerwas's quarrel is with the inherent violence of an enlightened liberal tolerance that can tolerate all things except any challenge to its hegemony. The death-dealing intolerance of tolerance is challenged by the radical exclusivity of the one who audaciously proclaims, "No one comes to the Father except through me." The exclusivity of Christ, however, "is not a burden, but a gift to all" that frees us from our violence-determined histories. This is on preeminent display in the life of the martyrs, that is, "those who have died in a manner that makes the cross of Christ unmistakable as God's victory over death." Like Bonhoeffer, Hauerwas understands that "the church's word gains weight and power not through concepts but by example."[20] The martyrs, Hauerwas preaches, "remain our most truthful form of persuasion."

17. I understand the desire to recover the ability to read Scripture *as Scripture* to be one of, if not the, animating concerns of Hauerwas's controversial book *Unleashing the Scripture*.

18. Radner, *Time and the Word*, 271.

19. Hauerwas, *Without Apology*, xviii–xix.

20. Dietrich Bonhoeffer, *Letters and Papers from Prison*, ed. John W. De Gruchy,

If Hauerwas is right in identifying the martyr with the specifically Christian form of rhetoric—and I believe he is—then this has significant implications for the practice of preaching. However, Hauerwas's own sermons and approach to preaching have not always been entirely consistent with his martyriological convictions. In what follows, I would like to subject two interrelated aspects of Hauerwas's homiletical reflections and performance to a friendly critique on grounds internal to his own theological commitments. The first line of critique will address the place of exemplification in Hauerwas's sermons, while the second will reflect further upon the previously adduced claim that sermons are best thought of as arguments.

The concluding lecture of Hauerwas's Gifford Lectures is fittingly entitled, "The Necessity of Witness." It is fitting at the material level in that the title aptly describes the central thesis of the chapter, namely that, "Christianity is unintelligible without witnesses."[21] However, it is also appropriate that what is perhaps Hauerwas's crowning academic achievement would conclude in this manner, as the importance of witness or exemplification has been a recurring theme throughout his work.[22] The importance of locating the saints for the life of the church is a note that is not only repeatedly sounded, but also exemplified in many of Hauerwas's writings.[23] While Hauerwas's essays are populated by saints—including Jean Vanier, Dorothy Day, the villagers of Le Chambon and the congregation of Broadway Methodist Church—interestingly, such exemplars of the faith are not nearly as prominent in his sermons.[24] I believe there may be a

trans. Best, Isabel et al., vol. 8, *Dietrich Bonhoeffer Works* (Minneapolis: Fortress, 2010), 504.

21. Stanley Hauerwas, *With the Grain of the Universe: The Church's Witness and Natural Theology* (Grand Rapids: Brazos, 2001), 214.

22. See, for example, the essay "Why Jean Vanier Matters: An Exemplary Exploration" in the present volume. For a monograph treating the place of witness in Hauerwas's theology, see Ariaan W. Baan, *The Necessity of Witness: Stanley Hauerwas's Contribution to Systematic Theology* (Eugene, OR: Pickwick, 2015).

23. For a mere sampling of places where Hauerwas emphasizes the importance of locating the saints, see Stanley Hauerwas and William H. Willimon, *Where Resident Aliens Live: Exercises for Christian Practice* (Nashville: Abingdon, 1996), 20; Stanley Hauerwas, *In Good Company: The Church as Polis* (Notre Dame: University of Notre Dame Press, 1995), 57; Stanley Hauerwas, *The Work of Theology* (Grand Rapids: Eerdmans, 2015), 106.

24. This is not to say that Hauerwas's sermons are devoid of exemplification. Hauerwas's telling of the story of Christian de Chergé in his meditation on the first of the seven last words is one place where he utilizes exemplification to great effect in

few factors contributing to Hauerwas's underemployment of exemplification in his sermons. First, Hauerwas is frequently preaching in pulpits at some remove from his home congregation. As a result, he may simply be unaware of the stories of particular congregations and therefore unable to convincingly identify the local saints in those contexts. In this regard, the parish priest or congregational pastor has a great advantage over the itinerant preacher.[25] Second, I believe Hauerwas is rightly nervous about how sermon illustrations can re-inscribe "the presumption that it is our 'common experience' that illumines the Gospel when in fact it should be the other way around."[26] However, exemplification is something different than illustration. Illustrations suggest that there is some underlying principle or idea that is more fundamental than the narrative of Scripture itself. Exemplification involves the work of discernment in attending and bearing witness to how the members of the body of Christ have been inscribed by the Spirit into the story of their crucified and risen Lord.

Paul Scott Wilson has proposed the simple homiletical rule: "good news should be experienced as good news."[27] While the conclusion of Hauerwas's sermons are frequently characterized by "surprising linguistic juxtapositions" that illumine the connections between the lectionary readings and the world that constitute our lives,[28] I fear that the relative absence of exemplification, in conjunction with the sheer proportion of time devoted in each sermon to exploring why we don't get it, may inhibit the reception of the Gospel in the fullness of its goodness. Interestingly, what may be needed is something like the final "WE" of Andy Stanley's relational outline. However, whereas Stanley casts this "WE" in terms of vision casting and imagining what life would be like if everyone embraced the preacher's one idea,[29] what I am envisioning is an exercise of dis-

---

Cross-Shattered Christ: Meditations on the Seven Last Words (Grand Rapids: Brazos, 2004), 31–33.

25. Funerals often provide preachers with a unique opportunity to help congregations locate the lives of the saints. See, for example, my attempt to do that through the figural interpretation of the stories of the raising of Dorcas and the raising of Lazarus in my funeral sermons "We Have to Give Thanks to God" and "Mary and Martha, Lucia and Lazarus" in Robert J. Dean, *Leaps of Faith: Sermons from the Edge*, foreword by Fleming Rutledge (Eugene, OR: Resource, 2017), 160–70.

26. Hauerwas, *Without Apology*, xxiv.

27. Wilson, *The Four Pages of the Sermon*, 25.

28. Brian Brock has drawn attention to "the surprising linguistic juxtapositions" at the climax of Hauerwas's sermons. Brock and Hauerwas, *Beginnings*, 249.

29. Stanley and Jones, *Communicating for a Change*, 129.

cerning where Christ is already at work, drawing all of creation through the Spirit under the umbrella of his royal rule. In a similar vein, Wilson argues that if the Gospel is to be proclaimed and received as good news, preachers will need to "be prepared to make bold claims in faith about where God is acting in the world."[30] Hauerwas's essays are full of such claims, for he knows that it is the lives of the saints that demonstrate that the world narrated in Scripture is eminently habitable. Good figural exegesis, I would suggest, will not only bring to the surface the intertextual connections that link the discrete books of the Bible together, but it will also dare to demonstrate how we have been written into (or figured into) the never-ending story of God's enduring love for the world in Christ.

While the saints might not be as prevalent in Hauerwas's sermons as we might expect, there is another subtle form of exemplification at work in Hauerwas's preaching that should not be overlooked. This takes the form of frequent references to the peculiar politics of the Christian community enacted in the liturgy. In the present sermon this takes the form of a reference to the "Reproaches" of the Good Friday liturgy and, ultimately, at the conclusion of the sermon, to the Eucharist. Almost two-thirds of the sermons in the present book contain some sort of reference to the Eucharist in their closing paragraphs. In holding forth the body and blood of Christ near the end of many of his sermons, Hauerwas is pointing us to the most concrete site of God's continuing action in the world. It is Christ's presence at the Table that is determinative for the Christian community in discerning God's action in the world. These closing Eucharistic moments that characterize many of Hauerwas's sermons resonate with the martyriological rhetoric described in "The Way, the Truth, and the Life" and suggest that what Hauerwas is doing is not so much advancing an argument, as he is bearing witness.

This brings us to the difficulties the witness of the martyrs raise for Hauerwas's conception of the sermon as an argument. I am not denying, however, that I sympathize with the sentiments lying behind the assertion that sermons are best thought of as arguments. On numerous occasions, I have heard homiletical offerings that could be described as "shotgun sermons" in which the hearer is left puzzling about how the various shards of the message are meant to fit together. In these instances, a more intentional focus upon the logical coherence of the argument or the "throughline" of the message would be salutary.[31] Furthermore, having recently

30. Wilson, *The Four Pages of the Sermon*, 24.

31. The term "throughline" is employed in TED settings to describe the overall arc

travelled through the season of Christmas into Epiphany, I am acutely aware of how the announcement of birth of the King of the Jews unsettles the petty tyrants of our world like Herod. However, I remain concerned that, to put it simply, conceiving of sermons as arguments may well be too argumentative. It must be remembered that the martyrs' "argument" with the world is an implication of their more determinative witness to Christ. There is the danger in conceiving of sermons as arguments that they end up being overly defined by what they are against rather than by the One for whom they are for. Furthermore, thinking of sermons as arguments may feed into an overly intellectual vision of preaching that serves to reinforce our modern conception of the autonomous rational human being sitting in judgement as the ultimate arbiter over all things. However, it is this autonomous individual that the Word seeks to kill and make alive through the sermon. For this reason, if it were not so cumbersome, I would propose that we think of sermons in terms of narrating (or re-narrating) reality. Perhaps we can do no better than to employ the classic terminology of proclamation. In a spirited defense of the importance of the practice of proclaiming the gospel, David Fitch writes:

> Because proclaiming the gospel does not immediately appeal to one's rationality but offers a new interpretation of events, it is an epistemological shift of sorts. It does not play on Western cognitive rational ways of knowing. Instead of putting myself forward as the control center of knowledge, it decenters my self. It decenters me from being the center of my world, and instead centers me before God and what he's doing in the world in Jesus Christ. The gospel does not come as "plausible words of wisdom," as a good teaching lesson. Instead it derives from "a demonstration of the Spirit and of power" (1 Cor. 2:4). The authority of preaching does not derive from a person's expertise in biblical knowledge, reasons for believing, or rhetoric, although these skills may be of help. Proclamation is spoken from a place of weakness and humility (1 Cor. 2:3). It tells the gospel from a place of having witnessed it, seen it, been humbled by it. It is unsettling. It calls for conversion (a response) every time.[32]

This conception of preaching as proclamation is highly congruent with Hauerwas's own best insights into and embodiment of the practice

---

that provides coherence to a talk. Chris Anderson, *TED Talks: The Official TED Guide to Public Speaking* (Toronto: Collins, 2016), 30–43.

32. David E. Fitch, *Faithful Presence: Seven Disciplines That Shape the Church for Mission* (Downers Grove: InterVarsity, 2016), 99.

of preaching. The emphasis upon how proclamation calls for conversion preserves the central soteriological insight lying behind Hauerwas's insistence that sermons are arguments, without becoming overly determined by argument through losing sight of the true subject of preaching. Because, as Robert Jenson has observed, "what the church lives for and what holds it together is rather a piece of alleged *news*—a *message* that is thought to be so important that it absolutely must be passed on,"[33] argument is best thought of as a subset of proclamation or tool in service of the more determinative task of bearing witness. Preachers are not primarily "arguers," but are first and foremost heralds proclaiming the news of the new creation that has dawned in the life, death, resurrection and ascension of Christ.

While Hauerwas's sermons are often argumentative, they almost always conclude with a moment of pure proclamation. These concluding moments of proclamation are not the result of the logical unfolding of an argument, but rather they come to us *extra nos*, as the purely gracious irruption of God in the midst of a sin-shattered world that must be received in faith. It may even be possible to read Hauerwas's sermons backwards, recognizing that the concluding paragraph of his sermons are often the premise upon which everything that has gone before has rested. Such a moment of pure proclamation is apparent in the Trinitarian flourish that marks the climax of "The Way, the Truth, and the Life" culminating in the doxology, "Alleluia!" Here, at the end of the sermon the rhetoric of argumentation ultimately fades away and we are left with the poetic language of proclamation and praise. The Trinitarian content and poetic character of this closing paragraph perhaps best reflects Hauerwas's formally stated convictions surrounding the Trinitarian nature of preaching. Preaching, for Hauerwas, is properly conceived of as pneumatological event through which the Word creates a world through the words of the preacher.[34] In short, "preaching creates reality."[35] There is, therefore, a properly poetic quality to sermonic speech that remains porous to the Spirit's work of drawing hearers into the web of connections through which the Word fashions a world that would otherwise remain unseen. Reflecting his in-

---

33. Robert W. Jenson, *A Theology in Outline: Can These Bones Live?*, ed. Adam Eitel (Oxford: Oxford University Press, 2016), 7–8.

34. See my earlier discussion of the implicit pneumatological convictions operative within Hauerwas's understanding of the practice of preaching in "Unapologetically (A)Political," 142–43.

35. Brock and Hauerwas, *Beginnings*, 272.

debtedness to Wittgenstein, Hauerwas is fond of saying, "You can only act in a world you can see, and you can only see by learning to say."[36] If we are to be "transformed by the renewing of our minds" (Rom 12:2), then the sermon will play a crucial role, for the sermon "is our fundamental speech act through which we learn the grammar of the faith."[37] Preachers, therefore, are teachers of language, whose exemplification of eloquent speech is employed by the Spirit to awaken listeners to the compelling beauty, truth and goodness of the God revealed in Jesus Christ, allowing each in turn to offer a more profound "Alleluia!"[38]

"Two Roads Diverged in a Wood . . ."

Those who have the opportunity to sit under the preaching of both Andy Stanley and Stanley Hauerwas will be exposed to two vastly different sensory experiences. In listening to the sermons of Andy Stanley, one encounters a world-class communicator, supported by audio and video resources embracing the highest production values, speaking in a winsome and conversational style, as he seemingly effortlessly patrols the platform of the North Point auditorium. Compared to Andy Stanley, Stanley Hauerwas cannot help but come across as a somewhat awkward academic behind a pulpit nervously shuffling his manuscript notes, from which he reads his sometimes dense and demanding prose in his distinctive Texas twang. While the differences in sensory experience provoked by the preaching of these two men is striking, what is more even more significant is the profound difference between the operative understandings of the nature of the Gospel and how that Gospel transforms our lives that underlies each of their approaches to preaching. It is at this theological level that Andy Stanley and Stanley Hauerwas stand as representatives for two homiletical paths that lie open before today's preachers.

36. Stanley Hauerwas, *Disrupting Time: Sermons, Prayers, and Sundries* (Eugene, OR: Cascade, 2004), 178. See also Stanley Hauerwas, *The Hauerwas Reader*, ed. John Berkman and Michael G. Cartwright (Durham: Duke University Press, 2001), 611; Stanley Hauerwas, *A Cross-Shattered Church: Reclaiming the Theological Heart of Preaching* (Grand Rapids: Brazos, 2009), 40–41.

37. Stanley Hauerwas, *Working with Words: On Learning to Speak Christian* (Eugene, OR: Cascade, 2011), 93.

38. For more on preachers as teachers of language, see Hauerwas, *Working with Words*, 84–93; Davis and Dennis, *Preaching the Luminous Word*, 89–105. *A More Profound Alleluia: Theology and Worship in Harmony* is the title of a book edited by Leanne van Dyk (Grand Rapids: Eerdmans, 2004).

One path seeks to establish the preacher as a master communicator who through the employment of clever communication techniques is able to inspire people to action; the other seeks to understand the preacher as a servant of the Word whose martyriological rhetoric cannot compel but only bear witness to the compelling beauty of the originary peace that characterizes the life of the Triune God. One asks "how the text 'applies' to us in our day and age, as if the important thing is to discover how the text relates to our world"; the other recognizes that "it is better to think in terms of inserting oneself into the world of the biblical text, which is the true story of the world."[39] One thinks the task of preaching is "to set out some reality in life and then go to the Bible to find extra wisdom"; the other recognizes the preacher's task is "to tell the story of the Bible so clearly that it calls into question and ultimately redefines what we think we know of reality and what we call wisdom in the first place."[40] One in its desire to demonstrate the usefulness of the Bible ends us essentially underwriting "a private, therapeutic, individualistic biblical discourse"; the other dares to proclaim the public truth of "God the Father's reclamation of all of creation from sin and death through the Son by the power of the Spirit" and in so doing confronts us with the question of how we are useful to the Lord of Scripture.[41] One reinforces the sovereignty of the autonomous, modern human subject by treating the Bible as an encyclopedia of tips that provide the necessary know-how (or *gnosis*) for getting by successfully in our world, the other decenters the self through re-inscribing men and women in a new narrative, in the recognition that "to save sinners, God seizes them by the imagination."[42] The former inevitably ends up preaching the law as it "assert[s] what we must do to build faith"; the latter is free to proclaim the gospel of "what God has done for us in the death and resurrection, in the continuous creation, in the sending of the Spirit."[43] One, as a result of its emphasis on application,

39. Kevin J. Vanhoozer, *Faith Speaking Understanding: Performing the Drama of Doctrine* (Louisville: Westminster John Knox, 2014), 133.

40. Long, *The Witness of Preaching*, 39.

41. John W. Wright, *Telling God's Story: Narrative Preaching for Christian Formation* (Downers Grove: IVP Academic, 2007), 19, 55.

42. Garrett Green, *Imagining God: Theology and the Religious Imagination* (San Francisco: Harper & Row, 1989), 149-50, quoted in Davis and Dennis, *Preaching the Luminous Word*, 92n.3.

43. Marva J. Dawn, *Powers, Weakness, and the Tabernacling of God* (Grand Rapids: Eerdmans, 2001), 94.

throws the hearer back upon him- or herself through its prescription of moral therapy; the other through the shape of its narration sends people forth from the sermon as those "re-enlisted in the company of those who follow Christ as witnesses and signs and agents of the rule of God in the life of the world."[44] Ultimately, perhaps the difference can be most succinctly stated by observing that one path insists that sermons should make a point, the other that faithful proclamation is not about making points, but pointing to the one who is "the Way, the Truth, and the Life."[45]

Two homiletical roads diverged in a wood, the one that is taken by the next generation of preachers will make all the difference.

44. Lesslie Newbigin, "Preaching Christ Today," (Joseph Smith Memorial Lecture, presented at Overdale College, Birmingham, U.K., 1979), http://newbiginresources.org/1979-preaching-christ-today/.

45. I'm grateful for a conversation with two of my theology students, Laura Puiras and Steven Latta, which illuminated the importance of distinguishing preaching that 'makes points' from preaching that 'points to' Jesus.

Name Index

Agamben, Giorgio, 202
Anscombe, Elizabeth, 157
Aquinas, 51, 152
Arendt, Hannah, 285n3
Aristotle, 45, 48–49, 105n17, 107
Armstrong, Regis J., 289n10
Augustine, 51, 265
Austen, Jane, 221

Baan, Ariaan W., 14n55, 302n22
Bachmann, E. Theodore, 279n5
Baehr, Peter, 285n3
Balthasar, Hans Urs von, 34
Bannon, Steve, 120
Barnett, Victoria J., 3n12, 60–61n2, 63n5, 65n8, 67n11, 288n9
Barrett, Lee C., 79n1
Barth, Karl, 6n21, 8n28, 9, 41, 158, 162, 213, 227, 265, 267
Berkman, John, 3n9, 307n36
Bernanos, Georges, 234, 236
Berry, Wendell, 109
Bertram, Martin H., 201n7
Best, Isabel, 60n2, 65n8, 67n11
Bethge, Eberhard, 63n5, 286n6
Blackledge, Paul, 102n15
Bloesch, Daniel W., 61n2
Bobbitt's, Philip, 101n12
Boers, Arthur, 2n3
Bogarde, Dirk, 264
Bonhoeffer, Dietrich, 3, 4, 4n12, 17n61, 60–74, 162, 272, 286–87, 288n9, 290, 301n20
Bowlin, John, 111
Braaten, Carl E., 285n4

Brierley, Justin, 5n20
Broadway, Michael, 110n23
Brock, Brian, 1n2, 3n9, 7n26, 9n31, 294n4, 299n11, 303n28
Brocker, Mark S., 3n12, 65n8, 286n6, 288n9
Bromiley, G. W., 213n1
Brooks, David, 48
Brown, Jeannine K., 281
Burrell, David, 81n6
Burrowes-Cromwell, Toni, 64n7
Burtness, James H., 61n2

Calhoun, Robert L., 15, 35–42, 46
Cartwright, Michael G., 3n9, 307n36
Cavanaugh, William, 5n18
Certeau, Michel de, 33
Chenu, Marie-Dominique, 34
Chergé, Christian de, 302–3n24
Clavier, Mark, 140–41
Clement, 40
Clements, Keith, 60n2
Clinton, Hillary Rodham, 115, 117, 120
Coles, Romand, 12n49
Collier, Charles M., 3n9, 16m59, 73n26, 161n1
Congar, Yves, 34
Corwin, Virginia, 36–37
Cramer, David, 146n4, 147n5–48n7
Cuarón, Alfonso, 113
Cushman, Robert, 37

Dahill, Lisa E., 286n6

Daniélou, Jean, 34
Davis, Ellen F., 157, 300n12
Dawn, Marva J., 308n43
Dean, Robert J., 1, 273, 284, 292, 303n25
deGruchy, John W., 67n11
Dennis, Austin McIver, 300n12
Dewar, Diana, 290n11
Duduit, Michael, 294n4
Dula, Peter, 139n10, 161n1

Eisenhower, Dwight, 256
Eitel, Adam, 306n33
Elizabeth I, Queen, 222
Elshtain, Jean Bethke, 5n19

Fitch, David, 305
Floyd, Wayne Whitson, Jr., 61n2, 62–63n4, 63n6, 69n21, 73n27
Flynn, Gabriel, 34n6
Fodor, James, 9, 12
Foot, Philippa, 157
Fortune, Marie, 157
Foucault, Michel, 51
Francis (pope), 237
Frei, Hans W., 7n26, 35–36, 38–39, 279n3

Garrigou-Lagrange, Reginald, 34
Godsey, John D., 73n27
Goff, Stan, 157
Goossen, Rachel, 142, 148
Gorman, Michael, 218
Gouwens, David J., 79n1
Green, Barbara, 73n27
Green, Clifford J., 17n61, 63n6, 69n21
Green, Garrett, 308n42
Green, Joel B., 281
Gregory, Brad, 198
Gregory of Nyssa, 254
Griffiths, Paul, 128
Gruchy, John W. De, 301n20
Gunton, Colin, 11n44
Guth, Karen, 156

Hall, Stuart, 119

Hans Ulrich, 127
Hargaden, Kevin, 1n2, 3n9, 7n26, 294n4
Harink, Douglas, 6, 6n23
Harn, Roger E. Van, 286n5
Hart, David, 191–92
Harvey, A. E., 127–37
Hauerwas, Stanley, 2, 4, 5–8, 8n28, 10, 11, 16, 16n59, 50, 127–30, 137–41, 143, 144, 292, 296n7, 297–309
Hays, Richard B., 9, 9n32
Heggen, Carolyn Holderread, 146, 153
Herder, 23
Herdt, Jennifer, 50, 161
Herman, Louis, 27
Higgins, David, 65n8
Holmer, Paul, 79n1, 81n7, 85–86
Hopkins, Gerard Manley, 6n22
Howell, Jenny, 146n4
Hunsinger, George, 41n21
Hybels, Bill, 292

Irenaeus, 6n23, 39, 40

James, 54
Jefferson, Thomas, 270
Jenson, Robert, 11n44, 35, 254, 306
John of the Cross, 136
John Paul II (pope), 289
Johnson, Kelly S., 16n59
Jones, Lane, 294

Kallenberg, Brad, 11–12n45
Kant, Immanuel, 38, 43, 49, 287
Katongole, Emmanuel, 14n55
Keen, Craig, 22–23, 28–30
Kelly, Geffrey B., 61n2, 67, 68n15, 68n16, 73n27
Kierkegaard, Søren, 18, 77–88
Kimbrough, S. T., Jr., 196n1
King, Martin Luther, 158, 163–64
Klein, Naomi, 113
Klinkenborg, Verlyn, 21–22
Knight, John Allen, 41n21
Knight, Kelvin, 102n15
Kolbe, Maximilian, 289–90

NAME INDEX

Krauss, Reinhard, 17n61, 63n6, 69n21
Krauss, Richard, 73n27

Lambert, William A., 279n5
Lear, Jonathan, 100n10
Lehmann, Helmut T., 201–2n7, 279n5
Lindbeck, George, 15, 35–36, 37–38, 39–42, 46
Lischer, Richard, 129n5, 161–64
Long, Thomas G., 300n14
Lowrie, Walter, 79, 82n8, 83n9
Lubac, Henri de, 32
Lukens, Michael B., 3n12, 65n8, 288n9
Lukens, Nancy, 63n6
Luther, Martin, 4, 66, 70, 198–202, 244, 272, 279, 282, 285
Lyon, John, 48

MacIntyre, Alasdair, 15, 22, 27–28, 35, 42–46, 49–56, 96n2, 100, 102n15, 102n16, 111, 151, 154–55
Mahn, Jason, 83n11
Mangina, Joseph, 298
Martens, Paul, 146n4, 147n5–48n7
Martyn, J. Louis, 6, 6n23
Matheny, Paul Duane, 62–63n4
May, Bill, 185
McBride, Jennifer, 70–72
McCabe, Herbert, 25, 273–74
McClendon, Jim, 144
McIntosh, Mark, 293
McMullin, Evan, 115, 117
Melville, Herman, 21
Metz, Johannes, 191
Meyer, Al and Mary Ellen, 144
Milbank, John, 1n1, 100–109, 111
Miller, Marlin, 142, 148, 149
Moo, Douglas J., 277n2
Moore, Sebastian, 152
Mulhall, Stephen, 30n22
Müller, Gerhard Ludwig, 61, 62, 68–69, 69n21
Murdoch, Iris, 157, 172
Murray, Paul, 34n6

Nation, Mark, 143n2
Nebelsick, Mary C., 62–63n4
Nelson, F. Burton, 68n16
Newman, 45
Niebuhr, H. Richard, 35
Niebuhr, Reinhold, 110, 110n23, 115
Nietzsche, Friedrich, 51
Noyes, John Humphrey, 149n8
Nussbaum, Martha, 157
Nyman, Heikki, 90n2

Ochs, Peter, 254
Origen, 39–40
Ortega y Gasset, José, 107n19
Orwell, George, 105
Owens, L. Roger, 73n27

Pabst, Adrian, 100–109, 111
Parker, Peter, 5
Patterson, David, 286n5
Paul (apostle), 170–72
Peirce, C. S., 54
Pelikan, Jaroslav, 199n2
Perrin, Nicholas, 281
Peterson, Eugene, 6n22, 292
Peterson, Ingrid J., 289n10
Pickstock, Catherine, 157
Pinches, Charles R., 16m59, 140n11, 161n1
Pinter, Harold, 264
Pius XI (pope), 208
Placher, William C., 41n21
Plant, Stephen, 64n7
Plato, 110, 154
Pliny, 274
Presley, Elvis, 256
Pugh, Jeffrey, 67n12
Purdy, Jedediah, 111

Radner, Ephraim, 300–301
Ramsey, Paul, 97n4
Rasmussen, Larry, 65n8
Rasmusson, Arne, 14n55
Rauschenbusch, Walter, 109–10
Rawls, John, 43
Rebanks, James, 90, 95–97, 108, 111

NAME INDEX

Reinders, Hans, 47–50, 56–59
Reno, Rusty, 101n11
Robinson, Haddon W., 300n14
Root, Andrew, 64–65, 65n8
Ross, Maggie, 26
Rouard, Christophe, 53n14, 54
Rowe, Kavin, 140, 141

Samuel Wells, 1n1
Sayers, Dorothy, 6–7, 7n25
Scarsella, Hilary, 158n20
Schenck, K., 281
Schick, George V., 199n2
Schlabach, Gerald, 156
Schleiermacher, Friedrich, 39, 40, 41
Schmidt-Lange, Anne, 3n12, 65n8, 288n9
Schönherr, Albrecht, 61, 62, 68–69, 69n21
Scott, John, 300n14
Seitz, Christopher R., 285n4
Sherman, Franklin, 201n7
Shield, Pretty, 100n10
Sider, Alex, 151–53
Sider, J. Alexander, 16m59
Socrates, 51
Spurgeon, Charles, 281
Stanley, Andy, 293–97, 307–9
Stanley, Charles, 294
Stassen, Glen, 144
Stott, Douglas W., 17n61, 62–63n4, 69n21
Stout, Jeff, 48
Sullivan, Andrew, 110–11

Taylor, Charles, 23, 168
Tertullian, 39, 40
Tessman, Lisa, 105n17
Thomson, John B., 14n55
Tietjen, Mark, 82n8
Tillich, Paul, 158
Tocqueville, Alexis de, 110
Torrance, T. F., 213n1

Tran, Jonathan, 16, 50, 113–26, 139, 146n4, 147n5–48n7, 161
Treece, Patricia, 290n12
Trenery, David, 42n25, 54–55
Trump, Donald, 97–98, 101, 109–11, 109n21, 113–21, 124, 243, 262
Turnbull, Ryan, 5n20

van Dyk, Leanne, 307n36
Vanhoozer, Kevin J., 308n39
Vanier, Jean, 12, 47–50, 56–57, 213–14, 302n22

Wadell, Paul J., 16m59
Webster, John, 14n53
Wells, Samuel, 3n9, 14n55, 50, 57n28, 87–88, 92, 161, 242
Wesley, Charles, 196
West, Charles C., 17n61, 69n21
Wilken, Robert, 35
Will, Frederick, 53–54
Williams, Rowan, 22–27, 32, 46, 302n23
Willimon, William H., 2n4, 11n43, 17n61, 216
Wilson, Paul Scott, 300n14, 303–4
Winch, Peter, 90n2
Wittgenstein, Ludwig, 11–12n45, 41n21, 57, 90n2, 92, 306
Wojhoski, Barbara, 60–61n2, 65n8, 65n9, 67n11
Wright, G. H. von, 90n2
Wright, John W., 308n41
Wyschogrod, Michael, 254

Yeago, David, 276n1
Yoder, John Howard, 6n23, 7n25, 12–13, 16n59, 80, 142–58

Zagano, Phyllis, 289n10

Subject Index

abduction, 54
abortion, 116–18
academy
    ethics, designation of, 4n11
    theological tradition, 77–81
    in today's world, 86–88
Advent, 167, 230–31
After Crucifixion (Keen), 28–29
After Virtue (MacIntyre), 35, 50, 55, 100
"Ambassadors for Christ" (sermon), 245–50
America
    churches, 98–99, 109, 256–58
    democracy, 109–11
    electoral process, 109n21, 262
American revival tradition, 267
amplification, 53
anarchy, 107
anti-foundationalists, 47
apologetics, 18
Apostles' Creed, 40
aristocracy, 106–7
Articles of Religion, 205
authority of a community, 44

Bampton Lectures (1982), 135–36
baptism, 152, 247, 273
Be Not Afraid: Facing Fear With Faith (Wells), 242
Becoming the Gospel (Gorman), 218
Bethel Confession, 67
"better off" term usage, 99–100
Bible, necessity of history, 32–33, 278

Bible stories, 129–30
Bonhoeffer, Dietrich
    Christ that is present, 72–74
    Dean on, 3, 4
    freedom, 272
    humanism, 71
    Lischer on, 162
    pastoral theology, 60–66
    religion, 66–67
    truth, 286–87
    visibility of the church, 66–72
    Westminster Abbey statue, 290
Bonhoeffer, Dietrich, works by
    Ecumenical, Academic, and Pastoral Work, 4n12, 288n9
    Ethics, 17n61, 69
    Letters and Papers from Prison, 66, 301n20
    Life Together, 61, 67–69
    Sanctorum Communio, 63
    Bonhoeffer as Youth Worker (Root), 64
Book of Common Prayer, The, 207n1, 208n4, 252, 273n1, 275
Borderline: Reflections on War, Sex and the Church (Goff), 157
boredom, 234–38
bread of life, 225, 227
Burdened Virtues (Tessman), 105n17

"Caesar Wants it All" (sermon), 269–72
capitalism, 119–20, 123

SUBJECT INDEX

Catholic theology
    law and forgiveness, 220
    ressourcement movement, 34
    Virgin Mary, 164, 165–69
"Celebration" (sermon), 256–59
Chalcedon Council and Creed, 40, 41
Christ
    existing as community, 63
    good life, storied by, 108–12
    presence, 72–74
    speaking directly, 260–63
    unity in, 170–75
Christian Attitudes to War, Peace, and Revolution (Yoder), 149
Christian Century (Hauerwas and Willimon), 2
Christian speech, 28
Christianity and Christendom
    in America, 98–99, 109
    being Christian, 81–86
    democracy and, 110
    hidden inwardness, 85
    persons, uniqueness of, 102
    political behaviors, 113–14
    relevance of, 46
    secular Christianity, 39
    story of, 32–35
    Western concerns, 14–15
Christological dogma, 4n11
church
    in America, 98–99, 109, 256–58
    defined, 108
    government and, 269–72
    militant church, 85
    nationalistic church, 65
    repentance for, 71–72
    sanctuary politics, 121–26
    seeker-sensitive church movement, 2
    triumphant church, 85
    visibility of, 66–72
    See also Councils
Church for the World, The (McBride), 70
"Citizens of Heaven" (sermon), 198–203

Commentary on Genesis (Luther), 199, 201
Communicating for a Change (Stanley and Jones), 293, 294–95
communication, direct, 82
community
    authority of, 44
    Christ existing in, 63
Community of Character, A, (Hauerwas), 110
compassion, fear of, 213–14
confession and repentance of sin, 71
consent, meaning of, 150
Constantinianism, 80, 88
Councils
    Chalcedon, 40, 41
    Ephesus, 166
    Federal Council of Churches, 36
    Nicaean, 40, 41, 45
    Vatican Second Ecumenical, 34
craft traditions, 51–52
creation and apocalyptic theology, 8, 8n28
creeds, 39, 40, 41, 253
crucifixion, 28–29, 33, 174, 231–32
Culture and Value (Wittgenstein), 90
culture of prosperity, 237

"dark night of the soul," 136
death, 182–86. *See also* martyrs and martyrdom
"Defeat of Boredom, The," 234–38
democracy
    American, 109–11
    liberalism and, 107–8
dependence on others, 56, 99
Dependent Rational Animals (MacIntyre), 27, 55–56, 96n2
Diary of a Country Priest, The (Bernanos), 234–37
direct communication, 82
disabled, persons, 57–58
discernment, 220
discipleship, 73, 84–85
"Do Not Be Afraid" (sermon), 239–44

SUBJECT INDEX

"Do You Love Me?" (sermons), 176–81
doctrine of recapitulation, 8n28
doctrines and dogma, 38, 40
Drawn Three Ways (Harvey), 128

Ecumenical, Academic, and Pastoral Work (Bonhoeffer), 4n12, 288n9
Edge of Words, The (Williams), 23, 24
Edith Stein (MacIntyre), 154
elderly generation, 105
"Elected" (sermon), 260–63
elections, political, 109n21, 262
Eleuthero Community, North Yarmouth, Maine, 72
elitism, 118–21
Elkhart Truth, The (newspaper), 143
Encyclopaedia tradition, 51, 52, 55
The End of Words (Lischer), 161
ending with a beginning, 46
endurance, 5
enframing account of language, 23
Enlightenment movement, 77–78, 102n15
Ephesus Council, 166
epistemological crisis, 44–45, 50, 55
epistemological foundation, 9
equality, 102, 102n15
ethical surplus, 54n17
ethical theory, 47
Ethics (Bonhoeffer), 17n61, 69
ethics, academic designation of, 4n11
Eucharist, 259, 304
exemplification, 47–50, 51n9, 53, 302–4
Exemplum (Lyon), 48
experimentation, 54

faith, 282
Faith in the City (Harvey), 135
"Fake News and Inconvenient Truths" (sermon), 284–91
falsity, 44
fear, 118–21, 239–44
Federal Council of Churches, 36

feminist theologians, 156–57
five word formula for preaching, 295
forgiveness, 68, 192, 247–49
"Fortuna," 140
freedom, 101n11, 102, 102n15, 272
friendship, 16
"Friendship, Alienation, Love" (Sider), 151–52
funerals, 303n25

genealogists, 51
generous orthodoxy, 36
globalized markets, 101, 101n12, 120
good life, the
    meaning of, 99
    politics of virtue, 100–108
    a shepherd's life, 95–100
    storied by Christ, 108–12
"good news," the, 277–79
Graduation Address, University of Aberdeen, 89
guilt, 152

Hannah's Child (Hauerwas), 4, 16n59, 137–41, 143, 144
happiness, 152
Harvey, A. E.
    Hauerwas on, 127–30
    memoir, 130–37
Hauerwas, Stanley
    apocalyptic character of Hauerwas's work, 5–8, 8n28
    on evangelical preaching, 296n7
    Gifford Lectures, 2, 302
    Harvey on, 127–30
    on pointless preaching, 297–307
    sermons by, 292 (See also sermons)
    Stanley, compared to, 307–9
    theology, defined by, 10
Hauerwas, Stanley, works by
    Christian Century, 2
    With the Grain of the Universe, 2
    Hannah's Child, 4, 16n59, 137–41, 143, 144
    "Making Connections," 50

Hauerwas, Stanley, works by (*cont.*)
  "Necessity of Witness, The" 2
  Resident Aliens, 2, 216
  Sanctify Them in the Truth, 11
  "A Sanctuary Politics," 16
"He is Our Peace" (sermon), 215–18
"A Heartfelt People" (sermon), 219–23
hegemonic liberal story, 101
heretics and heretical positions, 36, 41, 251, 252–53
hierarchy, defense of, 106–7
historians, 39
holiness, 258
Holy Spirit, gifts of, 255. See also Trinity, controversy over
honor, 104, 104n16
hope, 139–40, 255
humanism, Bonhoeffer on, 71
humanities, education in, 87, 91
humility, 29, 259
humility of the cross, 71, 259
hypocrisy, 221

Identity of Jesus Christ, The (Frei), 279
inconvenient truths, 288
individualism, 43, 110
insight, 151–53

Jesus and the Constraints of History (Harvey), 129
just or temperate persons, 48
justification, 198–203

Kierkegaard, Søren
  academia, 86–88
  academia theology, 77–81
  on being a Christian, 81–86
  on being Christian, 81–86
  getting the question right, 77–81
  Hauerwas influenced by, 18
"King Jesus" (sermon), 204–9
Kingdom and the Glory, The (Agamben), 202
Kolbe, Maximilian, 289–90

language
  Harvey on, 136
  MacIntyre on, 27–28
  Williams on, 23–27
L'Arche, 47, 57–58
law
  forgiveness and, 220
  natural law, 150–51
  perspective of, 219–23
Lent, 209–14, 266–67
Letters and Papers from Prison (Bonhoeffer), 66, 301n20
liberal cosmopolitans, 55
liberal elites, 120
liberal theology, 34–35
liberalism, 15, 38, 42–44, 101–3, 105n18, 107
Life Together (Bonhoeffer), 61, 67–69
listening, 174
living tradition, 35
love
  freely given, 249
  God as, 254
  God's, 176–81
  meaning of, 172
  romantic, 157
luck, 105, 105n17
lying, 90–92, 122, 286. See also truth

MacIntyre, Alasdair
  goals of Enlightenment, 102n15
  honor, 104n16
  language, 27–28
  philosophers, 154–55
  practical reason, 49–51, 51n9, 53–54, 56, 151
  rationality, 50–56
  tradition, 42–46
  whole human life concept, 100
  work, 111
MacIntyre, Alasdair, works by
  After Virtue, 35, 50, 55, 100
  Dependent Rational Animals, 27, 55–56, 96n2
  Short History of Ethics, A, 50
  Three Rival Versions of Moral Enquiry, 50–51

"Making Connections" (Hauerwas), 50
marriage, 147, 150, 157
martyrs and martyrdom, 84–85, 180, 189–91, 269–72, 289–90, 301. *See also* death
Mary, Virgin, 164, 165–69
"Mary: Mother of God" (sermon), 165–69
memoirs
    Hannah's Child, 137–41
    Harvey's memoir, 130–37
    theologians writing of, 127–30
mental illness, 129, 131–32, 137–40
methodism, 67
militant church, 85
ministry, 178–81, 234–38. *See also* preaching
modalism, heresy of, 252
modernity, 102n14
monasticism, 77
moral identity, 99n7
moral imagination, 153
moral reflection, 47
mule's attention story, 224–25

national elections, 109n21, 262
nationalism, 120
nationalistic church, 65
natural law, 150–51
Nature of Doctrine, The (Lindbeck), 40, 42, 42n25
"Necessity of Witness, The" (Hauerwas), 2
neo-orthodox theology, 37–38
neo-scholastic theology, 34
NeverEnding Story, The (movie), 282–83
"Never-ending Story, The" (sermon), 276–83
New Harmony community, 149, 149n8
news media, 121–22
Nicene Council and Creed, 40, 41, 45, 253
nonviolence, 204–9, 218

"Non-Violent Terrorist: In Defense of Christian Fanaticism, The" (Hauerwas), 49
novels, importance of, 153

On the Bondage of the Will (Luther), 4
One True Life (Rowe), 140
"Only Those We Need Can Betray Us" (Schlabach), 156

Paradox of Disability, The (Reinders), 56
past matters, theologically
    Christianity story, 32–35
    ending with a beginning, 46
    tradition, MacIntyre on, 42–46
    tradition at Yale, 35–42
pastoral theology, 60–66
peace, 57, 215–18
Performing the Faith (Hauerwas), 66
personhood, 107
persons, 57–58, 102
philosophers, 154–55
Philosophical Fragments (Kierkegaard), 83n10
Point of View for My Work as An Author, The (Kierkegaard), 81–82
political imagination, 114–18
political speech, 69–70, 91–92
"Politics of Martyrdom, The" (sermon), 273–75
politics of time, 57
politics of virtue, 100–108
Politics of Virtue, The (Milbank and Pabst), 100–108
populism, 119–20
pornography, 185
postliberal theology, 35, 41
post-liberalism, 103–6
poverty, 124
practical reason, 49–51, 51n9, 53–54, 56, 151
pragmaticism/pragmatism, 54
Pragmatism and Realism (Will), 53
preaching
    five word formula, 295

preaching (*continued*)
  point of, 292–94
  pointless sermons, 297–307 (*see also* sermons)
  significance of, "the" 164, 165–69
  silence of words, 26, 164, 170–75
  words matter, 161–64
pride, 29
priesthood, call to, 133–34
prosperity, culture of, 237
Protestant Reformation, 198–99, 220, 270
Protestant theology
  American revival tradition, 267
  on justification, 199
  liberal theology, 66–67
  mainstream traditions, 256
  survival of, 62, 266
  on tradition, 34–35
Psalms, reading of, 173
public vs. private religious matters, 78

Quas Primas (encyclical), 208

racism, 119–20
rational enquiry, 44–46
rationality
  Kant on, 49
  MacIntyre on, 50–56
realism, 41n21, 54
recapitulation doctrine, 8n28
redemption, 121
Reformation, 198–99, 220, 270
Reformed tradition, 40
Reinders, Hans
  as anti-foundationalists, 47
  exemplification and, 47–48
  Vanier's influence on, 56–59
  war alternative, 50
relativism, 55
religion, Bonhoeffer on, 66–67
"Repentance: A Lenten Meditation" (sermon), 210–14
repentance for the church, 71–72

Resident Aliens (Hauerwas and Willimon), 2, 216
respectable culture
  insight and wisdom, 151–53
  life and work, 154–55
  what now, 155–58
  Yoder, experimentation, 146–51
  Yoder, writing about, 142–46
responsibility, 17–18
ressourcement movement, 34
Resurrecting the Idea of a Christian Society (Reno), 101n11
"Resurrection" (sermon), 182–86
righteousness, 198–203
Road to Character, The (Brooks), 48
romantic love, 157
rule-theory, 40–41

sacred, language and, 26
saints, lives of, 302–4, 303n25
Sanctify Them in the Truth (Hauerwas), 11
Sanctorum Communio (Bonhoeffer), 63
sanctuary politics
  church's sanctuary politics, 121–26
  political imagination, 114–18
  populism, elitism, and fear, 118–21
  Trump supporters, 113–14
"Sanctuary Politics, A" (Hauerwas and Tran), 16
scholarly theological tradition, 77–81
sciences, education in, 87, 90–91
Second Ecumenical Council of the Vatican, 34
Secular Age, A (Taylor), 168
secular Christianity, 39
"Seeing Peace: L'Arche as a Peace Movement" (Hauerwas), 57
seeker-sensitive church movement, 2
self-knowledge, 58
sermons
  point of, 294–97
  purpose of, 300

SUBJECT INDEX 321

"Ambassadors for Christ,"
  245–50
"Caesar Wants it All," 269–72
"Celebration," 256–59
"Citizens of Heaven," 198–203
"Defeat of Boredom, The"
  234–38
"Do Not Be Afraid," 239–44
"Do You Love Me?," 176–81
"Elected," 260–63
"Fake News and Inconvenient
  Truths," 284–91
"He is Our Peace," 215–18
"Heartfelt People, A" 219–23
"King Jesus," 204–9
"Mary: Mother of God," 165–69
"Never-ending Story, The"
  276–83
"Politics of Martyrdom, The"
  273–75
"Repentance: A Lenten
  Meditation," 210–14
"Resurrection," 182–86
"Sin," 264–68
"Sound of Silence, The" 170–75
"Trinity," 251–55
"Waiting," 229–33
"Way, the Truth, and the Life,
  The" 187–92, 298
"Wounded," 193–97
See also preaching
Servant, The (Pinter), 264–65
*Several Short Sentences about
  Writing* (Klinkenborg), 21
sex, separated form intimacy, 185
Shepherd's Life, The (Rebanks), 90,
  95–100
Shield of Achilles, The (Bobbitt),
  101n12
Short History of Ethics, A
  (MacIntyre), 50
"Sign that is Christ, The" 224–28
silence of language, 26, 164, 170–75
sin
  repentance of, 71, 211–13
  understanding of, 83n11
"Sin" (sermon), 264–68
slogans, 167

social ethics, 98
"Sound of Silence, The" (sermon),
  170–75
speaking directly, 260–63
speech, 92
State of the University, The
  (Hauerwas), 80, 86–87
Stoics, 136, 140
subordinationism, heresy of, 252–53

Talmud, 286
teachers, 58
Tears of Silence (Vanier), 213–14
temperament, 105n17
temperate persons, 48
theologians
  audience for, 60
  as "doubtful Christians," 210–11
  life and work, 155
  writing memoirs (*See* memoirs)
theology
  in academia, 77–78
  defined by Hauerwas, 10
*Three Rival Versions of Moral
  Enquiry* (MacIntyre), 50–51
time
  politics of, 57
  significance of, 167–68
tradition
  attitude toward, 33–35
  craft traditions, 51–52
  living tradition, 35
  MacIntyre on, 42–46
  recovery of at Yale, 35–42
  scholarly theological, 77–81
traditionalist, 38, 40
traditions of inquiry, 42
"Trinity" (sermon), 251–55
Trinity, controversy over, 40, 41, 45
triumphant church, 85
Trump, Donald
  Christianity and democracy, 110
  Christian's alternative options,
    114–18
  as dangerous, 109
  description of, 101
  electoral process, 109n21, 262
  fear around, 118–21, 243

Trump, Donald (*continued*)
  news media, 120–21
  proposed bans, 124
  supporters of, 97–98, 111, 113–14
truth, 26, 84–85, 90–92, 122, 262–63, 284–91
Two Roads Diverged in a Wood, 307–9
Types of Christian Theology (Frei), 41

Unintended Reformation, The (Gregory), 198
unity in Christ Jesus, 170–75
universities
  theological tradition, 77–81
  in today's world, 86–88
University of Aberdeen, 89–92

Vatican II, 34
violence, 187–88, 192
Virgin Mary, 164, 165–69
virtue, 9n33, 103–4, 108–12, 153
virtue, politics of, 100–108
visibility of the church, 66–72

"Waiting" (sermon), 229–33
war, place of, 108, 108n20
"Way, the Truth, and the Life, The" (sermon), 187–92, 298

Western Christendom concerns, 14–15
What's the Matter with Liberalism (Beiner), 101–2
wisdom, 105, 153, 220
With the Grain of the Universe (Hauerwas), 2
word choices, 30
words, silence of, 26, 164, 170–75
words matter, 69–70, 161–64
work, purpose and, 111
"Wounded" (sermon), 193–97
"Wrestling Jacob" (Wesley), 196–97
writing
  Dean on, 21–23
  Keen on, 28–30
  truth in, 92

Yale, tradition at, 35–42
Yoder, John Howard
  abusive behavior of, 12–13, 142–46
  on Christological dogma, 7n25
  Constantinianism, 80
  experimentation, 146–51
  friendship and, 16n59
  insight and wisdom, 151–53
  life and work, 154–55
  on Lordship of Christ, 6n23
  what now, 155–58
  on writing about, 142–46